1000 Recipes
Slow Cooking

igloobooks

Published in 2012
by Igloo Books Ltd
Cottage Farm
Sywell
Northants
NN6 0BJ
www.igloobooks.com

Food photography and recipe development: PhotoCuisine UK
Front and back cover images © PhotoCuisine UK

SHE001 1112
4 6 8 10 9 7 5 3
ISBN: 978-0-85780-785-4

Printed and manufactured in China

1000 Recipes
Slow Cooking

CONTENTS

STARTERS AND SIDES

1

SERVES 4

Chicken Yakitori

PREPARATION TIME: 15 MINUTES
+ OVERNIGHT MARINATING

COOKING TIME:
3 HOURS 20 MINUTES

INGREDIENTS

8 chicken breast mini fillets
75ml / 3 fl. oz / ⅓ cup sake
75ml / 3 fl. oz / ⅓ cup mirin
75ml / 3 fl. oz / ⅓ cup dark soy sauce
2 tbsp honey
110g / 4 oz / 1 cup peanuts, finely
chopped
8 wooden skewers, soaked in water
for 30 minutes beforehand
1 tbsp tomato ketchup

GARNISH

4 sprigs chervil
2 chive stalks, roughly chopped

- Prepare the marinade by whisking together the sake, mirin, soy sauce and honey in a small mixing bowl.
- Add the chicken breast mini fillets to it and stir well.
- Cover and chill overnight.
- The next day, remove the chicken from the marinade, but reserve the marinade. Place the chicken in a slow cooker and cook on a medium setting for 3 hours.
- Remove and thread onto wooden skewers. Preheat the grill. Arrange on a tray and grill for 4-6 minutes.
- Meanwhile, place the marinade in a small saucepan and reduce over a moderate heat until thick and sticky.
- Brush the skewers with the reduced marinade and immediately roll in the chopped peanuts.
- Stir the tomato ketchup into the reduced marinade until incorporated.
- Arrange on serving plates and garnish with the marinade, sprigs of chervil and the chopped chives.

Turkey Yakitori

2

Swap the chicken breast for turkey
for a lean version of this recipe.

3

SERVES 4

Roast Potatoes

PREPARATION TIME :
15 MINUTES

COOKING TIME :
7 HOURS 10 MINUTES

INGREDIENTS

900 g / 2 lb / 6 cups potatoes, peeled
and diced
125 ml / 4 ½ fl. oz / ½ cup sunflower
oil
salt and pepper

- Place the potatoes in a slow cooker.
- Cover with water and cover with a lid before cooking on a medium setting for 6 hours until soft.
- Drain after 6 hours and pat dry.
- Preheat the oven to 200°C (180° fan) / 400F / gas 6.
- Pour the oil in a large roasting tray and heat in the oven for 10 minutes.
- Remove from the oven carefully after 10 minutes and add the potatoes.
- Add some seasoning and turn the potatoes over in the oil to coat them.
- Roast for 1 hour until golden brown in colour.
- Remove from the oven and spoon into serving dishes.

Garlic Roast Potatoes

4

Add 6 cloves of crushed garlic
to the roasting tray before roasting.

5

SERVES 4

Minestrone

Angel Hair Minestrone

6

Substitute the penne for angel hair pasta. Reduce the cooking time in the slow cooker by 30 minutes.

Minestrone with Olives

7

Substitute the basil for parsley and stir through some chopped, pitted black and green olives before serving.

Chicken Minestrone

8

Add 2 cooked chicken breasts diced into pieces, for a meaty flavour.

PREPARATION TIME: 15 MINUTES

COOKING TIME: 3 HOURS

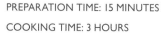

INGREDIENTS

4 tbsp olive oil
2 cloves garlic, minced
2 white potatoes, peeled and finely diced
2 large sticks celery, sliced
2 large carrots, peeled and sliced
110g / 4 oz / 1 ¼ cups penne
1 tbsp tomato puree
568 ml / 1 pint / 2 ¼ cups vegetable stock
1 bay leaf
2 tbsp basil leaves, finely chopped

GARNISH

4 sprigs of basil leaves

- Heat the olive oil in a large casserole dish over a medium heat until hot.
- Sweat the potatoes, garlic, carrot, celery and bay leaf with a little salt for 8-10 minutes until they start to soften, stirring occasionally.
- Stir through the tomato puree, then spoon everything into a slow cooker.
- Add the pasta and cover with the stock.
- Cook on a low setting for 3 hours until the pasta is tender.
- Discard the bay leaf and adjust the seasoning to taste.
- Stir through the chopped basil then spoon into serving bowls.
- Garnish with sprigs of basil leaves before serving.

9

SERVES 4

Mexican Soup

PREPARATION TIME: 15 MINUTES

COOKING TIME: 3 HOURS

INGREDIENTS

3 tbsp sunflower oil
2 chicken breasts cut into large chunks
2 onion, chopped
2 cloves garlic, minced
675 g / 1 lb 8 oz / 5 cups sweetcorn, drained
1.2 l / 2 pints / 4 ⅘ cups chicken stock, hot
2 ½ tsp dried oregano
2 tsp chilli powder
2 tsp paprika

GARNISH

1 tbsp coriander leaves, roughly chopped
1 green chilli

- Heat most of the oil in a large frying pan set over a moderate heat until hot.
- Season the chicken and seal in batches until deep golden.
- Remove from the pan and reduce the heat.
- Add the remaining oil to the pan and sweat the onion and garlic for 5-6 minutes with a little salt, stirring occasionally.
- Add the ground spices and stir well.
- Spoon into a slow cooker, then add the chicken, sweetcorn and stock.
- Cook on a low setting for 3 hours until the chicken is cooked and tender.
- Adjust the seasoning to taste before spooning everything into a serving pot.
- Garnish with the coriander and chilli before serving.

Crunchy Top Mexican Soup

10

Instead of using chilli to garnish the soup, crush some corn tortilla chips on top for an added crunch. Finish by sprinkling a pinch of smoked paprika on top as well.

11

SERVES 4

Saltimbocca

PREPARATION TIME: 10 MINUTES

COOKING TIME:
2 HOURS 120 MINUTES

INGREDIENTS

4 rose veal escalopes,
cut in half
55g / 2 oz / ½ stick unsalted butter
4 tbsp Marsala
1 tbsp sunflower oil
2 tbsp sage leaves

GARNISH

1 fennel bulb, trimmed and finely sliced
4 sage leaves

- Flatten the veal escalopes with a meat hammer until roughly ½ cm thick.
- Trim the edges so that you have rectangular shaped pieces of veal.
- Season the tops and cover with the sage leaves.
- Roll up into cylinders and secure using toothpicks.
- Melt some of the butter with the oil in a large frying pan set over a moderate heat.
- Season the outside of the veal generously and pan-fry in batches for 2-3 minutes until golden brown on the outside, transferring the veal to a slow cooker after each batch; make sure you use fresh butter for each batch.
- Deglaze the pan with the Marsala, then pour the contents of the pan into the slow cooker.
- Cook on a medium setting for 2 hours until tender.
- Spoon onto serving plates and garnish with the sage leaves and fennel.

Veal wrapped in Parma Ham

12

Wrap the veal in Parma ham after sealing in the pan. Secure using toothpicks before cooking in the slow cooker. Garnish with drained baby capers instead of fennel.

13

SERVES 4

Stewed Artichoke Hearts

- Heat a large frying pan over a moderate heat until hot.
- Saute the pancetta for a few minute until golden brown in colour on the outside.
- Remove from the pan and transfer to a slow cooker before adding the olive oil to the frying pan.
- Reduce the heat a little and sweat the onion for 5 minutes, stirring occasionally.
- Add the artichoke and cook for a further few minutes before spooning the onion and artichoke into the slow cooker.
- Cover with the stock and cover with a lid.
- Cook on a medium setting for 4 hours until softened.
- Adjust the seasoning to taste before serving.

PREPARATION TIME :
10-15 MINUTES

COOKING TIME :
4 HOURS 15 MINUTES

INGREDIENTS

4 Globe artichokes, trimmed and halved
30 ml / 1 fl. oz / 2 tbsp olive oil
1 onion, finely chopped
150 g / 5 oz / 1 cup pancetta, cut into thick strips
500 ml / 18 fl. oz / 2 cups vegetable stock
salt and pepper

Artichoke and Almond Stew

14

Garnish the dish with 30 g / 1 oz / ¼ cup flaked (slivered) almonds before serving.

15

SERVES 4

Chicken Nems

- Combine the vegetables, chicken, groundnut oil, soy sauce and pepper in a slow cooker.
- Cook on a high setting for 3 hours.
- Preheat the oven to 200°C (180° fan) / 400F / gas 6.
- Drain after 3 hours and use to fill the spring roll wrappers one at a time.
- Brush the rim of the wrappers with the beaten egg.
- Spoon the chicken and vegetable filling into the middle of the wrappers and fold the ends in and over the filling.
- Roll up tightly into cylinders and arrange on a baking tray.
- Bake for 15-20 minutes until golden and crisp.
- Remove from the oven and serve immediately.

PREPARATION TIME:
15 MINUTES

COOKING TIME:
3 HOURS 20 MINUTES

INGREDIENTS

8 spring roll wrappers, kept under a damp cloth
4 chicken breasts, cut into thin strips
2 carrots, peeled and julienned
4 spring onions, julienned
handful beansprouts
4 tbsp groundnut oil
4 tbsp dark soy sauce
1 egg, beaten

Red Onion Chicken Nems

16

Add julienned red onion and red peppers to the mixture instead of the carrot and spring onion.

17

SERVES 4

Spinach and Pine Nut Veal

Spinach and Hazelnut with Red Veal

18

Use toasted, chopped hazelnuts instead of pine nuts. Replace the Gruyere with slices of Parma ham.

Honey Veal with Spinach

19

Once the veal is removed from the slow cooker, lightly coat with honey and serve.

PREPARATION TIME: 15 MINUTES

COOKING TIME:
2 HOURS 20 MINUTES

INGREDIENTS

4 rose veal escalopes, cut in half
55 g / 2 oz / ½ stick unsalted butter
4 tbsp olive oil
225 g / 8 oz / 4 cups baby spinach
4 tbsp pine nuts, lightly toasted
4 tbsp Marsala
8 slices Gruyere

- Heat half of the olive oil in a large frying pan set over a medium heat until hot.
- Wilt the spinach in batches with a little seasoning for a minute or so, then drain in a colander and set to one side.
- Flatten the veal escalopes with a meat hammer and trim the edges so that you have rectangular shaped pieces of veal.
- Season the tops and position the wilted spinach in an even layer on top.
- Top with the pine nuts.
- Roll up into cylinders and secure using toothpicks.
- Melt some of the butter with the remaining olive oil in a large frying pan set over a moderate heat.
- Season the outside of the veal generously and pan-fry in batches, using fresh butter for each batch, for 2-3 minutes until golden brown.
- Once all the veal has been browned, wrap the Gruyere slices around them and secure using toothpicks.
- Deglaze the pan with the Marsala, then pour the contents of the pan into the slow cooker.
- Cook on a medium setting for 2 hours until the veal is tender and cooked.
- Spoon the veal and some of the accumulated juices onto serving plates.
- Serve immediately.

20

SERVES 4

Fish Soup

- Heat the olive oil in a large saucepan set over a moderate heat until hot and sweat the garlic and fennel for 4-5 minutes, stirring occasionally until softened.
- Spoon into a slow cooker and all the remaining ingredients apart from the chopped herbs and mussel meat.
- Cook on a low setting for 3 hours until the fish and seafood is tender and cooked; the soup should be thickened. If not, remove some of the liquid using a ladle.
- Adjust the seasoning to taste and discard the bay leaf.
- Add the mussel meat and warm through for 10 minutes.
- Spoon into serving bowls and garnish with the chopped herbs before serving.

PREPARATION TIME: 20 MINUTES

COOKING TIME:
3 HOURS 15 MINUTES

INGREDIENTS

2 tbsp olive oil
2 cloves garlic, minced
2 bulbs fennel, trimmed and finely chopped
300 g / 10 ½ oz / 2 cups prawns (shrimps), peeled and deveined
2 sea bass fillets, pin-boned and cut into chunks
150 g / 5 oz / 1 cup squid rings
150 g / 5 oz / 1 ½ cups cooked mussel meat
500 ml / 18 fl. oz / 2 cups fish stock
250 ml / 9 fl. oz / 1 cup passata
125 ml / 4 ½ fl. oz / ½ cup white wine
1 bay leaf
4 sprigs tarragon

GARNISH
1 tbsp tarragon leaves, finely chopped
1 tbsp chervil leaves, finely chopped

Fish Soup with Shrimp

21

Replace the sea bass with cod and change the prawns (shrimps) with brown shrimps for a British version of the soup.

22

SERVES 4

Cauliflower Cheese

- Place the cauliflower in a slow cooker and add half of the milk. Cook on a medium setting for 3 hours until the cauliflower florets are tender.
- Combine the onion halves and milk in a saucepan. Bring to the boil before removing and letting the milk infuse to one side.
- Once the cauliflower is tender, turn the slow cooker off but keep the lid on to keep the cauliflower warm.
- Strain the milk into a jug. Melt the butter in a saucepan.
- Whisk in the flour until you have smooth roux. Cook the roux for 1 minute before whisking in the milk in a slow, steady stream until you have a smooth sauce.
- Reduce the heat and simmer for 5 minutes, stirring occasionally until thickened. Adjust the seasoning
- Strain the cauliflower and arrange in serving bowls.
- Spoon the sauce on top and garnish with hazelnuts and Roquefort before serving.

PREPARATION TIME :
15 MINUTES

COOKING TIME :
3 HOURS 15 MINUTES

INGREDIENTS

2 heads of cauliflower, prepared into florets
30 g / 1 oz / 2 tbsp plain (all-purpose) flour, sifted
30 g / 1 oz / ¼ stick unsalted butter
1 l / 1 pint 16 fl. oz / 4 cups whole milk
1 onion, halved and studded with the bay leaf and cloves
1 bay leaf
6 cloves
salt and pepper

GARNISH
110 g / 4 oz / 1 cup Roquefort, cubed
55 g / 2 oz / ½ cup hazelnuts (cob nuts), roughly chopped

Cauliflower Cheese with Chorizo

23

To add a spicy kick to this dish, top this dish with slices of chorizo.

24

MAKES 18

Courgette Tajine

PREPARATION TIME :
10 MINUTES

COOKING TIME :
5 HOURS 5 MINUTES

INGREDIENTS

30 ml / 1 fl. oz / 2 tbsp olive oil
1 large courgette, sliced thinly
150 g / 5 oz / 1 ½ cups
broad beans, shelled
225 g / 8 oz / 2 cups mangetout
500 ml / 18 fl. oz / 2 cups
vegetable stock
salt and pepper

GARNISH

sprigs of mint leaves
2 tbsp mint leaves, finely sliced
1 tsp pink peppercorns

- Combine the courgette, broad beans, mangetout and stock in a slow cooker.
- Cover with a lid and braise on a low setting for 5 hours.
- Once the vegetables are tender, turn off the slow cooker.
- Adjust the seasoning to taste after cooking and stir through the olive oil.
- Ladle the tajine into serving bowls and garnish with the sliced mint and mint sprigs in the middle.
- Sprinkle over a few peppercorns before serving.

Courgette and Red Onion

25

For a more savoury version, add 1 sliced red onion to the slow cooker before cooking and cook as normal.

26

SERVES 4

Salé with Lentils

PREPARATION TIME: 10 MINUTES

COOKING TIME: 4 HOURS

INGREDIENTS

110 g / 4 oz / ⅔ cup salami, sliced
200 g / 7 oz / 1 cup Puy lentils
500 ml / 18 fl. oz / 2 cups
vegetable stock
2 tbsp flat-leaf parsley, finely
chopped
½ lemon, juiced
1 bay leaf

- Place the lentils, bay leaf and stock in a slow cooker.
- Cook on a low setting for 4 hours until the lentils have absorbed the stock and are tender.
- Drain if necessary and discard the bay leaf.
- Adjust the seasoning to taste with salt, pepper and lemon juice.
- Keep warm on a low setting.
- Preheat the grill to high.
- Grill the salami slices for a minute on both sides until they start to sizzle.
- Remove from the grill and drain on kitchen paper.
- Stir the parsley into the lentils, then ladle into serving bowls using a slotted spoon.
- Sit a couple of slices of salami on top and serve immediately.

Spicy Chorizo with Lentils

27

To add a spicy kick to this dish, top with slices of chorizo.

28

SERVES 4

Pumpkin and Cauliflower Soup

Orange and Cauliflower Soup

29

Squeeze the juice of half an orange into the stock and replace the pumpkin seed garnish with 1 tbsp of very finely chopped candied citrus peel.

Spicy Pumpkin Soup

30

Substitute the dried sage with 1 tsp chilli powder and garnish the soup with finely sliced green chilli instead of sage leaves for a spicier soup.

PREPARATION TIME :
15-20 MINUTES

COOKING TIME :
3 HOURS 15-20 MINUTES

INGREDIENTS

55 ml / 2 fl. oz / ¼ cup olive oil
1 kg / 2 lb 4 oz / 6 ½ cups pumpkin, peeled, deseeded and cubed
1 large head of cauliflower, prepared into large florets
1 clove garlic, minced
2 small onions, finely diced
1 tsp dried sage
1 ⅛ l / 2 pints / 4 ⅘ cups vegetable stock
250 ml / 9 fl. oz / 1 cup double cream
salt and pepper
To garnish
small handful of pumpkin seeds
small handful of picked sage leaves

- Heat the olive oil in a large saucepan set over a medium heat until hot.
- Sweat the onion and garlic with a little salt, stirring occasionally, until softened; 8-10 minutes.
- Add the dried sage, pumpkin and cauliflower and cover the mixture with the stock.
- Pour everything into a slow cooker and cook on a medium setting for 3 hours.
- After 3 hours, puree using a stick blender until smooth, then return to a large saucepan and cook over a low heat.
- Stir in the double cream until incorporated and adjust the seasoning to taste.
- Ladle into soup bowls and garnish with the sage leaves and a sprinkling of pumpkin seeds before serving.
- Serve any remaining pumpkin seeds in a serving bowl on the side.

31

SERVES 4

Peppers Stuffed with Cod

PREPARATION TIME :15 MINUTES

COOKING TIME :
4 HOURS 30 MINUTES

INGREDIENTS

1.2 l / 2 pints / 4 cups vegetable oil
8 green chilli peppers, tops removed and deseeded
600 g / 1 lb 5 oz / 4 cups salt-cod, rinsed in cold water overnight
55 g / 2 oz / ⅓ cup plain (all-purpose) flour
30 g / 1 oz / 2 tbsp cornflour
55 ml / 2 fl. oz / ¼ cup sparkling water, chilled
salt and pepper

FOR THE SAUCE

55 ml / 2 fl. oz / ¼ cup olive oil
2 cloves of garlic, minced
450 g / 1 lb / 3 cups vine tomatoes, cored and deseeded
30 ml / 1 fl. oz / 2 tbsp Cognac
½ tsp caster sugar
125 ml / 4 ½ fl. oz / ½ cup double cream

- Heat the olive oil in a saucepan and sauté the garlic with salt, stirring frequently before adding the tomatoes.
- Stir well then add the Cognac and the sugar. Pour into a slow cooker and cook on a low setting for 4 hours.
- Stir through the cream and pour into a food processor before pureeing.
- Adjust the seasoning to taste and pour into a saucepan.
- Cut the cod to size before stuffing the chilli peppers with it. Sift together the flour, cornflour and seasoning into a mixing bowl.
- Add a little of the sparkling water at a time and whisk until you have a thin batter.
- Heat the vegetable oil in a high-sided saucepan.
- Dip the stuffed chilli peppers in the batter and deep-fry in batches until lightly browned and crisp. Drain on kitchen paper and reheat the sauce.
- Pour the sauce into bowls and sit the peppers on top.

Peppers Stuffed with Tomato and Vodka

32

Replace the green chilli peppers with red chilli peppers and substitute the Cognac for Vodka.

33

SERVES 4

Channa Dal

PREPARATION TIME: 15 MINUTES

COOKING TIME: 4 HOURS

INGREDIENTS

2 tbsp sunflower oil
1 onion, finely chopped
3 cloves garlic, minced
5 cm / 2" ginger, peeled and minced
1 red chilli, deseeded and chopped
1 carrot, peeled and finely diced
225 g / 8 oz / 1 ¼ cup channa dal, soaked in water overnight then drained
500ml / 18 fl. oz / 2 cups vegetable stock
2 tsp ground cumin
2 tsp ground coriander seeds
1 tsp paprika
1 tsp turmeric
1 tsp garam masala
1 tsp amchoor (dried mango powder)

GARNISH

4 sprigs coriander
4 small red chillies

- Heat the oil in a large casserole dish set over a medium heat.
- Sweat together the onion, garlic, ginger and chilli with a little salt for 6-7 minutes, stirring occasionally until softened.
- Add the ground spices and stir well, then add the lentils and the stock.
- Stir well then pour into a slow cooker and cook on a low setting for 5 hours until the lentils have absorbed the stock and the mixture is akin to a thick soup.
- Adjust the seasoning to taste then ladle into soup bowls.
- Garnish with the coriander and a small chilli in each bowl.

Tarka Dal

34

Use tarka dal instead of the channa dal and green chilli instead of the red chilli. Follow the rest of the recipe and method in the same way. The amchoor powder can be replaced with the juice of ½ lemon at the end if it's too hard to source.

35

SERVES 4

Chicken Tikka Brochettes

- Combine the yogurt, oil, ginger, garlic, spices, sugar, food colouring, lemon juice, half of the chopped coriander and some seasoning in a large mixing bowl.
- Whisk until smooth, then add the chicken and stir well to coat.
- Cover and chill overnight.
- The next day, drain the chicken from the marinade and place in a slow cooker.
- Cook on a low setting for 2 hours then remove and thread onto wooden brochette skewers.
- Sprinkle with the remaining finely chopped coriander.
- Preheat the grill to hot.
- Grill the brochettes for 5-7 minutes, turning occasionally until the chicken is charred on the outside.
- Remove from the grill and serve immediately.

PREPARATION TIME: 15 MINUTES
+ OVERNIGHT MARINATING

COOKING TIME: 2 HOURS

INGREDIENTS

4 chicken breasts, cubed
2 tbsp sunflower oil
250 ml / 9 fl. oz / 1 cup plain yogurt
1 clove garlic, minced
2 cm / 1" ginger, peeled and minced
1 tbsp tandoori paste
1 tsp ground coriander seeds
1 tsp garam masala
½ tsp sugar
½ lemon, juiced
½ tsp red food colouring
2 tbsp coriander leaves, very finely chopped
8 wooden brochette skewers, soaked in cold water for 30 minutes

Lamb Tikka Brochettes

36

Replace the weight of chicken with lamb for a meatier dish.

37

SERVES 4

Leek and Potato Soup

- Heat the olive oil in a large saucepan set over a medium heat.
- Sweat the leek for 4-5 minutes with a little salt, stirring frequently, then add the potato and continue to sweat for 10 minutes until the potato starts to soften.
- Add the bay leaf, thyme and stock and stir well.
- Pour into a slow cooker and cook on a low setting for 4 hours.
- Adjust the seasoning after 4 hours and ladle into warm soup bowls.
- Garnish with the shaved Parmesan.
- Serve immediately.

PREPARATION TIME: 15 MINUTES

COOKING TIME: 4 HOURS

INGREDIENTS

2 tbsp olive oil
1 leek, sliced
2 large white potatoes, peeled and finely diced
500 ml / 18 fl. oz / 2 cups vegetable stock
1 bay leaf
1 sprig thyme

GARNISH
30 g / 1 oz / ¼ Parmesan, shaved

Leek Soup with Parmesan

38

Add a Parmesan rind to the soup before slow cooking. Puree the soup using a stick blender before garnishing with the Parmesan for a different texture.

39

SERVES 4

Tofu and Carrot Broth

Spicy Tofu Broth **40**

Add a dash (½ tsp) of Tabasco sauce at the end for a kick.

Tofu and Onion Broth **41**

Add 3 sliced spring onions to the slow cooker and use finely chopped chives instead of coriander to garnish.

PREPARATION TIME :10 MINUTES

COOKING TIME: 45 MINUTES

....

INGREDIENTS

30 ml / 1 fl. oz / 2 tbsp groundnut oil
250 g / 9 oz / 2 cups tofu, cubed
4 medium carrots, peeled and diced
4 medium eggs, beaten
2 small onions, finely chopped
2 cloves garlic, minced
½" piece of ginger, peeled and minced
568 ml / 1 pint / 2 ¼ cups vegetable stock
3 tbsp coriander leaves, finely chopped
salt and pepper

- Heat the groundnut oil in a large saucepan set over a medium heat until hot.
- Sweat the onion, garlic, ginger and carrots for 7-8 minutes, stirring frequently until they start to soften.
- Add the tofu and stock, stirring well.
- Pour into a slow cooker and cook for 2 hours on a medium setting.
- Pour back into a saucepan after 2 hours and simmer over a medium heat.
- Stir through the beaten egg and coriander until the egg starts to scramble and set.
- Adjust the seasoning to taste.
- Pour into warm soup bowls before serving.

42

SERVES 4

Curried Prawn Soup in Coconut Shell

- Combine the shallot, garlic, lemongrass, ginger, chilli, sunflower oil and seasoning in a food processor.
- Pulse until smooth then add the ground spices and sugar and pulse again until you have a paste.
- Heat the paste in a large saucepan set over a medium heat, stirring frequently for 2-3 minutes.
- Add the coconut milk and fish stock and whisk well until you have a broth.
- Pour into a slow cooker and add the shrimp and prawns.
- Cook on a low setting for 4 hours.
- Adjust the seasoning after 4 hours using lime juice, fish sauce, salt and pepper.
- Serve in hollowed out coconut halves (if available).
- Garnish with the basil leaves before serving.

Curried Chicken Soup

43

The prawns and shrimp can be replaced with two large skinless chicken breasts that have been cut into cubes.

PREPARATION TIME: 20 MINUTES

COOKING TIME: 4 HOURS

INGREDIENTS

2 tbsp sunflower oil
2 shallots, finely chopped
4 cloves garlic, chopped
10cm / 4" piece of lemongrass, chopped
5cm / 2" ginger, peeled and chopped
2 green chillies, deseeded and chopped
500 ml / 18 fl. oz / 2 cups coconut milk
250 ml / 9 fl. oz / 1 cup fish stock
8 king prawns (shrimps)
300 g / 10 ½ oz / 2 cups dried shrimp, thawed
1 tbsp Madras curry powder
1 tsp ground cinnamon
1 tsp turmeric
½ tsp paprika
1 tbsp light brown sugar
1 lime, juiced
1 tbsp fish sauce

GARNISH
4 sprigs of Thai basil leaves

44

SERVES 4

Tangy White Bean Soup

- Heat the olive oil in a large casserole dish set over a moderate heat until hot.
- Saute the leek with a little salt for 5 minutes, stirring occasionally.
- Add the remaining ingredients apart from the chives and stir well.
- Pour into a slow cooker and cover with a lid.
- Cook on a medium setting for 5 hours until the vegetables are tender.
- Adjust the seasoning to taste before ladling into serving bowls.
- Garnish with the chopped chives before serving.

White Bean and Seaweed

45

Stir through 30 ml / 1 fl. oz / 2 tbsp malt vinegar before ladling into serving bowls.

PREPARATION TIME :
15 MINUTES

COOKING TIME :
5 HOURS 10 MINUTES

INGREDIENTS

55 ml / 2 fl. oz / ¼ cups olive oil
400 g / 14 oz / 2 cups canned butter beans, drained
200 g / 7 oz / 1 cup canned sweetcorn, drained
450 g / 1 lb / 3 cups carrots, peeled with half sliced and half diced
450 g / 1 lb / 6 cups button mushrooms, halved
1 leek, sliced and washed
2 tbsp dried dulse seaweed, infused in the stock
500 ml / 18 fl. oz / 2 cups vegetable stock
salt and pepper

GARNISH
chive stalks, finely chopped

46

SERVES 4

Baked Potato and Cheese

PREPARATION TIME :
10 MINUTES

COOKING TIME :
4 HOURS 20-25 MINUTES

INGREDIENTS

30 ml / 1 fl. oz / 2 tbsp olive oil
4 baking potatoes, pricked a few
times with a fork
150 g / 5 oz / 1 ½ cups cheese, grated
salt and pepper

GARNISH
150 g / 5 oz / 2 cups baby spinach,
washed and dried
½ black truffle, shaved

- Place the potatoes in a slow cooker and cover with a lid.
- Cook on a medium setting for 4 hours until tender.
- Remove from the slow cooker and rub with the oil.
- Preheat the oven to 190°C (170° fan) / 375F / gas 5.
- Season the potatoes and arrange on a baking tray.
- Bake for 15-20 minutes until crisp on the outside.
- Remove from the oven and preheat the grill to hot.
- Open up the potatoes and sprinkle their tops with the grated cheese.
- Grill for a minute or so until the cheese is golden brown and bubbling.
- Remove from the grill and arrange on serving plates.
- Garnish with slices of the black truffle and the spinach on the side.

Baked Potato
with Blue Cheese

47

Replace the grated cheddar with the same
weight of cubed Roqeufort.

48

SERVES 4

Chicken Mulligatawny Soup

PREPARATION TIME: 15 MINUTES

COOKING TIME: 4 HOURS

INGREDIENTS

2 tbsp butter, unsalted
2 tbsp olive oil
1 leek, trimmed, sliced and washed
500 ml / 18 fl. oz / 2 cups coconut milk
500 ml / 18 fl. oz / 2 cups chicken stock
2 chicken breasts, diced
2 sticks celery, peeled and sliced
2 tsp ground cumin
2 tsp ground coriander seeds
½ tsp garam masala
2 tbsp sultanas
30 g / 1 oz / ¼ cup flaked (slivered)
almonds, toasted

- Melt the butter with the olive oil in a large, heavy-based saucepan set over a moderate heat.
- Sweat the leek and celery for 5-6 minutes, stirring occasionally, until they start to soften.
- Add the spices at this point along with 1 tsp of salt and stir well.
- Stir in the coconut milk, chicken stock and sultanas, then pour into a slow cooker.
- Cook on a low setting for 4 hours.
- Adjust the seasoning to taste after 4 hours.
- Spoon into balti dishes and garnish with the almonds and some black pepper.
- Serve immediately.

Sea Bass Mulligatawny Soup

49

Add the same weight of Sea Bass to the soup
for an alternative flavour.

50

SERVES 4

Cream of Orange Lentils

- Heat the olive oil in a large saucepan and sweat the onion and garlic with a little salt for 5 minutes.
- Add the ground cumin, ground coriander and cumin seeds, stirring well.
- Add the lentils and cover with the stock.
- Pour everything into a slow cooker and cook on a low setting for 4 hours until the lentils have absorbed most of the stock and are soft and tender.
- Once ready, stir through the carrot juice and cream and adjust the seasoning to taste.
- Pour the soup into a large saucepan and blitz until smooth using a stick blender.
- Reheat the soup over a medium heat until hot, stirring frequently.
- Spoon the soup into serving bowls and garnish each with a sprig of coriander.

PREPARATION TIME: 10 MINUTES

COOKING TIME:
4 HOURS 20 MINUTES

INGREDIENTS

2 tbsp olive oil
225 g / 8 oz / 1 ¼ cups orange split lentils
1 onion, finely chopped
1 clove garlic, minced
1 tsp cumin seeds, toasted
1 tsp ground cumin
½ tsp ground coriander seeds
500 ml / 18 fl. oz / 2 cups vegetable stock
125 ml / 4 ½ fl. oz / ½ cup carrot juice
125ml / 4 ½ fl. oz / ½ cup double cream

GARNISH
coriander

Stewed Red Cabbage

51

SERVES 4

PREPARATION TIME: 15 MINUTES

COOKING TIME :
6 HOURS 5 MINUTES

INGREDIENTS

1 large red cabbage, shredded
225 g / 8 oz / 1 ½ cups pickled beetroot, drained and sliced

125 ml / 4 ½ fl. oz / ½ cup red wine vinegar
55 g / 2 oz / ¼ cup caster (superfine) sugar
2 sticks of cinnamon
salt and pepper

GARNISH
2 bay leaves

- Combine the cabbage, red wine vinegar, sugar, cinnamon sticks and seasoning in a slow cooker.
- Cover with a lid and braise on a medium setting for 6 hours until the cabbage has softened.
- Adjust the seasoning to taste and discard the cinnamon.
- Spoon into a baking dish for presentation.
- Top with the slices of beetroot and the bay leaves in the middle.
- Serve warm or cold.

Stewed Tomatoes with Rosemary

52

SERVES 4

PREPARATION TIME: 15 MINUTES

COOKING TIME:
3 HOURS 30 MINUTES

INGREDIENTS

900 g / 2 lbs / 5 cups tomatoes
110 ml / 4 fl. oz / ½ cup olive oil
2 tsp dried rosemary
3 sprigs of rosemary

- Halve the tomatoes and set them on a tray with the cut side facing up.
- Remove the rosemary leaves from their sprigs and roughly chop them.
- Drizzle the tomato halves with half of the olive oil, seasoning, dried and fresh rosemary.
- Place in the slow cooker with the rest of the olive oil and cook on a medium setting for 3 hours until the tomatoes are soft and deep red in colour.
- Drain them and place on baking trays.
- Preheat the oven to 170°C / 325F / gas 3.
- Bake the tomatoes for 30 minutes until they have dried out.
- Serve on plates warm or cold.

53

SERVES 4

Fish Soup

PREPARATION TIME :
15-20 MINUTES

COOKING TIME :
3 HOURS 15 MINUTES

INGREDIENTS

30 ml / 1 fl. oz / 2 tbsp olive oil
2 cloves garlic, minced
2 bulbs fennel, trimmed and finely
chopped
300 g / 10 ½ oz / 2 cups prawns,
peeled and deveined
2 x 200 g / 7 oz sea bass fillets,
pin-boned and cut into large chunks
500 ml / 18 fl. oz / 2 cups fish stock
250 ml / 9 fl. oz / 1 cup passata
55 ml / 2 fl. oz / ¼ cup Cognac
30 g / 1 oz / ¼ cup fresh breadcrumbs
2 sprigs of tarragon
1 tbsp extra-virgin olive oil
salt and pepper

- Heat the olive oil in a large saucepan set over a
  moderate heat until hot and sweat the garlic and fennel
  for 5-6 minutes, stirring occasionally until softened.
- Deglaze the saucepan with the Cognac, letting it reduce
  by half.
- Spoon everything from the saucepan into a slow cooker
  and add all the remaining ingredients apart from the
  extra-virgin olive oil and the breadcrumbs.
- Cook on a low setting for 3 hours until the fish and
  seafood is tender and cooked; the soup should be
  thickened.
- Puree using a stick blender until smooth.
- If the soup is thin, thicken using the fresh breadcrumbs
  then adjust the seasoning to taste using the olive oil,
  salt and pepper.
- Ladle into warm soup bowls before garnishing.

Chunky Fish Soup **54**

Leave the soup unblended for a chunky
texture; do not use the breadcrumbs to
thicken it in this instance.

55

SERVES 4

Roasted Fennel

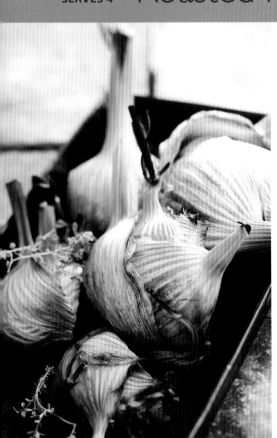

PREPARATION TIME : 5 MINUTES

COOKING TIME :
3 HOURS 30-35 MINUTES

INGREDIENTS

6 fennel bulbs
30 ml / 1 fl. oz / 2 tbsp olive oil
salt and pepper

GARNISH
sprigs of flowering thyme

- Cut half of the fennel bulbs in half.
- Arrange in a slow cooker and season.
- Cover with a lid and cook on a medium setting for 3
  hours until they start to soften.
- Remove from the slow cooker and pat dry.
- Preheat the oven to 190°C (170° fan) / 375F / gas 5.
- Arrange on a baking tray and drizzle with the olive oil
  and some more seasoning.
- Roast for 25-30 minutes until lightly coloured.
- Remove from the oven and garnish with the flowering
  thyme before serving.

Roasted Fennel with Tarragon **56**

Replace the thyme garnish with 1 small
bunch of tarragon that has been roughly
chopped.

Pork Brochettes

SERVES 4

Chicken and Pepper Brochettes  58

Replace the pork with 2" cubes of chicken breast to make chicken brochettes and add red and green chunks of peppers to the skewers.

Turkey Brochettes 59

Replace the pork with 2" cubes of turkey breast to make turkey brochettes. Cook in the slow cooker for 3 hours before threading onto skewers and grilling.

Beef Brochettes 60

Replace the pork with 2" cubes of beef fillet to make beef brochettes. Cook for 3 hours before threading onto skewers and grilling.

PREPARATION TIME :
15 MINUTES

COOKING TIME :
4 HOURS 15-20 MINUTES

INGREDIENTS

900 g / 2 lb / 6 cups pork fillet, trimmed and cut into 2" cubes
55 ml / 2 fl. oz / ¼ cup sunflower oil
1 tsp cayenne pepper
1 tsp ground cinnamon
1 tsp ground cumin
salt and pepper

GARNISH
small handful of Swiss chard, washed
8 large vine tomatoes, cored and quartered
30 ml / 1 fl. oz / 2 tbsp extra-virgin olive oil
sprigs of thyme
salt and pepper

- Combine the ground spices with a teaspoon of salt and pepper in a small pot and stir well.
- Mix the pork with half of the spice mixture in a slow cooker, then cook on a medium setting for 4 hours until tender.
- Remove from the slow cooker after 4 hours and pat dry.
- Preheat the grill to high.
- Thread the pork cubes onto 12 metal skewers and brush with the sunflower oil.
- Grill for 2-3 minutes, turning frequently until lightly coloured.
- Meanwhile, pulse the tomatoes, olive oil and some seasoning in a food processor until broken down and mushy.
- Spoon into 4 tumblers and garnish with some thyme leaves.
- Arrange the brochettes and tumblers on serving trays.
- Garnish the brochettes with pinches of the remaining spice mixture, sprigs of thyme and a few Swiss chard leaves before serving.

Peppers Stuffed with Vegetables

61

SERVES 4

PREPARATION TIME 15 MINUTES

COOKING TIME :
4 HOURS 30 MINUTES

INGREDIENTS

FOR THE STUFFED PEPPERS
30 ml / 1 fl. oz / 2 tbsp olive oil
4 large piquillo peppers (use regular red peppers if not available)
110 g / 4 oz / ½ cup quinoa
250 ml / 9 fl. oz / 1 cup vegetable stock
150 g / 5 oz / 1 ½ cups frozen petit pois, thawed
1 tbsp mint leaves, finely chopped
salt and pepper

FOR THE CREAM SAUCE
250 ml / 9 fl. oz / 1 cup double cream
1 small bunch of flat-leaf parsley leaves, finely chopped
salt and pepper

GARNISH
30 g / 1 oz / ¼ cup pine nuts, lightly toasted

- Place the quinoa in a saucepan and cook over a medium heat until the grains start to separate.
- Remove from the heat and stir through the stock.
- Pour into a slow cooker and cook on a low setting for 4 hours until the quinoa has absorbed the stock.
- Add the petit pois, mint and olive oil and set to one side.
- Preheat the grill and grill the peppers until blistered and blackened. Remove from the grill and place in a plastic bag. Tie it securely and leave for 10 minutes.
- After 10 minutes, remove the tops and the seeds.
- Fill with the quinoa mixture and place in the slow cooker to warm through as you prepare the sauce.
- Combine the cream and parsley in a saucepan and heat until it starts to thicken. Adjust the seasoning to taste before transferring to a blender.
- Arrange the peppers on a serving plate and spoon on some of the sauce. Garnish with pine nuts and serve.

Peppers Stuffed with Cous Cous

62

Replace the quinoa with the same weight of cous cous. Combine with the stock and stir before cooking on a medium setting for 2 hours.

63

SERVES 4

Red Kidney Beans with Vegetables

PREPARATION TIME :
10-15 MINUTES

COOKING TIME :
6 HOURS 10-15 MINUTES

INGREDIENTS

55 ml / 2 fl. oz / ¼ cup olive oil
800 g / 1 lb 12 oz / 4 cups canned red kidney beans, drained
75 g / 3 oz / ½ cup pancetta, cut into large cubes
2 green peppers, de-seeded and quartered
2 onions, peeled and roughly chopped
500 ml / 18 fl. oz / 2 cups vegetable stock
1 tsp smoked paprika
1 bay leaf
salt and pepper

GARNISH
1 large red chilli, de-seeded and finely sliced

- Heat a large casserole dish over a moderate heat.
- Saute the pancetta for 2-3 minutes until coloured all over, then add the peppers and onions to the dish.
- Stir well to combine and cover with a lid.
- Reduce the heat and cook until the vegetables are soft; usually 4-5 minutes.
- Remove the lid then add the kidney beans, stock, bay leaf and paprika.
- Stir well then pour into a slow cooker.
- Cover with a lid and cook on a medium setting for 6 hours until the beans are very soft.
- Remove the lid after 6 hours and discard the bay leaf.
- Adjust the seasoning to taste.
- Spoon into a ceramic serving dish and garnish the top with the sliced red chilli before serving.

Tabasco Kidney Beans

64

Add 1 tsp Tabasco sauce to the slow cooker after cooking for a spicier dish.

65

SERVES 4

Sauteéd potatoes with Tarragon

- Place the new potatoes in a slow cooker with some seasoning and cover with a lid.
- Cook on a medium setting for 4 hours until soft.
- Remove after 4 hours and pat dry.
- Place in a mixing bowl and drizzle with the olive oil and some more seasoning, tossing well.
- Heat a large frying pan over a moderate heat until hot.
- Saute the potatoes in batches with the tarragon sprigs until golden brown and crisp on the outside.
- Meanwhile, combine all the ingredients for the sauce in a food processor and blitz until smooth.
- Arrange the potatoes in a roasting tray for presentation and serve with the dipping sauce in pots.

PREPARATION TIME :
10-15 MINUTES

COOKING TIME :
4 HOURS 15-20 MINUTES

INGREDIENTS

55 ml / 2 fl. oz / ¼ cup olive oil
450 g / 1 lb / 3 cups new potatoes, halved
2 sprigs tarragon
salt and pepper

FOR THE DIPPING SAUCE
125 ml / 4 ½ fl. oz / ½ cup plain yoghurt
125 ml / 4 ½ fl. oz / ½ cup mayonnaise
2 cloves garlic, minced
2 tbsp tarragon leaves
salt and pepper

Sauteed Potatoes with Thyme

 66

Replace the tarragon with 4 sprigs of thyme and cook the same.

67

SERVES 4

Thai Red Curry Soup

- Combine half of the oil with the red chilli, garlic, ginger, soy sauce, lime juice and sugar in a food processor.
- Pulse until smooth.
- Heat the remaining oil in a large casserole dish set over a medium heat.
- Sweat the shallots with the paste for 4-5 minutes, stirring frequently.
- Add the chicken stock and the chicken and stir well.
- Pour into a slow cooker and add the rice noodle nests, making sure they are soaked in the liquid.
- Cook on a low setting for 4 hours.
- Adjust the seasoning after 4 hours using fish sauce, salt and pepper.
- Ladle into warm soup bowls and serve immediately.

PREPARATION TIME: 15 MINUTES

COOKING TIME: 4 HOURS

INGREDIENTS

2 tbsp groundnut oil
4 chicken breasts, sliced
4 shallots, finely sliced
2 cloves of garlic, minced
5cm / 2" ginger, peeled and minced
2 red chillies, deseeded and finely sliced
500 ml / 18 fl. oz / 2 cups chicken stock
4 rice noodle nests
1 lime, juiced
1 tbsp light brown sugar
1 tbsp fish sauce
1 tbsp dark soy sauce

Ginger Thai Soup

 68

Add 5cm / 2" ginger, sliced, to the slow cooker about 1 hour before the cooking is finished.

Round Courgette and Herb Tajine

Courgette and Coriander Tajine
70

Replace the chopped mint with a mixture of parsley, coriander and chervil.

Lamb Stuffed Courgette
71

Fill with lamb mince instead of cous cous for a meat version. Brown the mince in olive oil, then mix with the other ingredients before stuffing the courgette.

Sweet Courgette with Herbs
72

Coat the inside of the courgettes with honey before filling for a sweeter taste.

PREPARATION TIME: 15 MINUTES

COOKING TIME: 4 HOURS

⋯⋯⋯⋯⋯⋯⋯⋯⋯⋯⋯⋯⋯⋯⋯

INGREDIENTS

4 round courgettes, tops removed (but reserved) and insides scooped out
o 2 tbsp olive oil
175 g / 6 oz / 1 cup cous cous
500 ml / 18 fl. oz / 2 cups vegetable stock
2 onions, finely chopped
2 cloves garlic, minced
1 tsp ground cinnamon
1 tsp ground cumin
1 tsp ground ginger
1 tsp ground nutmeg
1 tsp paprika
1 tbsp honey
1 tbsp mint leaves, roughly chopped

- Place the cous cous in a large mixing bowl and cover with the olive oil and stock.
- Stir once then cover the bowl with clingfilm (plastic wrap); leave for 10 minutes.
- After 10 minutes, fluff with a fork and add the ground spices, chopped mint, honey, seasoning, onion and garlic.
- Stir well and fill the round courgettes with the cous cous.
- Place in a slow cooker and replace the tops on top of the cous cous.
- Cook on a low setting for 4 hours until the courgettes are soft and tender.
- Carefully lift out of the slow cooker and position on serving bowls.
- Spoon any accumulated juices around before serving.

SERVES 4

Veal Casserole with Gremolata Sauce

- Melt the butter with the sunflower oil in a large casserole dish sat over a moderate heat.
- Season the veal and seal well on all sides.
- Reduce the heat after the veal has been sealed and sweat the onion with a little salt until softened.
- Add the veal back to the dish and cover with the stock.
- Stir well and transfer to a slow cooker.
- Tuck the bouquet garni into the stock and cook on a low setting for 6 hours until the veal is tender.
- After 6 hours, discard the bouquet garni and adjust the seasoning to taste.
- Keep the casserole warm as you prepare the garnish.
- Mix together all ingredients for the gremolata in a small mixing bowl. Adjust the seasoning.
- Spoon the veal casserole into serving dishes and spoon the gremolata on top before serving.

PREPARATION TIME: 10 MINUTES

COOKING TIME: 6 HOURS

INGREDIENTS

FOR THE VEAL CASSEROLE
2 tbsp sunflower oil
1 tbsp butter
900 g / 2 lbs / 6 cups rose veal shoulder, cut into cubes
1 onion, chopped
500 ml / 18 fl. oz / 2 cups veal/beef stock
1 bouquet garni

FOR THE GREMOLATA SAUCE
3 tbsp, roughly chopped
4 tbsp olive oil
110 g / 4 oz / ½ cup pitted green olives
1 preserved lemon, drained and sliced
½ lemon, grated zest

Veal with Spicy Sauce

74

Add 1 tsp of chilli flakes to the gremolata sauce to add a spicy kick to this dish.

SERVES 4

Cream of Pumpkin Soup

- Heat the olive oil in a large saucepan over a medium heat and sweat the onions with some salt for 6-7 minutes until they start to soften.
- Add the pumpkin and continue to cook for 10 minutes, stirring occasionally.
- Spoon everything into a slow cooker and cover with the stock.
- Cook on a low setting for 3 hours.
- Pour everything back into a saucepan, stir through the cream and sour cream.
- Simmer the mixture for 5 minutes, then puree the soup with a stick blender until smooth.
- Adjust the seasoning to taste and ladle into warm soup bowls.
- Garnish each bowl with chives before serving.

PREPARATION TIME :
15 MINUTES

COOKING TIME :
3 HOURS 25 MINUTES

INGREDIENTS

55 ml / 2 fl. oz / ¼ cup olive oil
1 kg / 2 lb 4 oz / 6 ½ cups pumpkin, peeled, de-seeded and cut into chunks
2 small onions, finely diced
500 ml / 18 fl. oz / 2 cups vegetable stock
125 ml / 4 ½ fl. oz / ½ cup double cream
125 ml / 4 ½ fl. oz / ½ cup sour cream
salt and pepper

GARNISH
4 chive stalks, finely chopped

Peppered Pumpkin Soup

76

Add ½ tsp of cayenne pepper to the soup at the start when you are sweating the onions. Stir through the juice of ½ a lemon at the end instead of the sour cream.

SERVES 4

Clam Chowder

77

PREPARATION TIME: 10 MINUTES

COOKING TIME: 4 HOURS

....

INGREDIENTS

450 g / 1 lb / 3 cups clams, cleaned
1 cooked lobster tail, cut into chunks
75 ml / 3 fl. oz / ⅓ cup water
55 g / 2 oz / ½ stick unsalted butter
110 g / 4 oz / ⅔ cup thickly sliced
bacon, chopped
4 small onions, sliced
3 large white potatoes, peeled and
finely diced
250 ml / 9 fl. oz / 1 cup whole milk
125 ml / 4 ½ fl. oz / ½ cup double
(heavy) cream
500 ml / 18 fl. oz / 2 cups fish stock
1 bay leaf
pinch ground nutmeg

- Place a saucepan over a high heat and add the clams and water.
- Cover with a lid and cook for 2-3 minutes until the clams have opened; discard any that don't open.
- Strain the clams in a colander and collect the cooking liquor in a bowl underneath.
- Remove the clams from their shells and reserve to one side.
- Melt the butter in a large saucepan set over a medium heat and sauté the bacon until it browns, stirring occasionally.
- Add the onions and cook for a further 2-3 minutes until they start to soften.
- Add the potatoes, milk, cream, bay leaf, cooking juice and stock from the clams and nutmeg.
- Pour into a slow cooker and cook on a low setting for 4 hours until the potato starts to break down.
- Fish out the bay leaf and discard.
- Puree the mixture very briefly with a stick blender until you have thick soup-like texture.
- Stir the clams and lobster into the chowder and adjust the seasoning to taste.
- Spoon into serving bowls and serve immediately.

SERVES 4

Stewed Scallops

78

PREPARATION TIME:
120 MINUTES

COOKING TIME: 4 HOURS

....

INGREDIENTS

2 tbsp unsalted butter, melted
2 tbsp sunflower oil
12 queen scallops in their shells
½ lemon, juiced

GARNISH
flat-leaf parsley leaves
handful of rock salt

- Remove the scallops and their roe from the shells; reserve 4 of the shells but discard the rest.
- Remove the roe from the scallop flesh and reserve.
- Heat half of the sunflower oil in a large frying pan.
- Season the roe and flash fry for 1 minute, tossing and stirring frequently.
- Transfer to a food processor and blitz with half of the melted butter and some salt and pepper until smooth.
- Place the scallops in a slow cooker and season. Cook on a low setting for 4 hours until almost cooked.
- Remove after 4 hours and pat dry. Heat the butter in a pan and fry the scallops for 30 seconds on both sides.
- Reheat the roe sauce in a small saucepan set over a low heat, stirring frequently.
- Arrange rock salt on a serving platter in mounds.
- Sit the shells on the mounds of rock salt; pour the roe sauce into them, then arrange 3 scallops in each shell.

Stewed Scallops with Bacon 79

Replace the roe sauce with a bacon garnish – grill 8 rashers of thin smokey bacon and sit them on top of the scallops.

80

SERVES 4

Pistou Soup with Aged Mimolette

Breaded Pistou Soup   81

Toast 2 slices of crusty bread on both sides. Break into small chunks and add to the soup.

Pistou Soup with Parmesan   82

Change the Mimolette garnish to Parmesan. Add diced white potato to the soup as well.

Penne Pistou Soup   83

Replace the macaroni with penne for a different textured soup.

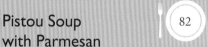

PREPARATION TIME: 15 MINUTES

COOKING TIME: 4 HOURS

....

INGREDIENTS

FOR THE SOUP
2 tbsp olive oil
1 courgette, finely diced
1 clove garlic, minced
110 g / 4 oz / 1 ½ cups green beans
110 g / 4 oz / 1 cup large macaroni
225 g / 9 oz / ½ cup canned
cannellini beans, drained
110 g / 4 oz / ¼ cup canned kidney
beans, drained
30 g / 1 oz / 2 tbsp preserved peppers,
drained and chopped
500 ml / 18 fl. oz / 2 cups vegetable
stock

FOR THE PISTOU
110 ml / 4 fl. oz / ½ cup olive oil
4 tbsp Parmesan, finely grated
2 tbsp basil leaves
2 cloves garlic, crushed

GARNISH
2 tbsp Mimolette, shaved

- Heat the olive oil in a large saucepan set over a medium heat.
- Sweat the courgette and garlic together with a little seasoning for 4-5 minutes, stirring frequently.
- Add the drained beans, green beans, stock, peppers and macaroni and stir well.
- Carefully pour into a slow cooker and cook on a low setting for 4 hours.
- After 4 hours, check to make sure the macaroni is cooked through.
- Adjust the seasoning to taste and keep warm on a low setting as you prepare the pistou.
- Blend the basil leaves, Parmesan, garlic, seasoning and a little of the oil until you have a smooth paste.
- Add the rest of the oil in a slow, steady stream as you keep the motor running until you have a thickened, pesto-like texture.
- Spoon into a bowl, ready to be used.
- Ladle the soup into warm serving bowls and spoon a tablespoon of the pistou into it.
- Garnish with shavings of the Mimolette before serving.

84

SERVES 4

Curried Pumpkin Soup

PREPARATION TIME: 15 MINUTES

COOKING TIME:
3 HOURS 25 MINUTES

....

INGREDIENTS

4 tbsp cup olive oil
1 kg / 2 lbs 4 oz / 6 ½ cups pumpkin,
peeled, de-seeded and cut into
chunks
2 small onions, finely diced
750 ml / 1 ½ pints / 3 cups vegetable
stock
1 tbsp Madras curry powder
2 tsp ground cumin
1 tsp ground coriander seeds
1 tsp Cayenne pepper

GARNISH
110 g / 4 oz / 1 cup cashews,
roughly chopped

- Heat the olive oil in a large saucepan over a medium heat and sweat the onions with some salt for 6-7 minutes until they start to soften.
- Add the ground spices and stir well.
- Add the pumpkin and continue to cook for 10 minutes, stirring occasionally.
- Spoon everything into a slow cooker and cover with the stock. Cook on a low setting for 3 hours.
- Pour everything back into a saucepan and remove half of the pumpkin using a slotted spoon.
- Puree the soup until smooth using a stick blender, then add the pumpkin back into the soup.
- Adjust the seasoning to taste and ladle into warm soup bowls.
- Garnish each bowl with chopped cashews and freshly ground black pepper before serving.

Curried Butternut Squash Soup

85

Swap the pumpkin for butternut squash for a nutritious alternative.

86

SERVES 3

Chinese Chicken Soup

PREPARATION TIME :
10-15 MINUTES

COOKING TIME :
3 HOURS 10 MINUTES

....

INGREDIENTS

30 ml / 1 fl. oz / 2 tbsp groundnut oil
1" piece of ginger, peeled and grated
2 large skinless chicken breasts,
diced
4 large carrots, peeled and cut into 2"
long thin batons
½ Chinese cabbage, shredded
1 red pepper, deseeded and finely
diced
1 red chilli, sliced
500 ml / 18 fl. oz / 2 cups
chicken stock
1 tbsp soy sauce, plus extra for
seasoning if needed
a pinch of caster sugar
pepper

GARNISH
sprigs of coriander leaves

- Heat the groundnut oil in a large frying pan set over a moderate heat.
- Season the chicken then pan-fry in the oil for 2-3 minutes until lightly coloured all over.
- Transfer to a slow cooker and add the carrot, cabbage, red pepper, chilli, chicken stock, soy sauce and sugar.
- Cook on a low setting for 4 hours.
- Adjust the seasoning to taste using pepper and a little more soy sauce if needed.
- Ladle into warm soup bowls and garnish with a sprig of coriander leaves before serving.

Chestnut Chicken Soup

87

Add 250 g / 9 oz / 1 cup drained water chestnuts to the slow cooker before cooking. Garnish with julienned fresh ginger as well as coriander.

88

SERVES 2

Ragout of Lentils

- Place the lentils, stock, bay leaf and olive oil in a slow cooker.
- Cook on a low setting for 6 hours until the lentils have absorbed most of the stock.
- Fish out the bay leaf and discard.
- Adjust the seasoning to taste.
- Stir through the chopped herbs.
- Ladle into warm serving bowls and serve immediately.

PREPARATION TIME: 10 MINUTES

COOKING TIME: 6 HOURS

INGREDIENTS

400 g / 14 oz / 2 cups Puy lentils, soaked in cold water overnight then drained
1 l / 1 pint 16 fl. oz / 4 cups vegetable stock
4 tbsp extra-virgin olive oil
1 bay leaf
2 tbsp mint, finely chopped
2 tbsp flat-leaf parsley, finely chopped

Paprika Ragout of Lentils

89

Season the ragout with the juice of 1 lemon and garnish with pinches of smoked paprika before serving.

90

SERVES 4

Cod, Herb and Cauliflower Purée

- Combine the cod, milk and bay leaf in a slow cooker and cook on a medium setting for 4 hours.
- Strain the cod, making sure you reserve the cooking juice; discard the bay leaf.
- Place the cooked cod in a bowl and crush. Season with tarragon, salt and pepper to taste.
- Cook the potato and cauliflower in separate saucepans of boiling salted water until tender; the cauliflower will take 5 minutes and the potato will take 20 minutes.
- Drain each vegetable when ready. Once the potato has cooled, mash with the butter and seasoning.
- Crush the cauliflower and fold it through the potato.
- Preheat the oven to 190°C (170° fan) / 375 F / gas 5.
- Spoon the cod into the base of a dish and top with the cauliflower and potato mixture.
- Sprinkle the cheese on top and bake for 15 minutes until golden brown. Garnish with the thyme.

PREPARATION TIME :
15-20 MINUTES

COOKING TIME :
4 HOURS 50 MINUTES

INGREDIENTS

2 heads cauliflower, prepared into florets
4 cod fillets, pin-boned and diced
500 ml / 18 fl. oz / 2 cups whole milk
1 bay leaf
1 kg / 2 lb 4 oz / 6 ⅔ cups potatoes, peeled and diced
110 g / 4 oz / 1 stick unsalted butter, softened
150 g / 5 oz / 1 ½ cups Parmesan, grated
1 small bunch of tarragon, finely chopped
salt and pepper

GARNISH
2-3 sprigs of thyme

Cod with Gruyere

91

Replace the chopped tarragon with chopped thyme and the Parmesan with the same weight of grated Gruyere.

92

SERVES 4

Oxtail with Lentils and Carrots

Oxtail with Cous Cous

 93

Remove the lentils from the dish and serve with cous cous instead.

Oxtail with Green Lentils

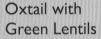 94

Add some chopped tomatoes to the slow cooker about an hour before the oxtail is ready. Substitute the brown lentils for green lentils.

Chicken with Lentils

 95

Use chicken instead of oxtail, creating a lighter dish.

PREPARATION TIME: 15 MINUTES

COOKING TIME:
6 HOURS 15 MINUTES

INGREDIENTS

2 tbsp sunflower oil
900 g / 2 lbs oxtail, cut into 4 large chunks
225 g / 8 oz / 1 ¼ cups brown lentils, soaked in water overnight then drained
2 carrots, peeled and sliced
500 ml / 18 fl. oz / 2 cups beef stock
2 bay leaves
2 sprigs rosemary

GARNISH
8 small bay leaves
4 small sprigs rosemary

• Heat the oil in a large frying pan set over a high heat until hot.
• Season the chunks of oxtail and seal in batches until golden brown.
• Remove from the pan and reduce the heat.
• Add the carrot to the pan along with the bay leaves and rosemary.
• Sauté for a couple of minutes before transferring to a slow cooker.
• Add the oxtail, stock and lentils and cook on a low setting for 6 hours.
• After 6 hours, remove the bay leaves and rosemary.
• Adjust the seasoning to taste.
• Spoon into serving bowls and garnish with fresh bay leaves and rosemary before serving.

96

SERVES 4

Green Curry Seafood Soup

- Prepare the curry paste by combining all the ingredients for it in a food processor.
- Pulse until you have a smooth paste.
- Heat a large saucepan over a moderate heat until hot then fry the green curry paste and the chopped red chilli for 2-3 minutes, stirring frequently.
- Add the fish stock and whisk well.
- Add the coconut milk and once simmering pour the mixture into a slow cooker.
- Add the seafood and cook on a medium setting for 3 hours until the seafood is cooked and tender to the touch.
- Adjust the seasoning using fish sauce, salt and pepper.
- Stir through the coriander (cilantro) leaves then ladle into serving bowls.
- Garnish with the sprigs of coriander before serving.

PREPARATION TIME. 20 MINUTES

COOKING TIME: 3 HOURS

INGREDIENTS

FOR THE CURRY PASTE
4 tbsp groundnut oil
2 green chillies, de-seeded and roughly chopped
2 tbsp coriander leaves
1 shallot, roughly chopped
1 piece of ginger, peeled and chopped
4 kaffir lime leaves
5 cm / 2" galangal, peeled and chopped
1 lemongrass stalk, chopped
1 clove of garlic, 1 lime, juiced
1 tsp light brown sugar
1 tsp fish sauce

FOR THE SOUP
300 g / 10 ½ oz / 2 cups king prawns
150 g / 5 oz / 1 cup squid rings
1.2 l / 2 pints / 5 cups fish stock
400 ml / 14 fl. oz coconut milk
1 red chilli, de-seeded and chopped
coriander leaves
1 tsp fish sauce

Red Curry Seafood Soup

97

Make this a red curry seafood soup by changing the green chillies for red chillies.

98

SERVES 4

Roasted Aubergines

- Arrange the aubergine halves skin-side down in a slow cooker.
- Season the tops and cover with a lid.
- Cook on a medium setting for 3 hours until tender.
- Remove after 3 hours and pat dry.
- Preheat the oven to 200°C (180° fan) / gas 6.
- Arrange the aubergine halves on a baking tray and drizzle with some of the olive oil.
- Layer the tomato slices on top and drizzle with more olive oil and some seasoning.
- Top each half with a thyme sprig and roast for 20-25 minutes until golden brown on top.
- Remove from the oven and serve on wooden platters.

PREPARATION TIME :
10 MINUTES

COOKING TIME :
3 HOURS 25-30 MINUTES

INGREDIENTS

55 ml / 2 fl. oz / ¼ cup olive oil
2 large aubergines, halved lengthways
4 large vine tomatoes, sliced
4 sprigs of thyme
salt and pepper

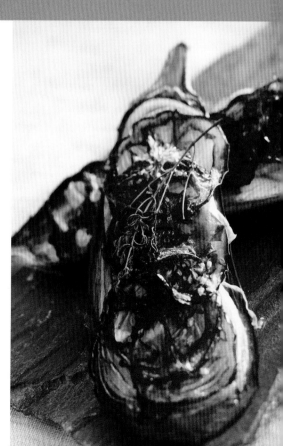

Glazed Aubergines

99

Paste onto the contents of the aubergine with honey for a sweet aubergine.

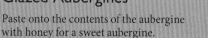

100

SERVES 4

Cipaille

- Heat the oil in a large casserole dish. Season the meats and brown them one by one in the casserole dish, moving them to the slow cooker once sealed.
- Add the onions, potatoes, bay leaf and stock. Cook on a low setting for 6 hours. Drain and pour the cooking juice into a saucepan.
- Reduce by half over a moderate heat until thickened.
- Preheat the oven to 170°C (150° fan) / 325F / gas 3.
- Arrange the meat and cooking juice in a pudding bowl.
- Roll the pastry out on a floured surface to ½ cm thick.
- Use it to cover the top of the pudding bowl. Bore a small hole in the middle of the pastry to let the steam escape.
- Bake for 35-45 minutes until the pastry is cooked through and the sauce is bubbling through the middle.
- Remove from the oven and let it sit for 5 minutes before garnishing with oregano and serving.

PREPARATION TIME: 25 MINUTES

COOKING TIME : 7 HOURS

INGREDIENTS

55 ml / 2 fl. oz / ¼ cup sunflower oil
450 g / 1 lb / 3 cups steak, cubed
450 g / 1 lb / 3 cups pork fillet, cubed
2 boneless chicken thighs, cubed
1 rabbit loin, trimmed and cubed
2 onions, finely chopped
4 white potatoes, peeled and diced
500 ml / 18 fl. oz / 2 cups beef stock
1 bay leaf
160 g / 5 ½ oz / 1 sheet ready-made shortcrust pastry
plain (all-purpose) flour, for dusting
salt and pepper

Cream of Courgette Soup

101

SERVES 4

PREPARATION TIME: 15 MINUTES

**COOKING TIME :
3 HOURS 20-25 MINUTES**

INGREDIENTS

30 ml / 1 fl. oz / 2 tbsp sesame oil
2 large courgettes, diced
1 leek, finely sliced and washed
500 ml / 18 fl. oz / 2 cups vegetable
stock
4 rice noodle nests
125 ml / 4 ½ fl. oz / ½ cup double cream
salt and pepper

GARNISH

2 tbsp sesame seeds
12 water biscuits/crackers

- Heat the sesame oil in a large saucepan set over a medium heat.
- Sweat the leek and courgette for 8-10 minutes, stirring occasionally, until softened.
- Add the stock then pour everything into a slow cooker.
- Cook on a low setting for 3 hours.
- Pour back into a saucepan and add the cream, stirring well.
- Cook over a medium heat for a few minutes before pureeing with a stick blender until smooth.
- Adjust the seasoning to taste and keep warm over a low heat.
- Blanch the rice noodles in a large saucepan of boiling, salted water for 1 minute until soft.
- Drain and reserve to one side.
- Ladle the soup into warm bowls and sit a rice noodle nest in the middle of the soup.
- Garnish with a sprinkle of sesame seeds before serving.

Lentil Soup with Tomatoes

102

SERVES 6

PREPARATION TIME: 10 MINUTES

**COOKING TIME:
4 HOURS 40 MINUTES**

INGREDIENTS

2 tbsp vegetable oil
1 onion, finely chopped
2 cloves garlic, minced
225 g / 8 oz / 1 ¼ cups
orange split lentils
500 ml / 18 fl. oz / 2 cups vegetable stock
175 g / 6 oz / 1 cup cherry tomatoes, halved

GARNISH

110 g / 4 oz / ⅔ cup chorizo, sliced
2 tbsp coriander leaves, chopped

- Heat the oil in a large saucepan set over a moderate heat.
- Sweat the onion and garlic for 5-6 minutes, stirring occasionally, until they start to soften.
- Add the lentils and stir well.
- Cover with the stock, then pour everything into a slow cooker.
- Cook on a low setting for 4 hours until the lentils have absorbed the stock.
- Add the tomatoes after 4 hours and continue to cook for 30 minutes.
- Adjust the seasoning to taste and keep on a low setting as you prepare the garnish.
- Preheat the grill to hot and grill the chorizo slices for a minute on both sides until crisp.
- Drain on kitchen paper.
- Ladle the soup into warm bowls and garnish with the coriander and chorizo slices before serving.

103

SERVES 4

Mixed Vegetable Tajine

- Heat half of the olive oil in a large saucepan set over a moderate heat until hot.
- Sweat the onion, garlic and carrot for 5 minutes until softened.
- Add the potato, courgette and prunes and stir again.
- Add the ground spices, stir thoroughly before adding the honey, prunes and stock.
- Pour into a slow cooker and cover with a lid.
- Cook on a medium setting for 4 hours until the vegetables are soft.
- Adjust the seasoning to taste before ladling into serving dishes.
- Garnish with the coriander leaves before serving.

PREPARATION TIME :
15 MINUTES

COOKING TIME :
4 HOURS 15-20 MINUTES

INGREDIENTS

55 ml / 2 fl. oz / ¼ cup olive oil
450 g / 1 lb / 3 cups white potatoes, peeled and diced
300 g / 10 ½ oz / 2 cups carrots, peeled and sliced
150 g / 5 oz / 1 cup prunes
1 courgette (zucchini), sliced
2 onions, sliced
4 cloves of garlic, lightly crushed
1 tsp ras al hanout
1 tsp ground cumin
1 tsp paprika
1 tbsp honey
500 ml / 18 fl. oz / 2 cups vegetable stock
salt and pepper

GARNISH
2 tbsp picked coriander leaves

Vegetable and Sultana Tajine

104

Add a handful of sultanas to the slow cooker just before serving to add a sweet taste.

105

SERVES 4

Curry and Shrimp Soup

- Heat the groundnut oil in a large saucepan set over a medium heat until hot.
- Sweat the celery and turnip for 6-7 minutes, stirring occasionally, until they start to soften.
- Add the ground spices and stir well.
- Add all the remaining ingredients apart from the baby spinach, then pour carefully into a slow cooker.
- Cook on a low setting for 4 hours.
- After 4 hours, add the spinach and stir well.
- Let it wilt, then turn off the slow cooker once wilted.
- Adjust the seasoning to taste before ladling into warm soup bowls.
- Serve immediately.

PREPARATION TIME: 15 MINUTES

COOKING TIME: 4 HOURS

INGREDIENTS

2 tbsp groundnut oil
300 g / 10 ½ oz / 2 cups prawns (shrimps)
150 g / 5 oz / 2 ½ oz baby spinach
500 ml / 18 fl. oz / 2 cups fish stock
1 turnip, peeled and diced
1 tsp Madras curry powder
1 tsp paprika
½ tsp Cayenne pepper
2 sticks of celery, sliced
2 tbsp pumpkin seeds, lightly toasted
1 tbsp soy sauce
1 tbsp fish sauce

Spicy Curry Shrimp Soup

106

Add julienned strips of ginger (2 tbsp) and a finely sliced red chilli to the soup before cooking in the slow cooker. Garnish with coriander sprigs.

107

SERVES 4

Stewed Cabbage

PREPARATION TIME :
10 MINUTES

COOKING TIME :
4 HOURS 15 MINUTES

INGREDIENTS

2 large Savoy cabbage
30 g / 1 oz / ¼ stick butter
100 g / 4 oz / ⅔ cup pancetta, cubed
250 ml / 9 fl. oz / 1 cup chicken stock
250 ml / 9 fl. oz / 1 cup water
salt and pepper

- Cut the cabbages in half; remove the hard inner cores, then cut the halves into large chunks.
- Melt the butter in a large casserole dish over a moderate heat until it stops foaming.
- Add the pancetta and sauté it for 3-4 minutes, stirring occasionally until the pancetta is golden in colour.
- Add the cabbage to the pan and cook, stirring a few times, for 1-2 minutes.
- Spoon the cabbage and pancetta into a slow cooker and cover with the stock.
- Cover with a lid and braise on a medium setting for 4 hours.
- Adjust the seasoning to taste before spooning into serving dishes.

108

SERVES 4

Orange Lentil Soup

PREPARATION TIME: 10 MINUTES

COOKING TIME: 4 HOURS

INGREDIENTS

FOR THE SOUP
2 tbsp olive oil
225 g / 8 oz / 1 ¼ cups orange split lentils
1 onion, finely chopped
1 clove garlic, minced
750 ml / 1 pint 6 fl. oz / 3 cups vegetable stock
1 bay leaf

GARNISH
110 g / 4 oz / ⅔ cup hazelnuts

- Heat the olive oil in a large saucepan set over a medium heat.
- Sweat the onion, garlic and bay leaf with a little salt for 5-6 minutes, stirring occasionally, until translucent and softened.
- Add the lentils and cover with the stock.
- Pour everything into a slow cooker and cook on a low setting for 4 hours until the lentils have absorbed ⅔rds of the stock and are soft and tender.
- Adjust the seasoning to taste and keep warm to one side.
- Lightly toast the hazelnuts in a dry frying pan set over a medium heat until they start to release their aroma.
- Roughly chop the hazelnuts and season to taste.
- Spoon the soup into serving bowls and garnish with the toasted hazelnuts on top before serving.

Tangy Orange Lentil Soup 109

Replace 110ml / 4 fl. oz / ½ cup of the stock with freshly squeezed orange juice for a tangy version.

110

SERVES 4

Crispy Chicken Breasts

Cripsy Paprika Chicken Breast

111

Season the flour with paprika, a pinch of Cayenne and some dried oregano before dipping the chicken in it.

Skewered Chicken with Yoghurt

112

Remove the salad garnish and thread the chicken onto skewers after they have been cooked. Serve with a yogurt dipping sauce.

Crispy Turkey Pops

113

Replace the chicken with turkey for a leaner option. Create bite size pieces and serve with dips.

PREPARATION TIME: 10 MINUTES

COOKING TIME:
1 HOUR 30 MINUTES

INGREDIENTS

FOR THE CRISPY
CHICKEN BREASTS
4 chicken breasts, cut into
8 large strips
55 g / 2 oz / ⅓ cup plain
(all purpose) flour
2 eggs, beaten
110 g / 4 oz / ½ cup panko
breadcrumbs

FOR THE SALAD GARNISH
2 tbsp extra-virgin olive
handful yellow cherry tomatoes,
halved
handful lamb's lettuce
handful beansprouts
½ courgette, sliced

- Place the chicken in a slow cooker and season.
- Cook on a high setting for 1 hour, then remove and pat dry.
- Preheat the oven to 190°C (170° fan) / 375F / gas 5.
- Season the flour with salt and pepper and dip the chicken in the flour, shaking off any excess.
- Dip in the egg, then roll in the breadcrumbs.
- Arrange on a baking tray and bake for 20-25 minutes until golden and crispy.
- Remove when ready and let them cool for a few minutes as you prepare the garnish.
- Arrange the salad garnish on serving plates and drizzle with the olive oil.
- Sit the chicken on top and serve immediately.

114

SERVES 4

Pea and Potato Tajine

PREPARATION TIME: 15 MINUTES

COOKING TIME:
4 HOURS 15 MINUTES

INGREDIENTS

2 tbsp olive oil
2 onions, sliced
3 cloves garlic, minced
350 g / 12 oz / 3 cups frozen petit
pois, thawed
450 g / 1 lb / 3 cups Maris Piper
potatoes, peeled and diced
1 tsp ras el hanout (Moroccan spice
blend)
1 tsp ground cumin
1 tsp paprika
750 ml / 1 pint 6 fl. oz / 3 cups
vegetables stock

GARNISH
pinch ground cinnamon

- Heat the olive oil in a large casserole dish set over a medium heat until hot.
- Sweat the onion and garlic with a little salt for 10 minutes, stirring occasionally until softened.
- Add the potato, peas and ground spices and stir thoroughly.
- Cover with the stock and pour into a slow cooker.
- Cover with a lid and cook on a medium setting for 4 hours until the potato is tender and soft.
- Adjust the seasoning to taste before ladling into serving bowls.
- Garnish with a pinch of ground cinnamon before serving.

Pea and Pumpkin Tajine

115

Swap the potato with pumpkin to brighten up this dish

116

MAKES 16

Ratatouille and Feta Savoury Cupcakes

PREPARATION TIME: 20 MINUTES

COOKING TIME:
4 HOURS 30 MINUTES

INGREDIENTS

FOR THE RATATOUILLE
110 ml / 4 fl. oz / ½ cup olive oil
1 aubergine, diced
1 courgette, diced
1 red pepper, diced
1 yellow pepper, diced
1 red green, diced
1 onion, chopped
2 gloves garlic, finely chopped
2 plum tomatoes, chopped
1 bouquet garni

FOR THE CUPCAKE BATTER
2 tbsp sunflower oil
350 g / 12 oz / 1 ⅔ cups plain (all
purpose) flour
2 tbsp butter, melted
225 g / 8 oz / 2 cups feta, cubed
4 eggs
2 tsp baking powder

GARNISH
4 sprigs marjoram

- In a large frying pan, heat a little of the olive oil and flash fry the vegetables for 2-3 minutes.
- Place all the vegetables in a slow cooker and mix in the bouquet garni and the chopped tomatoes.
- Cook on a low setting for 4 hours.
- Drain after 4 hours and set to one side to cool.
- Preheat the oven to 180°C (160° fan) / 350F / gas 4.
- Line two mini cupcake trays with 8 cases in each.
- In a large bowl, beat the eggs until light and frothy.
- Add the flour, melted butter, sunflower oil and baking powder and beat again until smooth.
- Fold in the feta and ratatouille and season the batter well with salt and black pepper.
- Spoon the batter into the cases and bake for 20 minutes.
- Remove from the oven and allow them to cool in the tins before turning out and removing from the cases.
- Serve warm or cold, garnished with marjoram.

Ratatouille and Cheddar Cupcakes

117

Add an English twist to these Mediterranean-style cupcakes but using smooth-tasting Cheddar.

118

SERVES 4

Scallop Brochettes

- Prepare the garnish by combining the mango, lime juice and sugar in a food processor.
- Pulse until you have a smooth puree, then spoon into a bowl, cover and chill until needed. Place the scallops in a slow cooker and season. Cook on a medium setting for 3 hours until firm.
- Remove from the slow cooker and pat dry. Melt the butter in a pan. Fry the pineapple for 1-2 minutes until starting to colour at the edges.
- Remove from the heat and set to one side. Preheat the grill to high. Thread 4 cubes of foie gras and 4 scallops onto each skewer.
- Season and grill for 3 minutes. Garnish with paprika.
- Spoon some of the mango puree onto serving plates.
- Top with slices of warm pineapple and handfuls of salad. Arrange the brochettes next to the salad and garnish the dish with some dill sprigs before serving.

PREPARATION TIME: 20 MINUTES

COOKING TIME: 3 HOURS

INGREDIENTS

16 queen scallops, roe removed
1 lobe of duck foie gras, cut into 16 cubes

GARNISH

½ pineapple, peeled, cored and cut into strips
2 mangoes, destoned and diced
1 lime, juiced
1 tsp caster (superfine) sugar
110 g / 4 oz / 2 cups mixed leaf salad
4 sprigs dill
pinch Cayenne pepper

Marinated Scallop Brochettes

119

Marinade the scallops in a mixture of olive oil (55 ml / 2 fl. oz / ¼ cup), orange juice (juice of 1) and star anise (2) before cooking in the slow cooker.

120

SERVES 4

Parsnips Soup with Pancetta

- Melt the butter with the olive oil in a large saucepan.
- Add the garlic and parsnip and sweat with a little salt for 15-20 minutes, stirring occasionally.
- Spoon everything into a slow cooker and cover with the stock and milk. Cook on a low setting for 3 hours.
- After 3 hours, pour everything back into a saucepan and puree using a stick blender until smooth.
- Add the double cream and simmer the soup as you prepare the garnish. Preheat the grill to high.
- Line a tray with greaseproof paper and line with the pancetta. Grill for 3-4 minutes until golden and crisp.
- Remove from the grill and drain on kitchen paper.
- Adjust the seasoning of the soup if necessary then ladle into serving bowls.
- Garnish with rashers of pancetta and a pinch of ground white pepper before serving.

PREPARATION TIME: 15 MINUTES

COOKING TIME:
3 HOURS 30 MINUTES

INGREDIENTS

2 tbsp butter
2 tbsp olive oil
1 kg / 2 lbs 4 oz / 6 ½ cups, peeled and diced
1 clove garlic, minced
500 ml / 18 fl. oz / 2 cups vegetable stock
250 ml / 9 fl. oz / 1 cup milk
4 tbsp double (heavy) cream

GARNISH

8 rashers pancetta
pinch ground white pepper

Carrot Soup with Pancetta

121

Change the weight of parsnips for the same weight of carrots for a colour filled soup.

122

SERVES 4

Spicy Rabbit and Clementine Casserole

Rabbit with Herbs 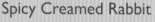 123

Remove the ground spices and replace with dried oregano, dried tarragon and dried thyme.

Spicy Creamed Rabbit 124

Add 125 ml / 4 ½ fl. oz / ½ cup double (heavy) cream after the rabbit has finished cooking in the slow cooker to make a cream sauce to go with it.

Spicy Beef Casserole 125

Replace the weight of rabbit with beef and cook until tender.

PREPARATION TIME: 20 MINUTES

COOKING TIME:
5 HOURS 20 MINUTES

INGREDIENTS

2 tbsp olive oil
1 tbsp butter
2 small rabbits, jointed
2 tbsp plain (all purpose) flour
2 onions, sliced
1 clove garlic, minced
3 sticks of cinnamon
4 clementines, peeled and segmented
2 tbsp Cognac
1 tsp ground cinnamon
1 tsp ground coriander seeds
½ tsp Cayenne pepper
½ tsp smoked paprika
500 ml / 18 fl. oz / 2 cups chicken stock
1 bay leaf

- Dust the rabbit pieces with the flour, shaking off any excess.
- Season well and set on a plate.
- Heat the butter and olive oil together in a large casserole dish set over a moderate heat.
- Seal the rabbit pieces, working in batches, until golden brown.
- Reduce the heat under the dish and add the onions, garlic, bay leaf, cinnamon sticks and ground spices and sweat for 5-6 minutes, stirring occasionally until softened.
- Deglaze the dish with the Cognac, then add the stock and stir well.
- Pour everything into a slow cooker.
- Cook on a low setting for 5 hours.
- Adjust the seasoning to taste after 5 hours and pour back into a casserole dish before serving.

126

SERVES 4

Saffron Mushrooms in Sauce

- Combine the mushrooms, olive oil, infused stock and seasoning in a slow cooker.
- Cover with a lid and cook on a medium setting for 4 hours until the mushrooms are tender.
- Adjust the seasoning to taste before pouring into a roasting tray.
- Preheat the oven to 180°C (160° fan) / 350F / gas 4.
- Sprinkle the chopped garlic on top and bake for 10 minutes.
- Remove after 10 minutes and let the dish stand for a few minutes before garnishing with rocket leaves.
- Serve immediately.

PREPARATION TIME :
10-15 MINUTES

COOKING TIME :
4 HOURS 15 MINUTES

INGREDIENTS

30 ml / 1 fl. oz / 2 tbsp olive oil
450 g / 1 lb / 3 cups field mushrooms, peeled
500 ml / 18 fl. oz / 2 cups vegetable stock
a pinch of saffron threads, infused in the stock
salt and pepper

GARNISH
small handful of rocket leaves

Saffron Tofu in Sauce

127

Substitute half the weight of the mushrooms for cubed tofu.

128

SERVES 4

Stuffed Cabbage

- Place 4 large cabbage leaves in a large saucepan of salted, boiling water for 1 minute until softened.
- Remove from the water and let them cool as you prepare the filling.
- Heat the vegetable oil in a large saucepan and sweat the onion, carrot and celery with the bay leaf and a little seasoning for 10-12 minutes until softened.
- Remove ⅓ of the sweated vegetables and place in a bowl to one side. Add the minced pork to the saucepan and stir well.
- Spoon the pork and vegetable filling into the middle of the cabbage leaves and bring the leaves around the filling to form balls. Tie securely with kitchen string and arrange in a slow cooker.
- Pour in the stock and the reserved vegetables.
- Cook on a medium setting for 5 hours. Adjust the seasoning to taste before spooning into a serving bowl, pouring the vegetable broth around them.

PREPARATION TIME :
10-15 MINUTES

COOKING TIME :
5 HOURS 20 MINUTES

INGREDIENTS

55 ml / 2 fl. oz / ¼ cup olive oil
1 large savoy cabbage, leaves removed
300 g / 10 ½ oz / 2 cups minced pork
3 onions, finely chopped
4 sticks of celery, peeled and finely diced
450 g / 1 lb / 3 cups carrots, peeled and finely diced
1 bay leaf
750 ml / 1 pint 6 fl. oz / 3 cups vegetable stock
salt and pepper

Stuffed Red Cabbage

129

Replace the Savoy cabbages with red cabbage for a colourful and tasty change.

130

SERVES 4

Mini Chicken Brochettes

PREPARATION TIME: 15 MINUTES

COOKING TIME:
2 HOURS 30 MINUTES

INGREDIENTS

FOR THE BROCHETTES
8 chicken breast mini fillets
2 eggs, beaten
55 g / 2 oz / ⅓ cup plain
(all purpose) flour
110 g / 4 oz / 1 cup breadcrumbs
1 tbsp paprika
1 tsp dried oregano
1 tsp dried rosemary
1 tsp garlic salt
1 tsp ground black pepper

FOR THE SAUCE
225 g / 8 oz / 1 cup peanut butter
4 tbsp light soy sauce
2 cloves garlic, minced
¼ tsp ground black pepper
125 ml / 4 ½ fl. oz / ½ cup hot water

GARNISH
1 cucumber, peeled and sliced

- Place all the ingredients for the sauce in a slow cooker and cook on a low setting for 2 hours.
- Puree in a food processor after two hours until smooth.
- Pour into a small saucepan and set to one side.
- Preheat the oven to 200°C (180° fan) / 400F / gas 6.
- Combine the flour with the herbs, spices and seasoning.
- Dip the chicken mini fillets into the flour, shaking off the excess.
- Dip into the beaten egg to coat evenly then in the breadcrumbs, making sure the fillets are evenly coated.
- Arrange on a baking tray. Bake for 15-20 minutes.
- Remove from the oven and thread onto bamboo skewers. Reheat the peanut sauce at the same time over a low heat.
- Arrange two brochettes on each plate and garnish with a wedge of cucumber. Pour the sauce on top and serve.

Spicy Turkey Brochettes
131

Replace the chicken fillets with strips of turkey breast. Add a dash of Tabasco to the peanut sauce as well for a chilli kick.

132

SERVES 4

Chickpea and Chorizo Soup

PREPARATION TIME: 15 MINUTES

COOKING TIME:
5 HOURS 25 MINUTES

INGREDIENTS

2 tbsp olive oil
1 onion, finely chopped
2 cloves garlic, minced
55 g / 2 oz / ⅓ cup chorizo, finely chopped
175 g / 6 oz / 1 cup dry chickpeas (garbanzo beans), soaked in cold water overnight then drained
1.2 l / 2 pint / 4 ⅘ cups vegetable stock

GARNISH
55 g / 2 oz / ⅓ cup chorizo, sliced
½ baguette, cut into thin slices
1 clove garlic, minced
110 g / 4 oz / ⅔ cup preserved sundried tomatoes, drained
110 ml / 4 fl. oz / ½ cup olive oil

- Prepare the garnish by pulsing together the garlic, sun-dried tomatoes and a little of the oil in a food processor.
- Transfer to a bowl and chill. Heat the olive oil for the soup in a large saucepan set over a medium heat.
- Sweat the onion, chorizo and garlic with a little salt for 5 minutes until they start to soften. Add the chickpeas and stock and stir well.
- Pour into a slow cooker and cook on a medium setting for 5 hours. Adjust the seasoning and keep warm on a low setting as you finish the garnish.
- Preheat the grill to high. Toast the baguette slices for 1 minute on both sides until golden in colour.
- Remove and grill the chorizo slices for the soup garnish for 1 minute on both sides.
- Ladle the soup into bowls and place a couple of slices of chorizo on each. Spread the baguette with the sun-dried tomato tapenade. Serve immediately.

Nutty Chickpea Soup
133

Use brown chickpeas instead of regular chickpeas for a nuttier flavour.

134

SERVES 4

Homemade Moussaka Casserole

Beef Moussaka Casserole

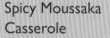 135

Change the lamb mince for beef mince. Stir the aubergine (eggplant) into the béchamel before layering.

Spicy Moussaka Casserole

136

Add ½ tsp of Cayenne pepper to the tomato sauce at the same time as the ground spices. Garnish the dish with sliced red chilli.

Red Pepper Moussaka Casserole

137

Remove ⅓ of the tomatoes and add a diced red pepper for extra crunch.

PREPARATION TIME: 20 MINUTES

COOKING TIME:
5 HOURS 30 MINUTES

INGREDIENTS

2 tbsp olive oil
1 onion, finely chopped
2 cloves garlic, minced
½ tsp dried oregano
½ tsp dried basil
½ tsp ground cinnamon
½ tsp ground cumin
350 g / 12 oz / 2 cups tomatoes, cored and chopped
2 tbsp sunflower oil
500 g / 1 lb 2 oz / 3 ⅓ cups lamb mince
½ tsp dried oregano
½ tsp paprika
2 tbsp olive oil
2 medium aubergines, thinly sliced
1 tbsp butter
1 tbsp plain (all purpose) flour
150 ml / 5 fl. oz / 3/5 cup milk

- Brown the lamb mince with half of the ground spices and some seasoning for 5-6 minutes, stirring and breaking up the mince with a wooden spoon.

- Heat the olive oil in a large saucepan and sweat the onion and garlic with a little salt for 4-5 minutes until softened. Add the remaining ground spices and tomatoes.

- Pour everything into a slow cooker and cook on a low setting for 3 hours.

- Meanwhile, griddle the aubergine in batches with a little salt until lightly charred.

- Prepare the béchamel by melting the butter in a small saucepan set over a medium heat.

- Whisk in the flour until you have a roux.

- Cook the roux for a minute, then whisk in the milk in a slow, steady stream until you have a smooth sauce.

- Simmer the sauce for 5 minutes over a low heat, adjusting the seasoning to taste.

- Assemble the casserole by spooning the tomato sauce into the base of 4, individual glass casseroles.

- Top with the aubergine, then the meat and repeat the layers.

43

138

SERVES 4

Bouillabaisse

PREPARATION TIME :
20 MINUTES

COOKING TIME :
6 HOURS 30 MINUTES

....

INGREDIENTS

450 g / 1 lb red mullet fillets, pin
boned and trimmed
450 g / 1 lb monkfish, cut into large
chunks
55 ml / 2 fl. oz / ¼ cup olive oil
55 ml / 2 fl. oz / ¼ cup Pernod
568 ml / 1 pint / 2 ¼ cups water
568 ml / 1 pint / 2 ¼ cups fish stock
450 g / 1 lb / 2 ½ cups vine tomatoes,
cut into wedges
1 tbsp tomato puree
1 fennel bulb, trimmed and sliced
2 onions finely chopped
4 cloves garlic, minced
2 tarragon stalks
1 bay leaf
salt and pepper

- Heat the olive oil over a moderate heat. Sweat the fennel, onion, garlic for 10 minutes with a little salt, stirring occasionally.
- Stir in the tomato puree, tomatoes, bay leaf and tarragon stalks.
- Stir well and cover with the fish stock and water.
- Pour into a slow cooker and cook on a low setting for 3 hours.
- Strain into a large, clean saucepan, pressing the tomatoes and all other ingredients through the sieve.
- Add the Pernod to the broth, then add the monkfish, red mullet fillets and return to the slow cooker for 3 hours on a low setting.
- After three hours, adjust the seasoning to taste and turn off the cooker but keep covered with a lid. Preheat the grill to high.
- Toast the baguette slices for a minute on both sides, then remove from the grill and sprinkle the Gruyere on top.
- Return to the grill for a minute until golden brown and bubbling.
- Ladle the Bouillabaisse into warm soup bowls and position the fish on top.

139

SERVES 4

Roast Potatoes with Béchamel

PREPARATION TIME :15 MINUTES

COOKING TIME : 2 HOURS
45-50 MINUTES

....

INGREDIENTS

FOR THE ROAST POTATOES
110 ml / 4 fl. oz / ¼ cup sunflower oil
450 g / 1 lb / 3 cups potatoes, peeled
and sliced
salt and pepper

FOR THE BECHAMEL SAUCE
30 g / 1 oz / 2 tbsp plain (all-purpose)
flour, sifted
30 g / 1 oz / ¼ stick unsalted butter
500 ml / 18 fl. oz / 2 cups whole milk
1 onion, halved and studded with the
bay leaf and cloves
1 bay leaf
6 cloves
salt and pepper

GARNISH
110 g / 4 oz / 1 ½ cups mixed leaf
salad

- Place the potatoes in a slow cooker and sprinkle with water. Cover and cook on a medium setting for 2 hours.
- Preheat the oven to 200°C (180° fan) / 400F / gas 6.
- Pour the oil into a roasting tray and place in the oven for 10 minutes. Remove after 10 minutes and add the potato slices.
- Coat in oil and return to the oven for 40-45 minutes.
- Combine the onion and the milk in a saucepan.
- Bring to the boil before removing. Strain the infused milk into a jug after 20 minutes.
- Melt the butter in a saucepan set over a medium heat.
- Whisk in the flour until you have smooth roux.
- Cook the roux for 1 minute before whisking in the milk in a slow, steady stream until you have a smooth sauce.
- Reduce the heat and simmer the sauce for 5 minutes..
- Spoon some of the sauce on top and garnish with the mixed leaf salad.

Roast Potatoes
with Mornay Sauce

140

Add 110 g / 4 oz / 1 cup grated Gruyere to the bechamel sauce and cook the same way.

141

SERVES 4

Sweet Potatoes with Honey

- Whisk together the olive oil and honey in a small mixing bowl.
- Coat the sweet potato in the honey and oil mixture and season generously.
- Place in a slow cooker and cover with a lid.
- Cook on a medium setting for 4 hours until tender.
- Remove from the slow cooker and arrange in a roasting tray along with the cloves and raisins.
- Preheat the oven to 200°C (180° fan) / 400F / gas 6.
- Roast the sweet potatoes for 20 minutes until coloured and golden at the edges.
- Remove from the oven and season a little more before spooning into serving dishes.
- Garnish with the coriander before serving.

PREPARATION TIME :
15 MINUTES

COOKING TIME :
4 HOURS 30 MINUTES

INGREDIENTS

55 ml / 2 fl. oz / ¼ cup olive oil
900 g / 2 lb / 6 cups sweet potatoes, peeled and diced
110 ml / 4 fl. oz / ½ cup honey
100 g / 4 oz / ½ cup golden raisins
1 tsp cloves
salt and pepper

GARNISH
sprigs of coriander (cilantro)

Maple Roasted Sweet Potatoes

142

Replace the honey with the same volume of maple syrup and cook the same.

143

SERVES 4

Fennel and Thyme Tajine

- Place the fennel bulb halves in a slow cooker and sprinkle with a little water.
- Cover with a lid and cook on a medium setting for 3 hours until softened.
- Remove after 3 hours and pat dry.
- Preheat the oven to 190° C (170° fan) / 375 F / gas 5.
- Place the fennel in a large mixing bowl and add the olive oil, ras al hanout, sugar and seasoning and toss well.
- Arrange the fennel bulbs with their cut sides facing up on a baking tray.
- Top with the tomato halves and place a thyme sprig on top.
- Roast for 20-25 minutes until lightly coloured.
- Remove from the oven and transfer to a serving platter.
- Serve immediately.

PREPARATION TIME: 10 MINUTES

COOKING TIME:
3 HOURS 20 MINUTES

INGREDIENTS

55 ml / 2 fl. oz / ¼ cup olive oil
4 large fennel bulbs, trimmed and halved
4 vine tomatoes, halved
8 sprigs of thyme
1 tsp ras al hanout
½ tsp caster (superfine) sugar
salt and pepper

Olive and Fennel Tajine

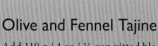

144

Add 110 g / 4 oz / ⅔ cup pitted black olives to the baking tray before roasting.

145

SERVES 4

Lentil and Chayote Stew

Lentil and Chorizo Stew

146

Add 55 g / 2 oz / ⅓ cup diced chorizo to the slow cooker before cooking.

Lentil and Butternut Squash

147

Instead of using chayote use butternut squash. Peel and core it, then cut into strips before adding to the slow cooker.

Peas and Chayote Stew

148

Adding another dimension to your stew, use the half the weight of peas and half lentils.

PREPARATION TIME: 15 MINUTES

COOKING TIME: 4 HOURS

....

INGREDIENTS

2 tbsp olive oil
1 onion, finely chopped
2 cloves garlic, minced
225 g / 8 oz / 1 ¼ cups brown lentils, soaked in water overnight then drained
500 ml / 18 fl. oz / 2 cups vegetable stock
1 chayote (Mexican pear squash), peeled, cored and cut into strips
1 lime, juiced
2 tbsp sundried tomatoes, finely chopped
2 sprigs rosemary

- Heat the olive oil in a large casserole dish set over a medium heat.
- Sweat the onion and garlic together with a little salt until softened.
- Add the lentils, sundried tomato, chayote, stock, rosemary and seasoning.
- Stir well then pour everything into a slow cooker.
- Cook on a low setting for 4 hours until the lentils are soft and have absorbed most of the stock.
- Adjust the seasoning to taste and discard the rosemary sprigs before ladling into soup bowls.
- Serve immediately.

149

SERVES 4

Courgette and Mint Tajine

- Heat the olive oil in a large casserole dish over a medium heat until hot.
- Sweat the onion and garlic for 5-6 minutes until softened.
- Add the tomato puree and stir well, cooking for a minute.
- Add the ground spices and stir in the honey at this point.
- Add the chopped tomato, golden sultanas and the courgette slices, stir well, then cover with the stock.
- Pour into a slow cooker and cover with a lid before cooking on a medium setting for 4 hours.
- Adjust the seasoning as necessary then stir in the chopped mint.
- Spoon into serving bowls and garnish with a sprig of mint leaves.

PREPARATION TIME :
15-20 MINUTES

COOKING TIME :
4 HOURS 20 MINUTES

INGREDIENTS

55 ml / 2 fl. oz / ¼ cup olive oil
3 large courgettes, sliced
2 small onions, roughly chopped
2 cloves garlic, minced
2 plum tomatoes, de-seeded and roughly chopped
1 tbsp tomato puree
1 tsp ground coriander
1 tsp ground cinnamon
½ tsp ground cumin
1 tbsp honey
55 g / 2 oz / ¼ cup golden sultanas
250 ml / 9 fl. oz / 1 cup light vegetable stock
small handful of mint leaves, chopped
salt and pepper
GARNISH
sprig of mint leaves

Courgette and Pine Nuts

150

Replace the mint garnish with 30 g / 1 oz / ¼ cup pine nuts that have been lightly toasted.

151

SERVES 4

Carrot and Apple Soup

- Melt the butter with the olive oil in a large saucepan set over a medium heat.
- Add the garlic and sweet potato and sweat with a little salt for 15-20 minutes, stirring occasionally, until the sweet potato is soft.
- Spoon everything into a slow cooker and cover with the stock, carrot and apple juice.
- Cook on a low setting for 3 hours.
- After 3 hours, pour everything back into a saucepan and puree using a stick blender until smooth.
- Add the double cream, stir well until incorporated then warm over a low heat for 5 minutes.
- Ladle into soup bowls and serve immediately.

PREPARATION TIME :
15 MINUTES

COOKING TIME :
3 HOURS 25-30 MINUTES

INGREDIENTS

30 g / 1 oz / ¼ stick unsalted butter
30 ml / 1 fl. oz / 2 tbsp olive oil
1 kg / 2 lbs 4 oz / 6 ½ cups sweet potato, peeled and diced
2 cloves of garlic, minced
500 ml / 18 fl. oz / 2 cups vegetable stock
125 ml / 4 ½ fl. oz / ½ cup carrot juice
125 ml / 4 ½ fl. oz / ½ cup double cream
55 ml / 2 fl. oz / ¼ cup apple juice
salt and pepper

Crunchy Carrot and Apple Soup

152

Garnish the soup with grilled, crispy pancetta and toasted pumpkin seeds for added crunch.

153

SERVES 4

Vegetable Tajine

PREPARATION TIME :
15-20 MINUTES

COOKING TIME :
4 HOURS 20 MINUTES

INGREDIENTS

75 ml / 3 fl. oz / ⅓ cup olive oil
1 onion, finely chopped
2 cloves of garlic, minced
2 large red peppers, deseeded and diced
2 large yellow peppers, deseeded and diced
2 courgettes, diced
1 aubergine, diced
1 tsp ras al hanout
1 tsp paprika
1 tsp ground cinnamon
500 ml / 18 fl. oz / 2 cups vegetable stock
1 large bunch of flat-leaf parsley, roughly chopped
salt and pepper

- Heat a little of the olive oil in a large casserole dish set over a medium heat until hot and sauté the vegetables in batches, using fresh olive oil for each vegetable.
- Transfer to a slow cooker and add the ground spices, stirring well.
- Cover with the stock and cover with a lid.
- Cook on a medium setting for 4 hours until the vegetables are soft.
- Stir through the chopped parsley once the vegetables are soft and adjust the seasoning to taste.
- Spoon into serving bowls and serve immediately.

Sweet Vegetable Tajine | 154

Add 55 g / 2 oz / ¼ cup raisins and 55 g / 2 oz / ⅓ cup apricot halves to the slow cooker before cooking.

155

SERVES 4

Cream of Pumpkin and Tomato Soup

PREPARATION TIME: 15 MINUTES

COOKING TIME:
3 HOURS 20 MINUTES

INGREDIENTS

4 tbsp olive oil
1 kg / 2 lb 4 oz / 6 ½ cups pumpkin, peeled, de-seeded and cut into chunks
2 onions, finely diced
500 ml / 18 fl. oz / 2 cups vegetable stock
200 ml / 7 fl. oz / ⅘ cup double (heavy) cream
1 tsp ground pink peppercorns
4 fresh tomatoes, chopped
GARNISH
1 tbsp pink peppercorns, lightly crushed

- Heat the olive oil in a large saucepan over a medium heat and sweat the onions with some salt and the ground pink peppercorns for 6-7 minutes until they start to soften.
- Add the pumpkin and tomatoes and continue to cook for 10 minutes, stirring occasionally.
- Spoon everything into a slow cooker and cover with the stock.
- Cook on a low setting for 3 hours.
- Pour everything back into a saucepan, stir through the cream and simmer the mixture for 5 minutes.
- Puree the soup with a stick blender until smooth.
- Adjust the seasoning and then ladle into serving bowls.
- Garnish each bowl with a pinch of the crushed peppercorns before serving.

Créme Fraiche Pumpkin Soup | 156

Replace the cream with crème fraiche for a lighter and healthier soup.

157

SERVES 4

Kefta Meatball and Tomato Tajine

Kefta and Apricot Tajine

158

Add 55 g / 2 oz / ⅓ cup dried apricot halves and 30 g / 1 oz / ¼ cup ground almonds to the slow cooker before cooking.

Beef Meatball Tajine

159

Use beef mince instead of lamb mince for the meatballs. Add 1 finely chopped shallot to the beef mince before mixing and shaping into meatballs.

Kefta Meatball with Pumpkin

160

Swap the potato for pumpkin as a lighter and fruity option.

PREPARATION TIME: 15 MINUTES

COOKING TIME: 6 HOURS

....

INGREDIENTS

2 tbsp olive oil
600 g / 1 lb 5 oz / 4 cups lamb mince
1 onion, chopped
2 cloves garlic, minced
4 medium white potatoes, peeled and diced
4 large tomatoes, cored and cut into wedges
2 tsp ground cumin
1 tsp ground coriander seeds
1 tsp ground cinnamon
1 tsp paprika
½ tsp Cayenne pepper
1 tbsp honey
1 tbsp mint, finely chopped
500 ml / 18 fl. oz / 2 cups lamb stock

GARNISH
4 sprigs of sage

- Combine the ground spices with the lamb mince, mint and seasoning in a large mixing bowl.
- Mix well with your hands until you have an even mixture, then shape into small balls and arrange on a tray.
- Cover and chill until needed.
- Heat the olive oil in a large casserole dish set over a medium heat.
- Sweat the onion and garlic with a little salt for 5-6 minutes, stirring frequently until softened.
- Add the potato, tomato and stock and stir well.
- Pour into a slow cooker then add the lamb meatballs.
- Cook on a low setting for 6 hours until the lamb is cooked and the potato is soft.
- Stir through the honey and some seasoning according to taste.
- Spoon into serving dishes and garnish with sprigs of sage.
- Serve immediately.

161

SERVES 4

Pumpkin with Sage

PREPARATION TIME :
10-15 MINUTES

COOKING TIME :
4 HOURS 30-35 MINUTES

INGREDIENTS

125 ml / 4 ½ fl. oz / ½ cup olive oil
1 medium-sized pumpkin, peeled,
deseeded and diced
2 sprigs of sage leaves
salt and pepper

- Combine the pumpkin and half of the olive oil in a slow cooker.
- Stir well and season generously before covering with a lid.
- Cook on a medium setting for 4 hours until the pumpkin is tender.
- Drain after 4 hours and pat dry.
- Preheat the oven to 190°C (170° fan) / 375F / gas 5.
- Arrange the pumpkin in a roasting tray and add the remaining oil and the sage.
- Stir well and roast for 25-30 minutes until the pumpkin starts to colour at the edges.
- Remove from the oven and spoon into serving dishes.
- Serve immediately.

Pumpkin and Pepper with Sage 162

Add 2 peppers, de-seeded and sliced, to the slow cooker for a fruity flavour.

163

SERVES 4

Artichoke Tajine

PREPARATION TIME: 15 MINUTES

COOKING TIME:
3 HOURS 45 MINUTES

INGREDIENTS

FOR THE TAJINE
4 tbsp olive oil
6 globe artichokes, trimmed, halved
and kept in cold water mixed with
juice of 1 lemon
1 tsp ground cumin
1 tsp ground coriander seeds
1 tsp paprika

FOR THE FILO PASTRY PIES
175 g / 6 oz frozen filo pastry, thawed
110 g / 4 oz / 1 sticks unsalted butter,
melted
12 quail eggs

GARNISH
2 tbsp coriander leaves, finely sliced

- Mix half of the oil with the ground spices and seasoning in a small mixing bowl, whisking briefly to combine.
- Pour over the artichoke halves and toss well. Place in a slow cooker and cook on a medium setting for 3 hours.
- Remove and arrange on a baking tray. Preheat the oven to 190°C (170°) / 375F / gas 5.
- Drizzle with oil and season. Cook the eggs in a pan of boiling water for 6 minutes. Peel and chop before moving to a bowl. Brush a tray with some melted butter.
- Cut a pastry sheet to size and lay one sheet on top of the melted butter. Brush the top with more melted butter.
- Repeat this process until you have a stack of 4 sheets of filo pastry. Do this twice. Sprinkle the egg on top of one set of layers and then cover with the other pastry layers.
- Bake the pastry and the artichokes for 30 minutes. Remove and arrange the artichokes in serving dishes.
- Let the pastry cool then cut into triangles. Sit on top of the artichokes and garnish with coriander.

Artichokes with Fruit and Nut Parcels 164

Replace the quail egg with a mixture of 110 g / 4 oz / 1 cup ground almonds and 110 g / 4 oz / ½ cup raisins mixed with 2 tbsp honey for the filo filling.

165

SERVES 4

Baked Potatoes with Bay Leaves

- Prick the potatoes a few times before placing in a slow cooker.
- Cover with a lid and cook on a medium setting for 5 hours until easily pierced with a sharp knife.
- Remove from the slow cooker and pat dry if wet.
- Preheat the oven to 190°C (170° fan) / 375F / gas 5.
- Rub the potatoes with the oil and season generously.
- Wrap in a large sheet of double-strength aluminium foil, tucking the bay leaves in next to them.
- Bake in the oven for 40-45 minutes until ready.
- Remove from the oven and open up the foil carefully before garnishing the top of each potato with a little of the flaked sea salt.

PREPARATION TIME: 5 MINUTES

COOKING TIME:

5 HOURS 40 MINUTES

INGREDIENTS

2 tbsp sunflower oil
4 baking potatoes
1 large sprig of bay leaves

GARNISH
1 tsp flaked sea salt

Smokey Baked Potatoes

166

Replace the sea salt garnish with smoked paprika.

167

SERVES 4

Fennel, Celery and Leek Soup

- Heat the olive oil in a large casserole dish set over a medium heat.
- Sweat the fennel, celery and leek with a little seasoning for 10-12 minutes, stirring frequently, until softened.
- Add the potato and stock and stir well.
- Pour everything into a slow cooker and cook on a low setting for 4 hours.
- After 4 hours remove a little of the leek which will act as a garnish.
- Puree with a stick blender until smooth.
- Adjust the seasoning to taste then ladle into warm soup bowls.
- Garnish with the leek and chives before serving.

PREPARATION TIME: 15 MINUTES

COOKING TIME: 4 HOURS

INGREDIENTS

3 tbsp olive oil
4 fennel bulbs, finely sliced
2 sticks celery, finely sliced
1 leek, finely sliced and washed
2 medium white potatoes, peeled and diced
500 ml / 18 fl. oz / 2 cups vegetable stock

GARNISH
2 chive stalks, finely chopped

Fennel and Apple Soup

168

Add 1 peeled, cored and diced apple to the mixture before slow cooking. Garnish with julienned strips of apple.

169

SERVES 4

Cabbage Stuffed with Salmon

Cabbage Stuffed with Chicken

170

Replace the salmon with the same weight of chicken mince and cook the same.

Cabbage Stuffed with Chestnuts

171

Substitute the salmon with the same weight of cooked, chopped chestnuts.

PREPARATION TIME :
15 MINUTES

COOKING TIME :
5 HOURS 20 MINUTES

INGREDIENTS

30 ml / 1 fl. oz / 2 tbsp cup olive oil
1 large savoy cabbage, leaves removed
450 g / 1 lb / 3 cups skinless salmon fillet, finely diced
2 onions, finely chopped
2 sticks of celery, peeled and finely diced
2 carrots, peeled and finely diced
500 ml / 18 fl. oz / 2 cups vegetable stock
salt and pepper

GARNISH
sprig of basil leaves

- Place 4 large cabbage leaves in a large saucepan of salted, boiling water for 1 minute until softened.
- Remove from the water and let them cool as you prepare the filling.
- Heat the vegetable oil in a large saucepan set over a medium heat until hot.
- Sweat the onion, carrot and celery with the bay leaf and a little seasoning for 8-10 minutes until softened.
- Add the finely diced salmon to the saucepan and stir well.
- Spoon the salmon and vegetable filling into the middle of the cabbage leaves and bring the leaves around the filling to form balls.
- Tie securely with kitchen string and arrange in a slow cooker.
- Pour in the stock, cover with a lid and braise on a medium setting for 5 hours.
- Adjust the seasoning to taste before spooning into a casserole dish, pouring the vegetable broth around them.
- Garnish with the basil before serving.

172

SERVES 4

Chorizo Soup

- Heat the olive oil in a large casserole dish set over a medium heat until hot.
- Sauté the onion, garlic and bacon with a little salt for 6-7 minutes, stirring occasionally until the onion has softened.
- Add the canned beans, chorizo, stock, tomatoes and seasoning and stir well.
- Pour into a slow cooker and cook on a low setting for 4 hours until the beans are tender and have absorbed the stock to leave you with a thickened soup.
- Adjust the seasoning to taste before ladling into warm soup bowls.
- Serve immediately.

PREPARATION TIME: 15 MINUTES

COOKING TIME: 4 HOURS

INGREDIENTS

2 tbsp olive oil
1 onion, finely chopped
2 cloves garlic, minced
2 rashers smokey bacon, chopped
225 g / 8 oz / ½ cup canned kidney beans, drained
450 g / 1 lb / 1 cup canned haricot beans, drained
110 g / 4 oz / ⅔ cup chorizo, cut into thin strips
4 tomatoes, chopeed
500 ml / 18 fl. oz / 2 cups vegetable stock

Spicy Chorizo Soup

173

Add 1 tsp Worcestershire sauce to the slow cooker before cooking for a spicier soup.

174

SERVES 4

Stuffed Yellow Peppers

- Heat the olive oil in a large saucepan set over a medium heat until hot.
- Sweat the onion and garlic with a little salt for 5 minutes, stirring occasionally.
- Add the dried herbs and minced beef and stir well.
- Brown the mince well before adding the chopped tomatoes and stirring well.
- Pour into a slow cooker and cover with a lid.
- Cook on a medium setting for 4 hours.
- Adjust the seasoning to taste after 4 hours before spooning into the peppers.
- Preheat the oven to 190°C / 375F / gas 5.
- Arrange the peppers in a roasting tray, replacing their tops.
- Bake for 15 minutes before removing and arranging on serving plates with any remaining sauce spooned around them.

PREPARATION TIME: 15 MINUTES

COOKING TIME:
4 HOURS 20 MINUTES

INGREDIENTS

4 tbsp olive oil
4 yellow peppers, tops removed (but reserved) and deseeded
500 g / 1 lb / 2 oz / 3 cups minced beef
1 onion, finely chopped
2 cloves garlic, minced
400 g / 14 oz / 2 cups chopped tomatoes
1 tsp dried oregano
1 tsp dried thyme

Stuffed Mixed Peppers

175

Use 1 yellow, 1 red, 1 orange and 1 green pepper instead of 4 yellow peppers.

176

SERVES 4

Ratatouille

PREPARATION TIME :
15-20 MINUTES

COOKING TIME :
4 HOURS 15 MINUTES

INGREDIENTS

125 ml / 4 ½ fl. oz / ½ cup olive oil
1 aubergine, diced
1 courgette, diced
2 red peppers, deseeded and diced
2 yellow peppers, deseeded and diced
1 onion, chopped
2 gloves garlic, finely chopped
2 plum tomatoes, deseeded and
chopped
1 bouquet garni
salt and pepper

GARNISH
sprigs of thyme

- In a large frying pan, heat a little of the olive oil over a medium-high heat and flash fry the peppers for 2-3 in separate batches, tossing occasionally.
- Remove to a sieve placed over a bowl to drain.
- Add a little more olive oil and flash fry the aubergine and courgette in separate batches, adding to the peppers to drain after 2-3 minutes of cooking.
- Finally, add a little more olive oil to the pan and flash fry the onion and garlic for 2-3 minutes, adding to the rest of the vegetables.
- Place all the vegetables in a slow cooker and cover with a lid.
- Cook on a medium setting for 4 hours until tender.
- Adjust the seasoning to taste after 4 hours and spoon into a casserole dish.
- Garnish with a few thyme sprigs before serving.

Tomato Ratatouille

177

Add 400 g / 14 oz / 2 cups canned chopped tomatoes to the slow cooker before cooking and cook the same.

178

SERVES 4

Tomato Soup with Cream and Basil

PREPARATION TIME: 20 MINUTES

COOKING TIME:
3 HOURS 30 MINUTES

INGREDIENTS

2 tbsp olive oil
1 kg / 2 lb 4 oz / 4 cups tomatoes,
cored and quartered
1 onion, finely chopped
1 carrot, finely chopped
1 stick celery, finely chopped
2 tbsp tomato puree
1 tsp sugar
1 bay leaf
1 tsp dried basil
1.2 l / 2 pints / 4 ⅘ cups vegetable
stock, hot
125 ml / 4 ½ fl. oz / ½ cup double
(heavy) cream

GARNISH
2 tbsp double (heavy) cream
4 sprigs basil leaves

- Heat the olive oil in a large saucepan over a medium-low heat for 1-2 minutes.
- Add the onion, carrot and celery and sweat for 8-10 minutes with a little salt. Stir in the tomato puree, then add the tomatoes.
- Add the sugar, bay leaf, dried basil and seasoning and cover the pot, allowing the tomatoes to stew for 10 minutes.
- Remove the cover after ten minutes and stir in the stock.
- Pour everything into a slow cooker and cook on a low setting for 3 hours.
- Pour everything from the slow cooker into a large saucepan. Discard the bay leaf.
- Blend the soup using a stick blender until smooth, then stir through the cream. Adjust the seasoning to taste.
- Ladle into bowls and garnish with a swirl of cream and a sprig of basil. Serve immediately.

Tomato and Pepper Soup

179

Replace the carrot with a red pepper,
de-seeded and sliced and cook in the same way.

180

SERVES 4

White Cabbage and Bacon Stew

- Heat the olive oil in a large saucepan set over a medium heat.
- Add the cabbage, seasoning, black peppercorns and bacon and stir well.
- Cover with a lid and sweat the cabbage for 10 minutes, stirring occasionally.
- Spoon into a slow cooker and cover with the wine.
- Cover with a lid and cook on a medium setting for 5 hours until the cabbage is tender.
- Adjust the seasoning to taste before spooning into serving dishes.

PREPARATION TIME :
15 MINUTES

COOKING TIME :
5 HOURS 15 MINUTES

....

INGREDIENTS

55 ml / 2 fl. oz / ¼ cup olive oil
2 white cabbages, finely sliced
4 rashers of back bacon, chopped
250 ml / 9 fl. oz / 1 cup aromatic white wine
1 tsp black peppercorns
salt and pepper

White Cabbage in Cider

 181

Substitute the white wine with the same volume of cider and continue cooking the same.

White Cabbage with Pancetta

 182

Replace the back bacon with 110 g / 4 oz / 1 cup pancetta that has been cut into lardons.

183

SERVES 4

Spiced Potatoes

- Coat the potatoes in the oil in a large mixing bowl and toss well.
- Add the ground and whole spices and toss again.
- Spoon into a slow cooker and cover with a lid.
- Cook on a medium setting for 5 hours until tender.
- Remove from the slow cooker and arrange in a roasting tray.
- Preheat the oven to 200°C (180° fan) / 400F / gas 6.
- Roast the potatoes for 20-25 minutes until crisp on the outside.
- Spoon into a serving bowl and season again.
- Garnish with the coriander leaves before serving.

PREPARATION TIME :
10 MINUTES

COOKING TIME :
5 HOURS 30-35 MINUTES

....

INGREDIENTS

55 ml / 2 fl. oz / ¼ cup sunflower oil
600 g / 1 lb 5 oz / 4 cups new potatoes
1 tbsp brown mustard seeds
1 tsp cumin seeds
1 tsp ground cumin
1 tsp ground fenugreek
salt and pepper

GARNISH
2 tbsp picked coriander leaves

Spiced Potatoes with Garlic

 184

Add 4 crushed cloves of garlic to the roasting tray before roasting.

MAIN DISHES

SERVES 6

Beef Bourguignon

PREPARATION TIME: 15 MINUTES

COOKING TIME: 8 HOURS

INGREDIENTS

1 ¾ kg / 4 lb silverside beef,
cut into 2 cm cubes
100 g / 4 oz streaky bacon, chopped
30 ml / 1 fl. oz / 2 tbsp vegetable oil
or lard
4 cloves, minced
2 large onions, sliced
1 stick celery, sliced
2 carrots, peeled and finely sliced
and blanched for 5 minutes
1 tbsp plain (all-purpose) flour
15 ml / 1 tbsp tomato puree
150 ml / ¼ pt / ⅔ cup beef stock
300 ml / ½ pt / 1 cup heavy red wine
(non oaked)
350 g / 12 oz / 1.5 cups mushrooms,
brushed and quartered
1 tbsp Dijon Mustard
bouquet garni
2 Bay leaves
salt and ground black pepper

- Pre-warm the slow cooker.
- Heat the oil and fry (sauté) the beef cubes until brown and transfer to the slow cooker.
- Fry the onions, bacon and vegetables for 5 minutes. Stir in the flour and fry for further minute.
- Pour the stock and wine into the pan, with the herbs and mustard and stir thoroughly. Bring to the boil.
- Transfer all the ingredients to slow cooker.
- Cover and cook on a low setting for 8 hours.
- Taste and adjust seasoning.

Mediterranean Olive Meatballs   187

Sliced black olives and ½ tsp of chilli flakes may be added to the sauce before cooking to add to the Mediterranean feel of the dish.

Beef Bourguignon with Mushrooms   188

Add a selection of wild mushrooms to the slow cooker.

SERVES 6

Shoulder of Lamb Mint

PREPARATION TIME: 15 MINUTES

COOKING TIME : 8 HOURS

INGREDIENTS

1 ½ kg / 3 lb shoulder of lamb
30 ml / 2 tbsp goose fat
30 ml / 2 tbsp butter
salt and ground black pepper
2 handfuls fresh mint
3 cloves of garlic, cut into slivers

- Pre-warm the slow cooker.
- Wipe the lamb and fry in the butter and fat until golden brown all over.
- Remove from the pan and sit inside the slow cooker. Sprinkle garlic and mint over the lamb. Season with salt and pepper.
- Cover and cook on a low setting for 8 hours.
- Remove the lamb and set in a roasting tray–place in the top of a hot over 220°C (200° fan) 425F / gas 7) for 20 minutes to crisp up the skin
- Remove and rest covered for 15 minutes before carving.
- Meanwhile, use the slow cooker juices to make a mint gravy.

190

SERVES 4

Lamb Tajine with Green Beans

Lamb Tajine
with Apricots

191

Replace the dried apricot
halves with dried prunes.

Lamb Fillet Tajine

192

Instead of using lamb shanks,
use 600 g / 1 lb 5 oz / 4 cups lamb
neck fillet. Reduce the cooking
time by 1 hour; add the beans
4 hours into cooking time.

Lamb Tajine
with Asparagus

193

Swap the green beans FOR
Asparagus and cook to
your own preference.

PREPARATION TIME: 15 MINUTES

COOKING TIME:
6 HOURS 20 MINUTES

....

INGREDIENTS

4 tbsp olive oil
4 lamb shanks, cut in half
300 g / 10 ½ oz / 3–3 ½ cups green
beans, trimmed
500 ml / 18 fl. oz / 2 cups lamb stock
55 g / 2 oz / ⅓ cup dried apricot
halves, roughly chopped
1 onion, chopped
2 cloves garlic, sliced
1 tsp ground cumin
1 tsp ground coriander seeds
1 tsp ground nutmeg
1 tsp ground cinnamon
1 tsp mild curry powder
½ tsp paprika
2 tbsp honey

- Heat half of the olive oil in a large casserole dish set over
  a moderate heat.
- Season the lamb and seal in batches until golden brown.
- Reduce the heat and add the remaining olive oil.
- Sweat the onion and garlic with a little salt for 4-5
  minutes, stirring occasionally.
- Add the ground spices into the dish, stir well, then add
  the lamb back.
- Add the apricots, honey and stock and stir well.
- Pour everything into a slow cooker and cook on a low
  setting for 6 hours until the lamb starts to come away
  from the bone.
- 1 hour before the lamb is ready, add the green beans to
  the slow cooker.
- When the lamb is ready, adjust the seasoning to taste.
- Spoon into serving bowls.
- Serve immediately.

194

SERVES 4

Pork and Veal Meatballs

PREPARATION TIME: 25 MINUTES

COOKING TIME : 4 HOURS

INGREDIENTS

MEATBALLS
650 g / 1 lb 8 oz / 2 ¾ cups veal mince
350 g / 12 oz / 1 ½ cups pork mince
2 tbsp Parmesan, freshly grated
1 garlic clove minced
1 medium onion, finely chopped
55 g / 2 oz / 1 cup breadcrumbs
1 egg, whipped with a fork
salt and black pepper
1 tsp oregano
3 tbsp olive oil

SAUCE
1 onion finely chopped
2 cloves garlic, minced
1 tsp dried oregano
2 bay leaves
110 g / 4 oz / ½ cup bacon lardons
1 x 400 g can chopped tomatoes
100 ml /3 fl. oz / ½ cup chicken stock
180 ml / 6 fl. oz / ⅓ cup whole milk

- Heat the oil. Mix the meatball ingredients and form into 40 meatballs. Fry evenly for 10 minutes and set to one side.
- To make the sauce, heat more oil and a knob of butter, fry the onion, bacon, garlic and herbs. Add the tomatoes with the basil and bring to the boil. Remove from heat and add the milk.
- Pour the sauce and the meatballs into the slow cooker and cook on a high setting for 4 hours.
- Taste when done and season accordingly.
- Garnish with grated Parmesan cheese and basil leaves.

Pork and Beef Meatballs   195
If veal is difficult to obtain, replace with the equivalent quantity of beef.

Mediterranean Olive Meatballs   196
Sliced black olives and ½ tsp of chilli flakes may be added to the sauce before cooking to add to the Mediterranean feel of the dish.

197

SERVES 4

Pan Roasted Scallops with Shallots

PREPARATION TIME: 30 MINUTES

COOKING TIME: 4 HOURS

INGREDIENTS

12 fresh scallops, taken from shell
3 shallots, finely sliced
30 g / 1 oz butter
1 tbsp vegetable oil
salt and pepper

STUFFED TOMATOES
4 large beef tomatoes
200 g / 7 oz / ¾ cup minced pork
60 g / 2oz / 1 cup breadcrumbs
1 egg yolk
½ small onion finely shredded
1 garlic clove, minced
1 tbsp basil, finely chopped
1 tbsp wholegrain mustard
250 g / 8 oz / 1 cup cooked rice
45 ml / 3 tbsp vegetable oil
1 tbsp Parmesan cheese, finely grated

- Pre-warm the slow cooker.
- Trim off the bottom each tomato to allow it to sit flat. Slice of the top about ⅓rd down and reserve the tops for later.
- Scoop out the tomato pulp, seeds and juices and place in a medium size bowl.
- Mix all the stuffing ingredients in the bowl with the tomato pulp and combine thoroughly.
- Sprinkle tomato shells inside with seasoning
- Split the stuffing mixture in the bowl into 4 portions and roll each one into a round shape and fill each tomato with it and replace the lid on each.
- Wipe oil thoroughly through the inside of the slow cooker (important to stop tomatoes sticking during cooking).
- Brush each tomato with a little olive oil and season.
- Transfer to the slow cooker and cook on a medium setting for 4 hours.
- Ten minutes before end of cooking time, heat butter, oil and a small pinch of salt (to prevent burning) in a heavy pan and fry shallots stirring for 4 minutes.
- Sprinkle salt and pepper on scallops and fry for 1 minute each side in hot oil.
- Serve immediately on a serving dish with the stuffed tomatoes to one side.

198

SERVES 4

Monkfish and Bell Pepper

- Heat the oil and fry the onion, peppers and garlic.
- Add the spices and chilli flakes, stir well and cook through for 3 minutes.
- Add the lemon juice, honey, stock and tinned tomatoes and stir. Add the dried fruit and simmer for 5 minutes.
- Dust the monkfish in flour and fry lightly on both sides.
- Place the monkfish, the stock, the fruit and vegetables into the slow cooker and cook on a low setting for 6 hours.
- Ten minutes before the end of cooking, stir in the chopped coriander

Spicy Monkfish Tagine

 199

For a slightly hotter tagine, double the chilli flakes to 1 tsp.

Monkfish with Dried Fruit

 200

The dried fruit may be replaced with raisins and sultanas.

PREPARATION TIME: 20 MINUTES

COOKING TIME: 6 HOURS

INGREDIENTS

1½ kg / 3 ⅓ lb / 6 ½ cups monkfish, skinned and cubed into 1.5" squares
flour for dusting
60 ml / 4 tsp / ¼ cup olive oil
4 garlic cloves, crushed
1 medium onion, finely sliced
½ tsp chilli flakes
1 tsp ginger powder
1 tsp cumin, 1 tsp turmeric
1 tsp cinnamon, ½ tsp paprika
½ tsp fennel seeds
1 x 440 g / 15 ½ oz can tomatoes
250 ml / 8 fl. oz / 1 cup fish stock
pinch of saffron soaked in stock
1 lemon zest and juice
fresh coriander, chopped finely
1 red pepper finely sliced
10 ml / 2 tbsp clear honey
125 g / 4 oz / ½ cup stoned dates
125 g / 4 oz / ½ cup dried apricots
1 green pepper, finely sliced

201

SERVES 4

Chicken Meatballs with Basil

- Combine meatball ingredients. Roll into 12 balls and refrigerate for 1 hour.
- Pre-warm the slow cooker.
- Heat the oil and fry the onion, lardons, garlic and herbs. Add tomatoes with basil and stock and bring to the boil. Take from heat and add the milk
- Pour the sauce into the slow cooker and gently spoon the meatballs into the sauce
- Replace the lid and cook on high for 4 hours.
- Taste when done and season accordingly
- Remove from heat and serve with a choice of pasta
- Garnish with grated Parmesan cheese and basil leaves.

PREPARATION TIME: 25 MINUTES

COOKING TIME: 4 HOURS

INGREDIENTS

MEATBALLS
1 kg / 2.2 lb / 3 cups chicken mince
4 tbsp Parmesan, freshly grated
4 garlic cloves minced
225 g / 8 oz / 2 cups breadcrumbs
1 eggs whipped with a fork
salt and black pepper
1 tsp oregano, finely chopped
1 tbsp basil, finely chopped
3 tbsp of vegetable oil

SAUCE
1 onion finely chopped
2 cloves garlic, minced
1 tsp dried oregano
2 bay leaves
110 g / 4 oz bacon lardons
1 x 400 g can chopped tomatoes
100 ml / ¼ pt / ½ cup chicken stock
180 ml / 6 fl. oz / ⅓ cup whole milk
salt and ground black pepper

202

SERVES 4

Sea Bream Tajine

Sea Bass Tajine

203

Use sea bass fillets instead of sea bream; brown them very briefly in the dish before moving to the slow cooker.

Tajine Aniseed

204

Instead of using white wine to deglaze the dish, you could use 55 ml / 2 fl. oz / ¼ cup of pastis instead. Finish the dish with chopped tarragon instead of the parsley to pick up the aniseed flavour from the pastis.

PREPARATION TIME: 25 MINUTES

COOKING TIME:
4 HOURS 20 MINUTES

....

INGREDIENTS

2 tbsp olive oil
2 sea bream, gutted, cleaned and cut into thick steaks
1 courgette, cut into strips using a vegetable peeler
2 onions, sliced
1 clove garlic, minced
1 tsp ground cumin
1 tsp ground coriander seeds
1 tsp ground cinnamon
500 g / 1 lb / 2 cups new potatoes, sliced
250 ml / 9 fl. oz / 1 cup fish stock
125 ml / 4 ½ fl. oz / ½ cup dry white wine
1 tbsp flat-leaf parsley, finely chopped
1 bay leaf

• Heat the olive oil in a large casserole dish set over a moderate heat.
• Season the sea bream steaks and seal until golden brown.
• Transfer to a slow cooker and set to one side.
• Reduce the heat under the casserole dish and add the onions and garlic.
• Sweat with a little salt for 5-6 minutes, stirring occasionally, until they start to soften.
• Add the ground spices and stir well.
• Deglaze the pan with the white wine, stirring the base and sides well, then add the fish stock.
• Add the potatoes, courgette and bay leaf and stir well.
• Pour over the bream in the slow cooker.
• Cook on a medium setting for 4 hours.
• Adjust the seasoning to taste and stir through the chopped parsley.
• Spoon into serving dishes and serve immediately.

205

SERVES 4

Chicken with Fruit Compote

- Preheat the slow cooker.
- Clean and dry the chicken breasts, season the skin with salt and pepper.
- Heat the oil and fry (sauté) the chicken pieces skin down until brown then turn and fry the underside. Transfer to the slow cooker
- Lightly fry the onions and garlic for 5 minutes, stirring all the time. Combine with the cinnamon and cloves.
- Add the chicken stock and mix in the fruit compote. Bring to a simmer.
- Pour the sauce over the chicken breasts, ensuring they are covered.
- Cover with the lid and cook on a low setting for 6 hours.

PREPARATION TIME: 15 MINUTES

COOKING TIME: 6 HOURS

INGREDIENTS

4 chicken breasts with skin on
30 ml / 2 tsp vegetable oil
500 g / 1.5 lb / 1 ¾ cups dried fruit compote from jar
1 medium onion, sliced
2 garlic cloves, minced
60 ml / 2 fl. oz / ¼ cup chicken stock
¼ tsp cinnamon
2 cloves
salt and ground black pepper

206

SERVES 4

Lamb with Apricot Tajine

- Preheat the slow cooker.
- Heat the oil and fry the lamb cubes until brown and sealed. Set to one side.
- Add more oil and sauté the onion, herbs, spices, and garlic for 3 minutes.
- Add the stock, honey and orange juice and zest and stir thoroughly. Bring gently to the boil. Add the potatoes, dates, apricots and simmer for 5 minutes.
- Place the spicy tagine sauce and lamb pieces into the slow cooker. Stir well and cook on a low setting for 8 hours.
- Serve hot with rice, couscous or pitta bread.

PREPARATION TIME: 20 MINUTES

COOKING TIME: 8 HOURS

INGREDIENTS

800 g / 28 oz / 3 cups lamb shoulder, diced
60 ml / 4 tsp / ¼ cup vegetable oil
4 garlic cloves, minced
1 medium onion, finely sliced
2 potatoes, peeled, quartered and blanched
1 tsp ground ginger
1 tsp cumin
1 tsp turmeric
½ tsp ground cinnamon
2 tsp ground cumin
2 tbsp ground coriander
2 garlic cloves minced
400 ml / ¾ pt / 1 ½ cups beef stock
125 g / 5 oz / ¾ cup dried apricots, finely chopped
125 g / 5 oz / ¾ cup dates, finely chopped
6 tbsp orange juice
10 ml / 2 tbsp clear honey

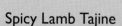

Spicy Lamb Tajine

207

For a slightly spicier tagine, add 2 tsp chilli flakes before slow cooking.

208

SERVES 2

Squid with Garlic

PREPARATION TIME: 25 MINUTES

COOKING TIME: 4 HOURS

INGREDIENTS

700 g / 1 ½ lb / 2 ¾ cups squid
3 tbsp fresh basil
4 spring onions sliced diagonally
juice of 1 lemon
30 ml / 2 tbsp vegetable oil
1 tsp chilli (chilli) flakes
4 garlic cloves, crushed
300 g / 10 oz / 2 cups fresh egg noodles
120 ml / 4 fl. oz / ½ cup fish stock
salt and black pepper
4 tbsp thick cream

GARNISH

chopped fresh parsley

- Cut off tentacles and keep for use. Cut off head, and remove quill from body and discard. Cut the body into rings. Return tentacles to mix.
- Heat the oil and fry the spring onions and squid for 3 minutes. Add the chilli flakes, garlic and basil and stir.
- Pour in the stock, noodles and lemon juice to deglaze the pan. Bring to the boil.
- Add the squid and boil for 1 minute. Pour all ingredients into the slow cooker and cook on a low setting for 4 hours. Stir in the cream gently.
- Sprinkle with chopped parsley and serve immediately.

Squid with Ink and Garlic Sauce

209

If you are lucky enough to have fresh squid, replace 2 tbsp of fish stock with 2 tbsp of squid ink, which will alter the colour and flavour of the final dish.

Sundried Tomato Squid

210

Add 2 tbsp of finely sliced sun-dried tomatoes to add to the authentic Mediterranean flavour of this recipe.

211

SERVES 4

Osso Bucco with Fennel

PREPARATION TIME: 30 MINUTES

COOKING TIME: 8 HOURS

INGREDIENTS

4 rose veal shanks
4 garlic cloves, crushed
60 ml / 4 tsp / ¼ cup olive or vegetable oil
2 large onions, finely chopped
400 ml / 14 fl. oz / 1 ½ cups red wine
400 ml / 14 fl. oz /1 ½ cups beef stock
2 tbsp sun-dried tomato puree
1 tbsp fresh thyme chopped
1 tbsp fresh rosemary
1 bay leaf
2 bulbs fennel, leaves separated
4 tbsp green pesto

- Heat the oil and fry the veal until golden brown. Remove and set aside.
- In the remaining oil, fry the fennel, onion, garlic and herbs until softened.
- Add the stock, wine, pesto and tomato puree and stir. Bring gently to the boil.
- Place the veal and sauce into the slow cooker and cook on a low setting for 8 hours.
- Serve warm with white rice.

212

SERVES 4

Vegetarian Stew with Beans

Butternut Stew with Beans

213

Replace the pumpkin with a butternut squash that has been peeled, cored and diced. Garnish with the butternut squash seeds.

Mixed Bean Stew

214

Instead of using butter beans, use a mixture of canned, drained kidney and cannellini beans. Stir through some chopped parsley before serving.

Spicy Stew with Beans

215

Add a few chilli flakes to spice this dish to your own preference.

PREPARATION TIME: 20 MINUTES

COOKING TIME: 5 HOURS

INGREDIENTS

4 tbsp olive oil
400 g / 14 oz / 2 cups canned butter beans, drained and rinsed
150 g / 5 oz / 1 ½ cups small portobello mushrooms
½ pumpkin, peeled, de-seeded and finely sliced
1 onion, finely chopped
2 cloves garlic, minced
500 ml / 18 fl. oz / 2 cups vegetable stock
1 bay leaf

GARNISH
pinch saffron strands

- Heat the olive oil in a casserole dish over a medium heat until hot.
- Sweat the onion and garlic with a little salt for 6-7 minutes, stirring frequently, until softened.
- Add the mushrooms, beans and pumpkin then cover with the stock, stirring well.
- Add the bay leaf and pour into a slow cooker.
- Cover and cook on a low setting for 5 hours.
- Adjust the seasoning after 5 hours and ladle into a serving dish.
- Garnish the dish with a few saffron strands before serving.

216

SERVES 6

Pork with Pineapple and Bacon

PREPARATION TIME: 25 MINUTES

COOKING TIME: 8 HOURS

INGREDIENTS

1.5 kg / 3 lb 3 oz boneless pork
roasting joint
30 ml / 2 tbsp clear honey
30 ml / 2 tbsp mild or Dijon mustard
1 tsp sage, fresh chopped or dried
1 garlic clove, minced
salt and ground black pepper
1 medium onion, thinly sliced
225 g / 8 oz / 1 cup crushed pineapple
225 g / 8 oz / 1 cup thin sliced bacon
120 ml / 4 oz / ½ cup chicken stock
350 g can sliced pineapple rings
(reserve 2 rings to garnish)
2 tbsp white wine vinegar
2 tbsp soy sauce
1 tbsp brown sugar
2 tbsp cornflour

- Wipe the pork joint and smear with honey and mustard. Fry the joint all over to seal until browned. Remove to the side.
- Mix together all the other ingredients, omitting the soy sauce and cornflour.
- Gently heat to simmer point and then pour into the slow cooker.
- Place the pork joint on top, cover with the lid and cook on low for 8 hours.
- Remove the Pork joint and pop into a hot over 230°C (210° fan) / 450F / gas 8 for 20 minutes.
- Meanwhile, place the sauce in a saucepan. Mix the cornflour and soy sauce thoroughly and pour into the sauce / gravy mixture stirring to thicken.
- Carve the pork, and spoon over the pineapple sauce mixture to serve. Garnish with slices of pineapple and sprinkled parsley.

Pork with Apple and Pineapple

217

The pineapple may easily be replaced with apple halves for a slightly less sweet flavour.

218

SERVES 4

Beef, Potato and Lentil Stew

PREPARATION TIME: 25 MINUTES

COOKING TIME: 8 HOURS

INGREDIENTS

1 kg / 2 lb silverside beef, cut into 2
cm cubes
30 ml / 2 tsp vegetable oil
1 stalk celery, chopped
1 tbsp plain (all-purpose) flour
6 small carrots, scrubbed, trimmed
and blanched for 5 minutes
1 courgette in ½" slices
1 bay leaf
4 medium potatoes, peeled,
quartered and blanched for
5 minutes
1 clove
2 tbsp fresh basil, finely chopped
1 x 400 g can of chopped tomatoes
1 onions, sliced
150 ml ¼ pt / ⅔ cup beef stock
salt and ground black pepper
salt and pepper

GARNISH

fresh Parsley

- Pre-warm the slow cooker.
- Heat the oil and fry (sauté) the beef cubes until brown and transfer to the slow cooker.
- Sweat the onions and vegetables for 5 minutes. Stir in the flour and cook for 1 further minutes.
- Add the stock and tomatoes, clove and herbs to the pan and season.
- Transfer all the ingredients to the slow cooker with the herbs
- Cover and cook on a low setting for 8 hours.
- Taste and adjust seasoning
- Pour into a casserole dish before serving and sprinkle with parsley.

219

SERVES 4

Crayfish and Broccoli Stew

Crayfish with Cashews Stew

220

Add 55 g / 2 oz / ⅓ cup chopped cashews to the slow cooker at the same time as the double cream. Garnish with chopped tarragon.

King Prawn Stew

221

Substitute the weight of the shrimp and crayfish for King prawns. The broccoli can be substitutes for 2 small heads of cauliflower.

PREPARATION TIME: 15 MINUTES

COOKING TIME:
4 HOURS 15 MINUTES

....

INGREDIENTS

110 ml / 4 fl. oz / ½ cup olive oil
4 cloves garlic, minced
2 large heads of broccoli
4 large crayfish
675 g / 1 lb 8 oz / 4 ½ cups whole shrimp
250 ml / 9 fl. oz / 1 cup fish stock
30 ml / 1 fl. oz / 2 tbsp Cognac
55 ml / 2 fl. oz / ¼ cup double cream
salt and pepper

- Remove the florets from the broccoli and finely dice the stems.
- Chop the florets into small pieces, reserving 4 large ones for the garnish.
- Heat the olive oil in a large saucepan set over a moderate heat.
- Season the crayfish and saute for 1-2 minutes, tossing and stirring occasionally.
- Remove from the pan and transfer to a slow cooker.
- Deglaze the pan with the Cognac and pour into the slow cooker.
- Add the fish stock, broccoli pieces and shrimp.
- Cook on a low setting for 4 hours.
- Pour in the cream after 4 hours and stir well.
- Adjust the seasoning to taste.
- Spoon into serving bowls and position the crayfish with the large pieces of broccoli in the centre of the dishes.
- Serve immediately.

222

SERVES 4

Spicy Fishball Tajine

PREPARATION TIME: 20 MINUTES

COOKING TIME: 4 HOURS

....

INGREDIENTS

600 g / 1¾ lb / 3 cups cod fillet
60 ml / 4 tbsp / ¼ cup olive oil
1 medium onion finely chopped
2 garlic cloves, crushed
⅛ tsp chilli flakes
1 tbsp capers finely chopped
2 tbsp coriander, finely chopped
1 tsp ground cumin
½ tsp harissa paste
100 g / 3 ½ oz / 2 cups breadcrumbs
1 egg lightly beaten
salt and pepper

SAUCE

2 tbsp olive oil
1 medium onion finely chopped
3 cloves garlic minced
1 x 400 g tin chopped tomatoes
250 ml / ½ pt / 1 cup fish stock
10 ml / 2 tbsp clear honey

- Blitz parsley, coriander, garlic, cumin, salt and pepper, onion and harissa paste and fish in a small blender until thoroughly chopped and mixed. Roll into 12 balls and fry in the oil until golden brown. Leave to one side.
- Pre-warm the slow cooker
- To make the sauce, heat the oil and fry the garlic and onion until softened. Add the stock, honey and chopped tomatoes. Bring to the boil and pour into the slow cooker.
- Gently place the fish balls onto the sauce in the slow cooker and cook on medium for 4 hours at medium.
- Serve hot with rice, couscous or pitta bread.

Spicey Tunaball Tagine

223

The white fish may be replaced with the same weight of canned drained tuna fish.

224

SERVES 4

Lamb with Dates

PREPARATION TIME :

20 MINUTES

COOKING TIME : 8 HOURS

....

INGREDIENTS

1 kg / 2 lb 2 oz / 6 cups lamb, cubed
45 ml / 3 tbsp vegetable oil
15 ml / 1 tbsp butter
1 tbsp plain (all-purpose) flour
2 large onions, finely chopped
2 medium green chillies, deseeded and finely chopped
4 garlic cloves, minced
4 beef tomatoes quartered
5 ml / 1 tsp tomato puree
350 ml / ¾ pint / 1 ½ cups beef stock
2 carrots, peeled and thinly sliced
120 g / 4 oz frozen peas
225 g / 8 oz / 1½ cups dates, finely chopped
1 tbsp each ground ginger, cumin, garam masala and cumin
1 tbsp fresh basil finely chopped
1 bunch coriander
1 cinnamon stick
salt and pepper

- Pre-warm the slow cooker.
- Heat the oil and fry (sauté) the lamb cubes until brown. Add a little more oil and fry the onions, garlic, and chillies until softened.
- Add all the spices and cook for 2 minutes stirring to draw out the flavour.
- Add the flour and cook another minute.
- Add the tomatoes, puree and stock and bring to a simmer.
- Transfer all the ingredients to the slow cooker.
- Cover and cook on a low setting for 8 hours.
- Taste and adjust seasoning.
- Pour into a casserole dish and serve with basmati or pilau rice.

Rabbit with Red Onions

225
SERVES 4

- Pre-warm the slow cooker.
- Heat the oil and fry (sauté) the rabbit until golden brown and transfer to the slow cooker.
- Fry the onions and garlic for 10 minutes. Mix in the mustard and cloves and stir for a further 2 minutes.
- Add stock, vinegar, brown sugar and rosemary and bring to the boil for 5 minutes.
- Pour the liquid into the slow cooker, over the rabbit.
- Cover and cook on a low setting for 8 hours.
- To serve, spoon the rabbit and onion sauce onto individual serving dishes.

Chicken with Red Onions   226

Replace the rabbit with a jointed chicken and cook in the same way.

Rabbit in Red Wine   227

Replace half the stock with red wine for a rich flavour.

PREPARATION TIME: 20 MINUTES

COOKING TIME: 8 HOURS

INGREDIENTS

1 prepared rabbit, chopped into 8 portions
salt and ground black pepper
oil for frying
3 red onions, thinly sliced
1 garlic clove, minced
30 ml / 2 tbsp clear honey
30 ml / 2 tbsp mild or Dijon mustard
4 sprigs of fresh rosemary
400 ml / 1 pt / 2 cups chicken stock
2 tbsp red wine vinegar
½ tsp ground cloves
1 tbsp brown sugar

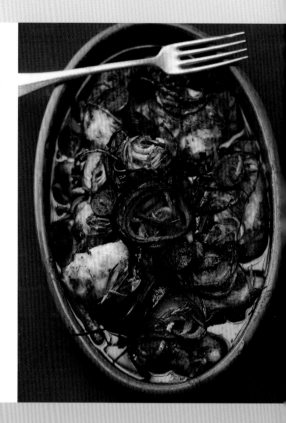

Chicken with Tropical Fruit

228
SERVES 4

- Warm the slow cooker.
- Heat the butter and oil in a heavy based pan over a medium heat.
- Add the onions and garlic and soften, then add guinea fowl pieces and brown all over. Sprinkle over the curry powder and stir for 1 minutes–remove to the slow cooker.
- Add the sugar, zest and juice of the lemon and lime, the chilli flakes, the coconut cream and the chicken stock.
- Pour into the slow cooker and cook for 4 hours on a medium setting.
- Taste and adjust seasoning. If required, thicken the sauce with cornflour (corn starch).

PREPARATION TIME :
15 MINUTES

COOKING TIME : 4 HOURS

INGREDIENTS

8 guinea fowl joints, skin on
30 ml / 2 tbsp vegetable oil
1 tbsp curry powder
juice and zest of 1 lemon
juice and zest of 1 lime
1 tsp brown sugar
450 g / 1 lb / 1 ¾ cup mixed tropical fruit (eg pineapple, papaya, mango)
2 large garlic cloves, minced
500 ml / 1 pint / 2 cups chicken stock
1 medium onion, finely chopped
1 garlic clove
½ tsp chilli (chili) flakes
60 ml / 2 oz / ¼ cup coconut cream
salt and freshly ground pepper

229

SERVES 6

Rose Rib Roast

PREPARATION TIME: 30 MINUTES

COOKING TIME: 8 HOURS

....

INGREDIENTS

1.5 kg / 3 lb 3 oz rose veal rib joint
salt and pepper
4 tbsp goose fat or vegetable oil
4 cloves garlic, cut into slivers
900 g / 2 lbs baby carrots, scrubbed
but with leaves and tops left on,
blanched for 5 minutes
4 tbsp red pesto

GARNISH
fresh basil leaves

- Slit the roasting joint and add slivers of garlic. Coat with pesto and season with salt and pepper. Heat the oil and fry the meat and carrots until golden brown all over.
- Transfer to the slow cooker and cook on a low setting for 8 hours.
- Remove from the slow cooker and rest, covered for 20 minutes. Carve and serve with carrots piled on top on a serving dish.
- Garnish with fresh basil leaves.

Rose Veal with Caramelized Carrots

230

Carrots may be caramelized with 1 tbsp honey, 1 tbsp water and 2 tsp sugar prior to cooking with the meat.

Pork Loin Joint

231

Substitute the rib joint for pork loin and cook in the same way.

232

SERVES 4

Veal and Chanterelle Mushroom Stew

PREPARATION TIME: 20 MINUTES

COOKING TIME: 8 HOURS

....

INGREDIENTS

1 kg / 2 lb / 4 cups rose veal, cubed
plain (all-purpose) flour for dusting
30 ml / 2 tbsp vegetable oil
3 tbsp butter
2 cloves garlic, minced
300 ml / ½ pt / 1¼ cups beef stock
1 glass red wine
500 g / 1 lb / 3 cups chopped carrots
2 carrots, sliced and blanched
1 bay leaves
bouquet garni
2 large onions, sliced
1 x 300 g can sweetcorn
300 g / 10 z / 34 cups Chanterelle
Mushrooms, chopped
salt and ground black pepper

GARNISH
chives, washed and snipped

- Pre-warm the slow cooker.
- Heat the oil in a pan. Dust the veal cubes with flour and seasoning and fry (sauté) until brown. Transfer to the slow cooker.
- Melt the butter and sauté the mushrooms. Transfer to the crockpot.
- Sweat the onions, garlic and carrots for 5 minutes. Stir in the herbs, sweetcorn, wine and stock and bring to the boil.
- Pour over the veal in the slow cooker. Cover and cook on a low setting for 8 hours.
- Taste and adjust seasoning. Thicken gravy with cornflour (cornstarch) if desired.
- Pour into a casserole dish before serving and sprinkle chopped chives.

233

SERVES 4

Vegetable Cocotte

- Combine the oil, new potatoes, carrots, cauliflower and stock in a slow cooker.
- Cover and cook on a low setting for 4 hours.
- After 4 hours, add the green beans and continue to cook for a further hour.
- After 1 hour, add the cocktail onions and peas and let them cook for a further hour.
- After 6 hours in total, turn off the slow cooker and adjust the seasoning to taste.
- Spoon into a casserole dish before serving.

PREPARATION TIME: 10 MINUTES

COOKING TIME: 6 HOURS

INGREDIENTS

30 ml / 1 fl. oz / 2 tbsp olive oil
450 g / 1 lb / 2 cups new potatoes
225 g / 8 oz / 2 cups green beans, trimmed
225 g / 8 oz / 2 cups baby carrots
225 g / 8 oz / 1 cup pickled onions, drained
110 g / 4 oz / 1 cup peas
1 head of cauliflower, cut into florets
375ml / 13 fl. oz / 1 ½ cups vegetable stock

234

SERVES 4

Paneer Jalfrezi

PREPARATION TIME: 10 MINUTES

COOKING TIME:
4 HOURS 45 MINUTES

INGREDIENTS

300 g / 10 ½ oz / 3 cups ready-made paneer, cut into 2cm / 1" cubes
2 tbsp sunflower oil
2 onions, chopped
1 red pepper, deseeded and chopped
1 green pepper, deseeded and chopped
4 cloves garlic, minced
5cm / 2" ginger, peeled and minced
1 green chilli, chopped
2 tsp ground coriander seeds
1 tsp ground cumin
1 ½ tsp paprika
1 ½ tsp garam masala
1 tsp chilli powder
1 tsp amchoor (dried mango powder)
1 tsp sugar
3 tomatoes, finely chopped
125 ml / 4 ½ fl. oz / ½ cup hot water

- Heat the oil in a large saucepan set over a medium heat.
- Sauté the onion, red and green pepper with a little salt for 4-5 minutes, stirring frequently.
- Meanwhile, combine the ground spices, sugar, tomatoes, water, garlic, ginger, chilli and seasoning in a food processor.
- Pulse until smooth then add to the onions and peppers.
- Cook for a further 5 minutes, stirring occasionally.
- Add the paneer and stir well to coat in the sauce.
- Pour into a slow cooker and cook on a low setting for 4 hours.
- Adjust the seasoning to taste after 4 hours.
- Spoon into serving bowls and serve immediately.

235

SERVES 4

Chicken Fricassée

PREPARATION TIME: 15 MINUTES

COOKING TIME:
6 HOURS 15-20 MINUTES

INGREDIENTS

30 ml / 1 fl. oz / 2 tbsp olive oil
30 g / 1 oz / ¼ stick unsalted butter
1 medium chicken, jointed
150 g / 5 oz / 2 cups mushrooms
250 ml / 9 fl. oz / 1 cup chicken stock
125 ml / 4 ½ fl. oz / ½ cup dry white wine
125 ml / 4 ½ fl. oz / ½ cup double cream
salt and pepper

GARNISH
sprigs of chervil
small bunch of chives stalks

- Heat the olive oil in a large casserole dish set over a moderate heat.
- Add the butter until it starts to foam, then season the chicken pieces and seal in the oil and butter mixture until golden brown in colour all over.
- Remove from the dish and place in a slow cooker.
- Add the mushrooms to the casserole dish and saute until golden brown in colour all over.
- Reduce the heat and deglaze the dish with the white wine, scraping the base and sides well.
- Add the chicken stock, stir well then pour over the chicken.
- Cook in the slow cooker on a medium setting for 6 hours.
- After 6 hours, stir through the cream and adjust the seasoning to taste.
- Spoon into serving bowls and garnish with the chervil and chive stalks before serving.

236

SERVES 4

Chicken and Cinnamon Tajine

PREPARATION TIME: 30 MINUTES

COOKING TIME: 8 HOURS

INGREDIENTS

1.5 kg / 4 lb chicken jointed and prepared
2 medium onions thinly sliced
1 red pepper, finely chopped
60 ml / 4 tbsp / ¼ cup Olive or vegetable oil
4 garlic cloves, crushed
¼ tsp chilli flakes
1 tsp ginger powder
1 tsp cumin
1 tsp turmeric
1 tsp cinnamon
½ tsp paprika
2 lemons cut into 8
1 lemon zested and juiced
1 x 440 g / 15 ½ oz can passata or pureed tomatoes
500 ml / 17 fl. oz / 2 cups stock
bunch of fresh coriander, chopped
10 ml / 2 tbsp clear honey

- Heat the oil and fry the chicken pieces until golden brown, remove to the side.
- Gently fry the onion, garlic, lemons and pepper until lightly browned. Stir in the spices and fry for 1 minute.
- Add the lemon zest and juice, honey, stock and passata and stir. Bring gently to the boil for 5 minutes.
- Place all the ingredients into the slow cooker and cook on low for 8 hours to let the flavours meld.
- At the end of cooking, stir in the chopped fresh coriander gently.
- Serve hot with rice, couscous or pitta bread.

Chicken Tajine with Dates **237**

Adding 110 g / 4 oz of chopped dates and 1 tbsp of brown sugar, adds a deeper flavour to this dish.

Chicken Tajine with Lemons **238**

Lemons may be replaced with oranges for a sweeter taste.

239

SERVES 6

Loin of Pork with Stewed Carrots

PREPARATION TIME: 30 MINUTES

COOKING TIME: 8 HOURS

INGREDIENTS

900 g / 2 lbs / 6 cups baby carroys, scrubbed
1 ½ kg / 3 lb 3 oz pork loin joint
salt and pepper
4 tbsp goose fat or vegetable oil
2 lbs baby carrots, scrubbed
1 onion chopped
sprig of rosemary
1 bay leaf
1 tbsp butter
120 ml / 4 fl. oz / ½ cup orange juice
¼ beef stock cube

GARNISH
fresh Parsley

- Heat the oil and sauté the pork until golden brown all over. Place in the slow cooker.
- Melt the butter and sauté the carrots and onions stirring for 5 minutes.
- Transfer to the slow cooker with the juice containing the crumbled ⅓ stock cube, bay leaf, rosemary
- Cover and cook on a low setting for 8 hours.
- Carve the pork and serve with carrots piled on top on a serving dish, spooning the liquid over it or thickening with cornflour if preferred.
- Garnish with fresh parsley.

240

SERVES 4-6

Pork with Lime Sauce

Pork with Creamy Lime Sauce

241

Replace the milk with double cream for a richer and creamier sauce.

Pork with Tarragon Top

242

Finely chop 2 tbsp of tarragon leaves and stir through the sauce at the end before serving.

PREPARATION TIME:
10-15 MINUTES

COOKING TIME:
6 HOURS 10 MINUTES

....

INGREDIENTS

55 ml / 2 fl. oz / ¼ cup sunflower oil
900 g / 2 lb piece of pork backbone, boned
125 ml / 4 ½ fl. oz / ½ cup pork stock
375 ml / 13 fl. oz / 1 ½ cups whole milk
1 bay leaf
3-4 leaves lime blossom / tilia
salt and freshly ground black pepper

- Tie the pork backbone with kitchen string at 1" intervals.
- Rub the pork with the sunflower oil and season generously.
- Heat a large frying pan over a moderate heat until hot, then seal the pork until golden in colour all over.
- Place in a slow cooker and cover with the stock, milk, bay leaf and lime blossom.
- Cover and cook on a low setting for 6 hours.
- Adjust the seasoning of the sauce after 6 hours, then lift the pork onto a serving dish.
- Spoon the sauce on top and garnish with the lime blossom before serving.

243

SERVES 4

Lamb Curry

PREPARATION TIME: 15 MINUTES

COOKING TIME:
6 HOURS 10-15 MINUTES

....

INGREDIENTS

55 ml / 2 fl. oz / ¼ cup vegetable oil
900 g / 2 lb / 6 cups lamb shoulder, diced
2 onions, chopped
4 cloves of garlic, chopped
2" ginger, peeled and chopped
1 green chilli, chopped
4 tomatoes, deseeded and diced
110 g / 4 oz / 1 cup frozen petit pois, thawed
1 tbsp ground coriander (cilantro)
1 tbsp ground cumin
1 tsp garam masala
1 tsp paprika, ½ tsp turmeric
½ tsp chilli powder
½ tsp caster (superfine) sugar
250 ml / 9 fl. oz / 1 cup lamb stock
250 ml / 9 fl. oz / 1 cup water
salt and pepper

- Combine the onion, garlic, ginger, chilli and a little salt in a food processor and pulse until you have a rough paste.
- Heat the oil in a large saucepan set over a medium heat and fry the onion paste for 5 minutes until it turns golden.
- Add the ground spices and sugar, stir well, then add the tomato and stir well again. Add the lamb, water and stock and stir before pouring into a slow cooker.
- Cover and cook on a medium setting for 6 hours. Add the peas after 5 hours of cooking.
- Cook the rice according to packet instructions. Spoon into serving bowls and place the lamb curry next to it.

244

Beef Madras

Replace the lamb with the same weight of diced beef braising steak and cook in the same way.

245

SERVES 4

Orange Lentils with Chicken

PREPARATION TIME: 20 MINUTES

COOKING TIME:
6 HOURS

....

INGREDIENTS

4 chicken breasts, flattened between 2 sheets of cling film
30 ml / 1 oz / 2 tbsp olive oil
2 cloves garlic, minced
250 g / 10 oz / 1 cup chopped parsley
200 g / 8 oz / 1 cup orange lentils
750 ml / 1 pt 6 fl. oz / 3 cups stock
salt and Pepper

CRUMB COATING

1 egg, lightly whipped
2 tbsp flour
150 g / 5 oz / ½ cup fresh breadcrumbs
3 tbsp vegetable oil

GARNISH

2 tbsp parsley leaves

- Wipe with oil and heat the slow cooker.
- In a pan, sweat the onion, parsley and garlic in the olive oil for 5 minutes. Drain off any juices.
- Cool slightly and spoon into each chicken breast before rolling up.
- Pour the lentils and stock into the slow cooker and cook for 2 hours on a medium setting.
- Place the chicken breasts, with the overlapping edge downwards, in the bottom of the slow cooker. Cook for a further 4 hours.
- Remove from the slow cooker and allow to cool.
- Dip each breast into the flour then dip into the whipped egg, and then the breadcrumbs. Set on a non-stick oiled baking tray.
- Drizzle the breasts with vegetable oil and cook in a hot oven set at 180˚ C (160˚ fan) / 350F / gas 4 for 20 minutes until crisp and golden.

246

Chicken Breast Stuffed with Sun Dried Tomato and Herbs

Replace half the parsley with 125 g / 5 oz / ½ cup finely chopped sundried tomatoes and 1 tbsp Parmesan.

247

SERVES 4

Lamb and Tomato Stew

- Heat the oil and fry the lamb pieces until golden brown. Remove and set aside. In the remaining oil, fry the onion, lardons, leeks and carrots.
- Stir in the flour and cook for 2 minutes. Pour over the wine and boil off the alcohol for 3 minutes.
- Add the stock, herbs, beans, cabbage and passata and bring to the boil. Place all ingredients (except the tomatoes) into the slow cooker.
- Cook on low heat, covered with a lid, for 8 hours.
- 1 hour before end of cooking, add the tomatoes
- Taste when done and season accordingly.

Lamb Chop and Tomato Stew   248

This recipe also works well replacing the neck fillet with the equivalent weight in lamb chops.

Lamb and Sundried Tomato Stew   249

Replace the beef tomatoes with 8 sliced sun-dried tomatoes for a more authentic Mediterranean flavour.

PREPARATION TIME: 15 MINUTES

COOKING TIME: 8 HOURS

INGREDIENTS

900 g / 2 lb / 3 ¾ cups lamb, diced
45 ml / 3 tbsp vegetable oil
150 g / 6 oz / ¾ cup bacon lardons
150 g / 6 oz / ¾ cup leeks, rinsed and chopped and blanched for 5 minutes
150 g / 6 oz / ¾ carrots, peeled, sliced and blanched for 5 minutes
225 g / 8 oz / 1 cup beef tomatoes, blanched, peeled and quartered
2 large cabbage leaves, chopped
1 x 400 g can haricot beans
1 tbsp plain (all-purpose) flour
1 tbsp sundried tomato puree
2 garlic cloves, crushed
1 small glass red wine
225 g / 8 oz / 1 cup tomato passata
150 ml ¼ pt / 2.3 cup chicken stock
2 tbsp basil, chopped
1 tsp mint, chopped
salt and black pepper

250

SERVES 4

Roast Duck with Cherries

- Grease and warm the slow cooker
- Wipe the duck with kitchen towel and prick the skin evenly with a fork. Rub salt into the skin.
- Heat the goose fat in a heavy pan and brown the duck all over. Stand to one side.
- To make the sauce, put all the sauce ingredients into a pan, except cornflour and vinegar.
- Bring to a boil and place in the slow cooker.
- Sit the duck on top of the sauce and cover with the lid.
- Cook for 8 hours on a low setting.
- Preheat the oven to 200˚ C (180˚ fan) / 400F / gas 6. Remove the duck carefully from slow cooker to avoid breaking it up and place on a baking tray. Roast it in the oven for 20 minutes to crisp the skin.
- Spoon off as much duck oil from the sauce as possible. Transfer the cherry sauce to a saucepan on the hob.
- Mix the cornflour with the vinegar and stir into the sauce. Bring to a simmer for a couple of minutes to thicken.
- Carve the duck and serve hot with the sauce.

PREPARATION TIME: 20 MINUTES

COOKING TIME: 8 HOURS

INGREDIENTS

1.75 kg / 4lb duck
30 ml / 2 tbsp goose fat
salt and pepper

CHERRY SAUCE

225 g / 8 oz / 1 cup de-stoned cherries
100 ml / 3 ½ fl. oz / ½ cup red wine
1 tbsp cornflour
1 tbsp red wine vinegar
1 tsp brown sugar
½ tsp cinnamon

251

SERVES 4

Olive and Lemon Thrush

252

Olive and
Lemon Poussin

Replace the thrush with 2
poussin and cook for 5 hours
on a medium setting in the slow
cooker.

253

Apricot and
Almond Thrush

Add 55 g / 2 oz / ⅓ cup dried
apricot halves and 55 g / 2 oz / ½
cup ground almonds to the slow
cooker before cooking.

PREPARATION TIME:
15-20 MINUTES

COOKING TIME:
6 HOURS 15-20 MINUTES

....

INGREDIENTS

55 - 75 ml / 2-3 fl. oz / ¼–⅓ cup
olive oil
2 thrush, plucked, cleaned and
jointed
2 preserved lemons, drained and
sliced
2 cloves garlic, minced
2 red peppers, deseeded and sliced
250 g / 9 oz / 2 cups preserved green
olives, drained
250 ml / 9 fl. oz / 1 cup chicken stock
1 tsp mild curry powder
1 tsp ground cumin
1 tsp ground coriander
½ tsp ground cinnamon
½ tsp paprika
1 tbsp honey
salt and pepper

- Heat the olive oil in large casserole dish set over a
  moderate heat until hot.
- Season the thrush and seal in the oil until golden brown
  in colour all over.
- Remove to a slow cooker and set to one side.
- Reduce the heat under the dish and add a little more
  olive oil if it looks too dry.
- Saute the garlic and red peppers in the oil for a minute
  then add the ground spices and stir well.
- Add the honey, olives, lemons and stock and stir well.
- Pour on top of the thrush in the slow cooker.
- Cover and cook on a medium setting for 6 hours until
  the thrush are cooked through.
- Adjust the seasoning to taste after 6 hours.
- Spoon into a serving dish using a slotted spoon and
  serve immediately.

Chicken in Vodka Casserole

254

SERVES 4

- Warm the slow cooker.
- Heat the butter and oil in a heavy based pan over a medium heat
- Add the onions and garlic and soften, then add chicken pieces and brown all over–remove to the slow cooker
- Add the sliced peppers and vegetables and stir well for 2 minutes
- Pour over the vodka, bulghar wheat and stock and bring to the boil. Add the herbs and spices.
- Pour the casserole into the slow cooker and cook for 6 hours on a low setting.
- Remove from the heat and stir in the cream.
- Taste and adjust seasoning
- Garnish with parsley leaves and serve.

Chicken in Brandy Casserole   255

Replace the vodka with brandy for a sweeter flavour and cook in the same way.

PREPARATION TIME: 25 MINUTES

COOKING TIME : 6 HOURS

....

INGREDIENTS

1 x 4 lb chicken jointed
salt and freshly ground pepper
30 ml / 2 tbsp vegetable oil
1 tbsp butter
2 large garlic cloves, minced
¼ tsp cayenne pepper
1 medium onion, finely chopped
4 sage leaves
2 tbsp bulghar wheat
1 tsp salt
60 ml / 2 oz / ¼ cup vodka
1 green pepper, thinly sliced
1 red pepper, thinly sliced
170 g / 6 oz cauliflower florets
170 g / 6 oz / 1 ½ cups mushrooms, quartered
500 ml / 1 pint chicken stock
100 ml / 4 fl. oz / ½ cup double cream

GARNISH
chopped parsley leaves

Fish Stew with Red Peppers

256

SERVES 4

- Warm the slow cooker.
- Heat the oil in a pan and gently sauté the onion, garlic, peppers and korma paste for 5 minutes.
- Add the chicken stock, sugar and pineapple juice, less 2 tbsp and bring to the boil
- Add the stew to the slow cooker, cover with the lid and cook for 6 hours on low.
- Transfer to a saucepan and bring to a simmer.
- Mix the cornflour (cornstarch) with the remaining 2 tbsp of pineapple juice, and stir into the stew gently to thicken.
- Spoon into serving dishes and garnish with the parsley and freshly ground black pepper.
- Serve warm alongside white rice.

PREPARATION TIME: 20 MINUTES

COOKING TIME: 6 HOURS

....

INGREDIENTS

500 g / 1 lb / 2 ½ cups mixed white fish (eg, cod, haddock, coley)
1 x 400 g can pineapple chunks with juice
1 red pepper, cut into small cubes
2 tbsp korma curry paste or powder
2 tbsp vegetable oil
2 garlic cloves, minced
1 medium onion, finely sliced
1 pinch saffron soaked in 100 ml / 4 fl. oz / ½ cup chicken stock
1 tbsp cornflour (cornstarch) in 2 tbsp of pineapple juice
50 ml / 4 fl. oz / ¼ cup plain yoghurt
½ tsp brown sugar

GARNISH
4 tbsp fresh parsley, chopped

257

SERVES 4

Stuffed Shoulder of Lamb

PREPARATION TIME:
15-20 MINUTES

COOKING TIME:
6 HOURS 20 MINUTES

INGREDIENTS

1.35 kg / 3 lb piece of boneless
shoulder of lamb
2 large courgettes, de-seeded and
diced
1 red pepper, de-seeded and diced
4-5 rosemary sprigs
55 ml / 2 fl. oz / ¼ cup olive oil
1 onion, diced
1 tomato, cored and chopped
250 ml / 9 fl. oz / 1 cup lamb stock
110 g / 4 oz / 1 ½ cups fresh
breadcrumbs
150 g / 5 oz / 1 cup sausage meat
1 tbsp finely chopped parsley
1 lemon, zested
salt and pepper

- Combine the breadcrumbs, sausage meat, parsley and seasoning in a bowl. Lay the lamb shoulder on a flat surface and season the inner side of it.
- Arrange the stuffing in the centre evenly and wrap up into a tight package. Tie using butcher's twine at 2" intervals to secure well.
- Rub the outside with olive oil and season well. Sear in a hot frying pan set over a high heat until golden all over.
- Tuck a sprig of rosemary under the twine.
- Arrange the vegetables in a slow cooker and pour the stock on top. Sit the lamb on top and cover with a lid.
- Cook on a medium setting for 6 hours until done.
- Garnishing with a remaining rosemary sprig.

Red Wine Braised Lamb   **258**

Replace the stock in the recipe with
750 ml / 1 pint 6 fl. oz / 3 cups red wine.

Lamb Stuffed with Olives   **259**

Replace the sausage meat with the same
weight of chopped green olives.

260

SERVES 6

Stewed Venison with Onion and Herbs

PREPARATION TIME: 20 MINUTES

COOKING TIME: 8 HOURS

INGREDIENTS

1 ½ kg / 3.3 lb venison fillet, cubed
salt and ground black pepper
oil for frying
1 medium onion, thinly sliced
3 medium carrots, slices and
blanched for 5 minutes
3 medium potatoes, slices and
blanched for 5 minutes
2 garlic cloves, minced
200 g / 8 oz mushrooms, sliced
125 ml / 4 fl. oz / ½ cup chicken stock
125 ml / 4 fl. oz / ½ cup red wine
250 ml / 8 fl. oz / 1 cup thick cream
2 bay leaves
bouquet garni

- Pre-warm the slow cooker.
- Heat the oil and fry (sauté) the venison until browned and transfer to the crockpot
- Fry the onions, mushrooms and garlic for 5 minutes.
- Add the wine and boil to reduce by half.
- Mix in the bay leaves, bouquet garni and stock and return to the boil. Add the carrots and potatoes and stir.
- Immediately transfer to the slow cooker.
- Cover and cook on a low setting for 8 hours.
- Check for seasoning and stir in the cream
- To serve, spoon onto individual serving dishes.

261

SERVES 6

Paella

Rabbit Paella

262

Replace the chicken with 2 small rabbits that have been jointed. Cook in the same way.

Monkfish Paella

263

Replace the chicken with 450 g / 1 lb of monkfish that has been cut into 2" cubes and cook in the same way.

PREPARATION TIME: 20 MINUTES

COOKING TIME:
6 HOURS 30 MINUTES

INGREDIENTS

1 small chicken, jointed and trimmed
300 g / 10 ½ oz / 2 cups prawns (shrimps)
150 g / 5 oz / 1 cup frozen squid rings, thawed
110 ml / 4 fl. oz / ½ cup sunflower oil
200 g / 7 oz / 1 cup calasparra rice
500 ml / 18 fl. oz / 2 cups chicken stock
125 g / 4 ½ oz / 1 cup peas, frozen or fresh
1 onion, finely chopped
2 cloves garlic, minced
1 green pepper, deseeded and finely diced
1 red pepper, deseeded and finely diced
1 tbsp smoked paprika
2 saffron strands, infused in the chicken stock
1 lemon, juiced

- Heat some of the olive oil in a wide frying pan or paella dish set over a moderate heat.
- Season the chicken pieces and seal until golden brown in colour all over.
- Remove from the pan and place in a slow cooker.
- Sweat the onion and garlic in a little more sunflower oil over a medium heat for 4-5 minutes until it starts to soften.
- Add the smoked paprika and the chicken stock infused with the saffron and stir well.
- Add the peppers, prawns (shrimps), squid rings and stock.
- Stir well, then pour into the slow cooker.
- Add the rice and stir well.
- Cover and cook on a low setting for 6 hours.
- After 6 hours, add the peas and adjust the seasoning to taste.
- Turn off the slow cooker and leave covered for 10 minutes.
- Stir again after 10 minutes and spoon the paella into a paella pan for presentation.
- Serve immediately.

264

SERVES 4

Chicken Pastilla

PREPARATION TIME: 25 MINUTES

COOKING TIME: 4 HOURS SLOW
COOKING PLUS 30 MINUTES

INGREDIENTS

4 chicken breasts, diced finely
3 garlic cloves, minced
1 large onion, finely chopped
pinch of salt
1 lemon, zested and juice
2 tsp ground cinnamon
10 eggs
1 pinch saffron, ground
½ tsp turmeric
1 tsp sugar
60 g / 2 oz sultanas
ground black pepper
1 tsp ground ginger
1 tbsp butter
250 ml / ½ pt / 1 cup water
300 g / 10 oz filo pasty

- Place the chicken, onions, spices, garlic, butter, sultanas, lemon zest and juice and a pinch of salt in the water and bring to the boil. Place in slow cooker for 4 hours on a high setting.
- Remove the chicken, chop very finely and reserve. Boil the stock down with the lid off to reduce by half.
- Whip the eggs with a whisk and pour into the reduced stock slowly, stirring continuously to allow to thicken.
- Preheat the oven to 200° C (180° fan) / 400F / gas 6.
- On a flat baking tray, wipe with butter. Lay a layer of filo pastry on this, brush it with butter, lay another layer of filo pastry and repeat until 6 sheets are covering the tin
- Place the chicken in a layer of the centre of the pastry. Drain the egg mixture and spoon this over the chicken.
- Bring the pastry edges up one by one and seal to form a large lozenge shaped pie. Very carefully, turn it over. Bake in the oven for 20 minutes. Serve immediately.

Moroccan Chicken Pastilla

265

60 g / 2 oz of finely chopped dates may be added to the chicken mix before forming the pie for a sweeter, but authentic Moroccan flavour.

266

SERVES 4

Beef, Lemon, Courgette and Almond Tagine

PREPARATION TIME: 30 MINUTES

COOKING TIME: 8 HOURS

INGREDIENTS

1 kg / 2 lb 3 oz stewing beef, diced
4 garlic cloves, minced
2 medium onions finely chopped
500 g / 18 oz / 3 cups diced courgettes
zest of 1 lemon
juice of 2 lemons
½ tsp salt
10 g / 2 tsp each of cumin, ground coriander and paprika
5 g / 1 tsp each of ginger and ground cinnamon
2 tbsp clear honey
170 g / 6 oz / ½ cup dried apricots, chopped
85 g / 3 oz / ½ cup flaked almonds, toasted
2 tbsp coriander, roughly chopped
500 ml / 1 pt / 2 cups beef stock

- Pre-warm the slow cooker.
- Toast the almonds for 5 minutes in a hot oven, then leave to cool.
- Heat the oil and fry the beef until golden brown. Place in the slow cooker.
- In the remaining oil, fry the onion and garlic until softened and add the spices, stir well and cook through for 3 minutes.
- Add the stock, lemon juice and zest and honey and stir. Bring gently to the boil. Add the apricots and mix.
- Place all ingredients (omitting the almonds) into the slow cooker, cover and cook on a low setting for 8 hours.
- Ten minutes before the end of cooking, stir in the almonds.
- Serve hot with rice, couscous or pitta bread.

267

SERVES 4

Traditional Loin of Lamb

- Wipe the leg of lamb and season with salt, pepper and paprika and fry in the fat until golden brown all over. Add the minced garlic and soften.
- Remove from the pan and sit inside the slow cooker sprinkled with the herbs and stock.
- Cover and cook on a low setting for 4 hours for a rare finish, or 6 hours for medium.
- Preheat the oven to 200° (180° fan) / 400F / gas 6. Remove the lamb and set in a roasting tray. Place in the oven for 15 minutes to crisp up the skin.
- Remove, cover and rest for 15 minutes before carving.

PREPARATION TIME: 15 MINUTES

COOKING TIME: 4-6 HOURS

INGREDIENTS

1 ½ kg / 3 lb rack or loin of lamb
(ensure it fits into the crockpot)
30 ml / 1 fl. oz / 2 tbsp vegetable oil
salt pepper and paprika
2 sprigs of fresh rosemary
1 cloves of garlic, cut into slivers
90 ml / 3 fl. oz / 6 tbsp chicken stock
10 g / ½ oz / 2 tbsp parsley, finely chopped

Lamb Loin with Sage   268

Pierce the skin of the lamb and smother with a mixture of oil and sage for extra flavouring.

Cajun Roast Loin of Lamb   269

Wipe the joint with oil and rub cajun spices into the skin, prior to initial frying.

270

SERVES 4

Lamb Meatball and Turmeric Tajine

- Heat the olive oil in a large tajine or casserole dish over a medium heat.
- Sweat the onion and cumin seeds for 6-7 minutes, stirring occasionally.
- Meanwhile, combine the lamb mince and ground spices (reserve ½ tsp of the turmeric) in a large mixing bowl with some seasoning.
- Mix well with your hands and take tablespoons of the mixture and shape into meatballs.
- Add the sweet potato to the onion and cumin and sprinkle over the remaining turmeric, mixing well.
- Cover with the stock and pour into a slow cooker.
- Sit the meatballs in the stock on top.
- Cover and cook on a medium setting for 6 hours.
- Add the sultanas when the meatballs are ready and adjust the seasoning to taste.
- Spoon into a serving dish.

PREPARATION TIME:
10-15 MINUTES

COOKING TIME:
6 HOURS 15 MINUTES

INGREDIENTS

450 g / 1 lb / 2 cups lamb mince
55 ml / 2 fl. oz / ¼ cup olive oil
½ tsp cumin seeds
1 tsp turmeric
2 tsp ground cumin
2 tsp ground cinnamon
1 tsp ground coriander
½ tsp chilli powder
1 large onion, finely sliced
4 medium sweet potatoes,
peeled and diced
500 ml / 18 fl. oz / 2 cups lamb stock
55 g / 2 oz / ¼ cup sultanas
salt and pepper

271

SERVES 4

Coconut Chicken

Raisin and Pistachio Chicken
272

Add 2 tbsp raisins and 2 tbsp shelled pistachios to the rice instead of the coconut.

Coconut Chicken Curry
273

Joint the chicken after cooking and roughly chop the flesh. Add to the coconut sauce to make a basic chicken curry.

Crispy Coconut Chicken
274

Add egg and breadcrumb along with the coconut to create a sweet crust.

PREPARATION TIME: 20 MINUTES

COOKING TIME: 6 HOURS

....

INGREDIENTS

FOR THE CHICKEN

1 medium chicken, cleaned
2 tbsp olive oil
110 g / 4 oz / 1 cup desiccated coconut
250 g / 9 oz / 1 cup basmati rice, cooked
400 ml / 14 fl. oz / 1 ¾ cups hot water
1 coconut, halved with flesh grated

FOR THE SAUCE

1 tbsp sunflower oil
1 onion, finely chopped
2 cloves garlic, minced
1 tbsp Madras curry powder
1 tsp ground coriander seeds
½ tsp sugar
250 ml / 9 fl. oz / 1 cup coconut milk

GARNISH

1 banana, peeled
4 sprigs coriander (cilantro) leaves

- Rub the chicken with the sunflower oil and season.
- Heat a frying pan over a moderate heat until hot and seal the chicken until golden brown.
- Transfer to a slow cooker and sprinkle over 1 tablespoon of the desiccated coconut. Cover and cook on a low setting for 6 hours.
- Cook the rice according to the packet instructions.
- Prepare the sauce by heating the oil in a saucepan set over a medium heat. Add the onion and garlic with a little salt for 5-6 minutes, stirring occasionally until softened.
- Add the ground spices and sugar and cook for a minute before adding the coconut milk.
- Stir well and simmer for 5 minutes over a low heat.
- Fluff the rice with a fork and stir through the grated coconut and 2 tbsp of the desiccated coconut.
- Season to taste and spoon onto a serving platter.
- Sit the chicken on top and sprinkle any remaining desiccated coconut on top.
- Reheat the sauce if necessary and pour into a serving bowl.
- Garnish the rice and chicken with the banana and sprigs of coriander before serving.

275

SERVES 4

Cockerel with Cabbage

- Warm the slow cooker.
- Heat the oil in pan and sauté the cockerel until golden. Place in the slow cooker. Surround the cockerel pieces with the chopped leeks and cabbage.
- Sauté the onions, garlic and lardons for 3 minutes. Add the flour and stir for another minute.
- Add the stock and seasoning to the pan to deglaze it, stirring to gather all the juices up. Pour into the slow cooker over the cockerel pieces.
- Place the lid over the pot and cook on low heat for 8 hours.

Cockerel with Juniper Cabbage
 276

Add 2 tsp of juniper berries when boiling the stock for a fruitier flavour.

Cockerel with Sauerkraut
277

The cabbage can be replaced with 225 g / 8 oz / 1 cup sauerkraut for a more acidic flavour.

PREPARATION TIME: 2 MINUTES

COOKING TIME: 8 HOURS

INGREDIENTS

1 ¾ kg / 4lb young cockerel cut into portions
1 Savoy cabbage, shredded
5 g / 1 tsp plain (all-purpose) flour
45 ml /1 ½ fl. oz / 3 tbsp vegetable oil
2 cloves garlic, minced
1 onion, finely chopped
15 ml / 1 tbsp honey
225 g / 8 oz / 1 cup leeks, finely sliced
60 ml / 2 fl. oz / ¼ cup chicken stock
salt and pepper

GARNISH
fresh parsley

278

SERVES 4

Ginger Chicken with Coriander

- Coat the chicken pieces in the oil and season with salt, pepper and ground coriander.
- Heat a large casserole dish over a moderate heat until hot and seal the chicken in batches until golden brown in colour all over.
- Transfer to a slow cooker and reduce the heat under the dish a little.
- Sweat the onion, garlic and ginger for 5-6 minutes stirring frequently until softened.
- Add the chicken stock and stir well before pouring over the chicken in the slow cooker.
- Cover with a lid and cook on a medium setting for 6 hours until the chicken is cooked through.
- Adjust the seasoning to taste once the chicken is ready before spooning into individual serving pots.
- Garnish with fresh coriander sprigs before serving.

PREPARATION TIME:
10-15 MINUTES

COOKING TIME:
6 HOURS 15 MINUTES

INGREDIENTS

55 ml / 2 fl. oz / ¼ cup olive oil
4 chicken legs, trimmed and jointed
2 large onions, finely chopped
1 clove of garlic, minced
4" ginger, peeled and minced
500 ml / 18 fl. oz / 2 cups chicken stock
½ tsp ground coriander (cilantro)
salt and pepper

GARNISH
sprigs of fresh coriander

279

SERVES 4

Lamb Ragout and Carrots

- Heat the olive oil in a large casserole dish set over a moderate heat until hot.
- Season then seal the lamb in batches until golden brown in colour all over. Remove from the dish and place in a slow cooker.
- Reduce the heat under the slow cooker and sweat the onion and garlic with a little salt for 3-4 minutes, stirring frequently until softened.
- Add the carrots and ground cumin and continue to cook for 4-5 minutes, stirring occasionally.
- Deglaze the dish with the white wine. Add the stock and bay leaf and stir well.
- Pour everything on top of the lamb in the slow cooker.
- Cover and cook on a low setting for 6 hours.
- Drain any excess liquid and adjust the seasoning.
- Spoon into a serving dish and garnish with the parsley.

PREPARATION TIME: 20 MINUTES

COOKING TIME:
6 HOURS 20 MINUTES

INGREDIENTS

55 ml / 2 fl. oz / ¼ cup olive oil
900 g / 2 lb lamb leg, cubed
450 g / 1 lb / 3 cups carrots, peeled and sliced
1 onion, finely chopped
2 cloves garlic, minced
2 tsp ground cumin
125 ml / 4 ½ fl. oz / ½ cup dry white wine
250 ml / 9 fl. oz / 1 cup lamb stock
1 bay leaf
salt and pepper

280

SERVES 4

Lentil Curry

281

SERVES 4

Curried Chicken Casserole

PREPARATION TIME: 15 MINUTES

COOKING TIME: 6 HOURS

INGREDIENTS

2 tbsp sunflower oil
2 cloves garlic, minced
5 cm / 2" ginger, peeled and chopped
350 g / 12 oz / 2 cups split brown lentils
2 large white potatoes, peeled and diced
2 tsp ground cumin
2 tsp ground coriander seeds
1 tsp garam masala
½ tsp chilli powder
½ tsp turmeric
1 bay leaf
500 ml / 18 fl. oz / 2 cups vegetables stock

- Heat the oil in a large casserole dish set over a medium heat until hot.
- Sauté the garlic and ginger for 2-3 minutes, stirring frequently.
- Add the ground spices and stir well.
- Add the lentils, stock, diced potato and bay leaf, then pour into a slow cooker.
- Cover and cook on a low setting for 6 hours until the lentils have absorbed most of the stock.
- Adjust the seasoning to taste before ladling into a serving bowl.
- Serve immediately.

PREPARATION TIME: 15 MINUTES

COOKING TIME: 6 HOURS

INGREDIENTS

4 tbsp sunflower oil
1 large chicken, cleaned and trimmed with wishbone removed
4 onions, cut into wedges
6 cloves garlic, peeled
4 bay leaves
2 tbsp Madras curry powder
2 tsp ground cumin
2 tsp ground coriander seeds
1 tsp ground paprika
1 tsp turmeric

- Truss the chicken using kitchen string so that it is securely tied.
- Mix the ground spices with some seasoning in a small mixing bowl.
- Rub the chicken with some of the oil and sprinkle over half of the spice mixture, reserving the rest for a garnish.
- Heat a large frying pan or casserole dish over a moderate heat until hot.
- Seal the chicken until golden brown, then remove to a plate to one side.

- Reduce the heat and add the remaining oil.
- Brown the onions and garlic in the oil until soft.
- Transfer to a slow cooker and sit the chicken on top.
- Cover and cook on a medium setting for 6 hours.
- After 6 hours, test to see if the juices run clean when the thickest part of the thigh is pierced.
- If so, the chicken is ready.
- Spoon everything into a casserole dish.
- Garnish the top of the chicken with the remaining spice mixture and the bay leaves.

SERVES 4

Chicken and Orange Stew

- Heat the olive oil in a large casserole dish set over a moderate heat until hot.
- Season and saute the chicken until golden brown.
- Add the pancetta and continue to saute for a few minutes until lightly coloured.
- Add the olives and orange to the dish and stir well.
- Cover with the stock, stir thoroughly and pour into a slow cooker.
- Cover with a lid and cook on a medium setting for 4 hours.
- Adjust the seasoning to taste after 4 hours.
- Pare the reserved orange zest into strips and stir into the slow cooker along with the finely chopped parsley.
- Spoon into serving dishes before garnishing with sprigs of parsley.

Chicken and Apricot Stew

283

Replace the oranges with 110 g / 4 oz / ⅔ cup dried apricot halves and cook the same.

PREPARATION TIME :
10-15 MINUTES

COOKING TIME :
4 HOURS 15 MINUTES

INGREDIENTS

55 ml / 2 fl. oz / ¼ cup olive oil
4 large skinless chicken breasts, diced
110 g / 4 oz / ⅔ cup green olives
55 g / 2 oz / ⅓ cup black olives
55 g / 2 oz / ⅓ cup pancetta, cut into lardons
2 oranges, peeled, segmented and chopped with pith reserved
500 ml / 18 fl. oz / 2 cups chicken stock
2 tbsp flat-leaf parsley, finely chopped
salt and pepper

GARNISH
flat-leaf parsley

SERVES 6

Roast Pork with Cinnamon

- Rub the pork knuckle with the oil and season generously.
- Heat a large frying pan over a high heat until hot.
- Seal the pork until golden brown in colour all over.
- Remove from the pan and place in a slow cooker.
- Add the cinnamon sticks and cover with a lid.
- Cook on a medium setting for 6-8 hours until the flesh is cooked.
- Once the flesh is cooked, baste in the vinegar before transferring the knuckle and any juices to a roasting dish for presentation.

PREPARATION TIME: 10 MINUTES

COOKING TIME:
6-8 HOURS 10 MINUTES

INGREDIENTS

30 ml / 1 fl. oz / 2 tbsp groundnut oil
1⅓ kg / 3 lb piece of pork knuckle, washed and patted dry
4 cinnamon sticks
30 ml / 1 fl. oz / 2 tbsp balsamic vinegar
salt and pepper

285

SERVES 4-6

Chicken with Roast Potatoes

PREPARATION TIME: 20 MINUTES

COOKING TIME:
7 HOURS 20-25 MINUTES

....

INGREDIENTS

FOR THE POTATOES
125 ml / 4 ½ fl. oz / ½ cup sunflower oil
900 g / 2 lb / 6 cups potatoes, peeled and cut into large chunks
salt and pepper

FOR THE CHICKEN
1 medium free range chicken, cleaned and with excess fat removed
30 ml / 1 fl. oz / 2 tbsp olive oil
250 g / 9 oz / 2 cups fresh breadcrumbs
55 g / 2 oz / ½ stick butter, softened
1 large egg
small bunch flat-leaf parsley
small handful of tarragon leaves
salt and pepper

- Preheat the oven to 190°C (170° fan) / 375F / gas 5.
- Blitz the breadcrumbs, herbs and seasoning. Melt the butter, then add the breadcrumb mix and egg.
- Loosen the skin of the chicken and stuff with the stuffing. Stuff the main cavity with the stuffing.
- Sit the chicken in a tray and rub with olive oil. Season and roast for 30 minutes. Transfer to a slow cooker. Cook on a medium setting for 6 hours.
- After 5 hours, preheat the oven to 190°C. Bring a saucepan of salted water to the boil and boil the potatoes for 15 minutes. Drain and cool. Pour the oil into a tray and place the potatoes in the oil.
- Season and shake, then roast for 50 minutes. Once cooked, remove and serve with the chicken.

Orange Glaze Chicken

286

Brush the outside of the chicken with 2 tbsp good-quality orange marmalade before roasting in the oven initially.

Chicken with Tied Herbs

287

Replace the stuffing with a bunch of herbs tied together– thyme, rosemary, bay leaf and marjoram.

288

SERVES 4

Lamb and Artichoke Stew

PREPARATION TIME:
10-15 MINUTES

COOKING TIME:
6 HOURS 15 MINUTES

....

INGREDIENTS

30 ml / 1 fl. oz / 2 tbsp sunflower oil
450 g / 1 lb / 2 cups lamb neck fillet, cut into 2" pieces
2 Globe artichokes, trimmed and sliced
300 g / 10 ½ oz / 2 cups broad beans
500 ml / 18 fl. oz / 2 cups lamb stock
salt and pepper

GARNISH
a few sprigs of thyme

- Heat the sunflower oil in a large casserole dish set over a moderate heat until hot.
- Season the lamb pieces generously and seal in the hot oil until golden brown in colour all over.
- Remove from the dish and transfer to a slow cooker.
- Reduce the heat under the dish and saute the artichoke for 4-5 minutes, stirring occasionally.
- Add the stock and stir well then pour into the slow cooker.
- Add the broad beans and cover with a lid.
- Cook on a low setting for 6 hours until the lamb is tender.
- Adjust the seasoning to taste before ladling the stew into serving bowls.
- Garnish with the thyme before serving.

289

SERVES 4

Mutton and Beans

Moroccan Mutton and Beans

290

Add 2 tsp of ras el hanout (Moroccan spice blend) to the onions and carrots when they are sweating, for a Moroccan flavour.

Mutton with Kidney Beans

291

Replace the haricot beans with 400 g / 14 oz / 2 cups drained kidney beans.

PREPARATION TIME: 15 MINUTES

COOKING TIME: 6 HOURS

....

INGREDIENTS

4 tbsp sunflower oil
900 g / 2 lbs mutton shoulder, diced into 5cm / 2" cubes
200 g / 7 oz / 1 cup dried haricot beans, soaked in water overnight and drained
500ml / 18 fl. oz / 2 cups lamb stock
2 onions, sliced
2 large carrots, peeled and sliced

GARNISH
2 bay leaves

- Season the mutton well.
- Heat the oil in a large casserole dish set over a moderate heat until hot.
- Seal the mutton in batches until golden brown in colour all over.
- Transfer each batch of mutton to a slow cooker.
- Reduce the heat under the dish and add the onions and carrots.
- Sweat for 5 minutes with a little salt, stirring occasionally.
- Add the drained beans and lamb stock to the dish and stir well.
- Pour everything on top of the lamb in the slow cooker.
- Cover with a lid and cook on a medium setting for 6 hours until the beans have absorbed most of the stock and the lamb is tender.
- Adjust the seasoning to taste before spooning back into a casserole serving dish.
- Garnish with the bay leaves before serving.

292

SERVES 4

Pork, Pepper and Olive Stew

PREPARATION TIME: 15 MINUTES

COOKING TIME:
6 HOURS 10-15 MINUTES

···

INGREDIENTS

55 ml / 2 fl. oz / ¼ cup olive oil
4 boneless pork chops, cut into large
chunks
1 onion, sliced
2 cloves garlic, minced
2 red peppers, deseeded and sliced
2 yellow peppers, deseeded and sliced
75 g / 3 oz / ⅓ cup pitted black olives
400 g / 14 oz / 2 cups canned
chopped tomatoes
500 ml / 18 fl. oz / 2 cups vegetable
stock
salt and pepper

GARNISH
1 sprig thyme
1 bay leaf

- Heat the olive oil in a casserole dish.
- Fry the onion and garlic together for 5 minutes.
- Add the peppers and stir well, cook for 4-5 minutes.
- Stir in the pork at this point and cook for 3-4 minutes before adding the chopped tomatoes and stock.
- Stir well before pouring into a slow cooker.
- Cover with a lid and cook on a medium setting for 6 hours until the pork is cooked through.
- Adjust the seasoning to taste, then stir in the black olives before spooning into a casserole dish for presentation.
- Garnish with the thyme and bay leaf before serving.

Creamy Paprika Stew   293

Add 1 tsp smoked paprika to the slow cooker before cooking. Garnish with dollops of sour cream instead of the herbs.

Cognac Pork Stew   294

Deglaze the saucepan with 55 ml / 2 fl. oz / ¼ cup Cognac before adding the stock.

295

SERVES 4

Sardine Bouillabaisse

PREPARATION TIME:
15-20 MINUTES

COOKING TIME:
6 HOURS 15 MINUTES

···

INGREDIENTS

55 ml / 2 fl. oz / ¼ cup olive oil
450 g / 1 lb sardines in brine, drained
55 ml / 2 fl. oz / ¼ cup Pernod
500 ml / 18 fl. oz / 2 cups fish stock
250 ml / 9 fl. oz / 1 cup water
400 g / 14 oz / 2 cups canned
chopped tomatoes
1 tbsp tomato puree
1 large white potato, peeled and
sliced thinly
1 fennel bulb, trimmed and sliced
2 onion finely chopped
4 cloves garlic, minced
sprigs of thyme, to garnish
1 bay leaf
salt and black pepper

- Heat the olive oil in a large casserole dish over a moderate heat.
- Sweat the onion, garlic for 10 minutes with a little salt, stirring occasionally until they are soft but not coloured.
- Stir in the tomato puree, fennel seeds, canned chopped tomatoes and bay leaf.
- Stir well and cover with the fish stock and water.
- Pour into a slow cooker and cover with a lid.
- Cook on a medium setting for 2 hours.
- Strain into a large, clean saucepan, pressing the tomatoes and all other ingredients through the sieve to extract as much flavour as possible.
- Add the Pernod to the broth, then add the potato and sliced fennel and pour back into the slow cooker.
- Add the sardines and cover with a lid.
- Cook on a medium setting for a further 4 hours until the fish is cooked.
- Adjust the seasoning as necessary, then ladle into a serving dish.
- Garnish with sprigs of thyme before serving.

296

SERVES 4

Sardine Boulettes

- Combine the breadcrumbs, sardine, seasoning and half of the parsley in a food processor.
- Pulse until smooth then scrape into a bowl.
- Shape into balls between your palms and arrange on a plate.
- Heat the olive oil in a saucepan set over a medium heat.
- Sweat the shallot and garlic with a little salt for 5 minutes, stirring occasionally.
- Add the passata, remaining parsley and some seasoning and stir well before pouring into a slow cooker.
- Add the sardine boulettes and cover the slow cooker with a lid.
- Cook on a medium setting for 6 hours.
- Adjust the seasoning to taste before spooning onto serving plates.
- Garnish with dill before serving.

Sardine Boulettes with White Wine

297

Replace 125 g / 4 ½ oz / ⅔ cup of the passata with 125 ml / 4 ½ fl. oz / ½ cup dry white wine.

PREPARATION TIME :
10-15 MINUTES

COOKING TIME :
4 HOURS 15 MINUTES

INGREDIENTS

30 ml / 1 fl. oz / 2 tbsp olive oil
450 g / 1 lb sardine fillets, pin boned and chopped
125 g / 4 ½ oz / 1 cup fresh breadcrumbs
4 cloves of garlic, sliced
2 shallots, minced
1 small bunch of flat-leaf parsley, finely chopped
500 g / 1 lb 2 oz / 2 ½ cups passata
salt and pepper

GARNISH
sprigs of dill

298

SERVES 4

Osso-Bucco Turkey Paupiettes

- Season the turkey strips.
- Thread 2 strips into each hollowed-out veal bone
- Tie securely using kitchen string before seasoning.
- Heat the olive oil for the paupiettes in a large casserole dish set over a moderate heat until hot and seal the turkey paupiettes until golden brown.
- Transfer to a slow cooker and reduce the heat under the casserole dish.
- Replace the lid and cook the paupiettes for 4 hours on a medium setting until cooked through.
- Add the olive oil for the sauce and saute the garlic for a minute.
- Add the passata, olives and seasoning and simmer for 10 minutes until thickened, stirring occasionally.
- Set to one side to be reheated later.
- Once the turkey paupiettes are ready, keep warm
- Cook the tagliatelle in a large saucepan of salted, boiling water until 'al dente'; usually 8-10 minutes.
- Drain the tagliatelle and toss with the olive oil.
- Arrange in the base of a tray and top with the paupiettes.
- Reheat the sauce gently and spoon over before garnishing with the tied bouquet garni and serving.

PREPARATION TIME:
15-20 MINUTES

COOKING TIME:
4 HOURS 25-30 MINUTES

INGREDIENTS

FOR THE PAUPIETTES
55 ml / 2 fl. oz / ¼ cup olive oil
4 x veal bone sections, marrow removed
4 x 250 g / 9 oz turkey escalopes, cut in half into even strips
salt and pepper

FOR THE PASTA
30 ml / 1 fl. oz / 2 tbsp olive oil
450 g / 1 lb Tagliatelle

FOR THE SAUCE
30 ml / 1 fl. oz / 2 tbsp olive oil
1 clove of garlic, minced
55 g / 2 oz / ¼ cup green olives
400 g / 14 oz / 2 cups passata
salt and pepper

GARNISH
1 fresh bouquet garni, tied

299

SERVES 4

Chicken with Thyme and Vanilla

Citrus Chicken with Vanilla

300

Add 1 quartered lemon and orange to the slow cooker before cooking, for a citrus flavour.

Chicken with Herb Sautéed Onions

301

Add 1 tsp dried thyme, ½ tsp dried oregano, ½ tsp dried rosemary and ½ tsp dried basil to the onions when you sauté them.

Turkey with Thyme

302

Swap the whole chicken for a turkey for a leaner option. Cook in the same way.

PREPARATION TIME: 15 MINUTES

COOKING TIME: 6 HOURS

INGREDIENTS

70 ml / 2 ½ fl. oz olive oil
1 tsp vanilla extract
1 medium chicken, cleaned and trussed
3 vanilla pods, tied together using straw
4 sprigs of thyme
2 large onions, cut into wedges
2 cloves garlic, crushed
4 tomatoes, roughly chopped

- Rub the chicken with the olive oil and vanilla extract.
- Season generously and heat a large frying pan over a moderate heat until hot.
- Seal the chicken until golden brown all over.
- Remove from the pan and add the onions, garlic, tied vanilla pod bundle and one of the thyme sprigs.
- Sauté for 2-3 minutes, tossing and stirring occasionally.
- Spoon the contents of the pan into the bottom of a slow cooker along with the tomatoes.
- Sit the chicken on top and cover with a lid.
- Cook on a low setting for 6 hours until the juice runs clear when the thickest part of the thigh is pierced.
- Spoon the onions, tomatoes and garlic into a roasting tray.
- Sit the chicken on top and garnish with the vanilla pod bundle and the remaining thyme before serving.

303
SERVES 4

Spicy Chorizo Stew

- Heat the olive oil in a large casserole dish set over a medium heat until hot.
- Sweat the onion, carrot, garlic and peppers for 5 minutes, stirring until the onion starts to soften.
- Add the chorizo, beans, cayenne pepper, passata and stock and stir well.
- Pour into a slow cooker and add a little seasoning.
- Cover with a lid and cook on a medium setting for 4 hours.
- Adjust the seasoning to taste after 4 hours.
- Ladle into bowls before garnishing with the parsley.

Chorizo Stew with Almonds   304

Add 55 g / 2 oz / ½ cup blanched whole almonds to the slow cooker before cooking.

Chorizo with Sun-dried Tomatoes   305

Replace the red peppers with the same weight of sun-dried tomatoes.

PREPARATION TIME :
15 MINUTES

COOKING TIME :
4 HOURS 15 MINUTES

INGREDIENTS

30 ml / 1 fl. oz / 2 tbsp olive oil
150 g / 5 oz / 1 cup chorizo slices
1 onion, sliced
2 large carrots, peeled and diced
4 cloves garlic, finely chopped
2 red peppers, deseeded and sliced
1 tsp cayenne pepper
400 g / 14 oz / 2 cups canned haricot beans, drained
250 ml / 9 fl. oz / 1 cup vegetables stock
250 ml / 9 fl. oz / 1 cup passata
salt and pepper

GARNISH
flat-leaf parsley leaves

306
SERVES 4

Pork and Artichoke Stew

- Heat the sunflower oil in a large casserole dish set over a moderate heat until hot.
- Season the pork and seal in batches until golden brown in colour all over.
- Move each sealed batch to a slow cooker when done.
- Add the sliced artichoke, stock, onion and garlic and stir well.
- Cover with a lid and cook on a low setting for 8 hours until the pork is starting to fall apart.
- Adjust the seasoning to taste before spooning into serving dishes.
- Serve immediately.

PREPARATION TIME: 15 MINUTES

COOKING TIME:
8 HOURS 10-15 MINUTES

INGREDIENTS

55 ml / 2 fl. oz / ¼ cup sunflower oil
900 g / 2 lb pork cheek, trimmed and diced
2 large Globe artichokes, trimmed and sliced
1 onion, very finely chopped
1 clove of garlic, minced
500 ml / 18 fl. oz / 2 cups ham stock
salt and pepper

307

SERVES 4

Beef Paupiette with Peppers

PREPARATION TIME:
15-20 MINUTES

COOKING TIME:
8 HOURS 15-20 MINUTES

INGREDIENTS

30 ml / 1 fl. oz / 2 tbsp sunflower oil
900 g / 2 lb piece of beef brisket, trimmed and butterflied
110 g / 4 oz / ⅔ cup sun-dried tomatoes, drained and chopped
900 g / 2 lb / 6 cups vine tomatoes, cored and diced
4 large red peppers, deseeded and diced
250 ml / 9 fl. oz / 1 cup vegetable stock
salt and pepper

- Place the brisket on a flat surface and fill the centre with the sun-dried tomatoes. Roll up into a cylinder before tying securely using kitchen string.
- Rub the outside with the oil and season generously.
- Heat a large casserole dish and eal the beef until golden brown. Transfer to a plate and set to one side.
- Reduce the heat under the dish before adding the vegetables. Cook for 5 minutes, stirring occasionally.
- Spoon into a slow cooker and add the stock. Stir and sit the beef on top. Cook on a low setting for 8 hours.
- Adjust the seasoning as necessary before spooning the stewed vegetables into a serving dish. Sit the beef on top and serve.

Beef Paupiette with Potatoes   308

Replace the tomatoes with 450 g / 1 lb / 3 cups of new potatoes, that have been halved.

Olive and Beef Paupiette   309

Replace the sun-dried tomtoes with the same weight of pitted green olives instead.

310

SERVES 4

Provençal Beef Stew

PREPARATION TIME :
10-15 MINUTES

COOKING TIME :
6 HOURS 15 MINUTES

INGREDIENTS

30 ml / 1 fl. oz / 2 tbsp sunflower oil
12 cloves of garlic, peeled
675 g / 1 lb 8 oz piece of beef fillet, trimmed
900 g / 2 lb / 6 cups carrots, peeled and chopped
150 g / 5 oz / 1 cup pitted black olives
375 ml / 13 fl. oz / 1 ½ cups beef stock
2 bay leaves
salt and pepper

- Coat the beef fillet in the oil and season generously.
- Heat a large casserole dish over a moderate heat until hot and seal the beef until golden brown in colour all over.
- Remove from the dish and transfer to a slow cooker.
- Reduce the heat under the dish and add the carrot, garlic and bay leaves and saute for 4-5 minutes stirring frequently.
- Add the beef stock and stir well, then pour into the slow cooker on top of the beef.
- Add the olives and seasoning before covering with a lid.
- Cook on a medium setting for 6 hours.
- Adjust the seasoning to taste before spooning into a serving dish.

Provençal Lamb Stew   311

For a richer taste, use lamb stock and cook in the same way, until tender.

312

SERVES 4

Pork Curry with Lime

Green Pork Curry

313

This dish can be made using green curry paste instead of red curry paste. Use the same quantities.

Pork Curry with Orange

315

Substitute the lime for sliced lemon or orange. If using orange, use 1 large orange in place of the 2 limes.

Pork and Apple Curry

316

Core and roughly cut 3 large apples and add for a fruity crunch in this dish.

PREPARATION TIME: 15 MINUTES

COOKING TIME: 6 HOURS

....

INGREDIENTS

30 ml / 1 fl. oz / 2 tbsp groundnut oil
2 cloves garlic, minced
2 large white potatoes, peeled and diced
450 g / 1 lb / 3 cups pork shoulder, diced
2 limes, sliced thinly
1 courgette, diced
500ml / 18 fl. oz / 2 cups coconut milk
1 tbsp Thai red curry paste

• Heat the oil in a large casserole dish set over a moderate heat until hot.
• Fry the garlic and red curry paste in the oil for 2-3 minutes, stirring frequently.
• Add the potato, courgette and pork and stir well.
• Add the coconut milk and half of the slices lime then pour into a slow cooker.
• Cook on a low setting for 6 hours.
• Adjust the seasoning to taste after 6 hours then ladle the curry into serving bowls.
• Garnish with the remaining sliced lime before serving.

317

SERVES 4

Beef and Orange Stew

PREPARATION TIME:
15-20 MINUTES

COOKING TIME:
8 HOURS 20-25 MINUTES

....

INGREDIENTS

55 ml / 2 fl. oz / ¼ cup sunflower oil
30 g / 1 oz / ¼ stick unsalted butter
900 g / 2 lb / 6 cups braising steak, diced
150 g / 5 oz / 1 cup pancetta, cut into lardons
4 shallots, finely sliced
2 carrots, peeled and finely diced
1 orange, juiced and zest pared
3 bay leaves
500 ml / 18 fl. oz / 2 cups beef stock
250 ml / 9 fl. oz / 1 cup ale
salt and pepper

- Coat the beef in the oil and season generously.
- Heat a large casserole dish and seal the beef in batches until golden brown in colour all over.
- Transfer the sealed beef to a slow cooker when done.
- Reduce the heat under the dish before adding the butter.
- Sweat the shallots, carrot, pancetta and bay leaf with a little salt until softened, stirring occasionally.
- Deglaze the dish with the ale before adding the orange juice, pared zest, stock and seasoning.
- Stir well before pouring into the slow cooker. Cook on a medium setting for 8 hours.
- Adjust the seasoning to taste before serving.

Beef and Onion Stew   318

Replace the shallots with 300 g / 10 ½ oz / 2 cups blanched and peeled pearl onions.

Red Wine Beef Stew   319

Replace the ale with the same volume of red wine and cook in the same way.

320

SERVES 4

Scallop and Vegetable Stew

PREPARATION TIME : 15 MINUTES

COOKING TIME :
4 HOURS 15-20 MINUTES

....

INGREDIENTS

55 ml / 2 fl. oz / ¼ cup olive oil
12 queen scallops, roe removed
450 g / 1 lb / 3 cups prawns, heads removed
75 g / 3 oz / 1 cup chanterelles, brushed clean
2 vine tomatoes, diced
1 tbsp tomato puree
1 red pepper, deseeded and finely diced
150 g / 5 oz / 1 ½ cups broad beans, shelled
2 large white potatoes, peeled and diced
250 ml / 9 fl. oz / 1 cup fish stock
250 ml / 9 fl. oz / 1 cup vegetable stock
125 ml / 4 ½ fl. oz / ½ cup double cream
flat-leaf parsley, finely chopped
salt and pepper

- Heat half of the olive oil in a large casserole dish set over a moderate heat until hot.
- Saute the scallops with a little seasoning for 1 minute, turning once.
- Remove to a slow cooker and cover with a lid.
- Add the remaining oil to the pan and saute the prawns for a few minutes, stirring occasionally.
- Remove to the slow cooker and reduce the heat under the dish before adding the potato, tomato puree and tomatoes.
- Stir well and cook for a few minutes before adding the remaining ingredients apart from the cream and parsley.
- Pour everything into a slow cooker and cover with a lid before cooking on a medium setting for 4 hours.
- Adjust the seasoning to taste before stirring through the cream and parsley. Serve immediately.

King Prawn Vegetable Stew   321

Swap the weight of scallops for king prawns for a light dish.

322

SERVES 4

Fish Stew with Carambola

- Coat the tilapia fillets in the oil and season generously.
- Heat a large non-stick frying pan over a moderate heat until hot and seal the fish for 1-2 minutes until golden brown.
- Arrange the star fruit in the base of a slow cooker and add the broad beans, stock and seasoning.
- Sit the fish on top and cover with a lid.
- Cook on a medium setting for 4 hours until the fish is firm yet springy to the touch.
- Adjust the seasoning to taste before stirring through the basil.
- Spoon the star fruit and broad beans into a serving dish and sit the fish on top before serving.

PREPARATION TIME :
10-15 MINUTES

COOKING TIME :
4 HOURS 10 MINUTES

INGREDIENTS

30 ml / 1 fl. oz / 2 tbsp olive oil
4 tilapia fillets, pin-boned
4 star fruit, sliced
300 g / 10 ½ oz / 2 cups broad beans, shelled
125 ml / 4 ½ fl. oz / ½ cup fish stock
2 tbsp basil leaves, finely sliced
salt and pepper
carambola, sliced

Fish Stew with Pears

323

Replace the star fruit with 4 cored, peeled and diced pears.

324

SERVES 4

Roast Pork with Vegetables

- Heat a large frying pan over a moderate heat until hot.
- Rub the pork with the oil and season before sealing in batches until golden brown in colour.
- Transfer to a slow cooker and deglaze the pan with the port. Pour the port into the slow cooker and add the artichoke and peppers.
- Cover with a lid and cook on a medium setting for 4 hours. Once the pork is ready, turn off the slow cooker but keep the lid on to let it rest.
- Melt the butter in a frying pan set over a moderate heat until it stops foaming. Add the beans and olives and fry for a few minutes, stirring occasionally.
- Adjust the seasoning to taste. Slice the pork steaks and arrange on serving plates.
- Spoon the peppers and artichokes next to the pork then add the olives and beans on top.
- Spoon the juices from the slow cooker on top and garnish with basil before serving.

PREPARATION TIME :10 MINUTES

COOKING TIME : 4 HOURS 15-20 MINUTES

INGREDIENTS

30 ml / 1 fl. oz / 2 tbsp olive oil
4 x 250 g / 9 oz pork rump steaks, trimmed
1 tbsp unsalted butter
2 Globe artichokes, trimmed and sliced
2 red Esplette peppers, deseeded and quartered
55 g / 2 oz / ½ cup broad beans, shelled
55 g / 2 oz / ⅓ cup pitted black olives
55 ml / 2 fl. oz / ¼ cup good-quality port
salt and peppercorn

GARNISH
basil leaves

Roast Pork and Figs

325

Combine the pork with figs instead of vegetables for a fresh summery dish.

326

SERVES 4

Squid and Cebette Stew

King Prawn Stew 327

Replace the octopus with the same weight of king prawns (shrimps).

Squid Stew 328

Leave out the Tabasco sauce and the chilli pepper garnish for a milder version.

Smokey Squid Stew 329

Add a little paprika into the slow cooker to create a smokier stew.

PREPARATION TIME: 15 MINUTES

COOKING TIME: 4 HOURS

INGREDIENTS

125 ml / 4 ½ fl. oz / ½ cup olive oil
450 g / 1 lb baby squid tentacles
450 g / 1 lb octopus tentacles, chopped
4 red onions, chopped
2 baby leeks, sliced
1 red pepper, deseeded and chopped
1 tbsp oyster sauce
1 tsp Tabasco sauce
1 lime, juiced

GARNISH

150 g / 5 oz / 1 cup tuna steak, diced
½ courgette, cored and finely sliced
2 green chilli peppers
4 sprigs of basil leaves

- Heat some of the olive oil in a large wok over a moderate heat until hot.
- Stir-fry the squid for 1 minute then transfer to a slow cooker.
- Add some more oil and stir-fry the octopus for a minute before adding to the slow cooker.
- Add more of the oil and stir-fry the spring onion, leek and red pepper for a few minutes.
- Stir in the oyster and Tabasco sauce as well as the lime juice.
- Pour the contents of the pan into the slow cooker and cook on a high setting for 4 hours.
- Adjust the seasoning to taste after 4 hours and spoon into a balti dish.
- Garnish with the courgette (courgette), chilli peppers and basil sprigs before serving.

330

SERVES 4

Chilli Con Carne

- Heat the oil in a large casserole dish set over a medium heat until hot.
- Sweat the onion and garlic with a little salt for 8-10 minutes until softened, adding the ground spices and oregano.
- Add the beef mince and brown off for 5 minutes, stirring occasionally.
- Add the stock and kidney beans and stir well.
- Meanwhile, pour into a slow cooker and cover with a lid and cook on a medium setting for 6 hours.
- Adjust the seasoning to taste after 6 hours.
- Heat the olive oil for the garnish in a frying pan set over a medium heat until hot.
- Sweat the onion and red pepper for a few minutes until the onion is just beginning to soften.
- Spoon the chilli into serving bowls and place the vegetable garnish on top before serving.

Chilli Con Carne with Steak

331

Replace half of the beef mince with the same weight of cubed chuck steak. Brown the steak at the same time as the mince.

PREPARATION TIME :15 MINUTES

COOKING TIME :
6 HOURS 20 MINUTES

INGREDIENTS

30 ml / 1 fl. oz / 2 tbsp sunflower oil
600 g / 1 lb / 5 oz / 4 cups beef mince
400 g / 14 oz / 2 cups canned kidney beans, drained
2 onions, finely chopped
2 cloves garlic, minced
1 tsp paprika
1 tsp cayenne pepper
½ tsp ground cumin
½ tsp dried oregano
500 ml / 18 fl. oz / 2 cups beef stock
salt and pepper

GARNISH
1 tbsp olive oil
1 red pepper, deseeded and finely diced
½ onion, diced

332

SERVES 4

Three Poultries in Broth

- Heat a large casserole dish over a moderate heat until hot.
- Season the duck and seal in the hot dish until golden brown in colour.
- Remove from the dish and move to a slow cooker.
- Season the chicken and pigeon breasts and seal in the casserole dish until golden brown before moving to the slow cooker.
- Add the potatoes, petit pois, asparagus, broad beans and stock and stir well.
- Cover with a lid and cook on a medium setting for 4 hours until the duck is firm yet springy to the touch.
- Adjust the seasoning to taste before ladling into serving bowls.
- Garnish with flaked sea salt and chervil before serving.

PREPARATION TIME:
10-15 MINUTES

COOKING TIME:
4 HOURS 20 MINUTES

INGREDIENTS

2 medium duck breasts, scored
2 medium chicken breasts, trimmed
2 pigeon breasts, trimmed
300 g / 10 ½ oz / 2 cups potatoes, peeled and sliced
150 g / 5 oz / 1 ½ cups frozen petit pois, thawed
110 g / 4 oz / 1 cup broad beans, shelled
110 g / 4 oz / 1 cup asparagus spears, trimmed
500 ml / 18 fl. oz / 2 cups chicken stock
salt and pepper

GARNISH
1 tsp flaked sea salt
sprigs of chervil

333

SERVES 4

Sage Roasted Sardines

- Place the sardines, tomatoes and onions in a slow cooker.
- Coat with the oil and season well.
- Cover and cook on a low setting for 4 hours.
- Remove after 4 hours and arrange side-by-side in a ceramic roasting tray.
- Preheat the oven to 190°C (170° fan) / 375F / gas 5.
- Arrange the slices of tomato and onion rings on top of the sardines and season a little more.
- Roast for 6-8 minutes until lightly coloured on top.
- Remove from the oven and let the sardines sit for 5 minutes before serving.

PREPARATION TIME: 10 MINUTES

COOKING TIME: 4 HOURS 10 MINUTES

INGREDIENTS

4 tbsp olive oil
8 sardines, gutted and cleaned
1 large beef tomato, sliced
1 onion, finely sliced into rings
sage leaves

334

SERVES 4

Lamb Korma

PREPARATION TIME: 15 MINUTES

COOKING TIME: 6 HOURS

INGREDIENTS

900 g / 2 lbs / 6 cups lamb shoulder, diced
2 large white potatoes, peeled and diced
2 sticks cinnamon
1 star anise
2 tbsp sunflower oil
1 onion, finely chopped
2 cloves garlic, minced

5cm / 2" ginger, peeled and minced
2 tsp ground cumin
2 tsp ground coriander seeds
1 tsp ground turmeric
1 tsp garam masala
1 tsp sugar
250ml / 9 fl. oz / 1 cup lamb stock
55ml / 2 fl. oz / ¼ cup double (heavy) cream

GARNISH

2 tbsp coriander (cilantro) leaves, finely chopped
4 sprigs of coriander (cilantro)

- Heat the sunflower oil in a large casserole dish set over a moderate heat.
- Sweat the onion, garlic and ginger with a little salt for 4-5 minutes, stirring occasionally.
- Add the cinnamon sticks, star anise, ground spices and sugar and stir well.
- Add the potato and lamb, stir well, then add the stock.
- Pour everything into a slow cooker and cook on a low setting for 6 hours until the lamb is soft and tender.
- Stir in the cream after 6 hours and adjust the seasoning to taste.
- Spoon into serving bowls and garnish with chopped coriander and a sprig of coriander before serving.

335

SERVES 4

Pike and Mackerel Soup

PREPARATION TIME: 15 MINUTES

COOKING TIME: 6 HOURS

INGREDIENTS

2 tbsp olive oil
4 peppered mackerel fillets
300 g / 10 ½ oz / 2 cups pike fillet, pin-boned
2 large white potatoes, peeled and cut into wedges

2 white radish, peeled and cut into wedges (reserve the tops)
2 sticks of celery, finely diced
2 red chilli peppers, sliced
1 tbsp chilli sauce
1 tbsp tomato puree
1 tbsp fish sauce
1 tbsp dark soy sauce
1 tsp sugar
250ml / 18 fl. oz / 2 cups fish stock

- Heat the olive oil in a large casserole dish set over a medium heat until hot.
- Sweat the celery, potato and radish for 5-6 minutes, stirring frequently.
- Add the chilli pepper, chilli sauce, soy sauce, fish sauce, tomato puree, sugar and fish stock, stirring well.
- Arrange the pike and the mackerel in a slow cooker and cover with the stock mixture.
- Cover with a lid and cook on low setting for 6 hours.
- Adjust the seasoning to taste then ladle the vegetables, pike and broth into serving bowls.
- Sit the mackerel on top and garnish with the radish tops.
- Serve immediately.

SERVES 4

Chicken and Vegetable Stew

- Heat the olive oil in a large casserole dish.
- Season the chicken breasts and seal in the hot oil until golden brown. Remove from the dish and transfer to a slow cooker.
- Reduce the heat under the casserole dish before adding the turnip and onion.
- Cook for 5 minutes before adding the stock. Stir well and pour into the slow cooker.
- Cover and cook on a medium setting for 4 hours.
- Add the Swiss chard to the slow cooker after 4 hours and let it wilt for 5-10 minutes.
- Remove 4 large wilted leaves and the chicken breast.
- Adjust the seasoning of the broth and stir through the sesame seeds and parsley.
- Finely chop the chicken breasts and pour into a casserole dish, then cover with the broth and serve.

PREPARATION TIME :
10-15 MINUTES

COOKING TIME :
4 HOURS 20-25 MINUTES

....

INGREDIENTS

30 ml / 1 fl. oz / 2 tbsp olive oil
4 skinless chicken breasts
2 turnips, peeled and sliced
300 g / 10 ½ oz / 4 cups Swiss chard
750 ml / 1 pint 6 fl. oz / 3 cups
chicken stock
6 spring onions (scallions), chopped
1 tbsp black sesame seeds
a handful of flat-leaf parsley, roughly
chopped
salt and pepper

Bok Choi Stew

337

Use sesame oil instead of the olive oil and replace 55 ml / 2 fl. oz / ¼ cup of the chicken stock with light soy sauce. Replace the Swiss chard with the same weight of bok choi and cook the same.

338

SERVES 4

Duck with Pineapple

- Heat a casserole dish over a moderate heat until hot.
- Coat the duck legs in the oil and honey and season generously.
- Seal in the casserole dish until golden brown all over before moving to a slow cooker.
- Add the pineapple, stock, star anise and seasoning and stir well.
- Cover with a lid and cook on a medium setting for 6 hours until the duck legs are cooked through.
- Adjust the seasoning to taste before spooning into serving dishes.

PREPARATION TIME :
10-15 MINUTES

COOKING TIME :
6 HOURS 10 MINUTES

....

INGREDIENTS

30 ml / 1 fl. oz / 2 tbsp sunflower oil
4 duck legs, trimmed
2 tbsp honey
600 g / 1 lb 5 oz / 3 cups canned
pineapple chunks, drained
500 ml / 18 fl. oz / 2 cups chicken
stock
1 star anise, crushed
salt and pepper

Duck with Passion Fruit

 339

Replacing the pineapple with a passion fruit, roast and glaze with honey alongside the duck.

340

SERVES 4

Meat and Vegetable Hotpot

PREPARATION TIME 20 MINUTES

COOKING TIME 6 HOURS
20 MINUTES

INGREDIENTS

55 ml / 2 fl. oz / ¼ cup sunflower oil
450 g / 1 lb / 3 cups steak, cubed
2 chicken legs, jointed
4 small onions, peeled and studded
with the cloves
12 cloves
450 g / 1 lb / 3 cups carrots, peeled
and halved
6 spring onions (scallions), trimmed
1 small white cabbage, roughly sliced
200 g / 7 oz / 1 cup canned butter
beans, drained
2 baby turnips, peeled
750 ml / 1 pint 6 fl. oz / 3 cups
chicken stock
salt and pepper

- Coat the steak and chicken pieces in the oil and season generously.
- Heat a large casserole dish over a moderate heat until hot and seal the meat in batches until golden brown in colour all over.
- Transfer to a slow cooker and reduce the heat under the casserole dish a little.
- Add the onions and carrots and saute for a few minutes before adding the remaining vegetables, the butter beans and stock.
- Stir well then pour into the slow cooker.
- Cover with a lid and cook on a medium setting for 6 hours.
- Adjust the seasoning to taste after 6 hours and spoon into a casserole dish for presentation.

Duck Leg Hotpot   **341**

Replace the chicken for duck legs that have
been jointed and trimmed and cook the same.

Chopped Tomato Hotpot   **342**

Replace half of the stock with the same
volume of canned chopped tomatoes.

343

SERVES 4

Rose Veal Casserole

PREPARATION TIME :
10-15 MINUTES
COOKING TIME :
4 HOURS MINUTES

INGREDIENTS

55 ml / 2 fl. oz / ¼ cup sunflower oil
900 g / 2 lb piece of rose veal
shoulder, cut in half
4 large vine tomatoes
1 garlic bulb, cut in half horizontally
150 g / 5 oz / 1 cup chorizo slices
800 g / 1 lb 12 oz / 4 cups canned
haricot beans, drained
500 ml / 18 fl. oz / 2 cups beef stock
salt and pepper

GARNISH
sprigs of sage
sage leaves

- Coat the veal pieces in the oil and season generously, meanwhile heat a large casserole dish over a moderate heat until hot and seal the veal pieces one at a time until golden brown in colour.
- Once browned, transfer the veal to a slow cooker.
- Reduce the heat under the casserole dish before adding garlic, beans and seasoning.
- Stir well before pouring in the stock and stirring again. Pour into the slow cooker and remove the veal pieces.
- Thread the veal onto skewers with chorizo slices bookended by the vine tomatoes.
- Add the remaining chorizo to the slow cooker and stir.
- Place the veal back in the slow cooker and cover with a lid; cook on a medium setting for 6 hours.
- Adjust the seasoning to taste once the veal is done.
- Spoon the bean mixture into the base of a casserole dish and sit the skewer of veal on top and garnish with sage leaves and sprigs.

344

SERVES 4

Chicken Stock with Ravioli

Mushroom Ravioli

345

Replace the chicken mince with 150 g / 5 oz / 1 cup chopped chanterelle mushrooms.

Vegetable Ravioli

346

Combine a few of your favourite part-cooked vegetables and place in the ravioli such as aubergines and courgettes.

Beef Ravioli

347

Replace the chicken mince with the same quantity of lean mince beef for a rich ravioli.

PREPARATION TIME: 15 MINUTES

COOKING TIME: 4 HOURS

INGREDIENTS

500 g / 1lb / 2 cups pasta dough
150 g / 5 oz / 1 cup chicken mince
500 ml / 18 fl. oz / 2 cups chicken stock
2 medium carrots, peeled and sliced
1 stick celery, sliced
2 sprigs thyme

- Combine the stock, carrot, celery and thyme in a slow cooker.
- Remove the pasta dough from the fridge and divide in half.
- Roll into a rectangular shape, thin enough to pass through the thickest setting of a pasta machine.
- Roll the pasta through the machine to smooth and thin, folding in half to control the size.
- Continue to decrease the thickness setting until you have reaching the thinnest setting on the machine.
- Rest the pasta dough on a lightly floured surface and use a circular fluted cookie cutter 2 inches in diameter to cut out rounds of the pasta.
- Place teaspoons of the chicken mince in the centre of the pasta dough and sandwich together against another round of pasta, sealing the rim well.
- Arrange the ravioli in the broth in the slow cooker.
- Cover and cook on a low setting for 4 hours until the pasta and the chicken mince is cooked.
- Adjust the seasoning of the broth to taste before ladling the broth and ravioli into serving bowls.
- Serve immediately.

348

SERVES 4

Chicken with Raisins

PREPARATION TIME :15 MINUTES

COOKING TIME :
4 HOURS 15-20 MINUTES

....

INGREDIENTS

55 ml / 2 fl. oz / ¼ cup olive oil
4 skinless chicken breasts, halved
150 g / 5 oz / 1 cup new potatoes, halved
1 red chilli, finely sliced
1 preserved lemon, drained, halved and sliced
200 g / 7 oz / 1 cup raisins
2 shallots, finely chopped
2 cloves of garlic, minced
2 tsp ras al hanout
1 tsp ground cinnamon
1 tsp ground cumin
1 tbsp honey
250 ml / 9 fl. oz / 1 cup chicken stock
salt and pepper

GARNISH
sprigs of coriander

- Coat the chicken pieces in half of the oil and season generously.
- Heat a large casserole dish over a moderate heat until hot and seal the chicken until golden brown.
- Remove to a slow cooker and reduce the heat under the casserole dish.
- Add the remaining oil and sweat the shallots, garlic and chilli in the oil for 5 minutes, stirring occasionally.
- Add the ground spices, honey, raisins, potatoes, lemon and stock.
- Stir well and pour into the slow cooker.
- Cover with a lid and cook on a medium setting for 4 hours until the chicken and the potatoes are cooked through.
- Adjust the seasoning to taste before spooning into serving bowls.
- Garnish with the coriander before serving.

Chicken with Sultanas

349

Instead of using raisins, replace with 200 g / 7 oz / 1 cup of golden sultanas. Do not add honey if using golden sultanas.

350

SERVES 4

Roast Duck with Vegetables

PREPARATION TIME :15 MINUTES

COOKING TIME :
6 HOURS 30-35 MINUTES

....

INGREDIENTS

1 medium duck, trimmed and cleaned
1 tbsp honey
55 g / 2 oz / ½ stick unsalted butter
450 g / 1 lb / 3 cups baby carrots, peeled
150 g / 5 oz / 2 cups chanterelles, brushed clean
150 g / 5 oz / 2 cups pleurotus mushrooms, roughly chopped
150 g / 5 oz / 2 cups oyster mushrooms, sliced
salt and pepper

- Preheat the oven to 190°C (170°C fan) / 375F / gas 5.
- Brush the duck with the honey and season generously and set in a roasting tray for 25-30 minutes until it starts to brown.
- Melt the butter in knobs in a large frying pan and saute the mushrooms in batches with salt for 2-3 minutes.
- Move the sauteed mushrooms to a slow cooker when finished. Meanwhile, saute the carrots in any remaining butter before spooning into the slow cooker.
- Remove the duck from the oven and sit on top of the vegetables in the slow cooker. Cover with a lid and cook on a medium setting for 6 hours until cooked thoroughly.
- Remove the duck from the slow cooker and cover loosely with aluminium foil to let it rest for 10 minutes.
- Spoon the mushrooms and carrots onto a serving plate and sit the duck on top.

Glazed Roast Duck

351

Brush the duck with honey and grill for 3 minutes to create a sweet crispy skin.

352

SERVES 4

Lamb and Spinach Curry

- Place the onion, ginger and garlic in a food processor and pulse until you have a paste.
- Heat the vegetable oil in a large casserole dish over a moderate heat until hot. Fry the whole spices for a few minutes, stirring occasionally.
- Add the onion, garlic and ginger paste to the dish, stirring frequently, for 3-4 minutes until it starts to turn golden in colour.
- Add the chopped tomatoes to the dish and cook for a few minutes. Add the diced lamb then sprinkle over the spices and a little seasoning, stirring well.
- Add enough water to cover the meat, then pour the mixture into a slow cooker.
- Cook on a medium setting for 6 hours until the lamb is tender. Adjust the seasoning to taste before stirring through the spinach.
- Let the heat of the curry wilt the spinach until soft, before spooning into serving bowl.

Lamb and Potato Curry   353

Replace half of the lamb with 300 g of diced white potato. Add the potatoes to the pan at the same time as the tomatoes.

PREPARATION TIME :
15-20 MINUTES

COOKING TIME :
6 HOURS 20 MINUTES

INGREDIENTS

55 ml / 2 fl. oz / ¼ cup vegetable oil
675 g / 1 lb 8 oz / 4 ½ cups diced lamb shoulder
225 g / 8 oz / 3 cups spinach, washed and dried
1 large onion, roughly chopped
1 inch piece of fresh ginger, peeled
3 cloves of garlic
a few cinnamon sticks
1 tsp cloves
1 tbsp Madras curry powder
2 tsp ground cumin
2 tsp ground coriander
1 tsp red chilli powder
1 tsp turmeric
½ tsp ground cinnamon
2 large plum tomatoes, de-seeded and chopped
salt and pepper

354

SERVES 4

Lamb Stew with Olives

- Heat the sunflower oil in a large, heavy-based casserole dish set over a moderate heat.
- Season well then seal the lamb until golden brown in colour all over.
- Remove from the dish to a slow cooker, then add the onion and sweat over a reduced heat for 4-5 minutes, stirring occasionally, until just softened.
- Increase the heat and add the red wine, allowing it to reduce by half.
- Add the lamb, cherry tomatoes, olives and bay leaf back to the dish.
- Cover with the stock and pour into the slow cooker.
- Cover with a lid and cook on a medium setting for 6 hours until the lamb is soft and coming apart.
- Adjust the seasoning to taste and discard the bay leaf before spooning into a serving dish.

Turkey Stew with Olives   355

For a leaner version of this meal, swap the quantity of lamb for turkey.

PREPARATION TIME :
15 MINUTES

COOKING TIME :
6 HOURS 15 MINUTES

INGREDIENTS

55 ml / 2 fl. oz / ¼ cup sunflower oil
600 g / 1 lb 5 oz / 4 cups lamb neck fillet, cut into large chunks
125 ml / 4 ½ fl. oz / ½ cup red wine
500 ml / 18 fl. oz / 2 cups lamb stock
1 onion, finely sliced
110 g / 4 oz / ⅔ cup cherry tomatoes
150 g / 5 oz / 1 cup green olives, pitted
1 bay leaf
salt and black pepper

356

SERVES 4

Swordfish with Tomatoes

Swordfish with Olives

357

Add 55 g / 2 oz / ⅓ cup pimento-stuffed green olives to the slow cooker before cooking.

Sweet Citrus Swordfish Tajine

358

Add 1 sliced, preserved lemon and 30 g / 1 oz / 2 tbsp dried apricot halves to the slow cooker before cooking.

Monkfish Tajine

359

Swap the swordfish for the same weight as monkfish for a sweeter taste.

PREPARATION TIME 10 MINUTES

COOKING TIME 45 MINUTES

INGREDIENTS

2 tbsp olive oil
4 x 225 g / 8 oz swordfish steaks
4 onions, sliced
4 cloves garlic, sliced
4 tomatoes, deseeded and sliced
2 orange peppers, deseeded and sliced
1 yellow pepper, deseeded and sliced
2 tsp ground coriander seeds
2 tsp ground cumin
1 tsp ground cinnamon
½ tsp paprika
1 tbsp honey
250ml / 9 fl. oz / 1 cup warm water
2 tbsp coriander (cilantro), roughly chopped
2 tbsp chervil leaves, finely chopped

GARNISH
4 sprigs of coriander

- Rub the swordfish steaks with the olive oil and season generously.
- Heat a large griddle pan over a moderate heat until hot.
- Seal the swordfish in the pan for a few minutes on both sides until marked.
- Move to one side as you prepare the vegetables.
- Add the onions and garlic to the pan and sauté for a few minutes.
- Transfer the onion and garlic to a slow cooker.
- Add the peppers and tomato to the pan and sauté for a few minutes, tossing occasionally.
- Add to the slow cooker along with the ground spices and honey.
- Stir well then sit the swordfish steaks on top.
- Pour in the warm water, cover and cook on a medium setting for 4 hours.
- Adjust the seasoning to taste after 4 hours before spooning the vegetables and swordfish into serving bowls.
- Sprinkle the chopped herbs on top and garnish with sprigs of coriander before serving.

360

SERVES 4

Roast Tuna Casserole

- Coat the tuna steak in the oil and season well.
- Heat a large frying pan over a high heat until hot and seal the tuna until golden brown in colour all over.
- Remove to a slow cooker and reduce the heat under the frying pan a little. Add the onions, mushrooms and carrot and saute with a little salt for 5 minutes, stirring occasionally.
- Spoon into the slow cooker and add the stock and water.
- Stir well before covering and cook on a medium setting for 5 hours until the tuna is just cooked through.
- Remove the tuna from the slow cooker and spoon the vegetables into serving dishes using a slotted spoon.
- Sit the tuna on top and garnish with chervil.

Tunas and Tomato Casserole   361

Add 4 diced vine tomatoes to the slow cooker before cooking for a Mediterranean casserole.

Tuna and Olive Casserole   362

Add 55 g / 2 oz / ⅓ cup chopped pitted green olives to the slow cooker before cooking.

PREPARATION TIME: 15 MINUTES

COOKING TIME:
5 HOURS 15 MINUTES

INGREDIENTS

45 ml / 1 ½ fl. oz / 3 tbsp sunflower oil
600 g / 1 lb 5 oz piece of tuna steak, cut in half
300 g / 10 ½ oz / 4 cups closed cup mushrooms, sliced
2 onions, finely sliced
2 large carrots, peeled and finely diced
250 ml / 9 fl. oz / 1 cup vegetable stock
250 ml / 9 fl. oz / 1 cup water
salt and pepper

GARNISH
2 tbsp picked chervil leaves

363

SERVES 4

Cassoulet

- Heat a large casserole dish and saute the pancetta for 3 minutes, until crisp. Drain on kitchen paper and season the duck pieces generously.
- Seal the duck in batches in the dish until golden brown in colour all over. Brown the sausages until dark brown in colour then add the contents to the slow cooker.
- Drain the dish of any excess fat and add the olive oil.
- Sweat the garlic and carrot for 5 minutes over a reduced heat until softened, then add the beans and stock.
- Pour into the slow cooker and stir well. Cook on a medium setting for 4-5 hours until the duck legs are cooked through. Adjust the seasoning to taste before spooning into a serving dish.
- Preheat the grill to hot and flash the gratin dish under the grill for 1 minute to lightly brown the top of the cassoulet.
- Remove from the grill and garnish with parsley.

English Cassoulet   364

An English spin on this French dish, add a chopped Cumberland sausage rather than Toulouse Sausage .

PREPARATION TIME :
15 MINUTES

COOKING TIME :
4-5 HOURS 20-25 MINUTES

INGREDIENTS

30 ml / 1 fl. oz / 2 tbsp olive oil
1 medium duck, jointed and scored on the skin side
4 large Toulouse sausages, pricked a few times
600 g / 1 lb 5 oz / 3 cups canned haricot beans, drained
2 large carrots, peeled and finely diced
150 g / 5 oz / 1 cup pancetta, cut into lardons
500 ml / 18 fl. oz / 2 cups chicken stock
salt and pepper

GARNISH
flat-leaf parsley

365

SERVES 4

Beef and Citrus Stew

PREPARATION TIME : 15 MINUTES

COOKING TIME :
6 HOURS 15-20 MINUTES

....

INGREDIENTS

55 ml / 2 fl. oz / ¼ cup sunflower oil
675 g / 1 lb 8 oz / 4 ½ cups chuck
steak, cut into 2" cubes
300 g / 10 ½ oz / 2 cups new potatoes,
halved
1 orange, juiced
4 shallots, halved
500 ml / 18 fl. oz / 2 cups beef stock
salt and pepper

GARNISH

2 tbsp flat-leaf parsley leaves, finely
chopped
2 large mandarins, peeled and
segmented
1 orange, zest pared and julienned

- Coat the chuck steak in the oil and season generously.
- Heat a large casserole dish over a moderate heat until hot.
- Seal the beef in batches until golden brown in colour all over.
- Transfer the sealed beef to a slow cooker and reduce the heat under the casserole dish a little.
- Saute the shallots and potatoes with a little seasoning for 5 minutes, stirring occasionally.
- Add the orange juice and stock and stir well.
- Pour into the slow cooker and cover with a lid before cooking on a medium setting for 6 hours until the beef is cooked through and the potatoes are soft.
- Adjust the seasoning to taste before spooning the stew into a serving dish using a slotted spoon.
- Garnish with the mandarin segments, orange zest and the parsley.

Beef and Marmalade Stew   366

Replace the orange juice with 2 tbs orange
marmalade for a richer texture.

367

SERVES 4

Roasted Palm's Heart

PREPARATION TIME :
10-15 MINUTES

COOKING TIME :
4 HOURS 20-25 MINUTES

....

INGREDIENTS

55 ml / 2 fl. oz / ¼ cup olive oil
10-12 palm hearts, trimmed
2 limes, juiced
small handful of basil leaves, finely
chopped
salt and pepper

GARNISH

2 limes, cut into wedges
sprigs of flat-leaf parsley

- Place the palm hearts in a large mixing bowl and combine with half of the olive oil, half of the lime juice and some seasoning.
- Toss well to coat in the mixture before moving to a slow cooker.
- Cover with a lid and cook on a low setting for 4 hours until softened.
- Once done, remove from the slow cooker and pat dry.
- Preheat the oven to 190°C (170° fan) / 375F / gas 5.
- Arrange the palm hearts on a roasting tray and coat in the remaining olive oil, adding more seasoning.
- Roast for 12-15 minutes until lightly coloured.
- Remove from the oven and toss with the remaining lime juice and the chopped basil.
- Arrange on serving plates and garnish with slices of lime and sprigs of parsley before serving.

Honey Glazed Palm's Heart   368

Brush the Palm's Heart with honey before
placing in the oven for a sweet coating.

369

SERVES 4

Beef and Okra Tajine

Smokey Mediterranean Beef Tajine

370

Add ½ tsp cayenne pepper and 2 tsp smoked paprika to the spices for a smokey, spicier flavour.

Beef and Potato Tajine

371

Replace the green beans with 2 large white potatoes that have been peeled and diced into cubes.

Spicy Beef Tajine

372

Add a few drops of Tabasco sauce (to your preferred taste) to create a spicier tajine.

PREPARATION TIME: 15 MINUTES

COOKING TIME:
6 HOURS 20 MINUTES

....

INGREDIENTS

4 tbsp sunflower oil
450 g / 1 lb / 3 cups braising steak, cut into 5 cm / 2" cubes
200 g / 7 oz / 1 okra
200 g / 7 oz / 2 cups green beans, trimmed
2 onions, sliced
2 cloves garlic, minced
2 tsp ras el hanout (Moroccan spice blend)
1 tsp ground cinnamon
1 tsp paprika
2 large tomatoes, chopped
375ml / 13 fl. oz / 1 ½ cups water

- Heat some of the oil in a large casserole dish set over a moderate heat until hot.
- Season the beef then seal in batches until golden brown.
- Move the sealed beef to a slow cooker when it is ready.
- Reduce the heat under the dish and add the remaining olive oil.
- Sweat the onion and garlic with a little salt for 5 minutes, stirring occasionally.
- Add the ground spices and stir well.
- Add the okra, tomatoes, beans and stock and stir thoroughly.
- Pour into the slow cooker and cover with a lid.
- Cook on a low setting for 6 hours until the beef is tender.
- Adjust the seasoning to taste after 6 hours before ladling into serving bowls.
- Serve immediately.

373

SERVES 4

Tuna with Stewed Vegetables

PREPARATION TIME :
10 MINUTES

COOKING TIME :
3-4 HOURS 10-15 MINUTES

....

INGREDIENTS

75 ml / 3 fl. oz / ⅓ cup olive oil
4 x 225 g / 8 oz tuna steaks
2 onions, finely sliced
30 g / 1 oz / 2 tbsp baby capers, drained
400 g / 14 oz / 2 cups canned chopped tomatoes
½ tsp caster sugar
salt and pepper

GARNISH
flat-leaf parsley

- Rub the tuna steaks with the olive oil and season well.
- Heat a large frying pan over a moderate heat until hot and seal the tuna for a minute on both sides.
- Transfer to a plate and set to one side.
- Combine the onions, capers, chopped tomatoes, sugar and seasoning in a slow cooker.
- Stir well and sit the tuna steak on top.
- Cover with a lid and cook on a medium setting for 3-4 hours until the tuna is just cooked; it should be firm yet a little springy to the touch.
- Adjust the seasoning once the tuna is cooked and remove from the slow cooker.
- Spoon the tomato, caper and onion stew onto a serving platter and top with the tuna steaks.
- Garnish with the parsley before serving.

Tuna with Butter Beans

374

Add 400 g / 14 oz / 2 cups canned butter beans to the slow cooker before cooking.

375

SERVES 4

Roasted Bass with Aniseed

PREPARATION TIME :
15 MINUTES

COOKING TIME :
5-6 HOURS 15 MINUTES

....

INGREDIENTS

125 ml / 4 ½ fl. oz / ½ cup olive oil
2 medium sea bass, gutted and cleaned
1 lemon, sliced
1 tbsp caraway seeds
1 tsp mustard seeds
4 red peppers, deseeded and sliced
150 g / 5 oz / 1 cup pitted green olives, sliced
150 g / 5 oz / 1 cup sun-dried tomatoes, roughly chopped
2 star anise
salt and pepper

- Heat half of the olive oil in a large casserole dish set over a medium heat until hot.
- Saute the peppers, olives and sun-dried tomatoes with the star anise for 2-3 minutes, stirring occasionally.
- Add half of the caraway and mustard seeds and stir well before spooning into a slow cooker.
- Make three slashes in one side of each sea bass and stuff with the lemon slices.
- Sit the sea bass on top of the vegetables in the slow cooker and cover with a lid.
- Cook on a medium setting for 5-6 hours until the sea bass is cooked through and the flesh is firm yet slightly springy to the touch.
- Discard the star anise and carefully remove the sea bass.
- Spoon the vegetables and olives into a serving dish and sit the bass on top before garnishing with the remaining caraway and mustard seeds.

Bass with Mixed Peppers

376

Add 2 red peppers, 1 yellow and 1 green pepper to create a bright summery dish.

377

SERVES 4

Fish Tajine

- Cut the mullet into 2" thick steaks.
- Coat in most of the oil and season well.
- Heat a large casserole dish over a moderate heat until hot and seal the fish until golden in colour all over.
- Remove to a slow cooker and reduce the heat under the dish a little.
- Add the remaining oil and saute the peppers and garlic for a few minutes, stirring frequently.
- Add the ground spices, stir well, add the wine, stock and potatoes.
- Pour into the slow cooker and cover with a lid.
- Cook on a medium setting for 5 hours until the fish is cooked through.
- Adjust the seasoning to taste before ladling into serving dishes.
- Garnish with coriander before serving.

Fish Tajine with Mint   378

Remove the saffron and add 2 tbsp chopped mint to the slow cooker at the end of cooking.

PREPARATION TIME :20 MINUTES

COOKING TIME :
5 HOURS 15-20 MINUTES

INGREDIENTS

75 ml / 3 fl. oz / ⅓ cup olive oil
2 large grey mullet, gutted and cleaned
450 g / 1 lb / 3 cups new potatoes, halved
2 yellow peppers, deseeded and sliced
2 cloves of garlic
500 ml / 18 fl. oz / 2 cups fish stock
125 ml / 4 ½ fl. oz / ½ cup dry white wine
½ tsp saffron threads, infused in the stock
1 tsp ras al hanout (Moroccan spice blend)
1 tsp paprika
½ tsp cayenne pepper
salt and pepper

GARNISH

sprigs of coriander leaves

379

SERVES 4

Okra and Quince Tajine

- Heat the olive oil in a large casserole dish set over a medium heat until hot.
- Sweat the onion, garlic and okra for 8-10 minutes, stirring occasionally, until the onion is softened.
- Add the ground spices and stir well before adding the quince.
- Stir well and add the honey and stock.
- Pour into a slow cooker and cover with a lid.
- Cook on a medium setting for 4 hours until the quince is soft.
- Adjust the seasoning to taste before spooning into a serving bowl.

Gombo and Pear Tajine   380

Replace the quince with pears. Core and roughly chop the pears to create a smoother tajine.

PREPARATION TIME :
10-15 MINUTES

COOKING TIME :
4 HOURS 10-15 MINUTES

INGREDIENTS

55 ml / 2 fl. oz / ¼ cup olive oil
450 g / 1 lb / 3 cups okra, chopped
450 g / 1 lb / 3 cups quince, halved and de-seeded
2 onions, sliced
2 cloves of garlic, minced
2 tsp ras al hanout (Moroccan spice blend)
1 tsp ground cumin
1 tsp ground cinnamon
2 tbsp honey
250 ml / 9 fl. oz / 1 cup vegetable stock
salt and pepper

381

SERVES 4

Chicken with Ceylon Spices

Coconut Chicken   382

Add 2 tbsp grated fresh coconut to the slow cooker before cooking.

Creamy Coconut Chicken   383

Replace the chicken stock with the same amount of coconut milk for a creamier version.

Parmesan Chicken   384

Add some Parmesan cheese to the slow cooker before cooking and grate some over the chicken before serving to create a cheesy twist.

PREPARATION TIME: 45 MINUTES
COOKING TIME:
4 HOURS 30 MINUTES

INGREDIENTS

2 tbsp olive oil
4 Bresse drumsticks, trimmed
150 g / 5 oz / 1 cup broad beans, shelled
250 g / 4 oz / 1 cup basmati rice
250ml / 9 fl. oz / 1 cup chicken stock
2 tbsp sultanas
2 tomatoes, blanched and sliced
1 tsp dried oregano
1 tsp Cayenne pepper
1 tsp paprika
½ tsp ground cumin

FOR THE POTATO GARNISH
500 ml / 18 fl. oz / 2 cups vegetable oil
2 large white potatoes, peeled and cubed
2 tbsp plain (all purpose) flour
1 egg, beaten
225 g / 8 oz / 1 cup panko breadcrumbs

GARNISH
4 sprigs chervil

- Heat the olive oil in a large casserole dish set over a moderate heat until hot. Season the chicken with the ground spices, salt and pepper.
- Seal in the oil until golden brown. Transfer to a slow cooker. Reduce the heat and add the rice.
- Stir well then add the stock, tomatoes and sultanas.
- Pour into the slow cooker and cover with a lid.
- Cook on a medium setting for 4 hours or until the chicken is cooked and rice is soft and tender.
- Add the broad beans and stir well then turn off the cooker but keep the lid on.
- Heat the vegetable oil in a deep saucepan.
- Coat the potato cubes in the flour and season well.
- Roll in the breadcrumbs and deep fry for 4-5 minutes until golden brown and drain on kitchen paper.
- Spoon the casserole from the slow cooker into serving bowls. Sit the chicken on top and garnish with the desiccated coconut.
- Sit the deep-fried potato next to the chicken and garnish with chervil before serving.

385

SERVES 4

Stewed Pork with Sprouts

- Rub the pork with the oil and season generously.
- Heat a large casserole dish over a moderate heat until hot and seal the pork until golden brown in colour all over.
- Remove to a slow cooker and reduce the heat under the dish a little.
- Add the butter and saute the shallots for 3-4 minutes until softened and starting to colour a little.
- Spoon into the slow cooker and add the Brussels sprouts, carrot and stock.
- Cover with a lid and cook on a medium setting for 8 hours until the pork is cooked and the brussels sprouts are tender.
- Adjust the seasoning to taste before spooning into a saucepan for presentation.

PREPARATION TIME :
15-20 MINUTES

COOKING TIME :
8 HOURS 15 MINUTES

....

INGREDIENTS

30 ml / 1 fl. oz / 2 tbsp olive oil
30 g / 1 oz / ¼ stick unsalted butter
2 shallots, finely sliced
1 large carrot, peeled and julienned
675 g / 1 lb 8 oz piece of boneless pork shoulder
675 g / 1 lb 8 oz / 4 ½ cups Brussels sprouts, scored on their bases
750 ml / 1 pint 6 fl. oz / 3 cups ham stock
salt and pepper

Stewed Pork with Apples   386

Replace the sprouts with apples and cook in the same way, for a sweeter dish.

387

SERVES 4

Roast Pork and Mustard

- Rub the pork with the oil and season.
- Heat a frying pan and seal the pork until golden brown.
- Transfer to a slow cooker and add the cider. Cover and cook on a medium setting for 4 hours.
- Pour the juices from the slow cooker into a saucepan.
- Preheat the oven to 190°C (170° fan) / 375F / gas 5.
- Meanwhile, soak the grated potato in cold water.
- Carve the pork into thin slices and set to one side.
- Coat the potato in the butter and separate into tablespoon-sized portions.
- Arrange the potato on a tray and flatten out with your palm. Bake for 12-15 minutes until golden brown.
- Remove from the oven and spread slices of the pork with the mustard. Layer with the potato rosti and arrange on a tray. Warm in the oven for 5 minutes.
- Spoon the sauce around and garnish with the chervil and Cos lettuce.

PREPARATION TIME :
15-20 MINUTES

COOKING TIME :
4 HOURS 35-45 MINUTES

....

INGREDIENTS

30 ml / 1 fl. oz / 2 tbsp olive oil
600 g / 1 lb 5 oz piece of pork loin roast, trimmed
900 g / 2 lb / 6 cups potatoes, peeled and grated
110 g / 4 oz / 1 stick unsalted butter, clarified
55 ml / 2 fl. oz / ¼ cup wholegrain mustard
250 ml / 9 fl. oz / 1 cup cider
salt and pepper

GARNISH
sprigs of chervil
1 Cos lettuce, chopped

Roast Pork and Cherry   388

Replace the mustard with the same volume of cherry jam and cook the same.

389

SERVES 4

Omelette with Stew

PREPARATION TIME :
10-15 MINUTES

COOKING TIME :
4 HOURS 30-35 MINUTES

INGREDIENTS

FOR THE OMELETTE
55 ml / 2 fl. oz / ¼ cup olive oil
3 large potatoes, peeled and finely diced
1 onion, finely chopped
6 large eggs
250 ml / 9 fl. oz / 1 cup whole milk
salt and pepper

FOR THE STEW
30 ml / 1 fl. oz / 2 tbsp olive oil
1 onion, finely chopped
4 cloves of garlic, mined
400 g / 14 oz / 2 cups canned chopped tomatoes
250 ml / 9 fl. oz / 1 cup passata
½ tsp caster (superfine) sugar
salt and pepper

- Prepare the stew by heating the olive oil in a large saucepan over a medium heat. Sweat the onion and garlic for 5 minutes.
- Add the sugar, chopped tomatoes, passata and seasoning and stir well. Pour into a slow cooker and cook for 4 hours on a low setting.
- Turn the slow cooker off and preheat the oven to 180°C (160° fan) / 350F / gas 4.
- Line a round cake tin with greaseproof paper. Heat the olive oil in a casserole dish over a medium heat. Sweat the onion and potato for 8-10 minutes.
- Meanwhile, whisk together the eggs, milk and seasoning in a bowl. Spoon the potato mixture into the base of the cake tin.
- Pour over the egg mixture and bake for 15-20 minutes. Remove from the oven and reheat the stew.
- Spoon the stew into serving dishes and turn the omelette out from the tin.
- Sit in the stew and garnish the dishes with the parsley.

Omelette with Soup

390

Blend the stew until smooth for an alternative soup-like texture.

391

SERVES 4

Petit Bacon with Lentils

PREPARATION TIME :
10-15 MINUTES

COOKING TIME :
6 HOURS 15 MINUTES

INGREDIENTS

450 g / 1 lb piece of gammon steak
110 g / 4 oz piece of pancetta
400 g / 14 oz / 2 cups puy lentils
750 ml / 1 pint 6 fl. oz / 3 cups chicken stock
4 bay leaves
salt and pepper

GARNISH
1 carrot, peeled and grated
celery leaves, chopped

- Heat a large casserole dish over a moderate heat until hot.
- Saute the piece of pancetta until golden brown in colour.
- Transfer to a slow cooker and add the gammon to the dish to brown all over.
- Add the lentils and bay leaves once sealed and cover with the stock.
- Stir well and cook for 10 minutes, stirring occasionally.
- Pour into a slow cooker and cover with a lid.
- Cook on a medium setting for 6 hours until the lentils are tender and the gammon is cooked through.
- Adjust the seasoning to taste before spooning into a shallow dish.
- Garnish with the celery leaf and carrot before serving.

Monkfish with Summer Vegetables

- Heat a large frying pan over a moderate heat until hot.
- Flash-fry the vegetables with a little seasoning in batches using fresh olive oil for each batch.
- Move the vegetables from the pan to a slow cooker after each batch is finished.
- Once all the vegetables have been flash-fried, sit the monkfish on top.
- Cover with a lid and cook on a medium setting for 4 hours.
- Remove the monkfish tail after 4 hours and cut into medallions.
- Adjust the seasoning of the vegetables to taste.
- Spoon the vegetables into a serving dish and sit the medallions of monkfish on top.
- Sprinkle with the chopped parsley and sprigs of parsley before serving.

PREPARATION TIME: 20 MINUTES

COOKING TIME:
4 HOURS 20 MINUTES

INGREDIENTS

450 g / 1 lb monkfish tail
75 ml / 3 fl. oz / ⅓ cup olive oil
2 aubergines, diced
2 onions, sliced
4 cloves garlic, minced
1 red pepper, deseeded and sliced
1 orange pepper, deseeded and sliced
1 green pepper, deseeded and sliced
GARNISH
2 tbsp flat-leaf parsley, chopped
4 sprigs of flat-leaf parsley

Lamb, Turnip and Sesame Seeds

PREPARATION TIME: 15 MINUTES

COOKING TIME:
6 HOURS 20 MINUTE

INGREDIENTS

4 tbsp olive oil
600 g / 1 lb 5 oz / 4 cups lamb shoulder, cut into cubes
4 onions, sliced

2 cloves garlic, crushed
1 turnip, peeled and cut into chunks
2 tbsp flaked (slivered) almonds
2 tbsp sesame seeds
1 tsp ras el hanout (Moroccan spice blend)
1 tsp ground cinnamon
1 tsp paprika
1 tbsp honey
500ml / 18 fl. oz / 2 cups lamb stock

- Heat some of the olive oil in a large casserole dish set over a moderate heat until hot.
- Season the lamb and seal in batches until golden brown.
- Transfer the sealed lamb to a slow cooker.
- Reduce the heat under the dish and add the remaining olive oil.
- Sweat the onion and garlic for 5 minutes stirring occasionally.
- Add the ground spices, honey and seasoning and stir well.
- Add the stock and turnip, stir well, then pour into the slow cooker.
- Cover and cook on a low setting for 6 hours.
- Adjust the seasoning to taste after 6 hours before ladling the tajine into serving bowls using a slotted spoon.
- Garnish with the sesame seeds and flaked almonds before serving

Cassoulet with Duck Confit

PREPARATION TIME: 15 MINUTES

COOKING TIME:
5 HOURS 30 MINUTES

INGREDIENTS

4 tbsp olive oil
2 onions, finely chopped
3 cloves garlic, minced
2 sticks celery, finely sliced

400 g / 14 oz / 2 cups flageolet beans, drained
400 g / 14 oz / 2 cups chopped tomatoes
110g / 4 oz / 2 cups breadcrumbs
500 ml / 18 fl. oz / 2 cups chicken stock
4 confit duck legs, pre-cooked
6 pork sausages
3 bay leaves
2 sprigs of thyme

- Heat the olive oil in a large casserole dish and seal the sausages until golden brown all over. Transfer to a slow cooker once sealed. Add the onion, celery and garlic to the dish and reduce the heat a little.
- Cook for 4-5 minutes until the vegetables start to soften. Add the stock, tomatoes, beans, duck legs, bay leaves and thyme sprigs. Stir thoroughly then pour on top of the sausages in the slow cooker.
- Cover and cook on a medium setting for 5 hours.
- Adjust the seasoning to taste after 5 hours and spoon everything from the slow cooker back into a casserole dish.
- Preheat the oven to 190°C (170° fan) / 375F / gas 5.
- Sprinkle the breadcrumbs on top of the cassoulet mixture in the casserole dish.
- Bake in the oven for 10-12 minutes until the breadcrumbs are starting to colour.
- Remove from the oven and let the cassoulet sit for 5 minutes before serving.

SERVES 4

Roast Beef with Bacon

PREPARATION TIME :
10 MINUTES

COOKING TIME :
4-5 HOURS 10-15 MINUTES

....

INGREDIENTS

45 ml / 1 ½ fl. oz / 3 tbsp groundnut oil
675 g / 1 lb 8 oz piece of beef fillet,
trimmed
6 rashers back bacon
110 g / 4 oz / 1 cup blackberries
small handful of flowering thyme
sprigs
salt and pepper

- Heat a large frying pan over a moderate heat until hot.
- Rub the beef fillet with the oil and season generously.
- Seal the beef until golden brown in colour all over then remove from the pan and make 6 incisions in the piece of beef fillet.
- Fill the incisions with the bacon rashers and move to a slow cooker.
- Cover with a lid and cook on a medium setting for 4-5 hours until the beef and bacon are cooked through.
- Remove from the slow cooker and cover loosely with aluminium foil before resting it for 10 minutes.
- Move to a cutting board after it has rested and garnish with the blackberries and thyme sprigs before serving.

Roast Beef with Strawberries 396

Replace the blackberries with strawberries and drizzle with balsamic vinegar and a sprinkle of sugar.

MAKES 18

Prune Stuffed Pork

PREPARATION TIME :
10-15 MINUTES

COOKING TIME :
6 HOURS 15 MINUTES

....

INGREDIENTS

55 ml / 2 fl. oz / ¼ cup olive oil
900 g / 2 lb pork loin roast
2 carrots, peeled and diced
2 shallots, finely sliced
2 cloves of garlic, finely chopped
75 g / 3 oz / ½ cup canned prunes,
drained
75 g / 3 oz / ½ cup cocktail onions,
drained
salt and pepper

GARNISH
small bunch of thyme sprigs
150 ml / 5 fl. oz / ⅔ cup barbecue
sauce

- Rub the pork with most of the oil and the chopped garlic. Meanwhile, heat a large frying pan over a moderate heat until hot.
- Seal the pork until golden brown in colour all over then transfer to a slow cooker.
- Reduce the heat under the casserole dish before adding the rest of the olive oil.
- Sweat the shallots and carrots until softened.
- Add the cocktail onions and prunes and stir well. Spoon contents into the slow cooker and cover with a lid. Cook on a medium setting for 6 hours.
- Remove from the slow cooker and arrange on a serving board before spooning the vegetables and prunes on top.
- Garnish with thyme sprigs and serve.

Roast Pork with Blackberries 398

Add 110 g / 4 oz / 1 cup drained canned cherries to the slow cooker before cooking for a sweeter taste.

399

SERVES 6

Roast Pork with Shallots

Roast Pork with Cherries
400

Add 55g / 2 oz / ⅓ cup pitted cherries to the cooker before cooking.

Roast Cider Pork
401

Add 250ml / 9 fl. oz / 1 cup cider to the slow cooker before cooking.

Roast Pork with Crackling
402

Remove the pork skin before slow cooking the meat and rub with some salt. Bake in the oven for 30 minutes to create crackling.

PREPARATION TIME: 10 MINUTES

COOKING TIME: 6 HOURS

INGREDIENTS

2 tbsp olive oil
900 g / 2 lbs pork loin
14 small shallots
2 cloves garlic, lightly crushed
2 sprigs thyme
1 bay leaf
GARNISH
2-3 sprigs of thyme

- Rub the pork loin roast with the olive oil and season generously.
- Heat a large frying pan over a moderate heat until hot.
- Seal the pork in the pan until golden brown.
- Transfer to a slow cooker and set to one side.
- Reduce the heat under the frying pan and add the shallots, garlic, thyme bay leaf and seasoning.
- Sauté for 2 minutes tossing and stirring occasionally.
- Spoon into the slow cooker and cover with a lid.
- Cook on a medium setting for 6 hours.
- Remove after 6 hours and arrange in a roasting tray.
- Garnish with the thyme before serving.

403

SERVES 4

Chicken with Ginger

PREPARATION TIME :
15 MINUTES

COOKING TIME :
5 HOURS 15 MINUTES

INGREDIENTS

55 ml / 2 fl. oz / ¼ cup olive oil
4 chicken legs, jointed and trimmed
2 onions, sliced
2 cloves of garlic, minced
4" ginger, peeled and finely chopped
2 preserved lemons, drained and
chopped
1 tsp ras al hanout
1 tsp smoked paprika
1 tsp ground cumin
½ tsp turmeric
½ tsp ground cinnamon
1 tbsp honey
75 g / 3 oz / 1 cup baby spinach,
chopped
500 ml / 18 fl. oz / 2 cups chicken
stock
salt and pepper

- Coat the chicken pieces in most of the oil and season generously.
- Heat a large casserole dish over a moderate heat until hot and seal the chicken in batches until golden brown in colour all over.
- Remove to a slow cooker and reduce the heat under the casserole dish a little.
- Add the remaining oil and sauté the onion, ginger and garlic for a few minutes, stirring occasionally.
- Add the ground spices, spinach, honey, preserved lemon and seasoning and stir well.
- Cover with the stock before pouring over the chicken in the slow cooker.
- Cover with a lid and cook on a medium setting for 5 hours until the chicken pieces are cooked through.
- Adjust the seasoning to taste before spooning into serving bowls.

Chicken with Star Anise   404

Replacing the ginger with star anise gives the meal a liquorice flavour.

405

SERVES 4

Moorish-style Lamb

PREPARATION TIME :
15 MINUTES

COOKING TIME :
5 HOURS 15 MINUTES

INGREDIENTS

55 ml / 2 fl. oz / ¼ cup groundnut oil
450 g / 1 lb / 3 cups lamb shoulder,
diced
3 sticks of celery, sliced
500 ml / 18 fl. oz / 2 cups passata
1 tbsp paprika
1 tbsp harissa
1 tsp honey
150 g / 5 oz / 1 cup pitted green olives
salt and pepper

- Coat the lamb in half of the oil and season generously.
- Heat a large casserole dish over a moderate heat until hot and seal the lamb in batches until golden brown in colour all over.
- Remove to a slow cooker when finished and reduce the heat under the casserole dish a little.
- Add the remaining oil and saute the celery with some salt and paprika for 2-3 minutes, stirring occasionally.
- Add the harissa, honey and passata and stir well.
- Pour into the slow cooker and add the green olives before stirring thoroughly.
- Cover with a lid and cook on a medium setting for 5 hours until the lamb is tender.
- Adjust the seasoning to taste before pouring into a serving dish.

Moorish-style Turkey   406

Swapping the lamb for turkey creates a lean dinner dish.

407

SERVES 4

Chicken Sauté

- Coat the chicken in the oil and season with the dried herbs and seasoning.
- Heat a large casserole dish over a moderate heat until hot then seal the chicken in batches until golden brown in colour all over.
- Remove to a slow cooker and add the chopped tomatoes, olives, mushrooms and stock.
- Cover with a lid and cook on a medium setting for 6 hours until the chicken is cooked through.
- Adjust the seasoning to taste when the chicken is ready and pour back into a casserole dish for presentation.
- Garnish with the oregano before serving.

Peanut Chicken Sauté   408

Add 1 tbsp of peanut butter to the dish for a nuttier flavour and crunch.

PREPARATION TIME :
15-20 MINUTES

COOKING TIME :
6 HOURS 10-15 MINUTES

INGREDIENTS

75 ml / 3 fl. oz / ⅓ cup olive oil
1 large chicken, jointed and trimmed
400 g / 14 oz / 2 cups canned chopped tomatoes
225 g / 8 oz / 1 ½ cups pitted black olives
300 g / 10 ½ oz / 4 cups button mushrooms, sliced
1 l / 1 pint 16 fl. oz / 4 cups chicken stock
1 tsp dried oregano
1 tsp dried basil
salt and pepper

GARNISH
sprigs of oregano leaves

409

SERVES 4

Pollack Casserole

- Heat the olive oil in a large casserole dish set over a moderate heat until hot.
- Saute the onion, garlic and potato for 5 minutes, stirring occasionally.
- Add the bay leaves, stock and wine and stir well.
- Pour into a slow cooker and position the pollack in the liquid.
- Cover with a lid and cook on a mediums setting for 4 hours until the fish is cooked and the potato is soft.
- Adjust the seasoning to taste before pouring back into a casserole dish for presentation.
- Garnish with a sprinkle of cayenne pepper and caraway seeds before serving.

Pollack and Shrimp Casserole   410

Add 225 g of prawns with their heads removed to the slow cooker for a richer seafood flavour.

PREPARATION TIME :
10-15 MINUTES

COOKING TIME :
4 HOURS 10 MINUTES

INGREDIENTS

55 ml / 2 fl. oz / ¼ cup olive oil
1 medium pollack, gutted, cleaned and cut into thick steaks
600 g / 1 lb 5 oz / 4 cups new potatoes, peeled
3 onions, sliced
4 cloves of garlic
3 bay leaves
500 ml / 18 fl. oz / 2 cups fish stock
125 ml / 4 ½ fl. oz / ½ cup dry white wine
salt and pepper

GARNISH
1 tsp cayenne pepper
1 tsp caraway seeds

411

SERVES 4

Roast Chicken with Onions

Orange Honey Roast Chicken

412

Add 2 tbsp honey and the juice of 1 orange to the slow cooker and stir well before cooking.

Roast Chicken with Chestnuts

413

Add 150 g / 5 oz / 1 cup cooked chestnuts to the slow cooker before cooking for a nutty variation.

Roast Chicken with Turnips

414

Use the same weight of turnips as you would onions and slow cook with the chicken to absorb the flavour.

PREPARATION TIME: 20 MINUTES

COOKING TIME: 5 HOURS

INGREDIENTS

4 tbsp olive oil
30 g / 1 oz / ¼ stick butter, unsalted
1 large chicken, jointed and trimmed
300 g / 10 ½ oz / 2 cups pearl onions, blanched
2 tbsp balsamic vinegar
1 tbsp light brown sugar
GARNISH
4 sprigs of chervil leaves
2 tbsp chervil leaves, chopped

- Rub the chicken pieces with the olive oil and season generously.
- Heat a large casserole dish over a moderate heat until hot and seal the chicken, in batches, until golden brown.
- Transfer the sealed chicken to a slow cooker.
- Reduce the heat under the dish and add the butter.
- Sauté the onions in the butter for 3-4 minutes, stirring occasionally.
- Deglaze the pan with the balsamic vinegar and sprinkle over the sugar.
- Spoon the contents of the dish into the slow cooker and cover with a lid.
- Cook on a medium setting for 5 hours until the chicken is cooked through.
- When the chicken is ready, spoon everything from the slow cooker back into a roasting dish for presentation.
- Garnish with the chopped chervil and sprigs of chervil leaves before serving.

415

SERVES 4

Roast Red Mullet with Tomatoes

- Rub the outside of the mullet with oil and season.
- Combine the shallot, tomatoes, stock, remaining oil and seasoning in a slow cooker. Sit the red mullet on top and replace lid.
- Cook on a medium setting for 4 hours until the fish is cooked.
- Prepare the fennel by melting the butter in a saucepan set over a medium heat.
- Sweat the fennel for 10 minutes, stirring occasionally until softened.
- Cover with milk and cook for 20 minutes at a gentle simmer.
- Strain and spoon the fennel into a food processor.
- Add a little cooking milk and puree until smooth; add more milk if too dry.
- Cover and chill until ready to serve.
- Pour everything from the slow cooker into a roasting dish and preheat the oven to 190°C (170°C fan) / 375F / gas 5.
- Place in the oven for 10 minutes.
- Spoon the puree onto a plate and garnish.
- Remove the red mullet from the oven and garnish before serving.

PREPARATION TIME :
10-15 MINUTES

COOKING TIME :
4 HOURS 15 MINUTES

INGREDIENTS

125 ml / 4 ½ fl. oz / ½ cup olive oil
2 red mullet, gutted and cleaned
450 g / 1 lb / 3 cups vine cherry tomatoes, picked
500 ml / 18 fl. oz / 2 cups fish stock
2 shallots, finely sliced
salt and pepper
For the pureed fennel
55 g / 2 oz / ½ stick unsalted butter
4 fennel bulbs, trimmed and sliced
250 ml / 9 fl. oz / 1 cup whole milk
salt and pepper
GARNISH
2 sprigs of rosemary

416

SERVES 4

Roast Pork with Red Cabbage

- Rub the pork with the oil and season generously.
- Heat a large casserole dish over a moderate heat until hot then seal the pork until golden brown in colour all over.
- Remove to a plate lined with kitchen paper to drain.
- Place the cabbage, vinegar, apple, cinnamon, bay leaf, sugar and seasoning in a slow cooker and stir well.
- Sit the pork on top and cover with a lid.
- Cook on a medium setting for 6 hours until the pork is cooked and the cabbage is tender.
- Adjust the seasoning to taste once the pork is ready and discard the bay leaf and cinnamon.
- Spoon back into a casserole dish before serving.

PREPARATION TIME :
15 MINUTES

COOKING TIME : 6 HOURS 10-15 MINUTES

INGREDIENTS

30 ml / 1 fl. oz / 2 tbsp olive oil
675 g / 1 lb 8 oz piece of boneless pork shoulder, trimmed
1 large red cabbage, shredded
2 large eating apples, peeled cored and diced
125 ml / 4 ½ fl. oz / ½ cup distilled white vinegar
55 g / 2 oz / ¼ cup caster (superfine) sugar
1 stick of cinnamon
1 bay leaf
salt and pepper

Pork with Savoy Cabbage

417

Replace the red cabbage with savoy cabbage and season to your preference.

418

SERVES 4

Beef Choucroute

PREPARATION TIME :
15 MINUTES

COOKING TIME :
6 HOURS 25-30 MINUTES

....

INGREDIENTS

30 ml / 1 fl. oz / 2 tbsp sunflower oil
450 g / 1 lb sirloin steak
2 white cabbages, shredded finely
1 stick of celery, julienned
750 ml / 1 pint 6 fl. oz / 3 cups
vegetable stock
250 ml / 9 fl. oz / 1 cup cider vinegar
salt and pepper

GARNISH
1 red pepper, finely diced
sprigs of coriander (cilantro)

- Combine the cabbage, celery, stock and vinegar in a slow cooker with a little seasoning. Cook on a low setting for 6 hours.
- Adjust the seasoning to taste and keep warm on a low setting as you cook the beef.
- Preheat the oven to 200°C (180° fan) / 400F / gas 6.
- Rub the beef with the oil and season generously.
- Heat a large heatproof frying pan over a moderate heat until hot then seal the beef until golden brown in colour all over.
- Transfer to the oven to finish cooking for 6-12 minutes depending on desired degree of cooking.
- Remove from the oven when ready and let it rest for 5 minutes before slicing.
- Spoon the cabbage into a metal wok and top with the slices of steak, the diced red pepper and a sprig of coriander before serving.

Lamb Choucroute

419

Replace the beef with lamb for an alternative taste to your dish, cook until tender.

420

SERVES 4

Mushroom Gratin Dauphinoise

PREPARATION TIME :
15 MINUTES

COOKING TIME :
4 HOURS 10 MINUTES

....

INGREDIENTS

55 g / 2 oz / ½ stick butter, softened
900 g / 2 lb / 6 cups Maris Piper
potatoes, peeled and sliced thinly on
a mandolin
250 ml / 9 fl. oz / 1 cup whole milk
250 ml / 9 fl. oz / 1 cup double cream
75 g / 3 oz / 1 cup chanterelles,
brushed clean
75 g / 3 oz / 1 cup porcini
mushrooms, brushed clean
a pinch of ground nutmeg
salt and pepper

- Combine the mushrooms, milk and double cream in a slow cooker with the nutmeg and some seasoning.
- Cover and cook on a medium setting for 3 hours until the mushrooms are soft.
- Preheat the oven to 180°C (160° fan) / 350F / gas 4.
- Grease a 2 lb baking dish with the butter and layer the potato slices with the mushrooms from the slow cooker, seasoning in between the layers.
- Pour the cooking liquor from the slow cooker into the dish and cover with aluminium foil.
- Bake for 1 hour then remove the foil and bake for a further 10 minutes to brown the top.
- Remove from the oven and let it sit for 10 minutes before serving.

Chorizo Gratin Dauphinoise

421

For that spicy, meaty meal use the same weight of chorizo as mushrooms.

422

SERVES 4

Crozets Casserole with Ham and Sage

Crozets Casserole with Chorizo

423

Replace the Parma ham with the same weight of finely diced chorizo.

Crozets Casserole with Tomato

424

Replace the sage with the same amount of basil and add 110g / 4 oz / ⅔ cup halved cherry tomatoes at the end before serving.

Crozets Casserole with Bacon

425

Add a little salt to the dish by frying bacon (crispy) and adding this to the slow cooker near the end of cooking.

PREPARATION TIME: 15 MINUTES

COOKING TIME: 6 HOURS

INGREDIENTS

2 tbsp olive oil
300 g / 10 ½ oz / 3 cups Crozets
110g / 4 oz / ⅔ cup Parma ham, diced
1 tbsp sage leaves, roughly chopped
500ml / 18 fl. oz / 2 cups chicken stock
110g / 4 oz / 1 cup Parmesan, grated

- Combine the crozets, olive oil, Parma ham, chicken stock and in a slow cooker.
- Cover and cook on a low setting for 6 hours until the crozets have absorbed the stock and are tender.
- Stir through the Parmesan and sage until the sage has wilted a little.
- Adjust the seasoning to taste.
- Spoon into a casserole dish.
- Serve immediately.

426
SERVES 4

Ostrich, Bacon and Carrot Stew

PREPARATION TIME :
15 MINUTES

COOKING TIME :
6 HOURS 15-20 MINUTES

INGREDIENTS

55 ml / 2 fl. oz / ¼ cup groundnut oil
450 g / 1 lb / 3 cups ostrich fillet, cut into 2" cubes
450 g / 1 lb / 3 cups carrots, peeled and sliced
4 rashers streaky bacon, chopped
2 onions, finely chopped
500 ml / 18 fl. oz / 2 cups chicken stock
1 small bunch of flat-leaf parsley, roughly chopped
salt and pepper

GARNISH
sprigs of oregano
1 tsp flaked sea salt

- Coat the ostrich in the oil and season generously.
- Heat a large casserole dish over a moderate heat until hot and seal the ostrich in batches until golden brown in colour over.
- Remove to a slow cooker and reduce the heat under the dish a little.
- Add the onion and carrot and sweat for 5 minutes, stirring occasionally.
- Add the stock and bacon and stir well.
- Pour into the slow cooker and cover with a lid.
- Cook on a medium setting for 6 hours until the ostrich is cooked and tender.
- Adjust the seasoning to taste before stirring through the parsley.
- Spoon into serving dishes and garnish with oregano and flaked sea salt before serving.

Ostrich, bacon and mint casserole

427

Replace the parsley with mint.

428
SERVES 4

Chicken Drumsticks with Bacon

PREPARATION TIME :
15 MINUTES

COOKING TIME :
4 HOURS 40-45 MINUTES

INGREDIENTS

55 ml / 2 fl. oz / ¼ cup olive oil
4 large chicken drumsticks
4 rashers streaky bacon
4 ripe pears, peeled, cored and sliced
250 ml / 9 fl. oz / 1 cup good-quality red wine
55 g / 2 oz / ¼ cup caster (superfine) sugar
salt and freshly ground black pepper

GARNISH
a few sprigs of lemon thyme

- Combine the wine and sugar in a saucepan and cook over a medium heat, stirring, until the sugar has dissolved.
- Add the pears and stir well.
- Pour into a slow cooker and cover with a lid.
- Poach the pears for 4 hours on a medium setting before removing and patting dry.
- Preheat the oven to 190°C (170° fan) / 375F / gas 5.
- Wrap the streaky bacon around the chicken drumsticks and season generously.
- Drizzle with the olive oil and arrange in a roasting tray.
- Add the pears and roast for 30-35 minutes until the chicken is cooked through.
- Remove from the oven and garnish with the thyme before serving.

Cheesy Chicken with Bacon

429

Before wrapping the chicken with bacon as a slice of cheese and allow to melt.

430

SERVES 4

Makfoul Tajine

- Coat the mutton in the oil and season generously.
- Seal in batches in a large casserole dish set over a moderate heat until hot.
- Remove from the dish and reduce the heat a little.
- Sweat the onion and garlic for 5 minutes, stirring occasionally until softened a little.
- Add the ground spices, stir well, then add the tomato, honey and stock.
- Stir again and pour into the slow cooker.
- Cover with a lid and cook on a moderate setting for 6 hours until the mutton is tender.
- Adjust the seasoning to taste before spooning into earthenware dishes.
- Sprinkle over the mint before serving.

PREPARATION TIME :
10-15 MINUTES

COOKING TIME :
6 HOURS 15 MINUTES

INGREDIENTS

55 ml / 2 fl. oz / ¼ cup olive oil
900 g / 2 lb / 6 cups mutton shoulder, diced
4 vine tomatoes, cored and chopped
2 onions, sliced
4 cloves of garlic, minced
2 tsp ras al hanout (Moroccan spice blend)
1 tsp paprika
½ tsp ground cinnamon
1 tbsp honey
500 ml / 18 fl. oz / 2 cups lamb stock
salt and pepper

GARNISH
2 tbsp mint leaves

431

SERVES 4

Caramelized Pork with Onions

- Heat most of the oil in a large frying pan until hot.
- Season the pork and seal in batches until golden brown in colour.
- Remove the pork from the pan and place in the slow cooker.
- Reduce the heat under the pan and add the remaining oil and the butter swirl together until the butter has melted.
- Saute the carrots and onions in the oil for 3-4 minutes, stirring occasionally.
- Spoon the vegetables and any liquid from the pan into the slow cooker.
- Cook on a medium setting for 4 hours.
- Heat the sunflower oil in a sauce pan over a medium heat.
- Fry the garlic for a minute, stirring constantly, then add the sugar, soy sauce and tomato ketchup.
- Stir well and simmer for 5-7 minutes until thickened.
- Adjust the seasoning then remove from the heat and keep to one side.
- When the pork and vegetables are ready, spoon into a roasting tray.
- Reheat the sauce and pour on top, mixing well.

PREPARATION TIME : 15 MINUTES

COOKING TIME :
4 HOURS 20-25 MINUTES

INGREDIENTS

FOR THE PORK STEW
55 ml / 2 fl. oz / ¼ cup groundnut oil
30 g / 1 oz / ¼ stick unsalted butter
450 g / 1 lb / 3 cups pork fillet, silver skin removed and cut into large chunks
250 g / 9 oz / 1 ⅔ cups baby carrots, peeled
250 g / 9 oz / 2 cups baby onions, peeled
sprig of sage leaves, to garnish

FOR THE SAUCE
1 tbsp sunflower oil
250 ml / 9 fl. oz / 1 cup tomato ketchup
55 ml 2 fl. oz / ¼ cup dark soy sauce
55 g / 2 oz / ⅓ cup dark brown sugar
2 cloves garlic, minced
salt and pepper

432

SERVES 8

Roast Pork Stuffed with Prunes

Apricot Stuffed Pork

433

Swap the same weight of prunes for apricot halves and garnish with chopped rosemary.

Chestnut Stuffed Pork

434

Stuff the middle with 150 g / 5 oz / 1 cup cooked chestnuts. Garnish with chopped tarragon.

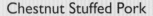

Stuffed Pork with Crackling

435

Remove the pork skin before slow cooking the meat and rub with some salt. Bake in the oven for 30 minutes to create crackling for this dish.

PREPARATION TIME 10 MINUTES

COOKING TIME 45 MINUTES

INGREDIENTS

FOR THE STUFFED PORK
4 tbsp sunflower oil
1.35 kg / 3 lbs rolled shoulder of pork
150 g / 5 oz / 1 cup prunes

FOR THE POTATO CAKES
2 tbsp olive oil
55 g / 2 oz / ½ stick unsalted butter
900 g / 2 lbs / 6 cups Maris Piper (or other floury) potato, peeled

GARNISH
3 sprigs thyme
1 sprig thyme, chopped

- Unfurl the shoulder of pork and arrange the prunes down the centre before gathering up either side of pork and rolling it around tightly, securing with string.
- Rub the outside of the pork with the oil and season generously, then transfer to a slow cooker.
- Cover and cook on a low setting for 8 hours.
- Meanwhile, finely slice the potatoes on a mandolin.
- Mix the slices of potato with half of the melted butter in a large mixing bowl.
- Gather handfuls of the potato together and shape into patties.
- Rub a large frying pan with some of the olive oil and heat over a medium heat until hot.
- Place a round metal ring in the middle of the frying pan and layer the handfuls of potato in the rings.
- Cook for a 2-3 minutes, then flip to cook the other side for a further 2-3 minutes until golden brown in colour on both sides.
- Drain the potato cakes on kitchen paper and season.
- Remove the pork from the slow cooker and place in a serving dish.
- Garnish with the chopped thyme, sprigs of thyme and potato cakes on one side.

436

SERVES 4

Veal, Chestnut and Artichoke Fricassée

- Place the chestnuts in a large saucepan of salted, boiling water and cook for 10-12 minutes until tender.
- Cut the pig's caul to size and wrap the veal shoulder portions in it, securing with toothpicks or kitchen string if necessary. Peel the chestnuts and keep aside.
- Heat the olive oil with the butter in a pan and brown the wrapped veal in the oil and butter.
- Put everything into a slow cooker and place the wrapped veal tucked into the chestnuts. Cook on a low setting for 6 hours.
- Heat the vegetable oil in a deep saucepan over a moderate heat. Make sure the slices of Jerusalem artichoke are dry, then deep-fry in the oil for 4 minutes.
- Drain and season immediately. Spoon the chestnuts and veal into serving bowls using a slotted spoon.
- Garnish the veal with the basil and sprinkle over some of the Jerusalem artichoke crisps before serving.

Lemon Chestnut Fricassée   437

Add 55 ml / 2 fl. oz / ¼ cup double cream to the fricassée before serving. Squeeze lemon juice at the same time and stir well before spooning over the veal.

PREPARATION TIME: 20 MINUTES

COOKING TIME:
6 HOURS 30 MINUTES

....

INGREDIENTS

2 tbsp olive oil
1 tbsp unsalted butter
600 g / 1 lb 5 oz rose veal shoulder, cut into 8 even portions
30cm x 30cm / 12" x 12" pig's caul, rinsed in cold water
900 g / 2 lbs / 8 cups chestnuts, scored on their undersides

GARNISH

1 l / 1 pint 16 fl. oz / 4 cups vegetable oil, for deep frying
4 Jerusalem artichokes, peeled and chopped
2 tbsp basil, finely chopped

438

SERVES 4

Monkfish in Garlic

- Heat half of the olive oil in a large frying or fish pan over a moderate heat until hot.
- Rub the monkfish tail with the remaining olive oil and season generously.
- Seal the monkfish until golden brown.
- Remove from the pan and add the peppercorns and cloves of garlic, sautéing them in the oil for a minute.
- Spoon them into the slow cooker and sit the monkfish on top.
- Cook in the slow cooker on high for 5 hours until the monkfish is firm yet springy to the touch and is starting to come away from the tailbone.
- Spoon everything back into a metal roasting pan.
- Garnish with the sprigs of thyme before serving.

Monkfish with Coriander Seeds   439

Replace the peppercorns with lightly toasted coriander seeds. Instead of garnishing with thyme, use fresh, finely chopped coriander instead.

PREPARATION TIME: 10 MINUTES

COOKING TIME: 5 HOURS

....

INGREDIENTS

4 tbsp cup olive oil
900 g / 2 lbs Monkfish tail
6 sprigs of thyme
6 cloves garlic, lightly crushed
1 tsp black peppercorns

440

SERVES 4

Veal with Ceps

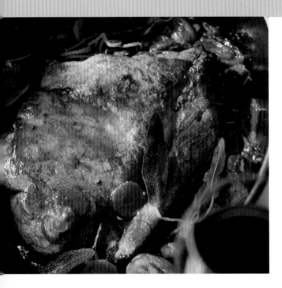

- Rub the piece of veal with some of the sunflower oil and season generously.
- Heat a large frying pan over a moderate heat until hot and seal the veal until golden brown.
- Transfer the veal to a slow cooker when sealed.
- Reduce the heat under the dish and add the remaining oil.
- Sweat the carrots for a few minutes then add the ceps and stir well.
- Spoon into the slow cooker and add the sage leaves and chicken stock.
- Cover and cook on a low setting for 8 hours.
- Spoon everything into a casserole dish after 8 hours before serving.

PREPARATION TIME: 15 MINUTES

COOKING TIME: 8 HOURS

INGREDIENTS

4 tbsp sunflower oil
900 g / 2 lb rose veal fillet, trimmed
2 carrots, peeled and finely sliced
handful of sage leaves
300 g / 10 ½ oz / 4 cups ceps, brushed clean
500 ml / 18 fl. oz / 2 cups chicken stock

Coconut Lobster Casserole

441

SERVES 4

PREPARATION TIME: 10 MINUTES

COOKING TIME: 6 HOURS

INGREDIENTS

FOR THE LOBSTER
900 g / 2 lb lobster
1 onion, chopped
1 carrot, chopped
2 sticks celery, chopped
1.75 l / 3 pints / 7 cups cold water
1 tsp black peppercorns

1 tsp salt
1 bay leaf

FOR THE BEAN STEW
200 g / 7 oz / 1 cup dried haricot beans, soaked in water overnight and drained
750 ml / 1 pint 10 fl. oz / 3 cups coconut milk
salt and pepper

- Combine the haricot beans, coconut milk and a little seasoning in a slow cooker. Stir and cover with a lid.
- Cook on a low setting for 6 hours until the beans are tender. Keep warm to one side as you cook the lobster.
- Prepare the cooking liquid for the lobster by combining the onion, carrot, celery, peppercorn, bay leaf, salt and water in a saucepan.
- Cook over a moderate heat until the liquid is simmering.
- Carefully lower the lobster into the simmering liquid and cook for 10-12 minutes until the lobster turns deep red in colour.
- Remove the lobster from the liquid and let it cool for 5 minutes.
- Remove the tail from the body and cut in half down the centre using a sharp knife.
- Crack the claws and extract the meat.
- Ladle the haricot beans into a casserole dish and top with the lobster. Serve immediately.

Veal Roast with Shallots

442

SERVES 4-6

PREPARATION TIME: 10 MINUTES

COOKING TIME: 6 HOURS 15 MINUTES

INGREDIENTS

4 tbsp olive oil
675 g / 1 lb 8 oz rose veal fillet roast, trimmed

2 onions, roughly sliced
12 shallots, blanched and peeled
4 cloves garlic, lightly crushed
2 tsp cumin seeds
1 tsp caraway seeds
1 tsp turmeric
1/2 tsp Cayenne pepper

- Combine the whole and ground spices with some seasoning in a small bowl.
- Rub the veal with half of the olive oil and season with the spice mixture.
- Heat a large frying pan over a moderate heat until hot and seal the veal until golden brown.
- Transfer to a slow cooker and reduce the heat under the frying pan.
- Add the remaining olive oil and sauté the onions, shallots and garlic for 2-3 minutes, tossing and stirring occasionally.
- Spoon the contents of the frying pan into the slow cooker and rearrange them so that the veal roast sits on top of the vegetables.
- Cover and cook on a medium setting for 6 hours until the veal is cooked through.
- Spoon everything back into a casserole dish and garnish with the remaining spice mixture before serving.

443

SERVES 4

Chicken in a Creamy Saffron Sauce

- In a large casserole dish, heat the sunflower oil.
- Season the pieces of chicken and seal well until golden brown in colour all over.
- Remove from the dish and drain in a colander placed over a bowl. Add the onion and reduce the heat.
- Add the chopped garlic after 2-3 minutes and continue cooking for a few minutes.
- At this point, turn the heat up and add the white wine, stirring the base of the dish to deglaze well; add any cooking juices collected from the draining chicken.
- Reduce the wine and add the stock. Pour everything into a slow cooker and cook on medium for 4 hours.
- After 4 hours, remove the chicken from the slow cooker and stir in the cream.
- Puree using a blender. Adjust the seasoning to taste. Arrange the chicken on serving plates and pour the sauce on top. Garnish with the chives and saffron.

Creamy Paprika Chicken   444

Replace the saffron with smoked paprika; whisk 1 tsp of smoked paprika into the stock instead of the saffron. Garnish with a pinch of smoked paprika instead of the saffron at the end.

PREPARATION TIME: 15 MINUTES

COOKING TIME: 4 HOURS

INGREDIENTS

4 tbsp cup sunflower oil
1 large chicken, jointed
1 onion, finely chopped
2 cloves garlic, finely chopped
125ml / 4 ½ fl. oz / ½ cup white wine
250ml / 9 fl. oz / 1 cup chicken stock, infused with a pinch of saffron strands.
250 ml / 9 fl. oz / 1 cup double (heavy) cream

GARNISH
1 tbsp chives, finely chopped
2 chive stalks
1 tbsp saffron strands

445

SERVES 4

Chicken Tikka Masala

- Heat the oil in a large saucepan set over a moderate heat.
- Add the onion and sweat with a little salt for 8-10 minutes, stirring frequently.
- Meanwhile, combine the remaining oil, garlic, ginger, chilli, ground spices, cardamom seeds, sugar, salt and pepper in a food processor and blitz until a smooth paste forms.
- Add the paste to the onions and cook for a further 5 minutes, stirring occasionally.
- Add the tomatoes and yogurt and stir well.
- Spoon into a food processor and pulse until smooth.
- Add the chopped coriander (cilantro) and pulse again.
- Adjust the seasoning to taste.
- Pour into a slow cooker and add the chicken.
- Cover and cook on a low setting for 6 hours.
- Adjust the seasoning if necessary before spooning into warm serving dishes.
- Serve immediately.

PREPARATION TIME: 15 MINUTES

COOKING TIME:
6 HOURS 20 MINUTES

INGREDIENTS

4 chicken breasts, cubed
4 tbsp sunflower oil
4 onions, finely chopped
8 cloves garlic, minced
7cm / 3" ginger, peeled and chopped
2 red chillies, chopped
1 tbsp ground coriander seeds
1 tbsp ground cumin
2 tsp garam masala
1 tsp paprika
1 tsp turmeric
2 cardamom pods, seeds extracted
1 tsp sugar
4 large tomatoes, finely chopped
30 ml / 1 fl. oz / 2 tbsp Greek yogurt
2 tbsp coriander (cilantro) leaves, chopped

446

SERVES 4

Cod with Peppers

PREPARATION TIME: 20 MINUTES

COOKING TIME: 6 HOURS

....

INGREDIENTS

4 tbsp olive oil
4 thick cod steaks
8 cloves garlic, peeled
4 red peppers, deseeded and diced
2 onions, peeled and sliced
1 fennel bulb, trimmed and sliced
1 red chilli pepper, deseeded and
finely sliced
250ml / 9 fl. oz / 1 cup fish stock

- Heat the olive oil in a large casserole dish set over a
  medium heat.
- Sweat the onion and fennel with a little salt for 5-6
  minutes, stirring occasionally.
- Add the peppers, garlic, stock and seasoning and stir
  well.
- Pour into a slow cooker and add the cod pieces.
- Cover and cook on a low setting for 6 hours.
- Adjust the seasoning to taste after 6 hours and stir
  through the sliced chilli pepper.
- Ladle back into a casserole dish before serving.

Cod with Mixed Peppers   447

Replace the red peppers with 1 orange, 1
yellow, 1 green and 1 red pepper instead of
using just red peppers.

448

SERVES 4

Lamb Tajine with Cashews

PREPARATION TIME: 10 MINUTES

COOKING TIME: 6 HOURS

....

INGREDIENTS

4 tbsp sunflower oil
900 g / 2 lbs / 6 cups lamb shoulder,
diced into 5 cm / 2" cubes
2 sticks cinnamon
1 onion, finely chopped
4 cloves garlic, sliced
110g / 4 oz / 1 cup cashew nuts,
chopped
1 tsp ground cumin
1 tsp ground coriander seeds
1 tsp ground cinnamon
½ tsp curry powder
½ tsp paprika
½ tsp ras el hanout (Moroccan spice
blend)
250ml / 9 fl. oz / 1 cup lamb stock
1 tbsp honey
GARNISH
4 sprigs of coriander (cilantro) leaves

- Heat the olive oil in a large casserole dish set over a
  moderate heat.
- Season the lamb chunks and seal in batches until
  golden brown.
- Remove from the dish and reduce the heat a little.
- Sweat the onion and garlic with a little salt for 4-5
  minutes, stirring frequently.
- Add the ground spices and honey and stir well.
- Add the lamb back to the dish along with the cashews,
  cinnamon sticks and stock.
- Stir well then pour into a slow cooker.
- Cover and cook on a low setting for 6 hours.
- Adjust the seasoning to taste after 6 hours, remove the
  cinnamon sticks and spoon onto serving dishes.
- Garnish with the coriander (cilantro) leaves before
  serving.

Lamb Tajine with Pistachios   449

Replace the cashews with pistachios. Add 55g
/ 2 oz / ½ cup chopped, pitted dates to the
mixture as well before slow cooking.

450

SERVES 4

Octopus and Chickpeas

Octopus and Bean Casserole

451

Replace the chickpeas with a mixture of kidney beans and flageolet beans.

Octopus and Prawn Casserole

452

Replace the vegetable stock with fish stock and replace the potatoes with 150 g / 5 oz / 1 cup thawed, frozen prawns (shrimps) before cooking.

Squid and Chickpea Casserole

453

Replace the weight of octopus with squid.

PREPARATION TIME: 10 MINUTES

COOKING TIME: 6 HOURS

INGREDIENTS

3 tbsp olive oil
200 g / 7 oz / 1 cup chickpeas (garbanzo beans), soaked in water overnight then drained
1 octopus, roughly chopped
2 medium white potatoes, peeled and cut into small chunks
500 ml / 18 fl. oz / 2 cups vegetable stock
2 tsp paprika
1 tsp ground cumin
1 lemon, juiced

GARNISH
pinch smoked paprika
handful frisee lettuce

- Heat the olive oil in a large frying pan set over a moderate heat.
- Sauté the octopus with the lemon juice, ground cumin, paprika and seasoning for a few minutes, stirring occasionally, before transferring to a slow cooker.
- Add the potatoes, chickpeas (garbanzo beans) and stock and stir well.
- Cover and cook on a low setting for 6 hours.
- Adjust the seasoning to taste after 6 hours and stir through the frisee lettuce.
- Spoon into serving dishes and garnish with pinches of smoked paprika before serving.

454

SERVES 4

Beef and Sorrel Stew

PREPARATION TIME: 20 MINUTES

COOKING TIME :
8 HOURS 20-25 MINUTES

....

INGREDIENTS

75 ml / 3 fl. oz / ⅓ cup sunflower oil
900 g / 2 lb / 6 cups chuck steak, cut
into 2" cubes
30 g / 1 oz / 2 tbsp plain (all-purpose)
flour
2 onions, chopped
2 cloves garlic, minced
1 tbsp tomato puree
125 ml / 4 ½ fl. oz / ½ cup white wine
30 g / 1 oz / 2 tbsp paprika
500 ml / 18 fl. oz / 2 cups beef stock
125 ml / 4 ½ fl. oz / ½ cup sour
cream
1 bay leaf
1 sprig of rosemary
salt and pepper

GARNISH
flat-leaf parsley
chive stalks

- Coat the cubes of chuck steak in the flour and toss well to shake off any excess. Season generously.
- Heat some of the sunflower oil in a large casserole dish set over a moderate heat until hot. Seal the beef in batches, using fresh oil for each batch.
- Transfer to a slow cooker. Reduce the heat under the casserole dish and add any remaining oil.
- Sweat the onion and garlic with some seasoning and the paprika for 5-6 minutes, stirring occasionally until the onion starts to soften.
- Deglaze the dish with the white wine, scraping the base and sides well.
- Stir in the tomato puree, bay leaf, rosemary sprig and beef stock then pour over the beef in the slow cooker.
- Cook on a medium setting for 8 hours. Adjust the seasoning and fish out the bay leaf and rosemary stem.
- Pour into a casserole dish and garnish with the herbs before serving.

Tomato Beef and Sorrel

 455

Replace 250 ml / 9 fl. oz / 1 cup of the beef stock with the same quantity of passata.

456

SERVES 4

Chicken and Pumpkin Tajine

PREPARATION TIME :
15 MINUTES

COOKING TIME :
6 HOURS 15 MINUTES

....

INGREDIENTS

30 ml / 1 fl. oz / 2 tbsp olive oil
1 medium chicken, jointed
1 onion, finely chopped
2 cloves garlic, minced
2 tsp mild curry powder
1 tsp ground cinnamon
1 tsp ground coriander
½ tsp paprika
250 ml / 9 fl. oz / 1 cup chicken stock
1 butternut squash, peeled, deseeded
and finely diced
4 large vine tomatoes, deseeded and
diced
30 ml / 1 fl. oz / 2 tbsp honey
salt and pepper

GARNISH
30 g / 1 oz / 2 tbsp unsalted
pistachios, finely chopped
1 tbsp pumpkin seeds

- Heat the olive oil in a large casserole dish set over a moderate heat until hot.
- Fry the ground spices with some salt in the oil for a minute, then add the chicken and stir well.
- Remove from the heat and pour into a slow cooker.
- Add the garlic, onion, butternut squash, tomatoes, honey and chicken stock to the slow cooker.
- Cover and cook on a low setting for 6 hours.
- After 6 hours, remove the chicken and keep warm to one side.
- Pour the contents of the slow cooker into a food processor and pulse until smooth.
- Arrange the chicken on serving plates and spoon the sauce from the processor on top.
- Garnish with pumpkin seeds and the finely chopped pistachios before serving.

Chicken and Apricot Tajine 457

Add 30 g / 1 oz / 2 tbsp dried apricot halves to the slow cooker before cooking.

458

SERVES 4 # Almond Chicken and Vegetables

- Whisk together the tomato puree, sugar, soy sauce, oyster sauce and pepper in a small mixing bowl until smooth.
- Cover and set to one side.
- Heat the oil in a large wok set over a moderate heat until hot.
- Stir-fry the onion, pepper, chilli, garlic, spring onion and bamboo shoots for 2 minutes, tossing and stirring frequently.
- Add the chicken, almonds and the prepared sauce then remove from the heat and stir well.
- Pour into a slow cooker, cover and cook on a medium setting for 4 hours.
- Adjust the seasoning to taste after 4 hours.
- Spoon into serving bowls and serve immediately.

PREPARATION TIME :
15-20 MINUTES

COOKING TIME :
4 HOURS 10 MINUTES

INGREDIENTS

55 ml / 2 fl. oz / ¼ cup groundnut oil
4 medium skinless chicken breasts, diced
1 onion, sliced
1 red onion, sliced
2 cloves garlic, minced
1 red pepper, deseeded and sliced
1 spring onion, finely sliced
1 red chilli, deseeded and very finely chopped
225 g / 8 oz / 1 ½ cups canned bamboo shoots, drained and sliced
75 g / 3 oz / ¾ cup blanched almonds
1 tbsp tomato puree
1 tbsp soft light brown caster sugar
30 ml / 1 fl. oz / 2 tbsp dark soy sauce
30 ml / 1 fl. oz / 2 tbsp oyster sauce
freshly ground black pepper

459

SERVES 4 # Rabbit Stew with Vegetables

- Shred the centre part of the cabbage. Heat the oil in a large casserole dish. Season the rabbit then seal in batches and transfer the pieces to a slow cooker.
- Add the carrots and onions to the casserole dish and cook for 4-5 minutes, stirring occasionally.
- Spoon into the slow cooker and add the cabbage, rabbit, mushrooms and cover with the stock.
- Cook on a medium setting for 6 hours. Adjust the seasoning to taste and reduce the setting to low to keep the rabbit warm as you prepare the sauce.
- Melt the butter in a saucepan. Whisk in the flour until you have a smooth roux. Cook for 1 minute.
- Add the milk in a slow, steady stream whisking until you have a thickened sauce. Simmer for 5-6 minutes.
- Adjust the seasoning to taste. Arrange the rabbit and vegetables in a large serving dish.
- Spoon the sauce over the rabbit before serving.

PREPARATION TIME: 10 MINUTES

COOKING TIME: 6 HOURS

INGREDIENTS

30 ml / 1 fl. oz / 2 tbsp olive oil
1 tbsp unsalted butter
2 small rabbits, jointed and trimmed
1 Savoy cabbage, large leaves removed
300 g / 10 ½ oz / 2 cups carrots, peeled and cut into thick batons
150 g / 5 oz / 1 cup pearl onions, peeled
75 g / 3 oz / 1 cup button mushrooms, chopped
250 ml / 9 fl. oz / 1 cup chicken stock
salt and pepper

FOR THE SAUCE

30 g / 1 oz / ¼ stick unsalted butter
30 g / 1 oz / 2 tbsp plain (all-purpose) flour, sifted
250 ml / 9 fl. oz / 1 cup whole milk
salt and pepper

Gruyere Rabbit Stew   460

Add 55 g / 2 oz / ½ cup grated Gruyere to the sauce and whisk until it has melted into the sauce.

461

SERVES 4

Roast Chicken with Lemon and Tarragon

Roast Chicken with Apple

462

Replace the lemon with apples– stuff the chicken with 1 eating apple.

Apple Brandy Roast Chicken

463

Deglaze the pan with 55 ml / 2 fl. oz / ¼ cup apple brandy instead of the wine. Replace the stock with the same volume of cider.

Citrus Roast Chicken

464

Add 1 lime and 1 ½ lemons to add a zesty flavour.

PREPARATION TIME 10 MINUTES

COOKING TIME 6 HOURS

....

INGREDIENTS

2 tbsp olive oil
30 g / 1 oz / ¼ stick butter, softened
1 chicken, cleaned and trussed
2 lemons
450 g / 1 lb / 3 cups pearl onions, blanched and peeled
450 g / 1 lb / 3 cups new potatoes
250ml / 9 fl. oz / 1 cup chicken stock
125ml / 4 ½ fl. oz / ½ cup dry white wine
1 tbsp tarragon leaves

GARNISH
4 tarragon sprigs

- Rub the chicken with the olive oil and butter.
- Pare the zest from one of the lemons and julienne for the garnish.
- Season generously and stuff with the tarragon and the lemon that was pared.
- Cut the other lemon into slices.
- Heat a large frying pan over a moderate heat until hot and seal the chicken until golden brown.
- Transfer to a slow cooker.
- Add the pearl onions, sliced lemon and potatoes to the pan and sauté them for a few minutes, tossing and stirring occasionally.
- Spoon into the slow cooker and deglaze the pan with white wine.
- Add the stock, stir well and pour into the slow cooker as well.
- Cover and cook on a medium setting for 6 hours.
- The chicken is ready when the juices run clear from the thickest part of the thigh when it is pierced.
- Pour everything back into a roasting tray and rearrange the chicken so that it rests on top of the vegetables.
- Garnish with the julienned lemon zest and the tarragon before serving.

Curried Lamb Tajine

465

SERVES 4

- Mix the ground spices with some seasoning in a small bowl.
- Rub the lamb cutlets in the oil and dip in the spice mixture.
- Heat a frying pan over a moderate heat until hot and seal the cutlets in batches until golden brown in colour all over.
- Transfer each sealed batch to a slow cooker.
- Cover and cook on a low setting for 6 hours.
- After 6 hours, stir through the ground almonds and adjust the seasoning to taste if necessary.
- Arrange the cutlets on serving plates and garnish with tablespoons of the chopped prunes and the harissa on the side.

PREPARATION TIME 10 MINUTES

COOKING TIME 45 MINUTES

INGREDIENTS

55 ml / 2 fl. oz / ¼ cup olive oil
8 lamb cutlets, trimmed
1 tbsp mild curry powder
1 tsp ground cumin
1 tsp ground coriander
½ tsp chilli powder
½ tsp smoked paprika
30 g / 1 oz / 2 tbsp ground almonds
salt and pepper

GARNISH

150 g / 5 oz / canned prunes, drained and roughly chopped
55 g / 2 oz / ¼ cup harissa

Sweet Curried Lamb Tajine

466

Add 2 tbsp of honey to the slow cooker after cooking at the same time as the ground almonds for a sweeter version.

Tuna Civet

467

SERVES 4

- Wrap the tuna loin tightly in film and roll into a cylinder. Refrigerate overnight. The next day, unwrap from the film and tie with kitchen string at 1" intervals.
- Rub with half of the olive oil and season well. Heat a pan and seal the tuna until golden in colour all over.
- Place in a slow cooker. Reduce the heat under the frying pan and add the remaining olive oil.
- Sauté the pancetta for 2-3 minutes, stirring frequently, then add the onions and potatoes.
- Cook for a further 3 minutes, then deglaze the pan with the red wine. Pour the contents of the pan over the tuna in the slow cooker.
- Cover and cook on a low setting for 5 hours.
- Adjust the seasoning to taste after 5 hours then spoon onto a serving dish.
- Garnish with the tarragon and some ground pepper before serving.

PREPARATION TIME: 20 MINUTES

COOKING TIME: 5 HOURS

INGREDIENTS

4 tbsp olive oil
675 g / 1 lb 8 oz tuna loin
1 onion, finely chopped
1 clove garlic, minced
150 g / 5 oz / 1 cup pancetta, cut into lardons
150 g / 5 oz / 1 cup pearl onions, peeled
300 g / 10 ½ oz / 2 cups charlotte potatoes, peeled
125ml / 4 ½ fl. oz / ½ cup red wine

GARNISH

2 sprigs tarragon, chopped

White Wine Tuna Civet

468

Replace the red wine with white wine when you deglaze the pan. Garnish with chopped flat-leaf parsley instead of the tarragon.

MAKES 18

469

Chinese Cabbage and Chicken Soup

PREPARATION TIME: 15 MINUTES

COOKING TIME: 4 HOURS

INGREDIENTS

2 tbsp sunflower oil
2 chicken breasts, skin removed and thinly sliced
1 bok choy (Chinese cabbage), chopped
250ml / 9 fl. oz / 1 cup chicken stock
250ml / 9 fl. oz / 1 cup coconut milk
2 tsp sugar
1 tbsp dark soy sauce
1 lime, juiced

GARNISH
2 tbsp coriander (cilantro) leaves
1 lime, grated zest and sliced
½ lime, sliced
1 red chilli, deseeded and sliced

- Heat the sunflower oil in a large frying pan set over a moderate heat.
- Season the chicken then pan-fry for 2-3 minutes, tossing and stirring occasionally until lightly coloured all over.
- Transfer to a slow cooker and add the cabbage, stock, coconut milk, soy sauce, chilli, sugar and lime juice.
- Cover and cook on a low setting for 4 hours.
- Adjust the seasoning to taste after 4 hours.
- Ladle into soup bowls and garnish with the lime slices, lime zest, sliced chilli and coriander (cilantro) leaves.

Spicy Chinese Chicken Soup **470**

Add 1 tbsp chilli sauce to the slow cooker before cooking for a spicier soup.

471

SERVES 4

Lamb with Yoghurt and Coriander

PREPARATION TIME: 20 MINUTES

COOKING TIME: 6 HOURS

INGREDIENTS

For the lamb
4 tbsp sunflower oil
900 g / 2 lbs / 6 cups lamb neck fillet, trimmed and cut into large chunks
150 g / 5 oz / 1 cup broad beans, shelled
2 large sweet potatoes, peeled and sliced
For the sauce
2 tbsp sunflower oil
500ml / 18 fl. oz / 2 cups plain natural yogurt
2 tsp ground cumin
1 tsp ground coriander seeds
½ tsp turmeric
1 tsp red chilli powder
2 tbsp coriander (cilantro), finely chopped

- Heat the sunflower oil for the lamb in a casserole dish. Season the lamb pieces and sear until golden brown.
- Add all the lamb back to the dish, then add the sweet potato slices. Pour in 500 ml of water and then pour everything into a slow cooker.
- Cover and cook on a low setting for 6 hours. Toast the spices in a frying pan over a medium heat for 1 minute, stirring occasionally.
- Add the sunflower oil to the pan and fry the spices for a few minutes. Add the yogurt to the pan and stir well until you have a smooth sauce.
- Simmer for a few minutes, then stir through the chopped coriander. Blanch the broad beans in a large saucepan of salted, boiling water for a minute.
- Spoon the lamb and sweet potato into a serving dish. Arrange the broad beans on top of the lamb then spoon the yoghurt sauce all over. Serve immediately.

Lamb with Yoghurt Potatoes **472**

Replace the sweet potato with 2 large white potatoes that have been peeled and sliced in the same way as the sweet potatoes. Garnish with 2 tbsp chopped coriander (cilantro) and a drizzle of olive oil.

473

SERVES 4

Beef Stew with Peaches

Beef Stew with Pear   474

Replace the peach with the same volume of canned, drained pear slices.

Tangy Beef Stew   475

Add 1 tbsp Worcestershire sauce to the slow cooker for a spicier stew.

Beef and Peach Soup   476

To create a sweet soup, before serving blitz until as smooth as preferred.

PREPARATION TIME: 15 MINUTES

COOKING TIME: 6 HOURS

....

INGREDIENTS

4 tbsp sunflower oil
900 g / 2 lbs / 6 cups braising steak, cut into cubes
2 onions, finely chopped
4 tomatoes, sliced
2 tbsp peach schnapps
400 g / 14 oz / 2 cups peach slices
500ml / 18 fl. oz / 2 cups beef stock

- Coat the beef in the sunflower oil and season generously.
- Heat a large casserole dish over a moderate heat until hot.
- Seal the beef in batches, moving each batch to a slow cooker when done.
- Reduce the heat and add the onion to the dish with a little salt.
- Sweat for 4-5 minutes until softened before deglazing the dish with the schnapps.
- Add the peaches, tomatoes and stock and stir well.
- Pour into the slow cooker and cover with a lid.
- Cook on a low setting for 6 hours until the beef is soft and tender.
- Adjust the seasoning to taste when the beef is ready and spoon back into a casserole dish for presentation.
- Serve immediately.

477

SERVES 4

Chickpea and Dried Fig and Bacon

PREPARATION TIME: 10 MINUTES

COOKING TIME: 4 HOURS

INGREDIENTS

150 g / 5 oz / 1 cup pancetta, cut into lardons
400 g / 14 oz / 2 cups canned chickpeas (garbanzo beans), drained
110g / 4 oz / 1 cup dried figs, chopped
250ml / 9 fl. oz / 1 cup vegetable stock

GARNISH
2 tbsp coriander (cilantro) leaves

- Heat a casserole dish over a moderate heat until hot.
- Add the pancetta lardons and sauté for 3-4 minutes.
- Add the chickpeas (garbanzo beans), stir well, then add the stock and figs.
- Pour into a slow cooker and cook on a low setting for 4 hours.
- Adjust the seasoning to taste after 4 hours.
- Spoon into serving dishes and garnish with the coriander leaves.
- Serve immediately.

Chickpea and Tomato Casserole   478

Add 1 finely chopped onion and 2 cloves of garlic to the dish after the pancetta has been cooked for 3-4 minutes. Add 2 diced tomatoes to the slow cooker as well.

479

SERVES 6

Ham Cooked in Cider with Apples

PREPARATION TIME: 15 MINUTES

COOKING TIME: 8 HOURS

INGREDIENTS

1.35kg / 3 lbs ham hock, soaked in cold water overnight then drained and dried
450 g / 1 lb / 3 cups carrots, peeled and chopped
1 leek, chopped
2 sticks celery, peeled and chopped
2 eating apples, cored and diced
4 baby turnips, peeled
500ml / 18 fl. oz / 2 cups cider

GARNISH
4-5 chive stalks, finely chopped
3 bay leaves

- Place the vegetables and apple in the bottom of a large slow cooker.
- Sit the ham hock on top and pour in the cider.
- Cover and cook on a low setting for 8 hours.
- Spoon everything into a serving dish after 8 hours and season well.
- Garnish with the chopped chives and bay leaves.
- Serve immediately.

Perry Cooked Ham   480

Replace the cider with perry for a pear-flavored ham.

481

SERVES 4

Cajun Tofu Stew with Vegetables

- Heat the groundnut oil in a large wok set over a moderate heat.
- Sauté the carrot, pepper, celery and tofu for 3-4 minutes, stirring frequently.
- Spoon into a slow cooker and add the pasta, kidney beans, seaweed and stock.
- Cover and cook on a medium setting for 4 hours.
- Adjust the seasoning to taste after 4 hours using the soy sauce.
- Spoon into serving bowls using a slotted spoon and garnish with a sprinkle of chopped parsley as well as a sprig of parsley leaves before serving.

PREPARATION TIME: 15 MINUTES

COOKING TIME: 4 HOURSS

INGREDIENTS

2 tbsp groundnut oil
300 g / 10 ½ oz / 2 cups tofu, cubed
2 large carrots, peeled and cubed
400 g / 14 oz / 2 cups canned kidney beans, drained and rinsed
2 sticks celery, sliced
110g / 4 oz / 1 cup lumache pasta
1 red pepper, deseeded and finely diced
2 sheets dried seaweed, cut into strips
250ml / 9 fl. oz / 1 cup vegetable stock
2 tbsp dark soy sauce

GARNISH

2 tbsp flat-leaf parsley, finely chopped
4 sprigs of flat-leaf parsley

Fish Etouffee and Vegetables   482

stir through 2 tbsp oyster sauce just before serving.

483

SERVES 4

Chicken with Ginger

- Rub the chicken pieces with some of the oil and season well.
- Heat a large casserole dish over a moderate heat until hot and seal the chicken pieces until golden brown.
- Move the sealed chicken pieces to a slow cooker when ready.
- Reduce the heat under the dish and add the lemons, ginger, olives and ground spices.
- Stir well, then spoon into the slow cooker alongside the chicken.
- Mix everything well and cook on a low setting for 6 hours until the juices run clear when the thickest part of the thigh is pierced.
- When ready, stir through the chopped parsley and seasoning to taste.
- Spoon into a serving dish and serve immediately.

PREPARATION TIME: 15 MINUTES

COOKING TIME: 6 HOURS

INGREDIENTS

4 tbsp cup olive oil
1 large chicken, jointed
2 lemons, cut into wedges
10 cm / 4" piece of ginger, peeled and sliced
110 g / 4 oz / ⅔ cup black olives
2 tsp mild curry powder
1 tsp turmeric
1 tsp paprika
1 tbsp flat-leaf parsley, finely chopped

Spicy Chicken with Olives   484

Change the same amount of black olives for green olives stuffed with pimento pepper for a spicier version of the dish.

485

SERVES 4

Spicy Lamb and Vegetable Tajine

Lamb Meatball and Vegetable Tajine

486

Replace the lamb with the same weight of minced lamb. Shape into golf ball-sized meatballs and add straight to the slow cooker instead of sealing in the oil.

Spicy Lamb and Olive Tajine

487

Add 55g / 2 oz / ⅓ cup Kalamata olives to the slow cooker before cooking.

Spicy Lamb and Tomato

488

Add an extra tomato, prepared the same for an extra saucy dish.

PREPARATION TIME: 15 MINUTES

COOKING TIME:
6 HOURS 20 MINUTES

....

INGREDIENTS

4 tbsp olive oil
900 g / 2 lbs / 6 cups lamb neck fillet, diced
1 large onion, chopped
2 cloves garlic, minced
1 small courgette, sliced
4 tomatoes, cored and chopped
2 tsp ras el hanout (Moroccan spice blend)
1 tsp ground cinnamon
½ tsp paprika
2 tbsp honey
500ml / 18 fl. oz / 2 cups lamb stock
1 small bunch of coriander (cilantro), finely chopped

- Coat the lamb in the olive oil and season generously.
- Heat a large casserole dish over a moderate heat until hot.
- Seal the lamb in batches until golden brown all over, moving each completed batch to a slow cooker once finished.
- Reduce the heat and add the onion and garlic, stirring well.
- Sweat for 4-5 minutes until softened before adding the ground spices.
- Stir well and add the tomato and courgette (courgette).
- Stir in the honey and the stock before pouring over the lamb in the slow cooker.
- Cover with a lid and cook on a medium setting for 6 hours.
- Adjust the seasoning to taste after 6 hours before stirring through the chopped coriander (cilantro).
- Spoon into serving bowls using a slotted spoon.
- Serve immediately.

489

SERVES 4

Pork in Red Wine

- Heat the oil in a large casserole dish set over a moderate heat until hot.
- Season the pork and seal in batches until golden brown.
- Transfer each batch to a slow cooker when ready.
- Reduce the heat under the dish and add the onions, carrot, bay leaf, rosemary, red wine and stock.
- Stir well then pour over the pork.
- Cover with a lid and cook on a low setting for 6 hours until the pork is tender.
- After 6 hours adjust the seasoning to taste.
- Ladle into serving bowls and garnish with a sprig of rosemary before serving.

PREPARATION TIME: 15 MINUTES

COOKING TIME: 6 HOURS

INGREDIENTS

4 tbsp sunflower oil
900 g / 2 lbs / 6 cups pork shoulder,
cut into 5cm / 2" cubes
150 g / 5 oz / 1 cup pearl onions,
peeled
2 carrots, peeled and chopped
500ml / 18 fl. oz / 2 cups red wine
250ml / 9 fl. oz / 1 cup pork stock
1 sprig of rosemary
1 bay leaf

GARNISH
4 sprigs of rosemary

Sour Pork in Vinegar 490

Replace half of the red wine for red wine vinegar for a sharper tasting stew.

491

SERVES 4-6

Salt Ham Hock with Lentils

- Heat the olive oil in a large casserole dish over a moderate heat until hot.
- Sweat the onion and carrot with a little salt for 5 minutes, stirring occasionally.
- Add the lentils, bay leaf and stock and stir well.
- Pour into a slow cooker and sit the ham hock in the lentils and stock.
- Cover and cook on a low setting for 8 hours.
- Adjust the seasoning after 8 hours and fish out and discard the bay leaf.
- Pour into a casserole dish before serving.

PREPARATION TIME: 15 MINUTES

COOKING TIME: 8 HOURS

INGREDIENTS

2 tbsp olive oil
1 onion, finely chopped
2 carrots, peeled and finely diced
450 g / 1 lb piece of ham hock, rinsed
in several changes of water
600 g / 1 lb 5 oz / 3 cups Puy lentils
750ml / 1 pint 6 fl. oz / 3 cups
vegetable stock
1 bay leaf

Spicy Salt Ham Hock 492

Stir through 1 tbsp of Worcestershire sauce through the lentils after they have finished cooking.

493

SERVES 4

Monkfish Glazed with Onions

PREPARATION TIME: 15 MINUTES

COOKING TIME: 4 HOURS

INGREDIENTS

4 tbsp groundnut oil
2 tbsp butter, unsalted
900 g / 2 lbs Monkfish tail, cubed
8 shallots, peeled and halved
2 tbsp honey
2 tbsp sesame seeds

GARNISH

4 sprigs of coriander (cilantro)

- Drizzle the monkfish with the oil and honey in a mixing bowl.
- Heat a large frying pan over a moderate heat until hot.
- Season the monkfish and seal in batches until golden brown.
- Move each batch to a slow cooker when ready.
- After the monkfish has been sealed, reduce the heat under the pan and add the butter and shallots.
- Sauté the shallot halves for 2-3 minutes until lightly coloured.
- Transfer the contents of the pan to the slow cooker.
- Cover the slow cooker and cook on a low setting for 4 hours.
- After 4 hours, stir through the sesame seeds and adjust the seasoning to taste.
- Spoon into serving dishes and garnish with the coriander before serving.

Poppy Seed Monkfish Glaze

494

Add 1 tbsp of black poppy seeds at the same time as the sesame seeds for a contrast.

495

SERVES 4

White Veal Casserole

PREPARATION TIME: 15 MINUTES

COOKING TIME: 8 HOURS

INGREDIENTS

4 tbsp sunflower oil
900 g / 2 lbs / 6 cups rose veal shoulder, diced
150 g / 5 oz / 1 cup pearl onions, blanched
450 g / 1 lb / 3 cups baby carrots, peeled
30g / 1 oz / ¼ stick butter, unsalted
30g / 1 oz / 2 tbsp plain (all purpose) flour
500ml / 18 fl. oz / 2 cups whole milk
1 bouquet garni

GARNISH

4 bay leaves
4 sprigs of thyme

- Heat the sunflower oil in a large casserole dish. Season the veal and seal in batches until golden brown.
- Transfer each batch to a slow cooker. Reduce the heat under the dish and sauté the onions and baby carrots for 4-5 minutes, stirring occasionally.
- Spoon into the slow cooker. Melt the butter in a large, clean saucepan set over a medium heat.
- Whisk in the flour until you have a smooth roux. Cook for 1 minute then whisk in the milk in a slow, steady stream until you a thickened sauce. Reduce the heat and simmer the sauce for 5-6 minutes, stirring occasionally.
- Adjust the seasoning then pour into the slow cooker.
- Add the bouquet garni to the slow cooker and cook on a low setting for 8 hours.
- Adjust the seasoning after 8 hours and ladle the stew into a casserole dish.
- Garnish with the thyme and bay leaves before serving.

Veal and Mushroom Casserole

496

Add 150 g / 5 oz / 2 cups button mushrooms to the slow cooker before cooking.

497

SERVES 4

Seafood Stew

- Heat half of the olive oil in a large frying pan set over a moderate heat until hot.
- Season the salmon and pan-fry for 1 minute on both sides until lightly coloured.
- Transfer to a slow cooker and add the rest of the olive oil to the frying pan.
- Sear the prawns and scallops with some seasoning for a few minutes.
- Transfer to the slow cooker.
- Add the vegetables, white wine, stock and tarragon stalks.
- Cover with a lid and cook for 4 hours on a medium setting.
- Adjust the seasoning after 4 hours and fish out the tarragon stalks.
- Ladle into serving bowls. Serve immediately.

PREPARATION TIME: 15 MINUTES

COOKING TIME: 4 HOURS

INGREDIENTS

4 tbsp olive oil
450 g / 1 lb salmon fillet, skinless
300 g / 10 ½ oz / 2 cups prawns
8 scallops, roe removed
4 white potatoes, peeled and halved
150 g / 5 oz / 1 cup carrots, peeled and cut into batons
110g / 4 oz / 1 cup green beans
75 g / 3 oz / ½ cup broad beans, shelled
500 ml / 18 fl. oz / 2 cups fish stock
125 ml / 4 ½ fl. oz / 1 cup white wine
2 tarragon stalks

Grouper with Urchin Sauce

498

SERVES 4

PREPARATION TIME: 15 MINUTES

COOKING TIME: 4 HOURS

INGREDIENTS

2 tbsp olive oil
4 225 g / 8 oz grouper fillets, skinned and pin-boned

2 sea urchins, halved with insides scooped out into a bowl
handful of white mushrooms, quartered
250ml / 9 fl. oz / 1 cup fish stock
1 tbsp pastis

GARNISH
4 sprigs of tarragon leaves

- Heat the olive oil in a large frying pan set over a moderate heat until hot.
- Season the group fillets and seal quickly in the oil on both sides for 30 seconds.
- Transfer to a slow cooker and add the insides of the sea urchins, the fish stock, pastis, mushrooms and a little seasoning.
- Cover and cook on a low setting for 4 hours.
- Adjust the seasoning of the sauce in the slow cooker to taste after 4 hours.
- Remove the grouper fillets and set them to one side covered loosely with aluminium foil.
- Spoon the sauce between 4 serving bowls.
- Place the grouper in the centre of the sauce and spoon a few mushroom quarters next to the fillets.
- Garnish with the tarragon before serving.

Grouper with Fennel

499

SERVES 4

PREPARATION TIME: 20 MINUTES

COOKING TIME: 4 HOURS

INGREDIENTS

2 tbsp olive oil
4 225 g / 8 oz grouper steaks, pin-boned
4 fennel bulbs, trimmed and

chopped
1 preserved lemon, sliced
2 cloves garlic, minced
2 tomatoes, cored and diced
450 g / 1 lb / 3 cups white potatoes, peeled and cut into chunks
125ml / 4 ½ fl. oz / ½ cup dry white wine
500ml / 18 fl. oz / 2 cups fish stock
2 bay leaves

- Heat the olive oil in a large frying pan set over a moderate heat until hot.
- Season the grouper and flash-fry for 30 seconds on both sides before moving to a slow cooker.
- Add the fennel, preserved lemon, garlic, tomato and potato and reduce the heat a little.
- Sauté for 4-5 minutes, stirring occasionally.
- Add the white wine and let it reduce by half before pouring everything into the slow cooker.
- Add the stock and bay leaves and stir carefully.
- Cover and cook on a medium setting for 4 hours.
- Adjust the seasoning to taste after 4 hours and ladle into serving bowls.
- Serve immediately.

500

SERVES 4

Fish Tajine

PREPARATION TIME:
15 MINUTES

COOKING TIME:
6 HOURS 15 MINUTES

INGREDIENTS

75ml / 3 fl. oz / ⅓ cup olive oil
4 large sea bream / sea bass fillets, pin-boned
200 g / 7 oz / 1 cup dried chickpeas
125ml / 4 ½ fl. oz / ½ cup water
4 cloves garlic, minced
110g / 4 oz / ⅔ cup pitted green olives, chopped
2 tbsp mint, chopped
2 tbsp coriander, chopped
2 tsp ground coriander seeds
1 tsp ground cumin
1 tsp ground cinnamon
½ tsp paprika, ½ tsp sugar

GARNISH
pinch saffron threads

- Combine half of the olive oil with the garlic, olives, chopped herbs, ground spices and sugar in a food processor.
- Pulse until you have a smooth paste; add a little warm water if it is too dry, it should be of a spreadable consistency.
- Rub the fish fillets with the paste and set to one side.
- Spoon the chickpeas into the base of a slow cooker and sit the fish on top.
- Add any remaining paste and the warm water to the slow cooker.
- Cover and cook on a low setting for 5-6 hours until the chickpeas are tender and the fish is cooked through.
- Adjust the seasoning when it is ready and spoon into serving bowls.
- Garnish with saffron threads before serving.

Fish and Prawn Tajine

501

Substitute half of the fish for 300 g / 10 ½ oz / 2 cups of king prawns (shrimps) to make a seafood tajine.

502

SERVES 4

Chicken Wing Stew with Chives

PREPARATION TIME: 20 MINUTES

COOKING TIME:
4 HOURS 30 MINUTES

INGREDIENTS

2 tbsp olive oil
2 tbsp unsalted butter
8 chicken wings, trimmed
2 tbsp dark soy sauce
125 ml / 4 ½ fl. oz / ½ cup dry white wine
1 leek, sliced
250 g / 9oz / 1 cup basmati rice, rinsed
400 ml / 14 fl. oz / 1 ⅔ cups boiling water
1 tbsp chives, finely chopped

- Heat the olive oil in a large, then sear the chicken wings for 3-4 minutes until golden brown.
- Remove from the saucepan and reduce the heat.
- Add the butter, then sweat the leeks for 2-3 minutes until they start to soften.
- Add the white wine and soy sauce to the saucepan and return the chicken wings as well, stirring well.
- Pour everything into a slow cooker, cover, and cook on a low setting for 4 hours.
- After 4 hours, adjust the seasoning to taste and keep the chicken warm on a low setting.
- Combine the rice and boiling water in a saucepan.
- Cover with a lid and cook over a low heat for 15-20 minutes until the rice has absorbed the water.
- Spoon into bowls and top with the chicken wing stew.
- Garnish with the chives and serve.

Sweet Chicken Wing Stew

503

Add 2 tbsp honey to the slow cooker before cooking for a sweet and sticky chicken wing stew.

504

SERVES 4

Mince Braised Spicy Beef Stew

Spicy Green Beef Stew 505

Substitute the red chilli for green chilli and garnish with finely chopped flat-leaf parsley.

Crunchy Minced Beef Stew 506

Add 110g / 4 oz / 1 cup panko breadcrumbs to meat for a crunchier texture.

Spicey Turkey Stew 507

For a leaner dish substitute the beef for turkey, using the same quantities.

PREPARATION TIME: 10 MINUTES

COOKING TIME: 6 HOURS

INGREDIENTS

675 g / 1 lb 8 oz / 4 ½ cups beef mince
4 cloves garlic, finely chopped
5cm / 2" piece of ginger, finely chopped
2 red chillies, finely chopped
1 tbsp tomato puree
1 tsp paprika
½ tsp Cayenne pepper
125 ml / 4 ½ fl. oz / ½ cup beef stock

- Combine all the ingredients apart from the beef stock in a large mixing bowl.
- Scrunch together using your hands until you have an even mixture.
- Shape into golf ball-sized rounds and arrange in a slow cooker.
- Add the stock, cover with a lid and braise for 6 hours on a medium setting.
- Spoon into a serving bowls and crush a little with a fork.
- Serve immediately.

508

SERVES 4

Chicken Tajine with Spices

PREPARATION TIME: 15 MINUTES

COOKING TIME:
4 HOURS 20 MINUTES

INGREDIENTS

4 tbsp olive oil
1 chicken, jointed and trimmed
6 cloves garlic, crushed
6-8 shallots, blanched and peeled
2 sticks cinnamon
1 tsp cloves
1 tsp coriander seeds
½ tsp cumin seeds
1 tsp saffron threads
1 tsp ground cumin
1 tsp ground coriander
1 tsp ras al hanout (Moroccan spice blend)
1 tbsp honey
500ml / 18 fl. oz / 2 cups chicken stock
2 tbsp coriander (cilantro) leaves, finely chopped

- Rub the chicken pieces with some of the olive oil.
- Season generously. Heat a pan and seal the chicken in batches until golden brown. Place in the slow cooker.
- Reduce the heat of the pan and add the olive oil.
- Sauté the shallots, garlic and whole spices for 4-5 minutes with a little salt.
- Add the ground spices, honey and some seasoning, stir well, then add the stock.
- Pour everything into the slow cooker and cook on a medium setting for 4 hours until the chicken is cooked through.
- Adjust the seasoning to taste when the chicken is ready and stir through the saffron.
- Ladle the tajine into serving bowls and sprinkle with the chopped coriander (cilantro).
- Serve immediately.

Tomato Chicken with Saffron

509

Add 4 quartered tomatoes and saffron to the slow cooker before cooking.

510

SERVES 4

Chicken in Tomatoes with Chickpeas

PREPARATION TIME: 15 MINUTES

COOKING TIME:
6 HOURS 20 MINUTES

INGREDIENTS

4 tbsp olive oil
1 chicken, jointed and trimmed
6 tomatoes, quartered
6 cloves garlic
200 g / 7 oz / 1 cup dried chickpeas (garbanzo beans), soaked in cold water overnight and drained
500ml / 18 fl. oz / 2 cups chicken stock
2 tsp ras el hanout (Moroccan spice blend)
1 tsp ground cinnamon
1 tsp paprika
1 tbsp honey

GARNISH

3 garlic chive stalks, whole
1 garlic chive stalk, chopped

- Heat half of the olive oil in a large casserole dish set over a moderate heat until hot.
- Season the chicken pieces and seal in the oil until golden brown.
- Move the sealed chicken to a slow cooker.
- Reduce the heat under the dish and add the remaining olive oil.
- Sauté the garlic and tomato for a few minutes before adding the ground spices, honey and chickpeas (garbanzo beans).
- Stir well then cover with the stock.
- Pour everything into the slow cooker and cook on a medium setting for 6 hours.
- Adjust the seasoning to taste. Spoon the tajine back into a cast iron casserole dish using a slotted spoon.
- Garnish with the chopped garlic chive and garlic chive stalks.

Chicken with Haricot Beans

511

Replace the chickpeas (garbanzo beans) with 400 g / 14 oz / 1 ⅔ cups canned, drained haricot beans.

512

SERVES 4

Chicken Stew with Cream Sauce

- Heat the sunflower oil in a large casserole dish set over a moderate heat until hot.
- Season the chicken and sprinkle with the flour.
- Seal until golden brown.
- Transfer the sealed chicken to a slow cooker when done.
- Reduce the heat under the dish and add the butter.
- Sweat the onion and mushrooms in the butter with a little salt for 3-4 minutes, stirring occasionally.
- Add the stock and bay leaf and stir well.
- Pour into the slow cooker and cover with a lid.
- Cook on a medium setting for 5 hours until the chicken is cooked.
- Stir through the double cream and adjust the seasoning when the chicken is ready.
- Spoon into a casserole dish before serving.

PREPARATION TIME: 20 MINUTES

COOKING TIME: 5 HOURS

INGREDIENTS

2 tbsp sunflower oil
1 tbsp butter, unsalted
1 chicken, jointed and trimmed
1 tbsp plain (all purpose) flour
2 onions, sliced
300 g / 10 ½ oz / 2 cups button mushrooms, chopped
250ml / 9 fl. oz / 1 cup double (heavy) cream
250ml / 9 fl. oz / 1 cup chicken stock
1 bay leaf

Chestnut Chicken with Sauce   513

Add 30g / 1 oz / 2 tbsp cooked chestnuts to the slow cooker before cooking for a nutty version of the dish.

514

SERVES 6

Roll of Pork with Ham

- Lay the slices of ham on a flat surface roughly in the shape of a rectangle, making sure there are no gaps.
- Sit the pork shoulder on top.
- Sprinkle the grated Comte in the centre and top with the parsley and some seasoning.
- Roll up the pork and ham on the outside into a cylindrical shape.
- Tie securely using kitchen string at 5 cm / 2" intervals.
- Rub the outside with the oil.
- Heat a large frying pan over a moderate heat until hot and seal the rolled pork in the oil until golden brown in colour all over.
- Transfer to a slow cooker and cover with a lid.
- Cook on a medium setting for 6 hours.
- Remove after 6 hours and sit on a serving dish.
- Garnish with rocket (arugula) leaves before serving.

PREPARATION TIME: 15 MINUTES

COOKING TIME: 6 HOURS

INGREDIENTS

2 tbsp sunflower oil
1.35 kg / 3 lbs boneless pork shoulder
250 g / 9 oz / 1 ⅔ cups cured ham slices
110g / 4 oz / 1 cup Comte, grated
2 tbsp flat-leaf parsley, finely chopped
GARNISH
110g / 4 oz / 2 cups rocket leaves

Pork Rolls with Roquefort   515

Replace the Comte with the same weight of cubed Roquefort for a more tangy filling.

516

SERVES 4

Rice with Chicken, Peas and Carrots

Chicken Rice with Pineapple

517

Add 200 g / 7 oz / 1 cup drained pineapple chunks to the slow cooker before cooking.

Chicken and Bacon Rice

518

Fry 4 diced rashers of back bacon at the same time as the chicken.

Wholegrain Rice with Chicken

519

Swap the white rice to wholegrain to create a fiber filled dish.

PREPARATION TIME 10 MINUTES

COOKING TIME 4 HOURS

INGREDIENTS

2 tbsp sunflower oil
2 chicken breasts, sliced
250 g / 9 oz / 1 cup basmati rice
500ml / 18 fl. oz / 2 cups chicken stock
150 g / 5 oz / 1 ½ cups peas, fresh or frozen
2 carrots, peeled and sliced
2 sticks celery, sliced
2 eggs, beaten
2 tbsp dark soy sauce

GARNISH
1 spring onion (scallion), very finely sliced

- Heat the oil in a large wok set over a moderate heat until hot.
- Season and stir-fry the chicken for 1 minute then add the carrots, celery, peas, egg, soy sauce and pepper.
- Cook for a minute stirring frequently then spoon into a slow cooker.
- Add the rice and stock and stir well.
- Cover with a lid and cook on a medium setting for 4 hours until the rice has absorbed the stock and is fluffy and tender.
- Fluff with a fork before spooning into serving bowls.
- Garnish with the sliced spring onion (scallion) before serving.

SERVES 4

Fish Casserole

520

- Heat the olive oil in a large casserole dish set over a moderate heat.
- Add the clams and half of the white wine and cover with a lid.
- Remove the dish from the heat after a few minutes and shake well with the lid in place.
- Strain the clam liquid into a slow cooker and discard any clams that haven't opened.
- Place the clams, sea bass, prawns, tomatoes, fennel, garlic, chorizo, stock and remaining wine in the slow cooker.
- Stir gently a few times and cover with a lid.
- Cook on a low setting for 6 hours until the seafood is cooked through.
- Adjust the seasoning and stir in the chopped parsley.
- Spoon into serving bowls and serve immediately.

PREPARATION TIME: 20 MINUTES

COOKING TIME: 6 HOURS

INGREDIENTS

4 tbsp olive oil
4 sea bass fillets, pin-boned
300 g / 10 ½ oz / 2 cups whole prawns (shrimps)
450 g / 1 lb / 3 cups clams, cleaned
55g / 2 oz / ⅓ cup chorizo, finely sliced
250ml / 9 fl. oz / 1 cup dry white wine
250ml / 9 fl. oz / 1 cup fish stock
4 tomatoes, cored and sliced
4 cloves garlic, minced
1 fennel bulb, trimmed and finely chopped
1 tbsp flat-leaf parsley, roughly chopped

Pastis Fish Casserole

521

Replace the dry white wine with 55ml / 2 oz / ¼ cup pastis. Replace the parsley garnish with the same amount of chopped tarragon.

SERVES 4

522

Chicken with Green Olives and Lemon

- Rub the chicken with the oil and the butter.
- Season generously and heat a large frying pan over a moderate heat until hot. Seal the chicken until golden.
- Transfer to a slow cooker and add the olives, garlic and lemon wedges.
- Rearrange so that the chicken is sitting on top of a bed of lemon, garlic and olives.
- Cover and cook on a medium setting for 6 hours until the juices run clear when the thickest part of the thigh is pierced.
- Remove from the slow cooker when the chicken is ready and let it rest covered loosely with aluminium foil for 10 minutes.
- Spoon the olives, garlic and lemon into a casserole dish and sit the chicken on top.
- Arrange any remaining olives, lemon wedges and garlic cloves on top of the chicken before serving.

PREPARATION TIME: 10 MINUTES

COOKING TIME: 6 HOURS

INGREDIENTS

2 tbsp olive oil
30g / 1 oz / ¼ stick butter, softened
1 chicken, cleaned and trussed
12-14 cloves garlic, lightly crushed
3 lemons, cut into wedges
150 g / 5 oz / 1 cup green olives

Chicken with Orange

523

Replace the lemon wedges with 2 oranges cut into large wedges for orange-roasted chicken.

524

SERVES 4

Chicken, Lemon and Olive Tajine

PREPARATION TIME: 15 MINUTES

COOKING TIME: 4 HOURS

INGREDIENTS

4 tbsp olive oil
4 chicken drumsticks, cleaned and trimmed
175 g / 6 oz / 1 cup sundried tomatoes
150 g / 5 oz / 1 cup garlic-stuffed green olives
55g / 2 oz / ⅓ cup Kalamata olives
55g / 2 oz / ⅓ cup green olives
150 g / 5 oz / 1 cup Charlotte potatoes, halved
1 preserved lemon, chopped
1 tsp mild curry powder
1 tsp paprika
½ tsp turmeric
1 tbsp honey
250ml / 9 fl. oz / 1 cup chicken stock
1 lemon, juiced
1 tbsp flat-leaf parsley, finely chopped

- Heat the olive oil in a large casserole dish set over a moderate heat until hot.
- Season and seal the chicken drumsticks until golden.
- Transfer to a slow cooker once sealed. Reduce the heat under the dish and add the potatoes, olives, sun-dried tomato and preserved lemon to the dish.
- Add the ground spices and seasoning and stir well.
- Sauté for 2 minutes then add the lemon juice, stock and honey and stir well.
- Pour on top of the chicken in the slow cooker and cover with a lid.
- Cook on a medium setting for 4 hours until the chicken is cooked through.
- Adjust the seasoning to taste and stir through the chopped parsley before spooning into serving dishes.
- Serve immediately.

Chicken and Artichoke Tajine

525

Replace the potatoes with the same weight of preserved artichoke hearts that have been drained and roughly chopped.

526

SERVES 4

Rabbit with Apricots

PREPARATION TIME: 15 MINUTES

COOKING TIME: 6 HOURS

INGREDIENTS

4 tbsp olive oil
4 rabbit loins, trimmed and cut into 5 cm / 2" cubes
300 g / 10 ½ oz / 2 cups dried apricot halves
125ml / 4 ½ fl. oz / ½ cup dry white wine
250ml / 9 fl. oz / 1 cup chicken stock
125 g / 4 ½ oz / 4 cups baby spinach, chopped

GARNISH

2 tbsp olive oil
250 g / 9 oz / 8 cups baby spinach

- Heat the olive oil in a large casserole dish set over a moderate heat until hot.
- Season the rabbit and seal, in batches, until golden brown.
- Transfer the sealed rabbit to a slow cooker.
- Add the white wine, stock, apricot halves and spinach.
- Stir thoroughly and cover with a lid.
- Cook on a low setting for 6 hours until the rabbit is tender.
- Adjust the seasoning to taste and keep warm on a low setting as you prepare the garnish.
- Heat the olive oil in a frying pan and wilt the spinach with some seasoning for a minute, stirring frequently.
- Spoon the spinach and any juices into a serving dish.
- Spoon the rabbit into a serving dish and serve alongside the spinach.

Armagnac Rabbit with Prunes

527

Replace the apricots with the same weight of prunes. Substitute half of the white wine for 55ml / 2 fl. oz / ¼ cup Armagnac.

Chicken Wings with Onion and Ginger

528

SERVES 4

Pineapple Chicken Wings

529

Peel and core half a fresh pineapple. Cut into thin wedges and add to the slow cooker instead of the spring onion (scallion).

Spicey Onion Chicken Wings

530

Add 1 tbsp chilli sauce to the slow cooker halfway through cooking time.

Onion Chicken Drumsticks

531

Swap the chicken wings for drumsticks (legs) and cook thoroughly.

PREPARATION TIME 10 MINUTES

COOKING TIME 3 HOURS
10 MINUTES

....

INGREDIENTS

4 tbsp sunflower oil
900 g / 2 lbs chicken wings, trimmed and cleaned
2 cloves garlic, minced
10 cm / 4" ginger, peeled and finely chopped
4 spring onions (scallions), sliced
250ml / 9 fl. oz / 1 cup cola
1 tbsp tomato puree
1 tbsp dark soy sauce

- Preheat the oven to 190C (170C fan) / 375F / gas 5.
- Coat the chicken wings in the oil and season generously.
- Arrange on a large baking tray and roast for 5 minutes.
- Meanwhile, whisk together the garlic, ginger, tomato puree, cola and seasoning until smooth.
- Pour into a slow cooker and add the spring onions (scallions).
- Remove the chicken from the oven and place in the slow cooker.
- Cover with a lid and cook on a medium setting for 3 hours.
- Adjust the seasoning of the sauce to taste before spooning the chicken wings and spring onions (scallions) onto serving plates.
- Serve immediately.

532
SERVES 6

Loin of Veal with Beets

PREPARATION TIME: 20 MINUTES

COOKING TIME: 8 HOURS

INGREDIENTS

2 tbsp olive oil
30g / 1 oz / ¼ stick butter, softened
900 g / 2 lb loin of rose veal, trimmed
450 g / 1 lb / 3 cups golden beets, peeled sliced
150 g / 5 oz / 1 cup green olives

- Rub the veal loin with the oil and butter and season generously.
- Heat a large frying pan over a moderate heat until hot.
- Seal the veal in the pan until golden brown.
- Transfer to a slow cooker.
- Reduce the heat under the pan and add the beets and olives.
- Sauté for 3-4 minutes stirring frequently.
- Add the beets and olives to the slow cooker along with a little seasoning.
- Cover the slow cooker with a lid and cook on a medium setting for 8 hours.
- Let the veal rest for 10 minutes after cooking before spooning everything onto a serving platter.
- Serve immediately.

Loin of Veal with Fennel
533

Substitute the beets for 4 trimmed and sliced fennel bulbs.

534
SERVES 4

Stewed Sausages

PREPARATION TIME: 15 MINUTES

COOKING TIME: 4 HOURS 20 MINUTES

INGREDIENTS

4 tbsp olive oil
55 g / 2 oz / ½ stick butter, unsalted
8 pork sausages
2 white onions, sliced
2 cloves garlic, chopped
1 large carrot, peeled and diced
4 tomatoes, chopped
4 sprigs of thyme
250ml / 9 fl. oz / 1 cup cider
250ml / 9 fl. oz / 1 cup beef stock

- Heat the oil and butter in a large casserole dish over a medium-high heat.
- Add the onion and carrot, reduce the heat a little and sweat for 5 minutes.
- Add the garlic and cook for a further 1-2 minutes.
- Deglaze the pan with the cider and stir the base well to remove any residue that has collected.
- Add the sausages and brown for 4-5 minutes and then add the tomatoes.
- Cover with the beef stock and add the thyme sprigs.
- Pour into a slow cooker and cover with a lid.
- Cook on a medium setting for 4 hours.
- Adjust the seasoning to taste after 4 hours before spooning into a large frying pan and serving.

Sausage and Leek Stew
535

Add 1 washed and sliced leek to the slow cooker before cooking. Garnish with 2 tbsp finely chopped flat-leaf parsley leaves.

536

SERVES 8

Pork Shoulder

- Rub the pork with the sunflower oil and season generously.
- Heat a large frying pan over a moderate heat until hot.
- Seal the pork until golden brown.
- Transfer the pork to a slow cooker.
- Add the onion, garlic and stock.
- Cover and cook on a medium setting for 8 hours.
- Pour the stock into a casserole dish after 8 hours and sit the pork in it.
- Let it rest for 10 minutes before serving.

PREPARATION TIME: 10 MINUTES

COOKING TIME: 8 HOURS

INGREDIENTS

4 tbsp sunflower oil
1.35 kg / 3 lbs pork shoulder, trimmed of excess fat
500ml / 18 fl. oz / 2 cups beef stock
1 onion, sliced
2 cloves garlic, crushed

Pork and Potato 537

Add 2 large peeled and diced white potatoes, 2 large peeled and chopped carrots and another onion to the slow cooker to turn the dish into a pork and vegetable pot roast.

538

SERVES 4

Fish Stew

- Heat the olive oil in a large frying pan set over a moderate heat until hot.
- Season the fish fillets and flash-fry with the garlic for 1 minute.
- Transfer to a slow cooker.
- Add the prawns (shrimps) and mussels and flash-fry for a minute as well before transferring to the slow cooker.
- Deglaze the pan with the Cognac before reducing the heat and adding the infused stock and cream.
- Stir well and pour into the slow cooker.
- Add the tomatoes and cover with a lid.
- Cook on a medium setting for 4 hours.
- Adjust the seasoning to taste after 4 hours.
- Ladle the broth and seafood into serving bowls.
- Garnish with sprigs of basil leaves before serving.

PREPARATION TIME: 20 MINUTES

COOKING TIME: 4 HOURS

INGREDIENTS

4 tbsp olive oil
450 g / 1 lb red mullet fillets, pin-boned
225 g / 8 oz sea bass fillets, pin-boned
225 g / 8 oz / 2 cups mussels
4 whole prawns (shrimps), peeled and de-veined
4 tomatoes, cored and cut into wedges
2 cloves garlic, minced
2 tbsp Cognac
250ml / 9 fl. oz / 1 cup double (heavy) cream
250ml / 9 fl. oz / 1 cup fish stock
1 tsp saffron threads, infused in the stock

GARNISH
4 sprigs basil leaves

Fish and Potato Stew 539

Add 150 g / 5 oz / 1 cup Charlotte potatoes to the slow cooker before cooking. Garnish with tarragon sprigs instead of basil.

540

SERVES 4

Chicken Breasts with Cauliflower

Chicken Breasts with Mustard

541

Replace the wholegrain mustard with the same volume of Dijon mustard. Add 2 tbsp mayonnaise to the mustard and whisk before warming gently.

Chicken Breasts with Onions

542

Add 110g / 4 oz / 1 cup drained cocktail onions to the slow cooker at the same time as the other vegetables.

Turkey Breasts with Cauliflower

543

Replace the chicken breasts with the same amount of turkey breasts, and cook the same.

PREPARATION TIME: 15 MINUTES

COOKING TIME:
4 HOURS 20 MINUTES

INGREDIENTS

4 tbsp olive oil
4 chicken breasts
1 head cauliflower, prepared into small florets
4 tbsp wholegrain mustard
150 g / 5 oz / 1 cup new potatoes, halved

GARNISH
4 sprigs of flat-leaf parsley

- Combine the cauliflower, potatoes, half of the olive oil and some seasoning in a slow cooker.
- Cover with a lid and cook on a low setting for 4 hours until the vegetables are soft.
- Once the vegetables are soft, turn the slow cooker off but keep covered with the lid.
- Preheat the oven to 190C / 375F / gas 5.
- Rub the chicken breasts with the remaining olive oil and season generously.
- Arrange on a baking tray and roast for 12-15 minutes until firm yet springy to the touch.
- Remove from the oven and let them rest on the tray for a few minutes before slicing.
- Place the mustard in a small saucepan and warm gently over a low heat for a few minutes to loosen it.
- Arrange the cauliflower and potato on serving plates and position the sliced chicken breasts around them.
- Spoon some of the warmed mustard on top and garnish with a sprig of parsley before serving.

Squid and Lentil Casserole

544

SERVES 4

- Heat the olive oil in a casserole dish set over a medium heat until hot.
- Sweat the onion and carrot with the bay leaf and some salt for 4-5 minutes until softened.
- Add the lentils, white and stock and boil for 5 minutes, stirring occasionally.
- Add the squid, stir thoroughly, and pour into a slow cooker.
- Cover with a lid and cook on a low setting for 6 hours.
- Adjust the seasoning to taste after 6 hours and discard the bay leaf.
- Ladle into a serving dish and garnish with the chopped chives and chive stalks.
- Serve immediately.

PREPARATION TIME: 15 MINUTES

COOKING TIME: 6 HOURS

INGREDIENTS

1 squid, divided into parts
200 g / 7 oz / 1 cup brown lentils, soaked in cold water overnight and drained
2 tbsp olive oil
2 carrots, peeled and diced
1 onion, chopped
125ml / 4 ½ fl. oz / ½ cup white wine
500ml / 18 fl. oz / 2 cups vegetable stock
1 bay leaf
GARNISH
2 chive stalks
2 chive stalks, chopped

Squid Casserole with Pancetta

545

Add 110g / 4 oz / ⅔ cup pancetta lardons to the saucepan at the same time as the onion and carrot.

Pork Tenderloin Casserole

546

SERVES 8

- Tie the pork tenderloins securely using kitchen string.
- Season generously.
- Melt the butter with the oil in a large casserole dish set over a moderate heat.
- Seal the tenderloins until golden brown.
- Transfer to a casserole dish when done.
- Reduce the heat under the dish and add the pearl onions and garlic.
- Sauté for a few minutes then add the stock and bay leaf.
- Pour everything into the slow cooker and cover with a lid.
- Cook on a low setting for 6 hours.
- Adjust the seasoning to taste after 6 hours and pour back into a casserole dish before serving.

PREPARATION TIME: 20 MINUTES

COOKING TIME: 6 HOURS

INGREDIENTS

2 tbsp sunflower oil
30g / 1 oz / butter, unsalted
900 g / 1 lb pork tenderloin, trimmed
300 g / 10 ½ oz / 2 cups pearl onion, blanched
4 cloves garlic, lightly crushed
500ml / 18 fl. oz / 2 cups ham stock
1 bay leaf

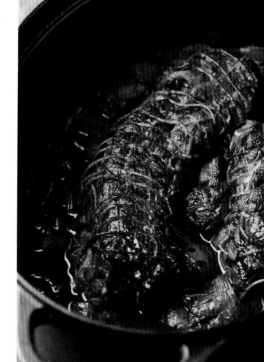

Pork Tenderloin with Cider

547

Replace the stock with the same volume of cider for a fruitier version of the dish.

548

SERVES 4

Guinea-fowl with New Potatoes

- Rub the guinea-fowl with the olive oil and season.
- Tie securely at 2" intervals using kitchen string.
- Heat a large casserole dish over a high heat until hot.
- Seal the guinea-fowl until golden brown.
- Reduce the heat under the dish and add the potatoes and 125ml / 4 ½ fl. oz / ½ cup of the chicken stock.
- Stir the base well to loosen any debris.
- Add the remaining stock, chanterelles and the sage and stir well.
- Pour into the slow cooker and position the guinea-fowl so that it sits on top of the potatoes and mushrooms.
- Cover and cook on a medium setting for 6 hours.
- Adjust the seasoning to taste and stir in the cream.
- Pour the contents of the slow cooker back into the casserole dish and rearrange the guinea-fowl on top before serving.

PREPARATION TIME: 15 MINUTES

COOKING TIME: 6 HOURS

INGREDIENTS

2 tbsp olive oil
1 guinea-fowl, cleaned and trimmed
300 g / 10 ½ oz / 2 cups Grenaille potatoes
150 g / 5 oz / 2 cups chanterelles, brushed clean
1 tbsp sage leaves
500ml / 18 fl. oz / 2 cups chicken stock
2 tbsp double (heavy) cream

Chicken Breast with Bulgur

549

SERVES 4

PREPARATION TIME: 15 MINUTES

COOKING TIME: 1 HOUR

INGREDIENTS

PESTO
30g / 1 oz basil leaves
125ml / 4 ½ fl. oz / ½ cup olive oil
30g / 1 oz / ⅓ cup pine nuts, toasted
55g / 2 oz / ½ cup Parmesan, grated
1 clove garlic, crushed

CHICKEN AND BULGUR
2 tbsp olive oil
4 chicken breasts, skin-on
1 red pepper, deseeded and finely diced
110g / 4 oz / ½ cup bulgar wheat

- Prepare the pesto by placing the basil, pine nuts, olive oil, garlic and a seasoning in a food processor and mix until smooth. Add the Parmesan and pulse until a thicker consistency is reached.
- Cover and chill until needed. Place the bulgar wheat in a slow cooker and cover with boiling water. Add red pepper and seasoning and stir.
- Cover with a lid and cook on a low setting for 1 hour. Meanwhile, preheat the oven to 190°C (170° fan) / 375F / gas 5.
- Fluff the bulgar after 1 hour and stir through 1 tbsp of the pesto.
- Turn the slow cooker off and keep the bulgar covered with a lid.
- Coat the chicken breasts in the oil and season well.
- Arrange on a baking tray and bake for 12-15 minutes until firm yet springy to the touch.
- Remove from the oven and let them rest for a few minutes before slicing thinly.
- Spoon some of the pesto bulgar wheat onto serving plates.
- Arrange the sliced chicken breast next to the bulgar and spoon some extra pesto next to it before serving.

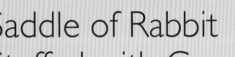

Saddle of Rabbit Stuffed with Capers

550

SERVES 4

PREPARATION TIME: 15 MINUTES

COOKING TIME 6 HOURS

INGREDIENTS

2 tbsp sunflower oil
1 saddle of rabbit, boned
250 g / 9 oz / 1 ⅔ cups sausage meat
55 / 2 oz / ⅓ cups capers, drained
2 tbsp olives

- Lay the saddle on a flat surface and season the inside.
- Stuff the inside with the sausage meat and capers and wrap the saddle around the stuffing.
- Tie the saddle securely with the kitchen string at intervals.
- Rub the outside with the oil and season generously.
- Heat a large frying pan over a moderate heat until hot.
- Seal the rabbit until golden brown.
- Transfer to a slow cooker and add the olives.
- Cover with a lid and cook for 6 hours until the rabbit is done.
- Remove from the cooker after 6 hours and cover loosely with aluminium foil for 10 minutes.
- Slice into portions and present on a serving platter with the olives and any roasting juices spooned around.

551

SERVES 4

Oxtail Casserole

- Rub the oxtail with the olive oil and season generously.
- Heat a large casserole dish over a high heat until hot.
- Seal the oxtail chunks until golden brown.
- Transfer to a slow cooker and reduce the heat under the dish.
- Add the butter and let it melt.
- Sauté the potatoes and carrots for 5 minutes, stirring occasionally.
- Spoon into a slow cooker and add the peas, stock, rosemary and bay leaf.
- Cover and cook over a low setting for 6 hours.
- After 6 hours, adjust the seasoning to taste and spoon into serving dishes.
- Discard the bay leaf and rosemary before garnishing with sprigs of rosemary.
- Serve immediately.

Oxtail Casserole with Tomatoes   552

Substitute the peas for 4 quartered tomatoes.

PREPARATION TIME: 15 MINUTES

COOKING TIME: 6 HOURS

INGREDIENTS

2 tbsp olive oil
1 tbsp butter, unsalted
900 g / 2 lbs oxtail, cut into 4 large chunks
450 g / 1 lb / 3 cups white potatoes, peeled and cut into chunks
450 g / 1 lb / 3 cups carrots, peeled and chopped
225 g / 8 oz / 2 cups peas, fresh or frozen
500ml / 18 fl. oz / 2 cups beef stock
1 bay leaf
1 sprig of rosemary
4 sprigs of rosemary

553

SERVES 4

Chicken and Vegetable Tajine

- Coat the chicken drumsticks with the oil and season generously.
- Heat a large casserole dish over a moderate heat until hot.
- Seal the chicken until golden brown in colour.
- Transfer to a slow cooker once sealed and reduce the heat under the dish.
- Add the vegetables, ground spices, honey and seasoning.
- Stir well and cook for 4-5 minutes.
- Spoon into the slow cooker and cover with the stock.
- Cover and cook on a low setting for 6 hours until the chicken is cooked and the vegetables are soft.
- Adjust the seasoning to taste before spooning into serving bowls.
- Serve immediately.

Chicken and Apricot Tajine   554

Add 2 tbsp dried apricot halves and 2 tbsp flaked (slivered) almonds to the slow cooker halfway through cooking.

PREPARATION TIME: 15 MINUTES

COOKING TIME : 6 HOURS

INGREDIENTS

4 tbsp olive oil
4 chicken drumsticks, cleaned and trimmed
450 g / 1 lb / 3 cups carrots, peeled and chopped
4 white potatoes, peeled and cut into large wedges
1 onion, finely chopped
2 cloves garlic, minced
1 tsp mild curry powder
1 tsp turmeric
½ tsp ground cinnamon
½ tsp ground cumin
1 tbsp honey
250 ml / 9 fl. oz / 1 cup chicken stock

SERVES 4

Chicken Stuffed with Pasta

PREPARATION TIME: 15 MINUTES

COOKING TIME: 6 HOURS

INGREDIENTS

55g / 2 oz / ½ stick butter, softened
1 chicken, cleaned and trussed
250 g / 9 oz / 1 ⅔ cups duck fois gras
110g / 4 oz / 1 cup spirali pasta
250ml / 9 fl. oz / 1 cup chicken stock
250ml / 9 fl. oz / 1 cup dry white wine

- Blanch the pasta in a large saucepan of salted, boiling water for 2 minutes. Drain and refresh in iced water.
- Stuff the chicken with the pasta and the foie gras.
- Rub the outside with the butter and season generously.
- Heat a large frying pan over a moderate heat until hot and seal the chicken until golden brown.
- Transfer to a slow cooker and cover with the stock.
- Deglaze the pan with the white wine until reduced by half.
- Pour into the slow cooker and cover with a lid.
- Cook on a medium setting for 6 hours.
- The chicken is ready when the juices run clear from the thickest part of the thigh when pierced.
- When the chicken is ready, spoon the contents of the slow cooker into a roasting tray for presentation.
- Serve immediately.

Chicken Stuffed with Pearl Barley   556

Replace the pasta with 110g / 4 oz / ½ cup pearl barley that has been soaked in cold water overnight.

SERVES 4

Stewed Rabbit with Raisins

PREPARATION TIME: 15 MINUTES

COOKING TIME: 6 HOURS

INGREDIENTS

2 tbsp olive oil
2 rabbit loins, trimmed and cut into chunks
2 onions, finely chopped
1 clove garlic, minced
4 tbsp Armagnac
250ml / 9 fl. oz / 1 cup chicken stock
110g / 4 oz / ½ cup raisins

- Heat the olive oil in a large casserole dish set over a moderate heat until hot.
- Season the rabbit and seal in batches until golden brown.
- Transfer the sealed rabbit to a slow cooker.
- Reduce the heat and add the onion and garlic.
- Sweat for a few minutes stirring occasionally, then deglaze the dish using the Armagnac.
- Add the stock and raisins and stir well.
- Pour into the slow cooker and cover with a lid.
- Cook on a medium setting for 6 hours until the rabbit is tender and soft.
- Adjust the seasoning to taste and ladle into serving dishes using a slotted spoon.
- Serve immediately.

Stewed Rabbit with Apples   558

Replace the raisins with 2 cored and diced eating apples.

559

SERVES 4

Three Meat Stew

Stew with Lamb Shoulder

560

Replace the oxtail with the same weight of lamb shoulder that has been cut into cubes.

Stew with Turnips

561

Substitute the carrot with 300 g / 10 ½ oz / 2 cups baby turnips that have been peeled and halved.

Stew with Turkey

562

Replace the same amount of chicken breast with turkey and cook the same.

PREPARATION TIME: 15 MINUTES

COOKING TIME: 8 HOURS

....

INGREDIENTS

4 tbsp olive oil
450 g / 1 lb oxtail, cut into 2 pieces
450 g / 1 lb rose veal bones
2 chicken breasts, trimmed
1 Cos lettuce, trimmed and chopped
2 carrots, peeled and chopped
4 spring onions (scallions), chopped in half
500ml / 18 fl. oz / 2 cups chicken stock

- Preheat the oven to 190C / 375F / gas 5.
- Arrange the oxtail and veal bones on a roasting tray and drizzle with the olive oil and some seasoning.
- Roast for 10 minutes then remove from the oven and transfer to a slow cooker.
- Add the chicken, carrot, spring onion (scallion) and stock.
- Cover with a lid and cook on a medium setting for 8 hours.
- Adjust the seasoning to taste after 8 hours and stir through most of the lettuce.
- Spoon into a casserole dish and arrange more lettuce in and around the meat before serving.

563

SERVES 4

Goose and Sweet Potato Tajine

PREPARATION TIME: 15 MINUTES

COOKING TIME:
6 HOURS 20 MINUTES

....

INGREDIENTS

4 tbsp olive oil
2 goose legs, jointed and trimmed
4 sweet potatoes, peeled and diced
3 star anise
2 sticks cinnamon
1 tsp ras el hanout (Moroccan spice blend)
½ tsp ground cinnamon
½ tsp turmeric
1 tbsp honey
250ml / 9 fl. oz / 1 cup chicken stock

GARNISH

30g / 1 oz / 2 tbsp pine nuts, lightly toasted
4 sprigs coriander (cilantro) leaves

- Heat half of the olive oil in a large casserole dish set over a moderate heat until hot.
- Season the goose and seal in batches until golden.
- Remove from the dish and transfer to a slow cooker.
- Add the remaining olive oil and reduce the heat.
- Add the whole and ground spices and stir well, cooking them for a minute.
- Add the sweet potato and stir well, cooking for a further 2-3 minutes.
- Stir in the honey and stock then pour over the goose in the slow cooker.
- Cover with a lid and cook on a low setting for 6 hours.
- Adjust the seasoning to taste after 6 hours and spoon into serving dishes using a slotted spoon.
- Garnish with a sprinkling of the pine nuts and a sprig of coriander leaves before serving.

Goose and New Potato Tajine

564

Replace the sweet potato with the same volume of new potatoes. Garnish with sprigs of flat-leaf parsley.

565

SERVES 4

Duck and Pear Tajine

PREPARATION TIME: 15 MINUTES

COOKING TIME: 6 HOURS

....

INGREDIENTS

4 duck legs, cleaned and trimmed
4 eating pears, peeled and quartered
2 cinnamon sticks
2 tsp ras el hanout (Moroccan spice blend)
1 tsp ground cumin
½ tsp ground cinnamon
2 tbsp honey
250ml / 9 fl. oz / 1 cup chicken stock
2 tbsp coriander (cilantro) leaves, finely chopped

- Heat a large frying pan over a medium heat until hot.
- Season the duck legs and seal until golden brown.
- Transfer to a slow cooker once sealed.
- Add the pears to the rendered duck fat in the pan and sauté for a few minutes before adding the ground spices and cinnamon sticks.
- Stir well then stir through the honey.
- Pour into slow cooker and cover with the stock.
- Cover with a lid and cook on a medium setting for 6 hours.
- Adjust the seasoning to taste after 6 hours before stirring through the chopped coriander.
- Spoon into serving dishes and serve immediately.

Duck and Apple Tajine

566

Replace the pear quarters with 2 cooking apples that have been peeled and cut into large wedges.

567

SERVES 4

Chicken and Mushroom Casserole

- Heat the sunflower oil and butter together in a large casserole dish set over a moderate heat until hot.
- Season the chicken pieces and seal until golden brown.
- Transfer to a slow cooker. Deglaze the dish with the white wine and pour on top of the chicken.
- Melt the butter for the sauce in a pan and whisk in the flour until you have a roux. Cook for 1-2 minutes.
- Add the milk in a slow, steady stream whisking until you have a smooth, thickened sauce. Add the bay leaf and simmer for 8-10 minutes, stirring occasionally.
- Adjust the seasoning and pour on top of the chicken and wine in the slow cooker. Add the chanterelles and some seasoning and cover with a lid.
- Cook on a low setting for 6 hours until the chicken is cooked through.
- Serve immediately.

PREPARATION TIME: 15 MINUTES

COOKING TIME: 6 HOURS

INGREDIENTS

2 tbsp sunflower oil
1 tbsp butter
1 chicken, jointed and trimmed
125ml / 4 ½ fl. oz / ½ cup white wine
300 g / 10 ½ oz / 4 cups chanterelles, brushed clean

FOR THE SAUCE
55g / 2 oz / ½ stick butter
55g / 2 oz / ⅓ cup plain (all purpose) flour
750ml / 1 pint 6 fl. oz / 3 cups milk
1 bay leaf

Casserole with Oysters and Mushrooms

568

Replace the chanterelles with a mixture of oyster, chestnut and button mushrooms.

569

SERVES 4

Sweet and Sour Beef Stew

- Coat the rump steak in the oil and season generously.
- Heat a large frying pan over a moderate heat until hot.
- Seal the beef in batches for 30 seconds, tossing and stirring before moving to a slow cooker.
- Add the carrots, leek, red pepper, vinegar, sugar, stock, raisins, lemon juice and beef stock to the slow cooker.
- Cover with a lid and cook on a medium setting for 4 hours.
- Adjust the seasoning to taste before stirring through the coriander.
- Spoon into big serving bowls before serving.

PREPARATION TIME: 15 MINUTES

COOKING TIME: 4 HOURS

INGREDIENTS

4 tbsp sunflower oil
675 g / 1 lb 8 oz / 4 ½ cups rump steak, sliced
2 carrots, peeled and diced
1 leek, washed and sliced
2 red peppers, deseeded and diced
4 tbsp rice vinegar
2 tbsp caster sugar
500ml / 18 fl. oz / 2 cups beef stock
2 tbsp raisins
1 lemon, juiced
1 tbsp (cilantro), finely chopped

Sweet and Sour Beef with Mushrooms

570

Add 150 g / 5 oz / 2 cups sliced shiitake mushrooms and 1 tsp Tabasco sauce to the slow cooker before cooking.

571

SERVES 4

Beef and Olive Stew

Beef and Mushroom Stew

572

Add 150 g / 5 oz / 2 cups button mushrooms to the slow cooker before cooking.

Beef and Pancetta Stew

573

Add 110g / 4 oz / ⅔ cup cubed pancetta to the casserole dish at the same time as the beef is being sealed.

Beef and Wine Stew

574

Add another ½ cup of red wine to the slow cooker while cooking.

PREPARATION TIME: 15 MINUTES

**COOKING TIME:
6 HOURS 20 MINUTES**

INGREDIENTS

4 tbsp sunflower oil
675 g / 1 lb 8 oz / 4 ½ cups chuck steak, cut into cubes
150 g / 5 oz / 1 cup pearl onions, blanched
110 g / 4 oz / ⅔ cup black olives, pitted
750ml / 1 pint 6 fl. oz / 3 cups beef stock
1 carrot, peeled and diced
125ml / 4 ½ fl. oz / ½ cup red wine

- Coat the beef in the oil and season well.
- Heat a large casserole dish over a moderate heat until hot.
- Seal the beef in batches until golden brown in colour all over before moving to a slow cooker.
- Reduce the heat and add the onions, carrot and olives to the dish.
- Sauté for a few minutes before deglazing the dish with the red wine.
- Let the wine reduce by half before pouring in the stock.
- Pour the contents of the casserole dish into the slow cooker and stir well.
- Cover and cook on a low setting for 6 hours until the beef is tender.
- Adjust the seasoning to taste after 6 hours before ladling into a casserole dish for presentation.
- Serve immediately.

575

SERVES 4

Chicken in Kung Po Sauce

- Heat the oil in a large wok set over a high heat until hot.
- Season and flash-fry the chicken for 1 minute before spooning into a slow cooker.
- Reduce the heat a little under the wok and add the chilli peppers, garlic and peanuts.
- Stir-fry for a minute.
- Briefly whisk together the ingredients for the sauce and pour into the wok.
- Stir well and cook for 1 minute before pouring everything into the slow cooker.
- Cover with a lid and cook on a high setting for 2 hours.
- Spoon into serving bowls using a slotted spoon.
- Serve with a bowl of the soy sauce on the side as a garnish.

PREPARATION TIME: 15 MINUTES

COOKING TIME: 2 HOURS

INGREDIENTS

2 tbsp groundnut oil
4 chicken breasts, diced
2 cloves garlic, minced
2 green chilli peppers, chopped
2 red chilli peppers, chopped
110g / 4 oz / ½ cup salted peanuts

FOR THE SAUCE
1 tbsp white wine
1 tbsp distilled white vinegar
1 tbsp light soy sauce
1 tbsp sesame oil
1 tbsp red chilli paste
1 tbsp brown sugar
1 tbsp cornflour (cornstarch)
1 tbsp water, combined with the cornflour (cornstarch)
GARNISH
125ml / 4 ½ fl. oz / ½ cup dark soy sauce

Chicken with Chestnuts and Spring Onions

576

Add 200 g / 7 oz / 1 cup canned, drained water chestnuts to the slow cooker before cooking. Garnish with 2 sliced spring onions.

577

SERVES 4

Spicy Pollock

- Whisk together the yogurt, ground and whole spices with some seasoning in a mixing bowl.
- Add the pollock and stir well to coat.
- Heat the oil in a large frying pan set over a moderate heat until hot.
- Sweat the onion and carrot with a little seasoning for 5 minutes, stirring frequently until the vegetables start to soften.
- Spoon the vegetables into a slow cooker and sit the marinated pollock on top.
- Cover with a lid and cook on a medium setting for 4 hours.
- Adjust the seasoning to taste after 4 hours before spooning into individual casserole dishes.
- Garnish with the chervil before serving.

PREPARATION TIME: 15 MINUTES

**COOKING TIME:
4 HOURS 15 MINUTES**

INGREDIENTS

2 tbsp sunflower oil
4 x 200 g / 7 oz pollock fillets, skinned, pin-boned and sliced
1 onion, finely sliced
2 carrots, peeled and finely sliced
2 tsp Madras curry powder
1 tsp cumin seeds
½ tsp caraway seeds
125ml / 4 ½ fl. oz / ½ cup plain yogurt

GARNISH
4 sprigs chervil

Spicy Pollock with Chili

578

Add 1 finely sliced red chilli to the slow cooker before cooking.

579

SERVES 4

Wild Boar Stew with Beer

PREPARATION TIME: 15 MINUTES

COOKING TIME:
6 HOURS 20 MINUTES

....

INGREDIENTS

4 tbsp sunflower oil
675 g / 1 lb 8 oz / 4 ½ cups wild boar
fillet, cut into cubes
2 tbsp plain (all purpose) flour
1 onion, chopped
300 g / 10 ½ oz / 4 cups mixed exotic
mushrooms, brushed cleaned
250ml / 9 fl. oz / 1 cup lager
400ml / 14 fl. oz / 1 ⅔ cups beef stock
900 g / 2 lbs / 6 cups floury potatoes,
peeled and cut into chunks
55g / 2 oz / ½ stick unsalted butter

GARNISH
4 sprigs of thyme
250ml / 9 fl. oz / 1 cup lager

- Coat the boar with the flour and season.
- Heat the oil in a pan and seal the boar in batches until golden, then move to the slow cooker.
- Add the remaining oil and reduce the heat a little. Add the mushrooms and sauté for a few minutes.
- Deglaze the dish with the lager before adding the stock and stirring well. Pour into the slow cooker and cook on a medium setting for 6 hours. Adjust the seasoning.
- Cook the potatoes in a saucepan of salted, boiling water for 15-20 minutes until tender.
- Drain and let the potato steam off for 5 minutes before mashing with the butter and seasoning until smooth.
- Spoon the mash onto serving plates.
- Spoon the wild boar stew on top and garnish with the thyme.

Wild Boar Stew with Red Wine

580

Replace the lager with the same volume of red wine for a red wine stew.

581

SERVES 4

Chestnut Stuffed Capon

PREPARATION TIME: 20 MINUTES

COOKING TIME:
6 HOURS 20 MINUTES

....

INGREDIENTS

2 tbsp olive oil
2 capon breasts, with skin on
For the stuffing
200 g / 7 oz / 1 cup cooked
chestnuts, peeled
150 g / 5 oz / 1 cup sausage meat
½ tsp dried thyme
½ tsp dried rosemary

GARNISH
4 sprigs rosemary
4 sprigs thyme
4 whole chestnuts
4 peeled chestnuts, halved

- Combine the chestnuts, sausage meat, dried herbs and seasoning in a blender. Pulse until it comes together.
- Separate most of the skin away from the capon breasts, making sure they are still attached to the meat.
- Pack the stuffing onto the insides of the breast meat and shape so that you have cylinder shapes. Bring the loose skin around the stuffing to cover it.
- Tie the breasts with kitchen twine / string at even intervals, then rub all over with the olive oil.
- Season well and place in a slow cooker. Cover with a lid and cook on a medium setting for 6 hours.
- Preheat the oven to 190°C (170° fan) / 375F / gas 5.
- Arrange the capon on a roasting tray and roast for 8-10 minutes until golden brown on the outside.
- Cut into slices with a sharp knife and arrange on serving plates. Garnish with the chestnuts. Lay rosemary and thyme sprigs across the meat and serve.

Chestnut Stuffed Capon with Apricot

582

Add 55g / 2 oz / ⅓ cup chopped, dried apricot halves to the stuffing mixture before using.

Sicilian-style Tuna

583

SERVES 4

Sicilian-style Tuna with Beans

584

Add 400 g / 14 oz / 2 cups canned, drained cannellini beans to the slow cooker before cooking.

Sicilian-style Capers

585

Replace the peas with 55g / 2 oz / ⅓ cup drained baby capers.

Sicilian-style Tuna with Olives

586

Add ½ cup of pitted olives to the slow cooker and cook the same.

PREPARATION TIME: 15 MINUTES

COOKING TIME: 4 HOURS

INGREDIENTS

4 tbsp olive oil
450 g / 1 lb tuna steak, diced
2 onions, sliced
2 large potatoes, peeled and finely diced
2 carrots, peeled and finely diced
400 g / 14 oz / 2 cups chopped tomatoes
250ml / 9 fl. oz / 1 cup vegetable stock
125ml / 4 ½ fl. oz / ½ cup dry white wine
110g / 4 oz / 1 cup peas, frozen or fresh

- Heat the olive oil in a large casserole dish set over a moderate heat until hot.
- Season the tuna and flash-fry in batches before moving to a slow cooker.
- Reduce the heat under the dish and add the onions, potatoes, carrots and a little seasoning.
- Sauté for a few minutes, stirring occasionally, before deglazing with the white wine.
- Let it reduce by half before adding the stock, chopped tomatoes and peas.
- Pour into the slow cooker and cover with a lid.
- Cook on a medium setting for 4 hours.
- Adjust the seasoning to taste after 4 hours before spooning into a baking dish for presentation.
- Serve immediately.

587

SERVES 4

Lamb and Apricot Tajine

PREPARATION TIME: 15 MINUTES

COOKING TIME: 6 HOURS

....

INGREDIENTS

4 tbsp olive oil
900 g / 2 lbs / 6 cups lamb shoulder, diced into 2" cubes
2 tsp ras el hanout (Moroccan spice blend)
1 tsp ground cinnamon
1 tsp ground cumin
1 tsp ground coriander seeds
1 tsp paprika
2 tbsp honey
150 gg / 5 oz / 1 cup dried apricot halves
2 tbsp ground almonds
500ml / 18 fl. oz / 2 cups lamb stock

- Coat the lamb in the olive oil and season generously with the ground spices, salt and pepper.
- Heat a large casserole dish over a moderate heat until hot.
- Seal the lamb in batches until golden brown.
- Transfer to a slow cooker and cover with the stock.
- Add the ground almonds, apricot halves and honey and stir well.
- Cover with a lid and cook on a medium setting for 6 hours.
- Adjust the seasoning to taste after 6 hours before spooning into serving dishes.

Lamb and Sweet Potato Tajine

588

Add 2 peeled and diced sweet potatoes to the slow cooker before cooking.

589

SERVES 6

Gammon

PREPARATION TIME: 10 MINUTES

COOKING TIME: 7 HOURS

....

INGREDIENTS

2 tbsp olive oil
900 g / 2 lbs gammon joint
2 sticks celery, chopped
2 carrots, peeled and chopped

- Rub the gammon with the olive oil and season generously.
- Heat a large frying pan over a moderate heat until hot.
- Seal the gammon until golden brown.
- Add the celery and carrot halfway through sealing.
- Transfer everything to a slow cooker.
- Cover with a lid and cook on a medium setting for 7 hours.
- Remove from the slow cooker after 7 hours and arrange on a serving plate.
- Season with a little more flaked sea salt and black pepper before serving.

Gigot with Ham Stock

590

Add 500ml / 18 fl. oz / 2 cups ham stock to the slow cooker and braise the gammon in the stock.

Roast Pork with Sage

591

SERVES 8

- Tie the pork with butcher's twine, securing well using a cross pattern.
- Rub with the olive oil and season well.
- Heat a frying pan until hot over a medium-high heat and seal the pork until golden.
- Arrange the potatoes, onion and sage leaves in the base of a slow cooker.
- Sit the pork on top and pour in the stock and cider.
- Cover with a lid and cook on a medium setting for 8 hours.
- Remove the pork after 8 hours and let it rest for 10 minutes covered loosely with aluminium foil.
- Pour the stock and vegetables into a casserole dish before replacing the rested pork and serving.

PREPARATION TIME: 15 MINUTES

COOKING TIME:
8 HOURS 25 MINUTES

INGREDIENTS

4 tbsp cup olive oil
2 kg / 4 ½ lb piece of rolled pork shoulder
250ml / 9 fl. oz / 1 cup cider
500ml / 18 fl. oz / 2 cups chicken stock
2 onions, sliced
300 g / 10 ½ oz / 2 cups new potatoes, halved
Handful sage leaves

Roast Pork with Prunes

592

Add 150 g / 5 oz / 1 cup of prunes to the slow cooker before cooking.

Lamb Confit and Cheese

593

SERVES 4

- Heat the olive oil in a pan. Season the lamb and seal in batches until golden, then move to a slow cooker.
- Reduce the heat a little and add the butter to the dish and sweat the onion, garlic and ground coriander with a little salt for 8-10 minutes until softened.
- Add the stock and stir well before pouring over the lamb in the slow cooker.
- Cover with a lid and cook on a medium setting for 6 hours until the lamb is tender and pulling apart easily.
- Preheat the oven to 190°C (170° fan) / 375F / gas 5.
- Cook the potato in a large saucepan of salted, boiling water for 15-20 minutes.
- Drain and let them steam off for 5 minutes before mashing with butter and coriander until smooth.
- Fold through the cheese. Spoon the lamb into a casserole dish and top with the mashed potato mixture.
- Sprinkle over the breadcrumbs and bake for 10 minutes.

PREPARATION TIME 10 MINUTES

COOKING TIME 45 MINUTES

INGREDIENTS

2 tbsp olive oil
1 tbsp butter
450 g / 1 lb / 3 cups lamb neck fillet
3 onions, finely sliced
2 cloves garlic, minced
½ tsp ground coriander seeds
250ml / 9 fl. oz / 1 cup lamb stock
For the topping
675 g / 1 lb 8 oz / 4 ½ cups floury potatoes, peeled and diced
55 g / 2 oz / ½ stick butter
2 tbsp coriander (cilantro), roughly chopped
55g / 2 oz / ½ cup Cheddar, finely grated
2 tbsp panko breadcrumbs

Lamb Confit with Tarragon

594

Replace the ground coriander seeds with dried tarragon and the chopped coriander (cilantro) with chopped tarragon.

595

SERVES 4

Lamb and Potato Stew

Lamb Stew with Almonds

596

Stir through 2 tbsp ground almonds into the slow cooker before cooking. Garnish with 1 tbsp toasted, flaked almonds.

Lamb Stew with Rum

597

Deglaze the dish with 4 tbsp white rum after you have sautéed the vegetables.

Lamb Stew with Beans

598

Five minutes before the lamb has cooked, add 150 g / 5 oz of beans and cook the same.

PREPARATION TIME: 20 MINUTES

COOKING TIME: 6 HOURS 20 MINUTES

....

INGREDIENTS

4 tbsp olive oil
900 g / 2 lbs / 6 cups lamb shoulder, cut into cubes
2 onions, chopped
2 large sweet potatoes, peeled and diced
2 tsp mild curry powder
1 tsp ground coriander seeds
1 tsp dried oregano
1 tsp paprika
400 g / 14 oz / 2 cups canned pineapple chunks, drained
500 ml / 18 fl. oz / 2 cups coconut milk
250 ml / 9 fl. oz / 1 cup lamb stock

GARNISH
2 tbsp coriander (cilantro) leaves, finely chopped

- Coat the lamb in the olive oil and season generously.
- Heat a large casserole dish over a moderate heat until hot and seal the lamb in batches until golden brown.
- Transfer each batch to a slow cooker when ready.
- Reduce the heat under the dish and add the onion, sweet potato and spices, stirring thoroughly.
- Sauté for 2-3 minutes, stirring occasionally before adding the pineapple chunks, coconut milk and stock.
- Stir well and pour into the slow cooker.
- Cover and cook on a medium setting for 6 hours until the lamb is tender and pulls apart easily.
- Adjust the seasoning to taste before ladling into a casserole dish and garnishing with the chopped coriander (cilantro).
- Serve immediately.

599
SERVES 4
Monkfish with Vegetables

- Coat the monkfish in the olive oil and season generously.
- Heat a large frying pan over a moderate heat until hot and seal the monkfish all over before moving to a slow cooker.
- Reduce the heat a little and add the peas, courgette and runner beans to the pan.
- Spoon the vegetables into the slow cooker and cover with the stock and saffron threads.
- Cover with a lid and cook on a medium setting for 6 hours until the fish is cooked and firm yet springy to the touch.
- Adjust the seasoning to taste before spooning into a wok for presentation.

PREPARATION TIME :
10-15 MINUTES

COOKING TIME :
6 HOURS 15 MINUTES

INGREDIENTS

4 tbsp olive oil
450 g / 1 lb monkfish tail, cut into chunks
1 medium courgette (courgette), sliced
110g / 4 oz / 1 cup peas, frozen or fresh
225 g / 8 oz / 2 cups runner beans, trimmed
1 tbsp saffron threads
500ml / 18 fl. oz / 2 cups fish stock

Monkfish Wrapped in Parma Ham
600

Wrap the chunks of monkfish in strips of Parma ham before sealing.

601
SERVES 4
White Salmon and Mussels

- Heat a large saucepan and add the mussels and white wine. Cover and let the steam cook the mussels for 3-4 minutes. Drain and discard any mussels that haven't opened during cooking.
- Remove the mussels from their shells carefully and reserve to one side in a bowl.
- Melt the butter in a saucepan and whisk in the flour to make a roux. Cook for 1-2 minutes, then whisk in the milk in a slow stream until you have a thickened sauce.
- Simmer for a few minutes, then season to taste with the nutmeg and seasoning.
- Combine the mussels and salmon fillet in a slow cooker.
- Pour the sauce on top and cover with a lid.
- Cook on a low setting for 4 hours before adjust the seasoning to taste.
- Spoon into serving bowls and garnish with black pepper and chive stalks before serving.

PREPARATION TIME: 15 MINUTES

COOKING TIME:
4 HOURS 30 MINUTES

INGREDIENTS

450 g / 1 lb salmon fillet, cubed
450 g / 1 lb / 3 cups mussels, beards removed and cleaned
125ml / 4 ½ fl. oz / ½ cup dry white wine
2 tbsp plain (all purpose) flour
2 tbsp butter
500ml / 18 fl. oz / 2 cups milk
Nutmeg, grated to taste
GARNISH
4 chive stalks

White Salmon with Mushrooms
602

Before cooking the roux, add 150 g / 5 oz of button top mushrooms and sauté for 5 minutes in a knob of butter over a medium heat.

Vanilla Rose Veal

603

SERVES 4

PREPARATION TIME: 15 MINUTES

**COOKING TIME:
6 HOURS 20 MINUTES**

INGREDIENTS

2 tbsp olive oil
2 tbsp butter
900 g / 2 lbs / 6 cups rose veal fillet, diced
300 g / 10 ⅓ oz / 4 cups closed cup mushrooms, sliced
1 vanilla pod, split lengthwise
1 tsp vanilla extract
250ml / 9 fl. oz / 1 cup milk
250ml / 9 fl. oz / 1 cup beef stock
4 tbsp double (heavy) cream

- Heat together the olive oil and butter in a large casserole dish set over a moderate heat.
- Season the veal generously and seal in batches until golden brown, transferring the sealed veal to a slow cooker when ready.
- Reduce the heat and add the mushrooms, vanilla pod and stir well.
- Sauté for a few minutes before adding the milk, vanilla extract and stock.
- Stir well before pouring into the slow cooker.
- Cover with a lid and cook on a medium setting for 6 hours until the veal is soft and can be pulled apart easily between your fingers.
- Stir through the double cream and adjust the seasoning to taste before discarding the vanilla pod and ladling into serving bowls.
- Serve immediately.

Rose Veal with Bay Leaves

604

Remove the vanilla pod and extract and replace with 2 bay leaves.

Orange Duck

605

SERVES 4

PREPARATION TIME: 10 MINUTES

COOKING TIME: 6 HOURS 30 MINUTES

INGREDIENTS

2 tbsp sunflower oil
1 duck, cleaned and trimmed of excess fat
1 orange, pared zest and juiced
2 tbsp honey

TO GARNISH
2 blood oranges, peeled and segmented
1 heart Romaine lettuce, chopped

- Preheat the oven to 200°C (180° fan) / 400F / gas 6.
- Julienne the pared orange zest and set to one side.
- Rub the duck with the oil and season generously inside and out.
- Place on a roasting tray and roast in the oven for 20-25 minutes until golden brown.
- Remove from the oven and transfer to a slow cooker.
- Cover with a lid and cook on a low setting for 6 hours.
- Baste halfway through with the honey and orange juice.
- Place the roast duck on a serving platter and garnish with the julienned orange zest on top.
- Serve with the lettuce and orange segments on the side.

Duck Stuffed with Cherries

606

Stuff the duck with 400 g / 14 oz / 2 cups canned, drained cherries.

SERVES 4

Moroccan Soup

- Coat the lamb in half of the olive oil and season generously.
- Heat a large casserole dish over a moderate heat until hot.
- Seal the lamb in batches until golden brown.
- Transfer to a slow cooker and reduce the heat under the dish a little.
- Add the remaining olive oil and sauté the onion, garlic and carrots for a few minutes.
- Stir well then add the harissa and chickpeas (garbanzo beans).
- Stir thoroughly before adding the stock, chopped tomatoes, peas and seasoning.
- Pour into the slow cooker and cover with a lid.
- Cook on a medium setting for 6 hours. Adjust the seasoning before ladling into serving bowls.
- Garnish with coriander before serving.

PREPARATION TIME: 20 MINUTES

COOKING TIME: 6 HOURS

INGREDIENTS

4 tbsp olive oil
450 g / 1 lb / 3 cups lamb, diced
400 g / 14 oz / 2 cups canned chickpeas (garbanzo beans), drained
400 g / 14 oz / 2 cups chopped tomatoes
110g / 4 oz / 1 cup peas
1 onion, chopped
2 carrots, peeled and sliced
3 sticks celery, sliced
2 cloves garlic, minced
1 tbsp harissa
500ml / 18 fl. oz / 2 cups lamb stock

SERVES 4

Chicken Tajine

PREPARATION TIME: 15 MINUTES

COOKING TIME: 6 HOURS

INGREDIENTS

4 tbsp olive oil
4 chicken legs, jointed and trimmed
2 carrots, peeled and diced
2 onion, diced
1 clove garlic, minced

1 tsp ras el hanout (Moroccan spice blend)
1 tsp ground cumin
1 tbsp honey
1 preserved lemon, diced
55g / 2 oz / ⅓ cup Kalamata olives
500ml / 18 fl. oz / 2 cups chicken stock

GARNISH

4 sprigs coriander (cilantro)

- Coat the chicken in half of the olive oil and season generously.
- Seal the chicken pieces in a hot casserole dish set over a moderate heat until golden brown all over.
- Transfer to a slow cooker.
- Add the remaining olive oil to the casserole dish and reduce the heat a little.
- Sauté the vegetables with the ground spices and honey for 5 minutes, stirring occasionally.
- Add the preserved lemon, olives and stock before pouring into the slow cooker.
- Cover with a lid and cook on a medium setting for 6 hours.
- Adjust the seasoning to taste after 6 hours before spooning into serving dishes.
- Garnish with the coriander and serve immediately.

SERVES 4

Seafood Saffron Casserole

PREPARATION TIME: 15 MINUTES

COOKING TIME: 4 HOURS

INGREDIENTS

450 g / 1 lb / 3 cups frozen prawns (shrimps), thawed
300 g / 10 ½ oz / 2 cups mussels, cleaned with beards removed
125ml / 4 ½ fl. oz / ½ cup

dry white wine
450 g / 1 lb baby squid, chopped
250ml / 9 fl. oz / 1 cup double (heavy) cream
500ml / 18 fl. oz / 2 cups fish stock

GARNISH

Pinch saffron threads

- Heat a large saucepan over a high heat until hot then reduce the heat a little.
- Add the mussels and white wine to the saucepan and cover with a lid.
- Steam cook for 2-3 minutes, shaking the pan occasionally, until the mussels have opened.
- Strain the mussels and reserve the liquor; discard any that haven't opened.
- Remove the mussel meat from the shells and combine with the fish stock, cream, prawns, baby squid, cooking liquor from the mussels and some seasoning.
- Cover with a lid and cook on a medium setting for 4 hours.
- Adjust the seasoning to taste after 4 hours before ladling into soup bowls.
- Garnish with a pinch of saffron threads before serving.

610
SERVES 6

Mullet Stew

PREPARATION TIME: 20 MINUTES

COOKING TIME: 6 HOURS 45 MINUTES

INGREDIENTS

4 red mullet, gutted, cleaned and roughly chopped
4 grey mullet, gutted, cleaned and roughly chopped
4 tbsp olive oil
4 tbsp Pernod
1.2 l / 2 pints / 4 ⅘ cups fish stock
500 ml / 18 fl. oz / 2 cups water
1 tbsp tomato puree
6 plum tomatoes, cut into wedges
1 fennel bulb, trimmed and sliced
2 onions, finely chopped
4 cloves garlic, minced
pinch cayenne pepper
pinch paprika
1 bay leaf

GARNISH

4 chive stalks

- Heat the olive oil in a large casserole dish set over a moderate heat.
- Sweat the fennel, onion, garlic for 10 minutes with a little salt, stirring occasionally until they are soft but not coloured.
- Stir in the tomato puree, tomatoes, bay leaf, paprika and Cayenne pepper.
- Stir well and cover with the fish stock and water. Pour into a slow cooker and cook on low for 3 hours.
- Strain after 3 hours into a saucepan, pressing the tomatoes and all other ingredients through the sieve.
- Reduce the broth a little by boiling it for 5 minutes.
- Add the Pernod to the broth, then add fish and pour back into a slow cooker. Cover and cook on a medium setting for 4 hours.
- Adjust the seasoning to taste then ladle the into serving bowls. Garnish with black pepper and sprigs of chervil.

Fish Stew with Toasted Baguette
611

Serve with toasted slices of baguette that have been rubbed with crushed garlic.

612
SERVES 4

Chicken with Stuffing

PREPARATION TIME:
15 MINUTES

COOKING TIME:
6 HOURS 20 MINUTES

INGREDIENTS

1 chicken, cleaned
55g / 2 oz / ½ stick butter
300 g / 10 ½ oz / 2 cups sausage meat
150 g / 5 oz / 1 ½ cups fresh breadcrumbs
1 orange, juiced
2 tbsp flat-leaf parsley, roughly chopped

GARNISH

1 orange, sliced

- Preheat the oven to 190°C (170° fan) / 375F / gas 5.
- Combine the sausage meat, breadcrumbs, butter, orange juice, parsley and seasoning in a bowl.
- Mix well with your hands. Loosen the skin away from the chicken meat by working your hand between the skin and the meat on the breast.
- Do the same with the chicken legs as well. Carefully push the stuffing into the loosened space and spread it out evenly on top of the chicken breasts and between the legs and the skin.
- Place in a roasting tray and roast for 20 minutes Remove from the oven and transfer to a slow cooker.
- Cover with a lid and cook on a medium setting for 5-6 hours or until the juices run clear when the thicken part of the thigh is pierced.
- Remove from the slow cooker and place on a serving platter. Garnish with the sliced orange before serving.

Chicken with Apple Stuffing
613

Add 4 cored, peeled and finely diced eating apples to the stuffing mixture instead of the sausage meat.

614

SERVES 4

White Rose Veal

White Rose Veal with Cashews

615

Replace the gherkin garnish with 30g / 1 oz / ¼ cup cashews.

Rose Veal with Pancetta

616

Sauté 110 g / 4 oz / ⅔ cup pancetta lardons in a frying pan until golden and crisp. Drain on kitchen paper before using as a garnish.

Rose Veal with Parsnips

617

Omit the mushrooms and substitute with the same amount of parsnips.

PREPARATION TIME: 10 MINUTES

COOKING TIME: 6 HOURS 20 MINUTES

....

INGREDIENTS

2 tbsp sunflower oil
2 tbsp butter
900 g / 2 lb / 6 cups rose veal shoulder, diced into cubes
150 g / 5 oz / 2 cups button mushrooms
150 g / 5 oz / 1 cup pearl onion, blanched
250ml / 9 fl. oz / 1 cup crème fraiche

GARNISH
2 tbsp butter
2 cocktail gherkins, sliced
2 baby leeks, washed and chopped
handful cherry tomatoes, halved

- Coat the veal in the oil and season well.
- Heat a large casserole dish over a moderate heat until hot and seal the veal in batches until golden brown.
- Transfer the sealed veal to a slow cooker and reduce the heat under the casserole dish.
- Add the butter and sauté the onions and mushrooms for 3-4 minutes with some seasoning until the mushrooms are golden brown.
- Add to the veal in the slow cooker and cover with a lid.
- Cook on a medium setting for 6 hours until the veal is tender.
- Remove from the slow cooker after 6 hours and separate the mushrooms and onions from the veal.
- Stir the crème fraiche into the veal until coated and season again.
- Keep warm to one side.
- Melt the butter for the garnish in a large frying pan set over a moderate heat.
- Sauté the baby leeks with a little seasoning for 4-5 minutes, stirring occasionally until softened.
- Combine the veal, onions, mushrooms and baby leeks in a casserole dish.
- Garnish with the cherry tomato halves and sliced gherkin before serving.

618

SERVES 4

Irish Stew

PREPARATION TIME: 15 MINUTES

COOKING TIME: 6 HOURS

....

INGREDIENTS

4 tbsp sunflower oil
450 g / 1 lb / 3 cups lamb shoulder, diced
300 g / 10 ½ oz / 2 cups new potatoes, peeled and sliced
2 carrots, peeled and sliced
2 onions, chopped
1 tbsp juniper berries, lightly crushed
3 bay leaves
500 ml / 18 fl. oz / 2 cups lamb stock

GARNISH

1 tbsp curly leaf parsley leaves, finely chopped

- Heat half of the oil in a large casserole dish set over a moderate heat until hot.
- Season the lamb generously and seal in batches until golden brown.
- Transfer the sealed lamb to a slow cooker and reduce the heat under the casserole dish a little.
- Add the remaining oil and sauté the onions and carrots for 4-5 minutes, stirring occasionally.
- Add the bay leaves, potatoes, juniper berries, stock and a little seasoning and stir well.
- Pour on top of the lamb in the slow cooker and stir thoroughly.
- Cover and cook on a medium setting for 6 hours.
- Adjust the seasoning to taste after 6 hours and ladle the stew into serving dishes.
- Garnish with the chopped parsley before serving.

Irish Stew with Pearl Barley

619

Add 55 g / 2 oz / ¼ cup pearl barley to the slow cooker before cooking.

620

SERVES 6

Blanquette-Style Rose Veal

PREPARATION TIME :
15 MINUTES

COOKING TIME :
8 HOURS 25-30 MINUTES

....

INGREDIENTS

30 ml / 1 fl. oz / 2 tbsp sunflower oil
30 g / 1 oz / ¼ stick butter
900 g / 2 lb piece of veal roast
3 carrots, peeled and diced
75 g / 3 oz / 1 cup morels, brushed clean
30 g / 1 oz / ¼ stick unsalted butter
30 g / 1 oz / 2 tbsp plain (all-purpose) flour
500 ml / 18 fl. oz / 2 cups whole milk
salt and pepper

- Rub the veal roast with the oil and season well.
- Melt the butter in a pan set over a moderate heat.
- Seal the veal in the butter until golden brown in colour all over. Transfer to a slow cooker once sealed.
- Add the carrots and rearrange so that the veal roast is on top of the carrots.
- Melt the unsalted butter in a saucepan set over a medium heat.
- Whisk in the flour until you have a smooth roux.
- Cook for 1 minute before whisking in the milk in a slow, steady stream until you have a thickened sauce.
- Reduce the heat and simmer for 6-8 minutes.
- Season the sauce to taste before pouring over the veal in the slow cooker. Cook on a medium setting for 8 hours.
- Two hours before the veal is ready, add the morels.
- When the veal is ready, spoon the contents of the slow cooker into a casserole dish for presentation.

Rose Veal with Mornay Sauce

621

Add 150 g / 5 oz / 1 ½ cups grated Gruyere to the sauce to make a Mornay sauce.

622

SERVES 4

Chicken Tajine

- Heat the olive oil in a large casserole dish set over a moderate heat until hot.
- Season the chicken pieces and seal in batches until golden brown in colour all over.
- Transfer to a slow cooker and lower the heat under the casserole dish.
- Add the onion and garlic and sweat with a little salt for 5 minutes, stirring occasionally, until soft.
- Add the ground spices, honey, lemon, tomato, olives and stock and stir thoroughly.
- Pour over the chicken in the slow cooker and stir again.
- Cover with a lid and cook on a medium setting for 4 hours until the chicken is cooked through.
- Adjust the seasoning taste after 4 hours before ladling into serving dishes.
- Garnish with the basil and saffron before serving.

Chicken Tajine with Turnip

623

Add 1 peeled and finely diced turnip to the slow cooker before cooking.

PREPARATION TIME : 10 MINUTES

COOKING TIME :
4 HOURS 15-20 MINUTES

INGREDIENTS

55 ml / 2 fl. oz / ¼ cup olive oil
4 chicken legs, jointed
4 small lemons, quartered
4 large vine tomatoes, cored and cut into wedges
110 g / 4 oz / ⅔ cup pitted green olives
110 g / 4 oz / ⅔ cup pitted black olives
2 onions, finely chopped
2 cloves garlic, minced
2 tsp ras al hanout
1 tsp ground cinnamon
1 tsp ground cumin
1 tbsp honey
250 ml / 9 fl. oz / 1 cup chicken stock
salt and pepper

GARNISH
2 tbsp basil leaves, finely sliced
1 tsp saffron threads

624

SERVES 4

Rabbit and Mushroom Casserole

- Melt the half of the butter with the oil in a large casserole dish set over a moderate heat until hot.
- Season the rabbit pieces and seal in batches until golden brown in colour all over.
- Remove from the dish and transfer to a slow cooker before reduce the heat under the dish a little.
- Add the remaining butter and sweat the celery, wild button mushrooms and porcini mushrooms for a few minutes before deglazing the dish with the white wine.
- Stir well then add the herbs and stock.
- Pour over rabbit in the slow cooker and cover with a lid.
- Cook on a medium setting for 6 hours until the rabbit is cooked through.
- Adjust the seasoning to taste before spooning into a casserole dish with a slotted spoon.
- Serve immediately.

PREPARATION TIME :
15 MINUTES

COOKING TIME :
6 HOURS 15 MINUTES

INGREDIENTS

30 ml / 1 fl. oz / 2 tbsp sunflower oil
30 g / 1 oz / ¼ stick unsalted butter
2 small rabbits, jointed
4 sticks celery, peeled and chopped
150 g / 5 oz / 2 cups porcini mushrooms, sliced
75 g / 3 oz / 1 cup wild button mushrooms, brushed clean
125 ml / 4 ½ fl. oz / ½ cup dry white wine
500 ml / 18 fl. oz / 2 cups chicken stock
small handful of thyme sprigs
3 bay leaves
salt and pepper

625

SERVES 6-8

Roast Turkey with Grapes

Roast Turkey with Macadamia Nuts

626

Replace the chestnuts with the same volume of macadamia nuts.

Roast Turkey with Duck

627

Stuff the inner cavity of the turkey with 1 small lobe of duck foie gras.

Roast Turkey with Apples

628

Substitute the grapes for 1 sliced apple glazed in cinnamon and cook the same.

PREPARATION TIME: 15 MINUTES

COOKING TIME:
8 HOURS 30 MINUTES

INGREDIENTS

110g / 4 oz / 1 stick butter, softened
1 turkey, giblets removed
150 g / 5 oz / 1 cup white seedless grapes
150 g / 5 oz / 1 cup cooked chestnuts, peeled
3 pearl onions, peeled and halved

- Rub the chicken with the butter and season generously.
- Arrange the chestnuts, onion halves and grapes in the base of a slow cooker.
- Sit the turkey on top and cover with a lid.
- Cook on a medium setting for 8 hours.
- Remove after 8 hours and transfer the turkey and onions to a roasting tray.
- Preheat the oven to 190°C / 375F / gas 5.
- Cover the turkey with a sheet of aluminium foil and roast in the oven for 30 minutes until golden brown.
- Remove from the oven and let it rest for at least 20 minutes.
- Transfer to a serving platter and serve with the grapes, chestnuts and onion halves on the side.

629

SERVES 8

Roast Goose with Apple

- Heat the oven to 180°C (160°C fan) / 350F / gas 4. Roll the pastry on a floured surface to ½ cm thickness.
- Cut 4 tartlet moulds and press the pastry around the base. Prick the bases before lining with greaseproof paper, fill with beans and refrigerate.
- Sweat the shallots in a pan with butter and salt for 10 minutes adding apples and sugar; cook for 10 minutes.
- Combine the sausage, cranberries and seasoning and stuff the main cavity of the goose.
- Cover the goose with honey and season, placing in the oven for 1 hour; once cooked, transfer to a slow cooker on a medium setting for 8 hours.
- Transfer to a tray and cover with foil. Preheat the oven to 180°C (160°C fan) / 350F / gas 4. Remove the pastry from the fridge and fill with the apple filling.
- Bake in the oven for 25 minutes. Remove the tartlets and place alongside the goose and garnish with parsley.

Roast Goose with Pears

630

Replace the apple with the same amount of sliced pear and cook the same. with tarragon instead of parsley.

PREPARATION TIME :
20-25 MINUTES

COOKING TIME :
9 HOURS 15 MINUTES

INGREDIENTS

For the goose

55 g / 2 oz / ½ stick unsalted butter
1 goose, cleaned and trussed
450 g / 1 lb / 3 cups sausage meat
150 g / 5 oz / 1 cup dried cranberries
2 tbsp honey
salt and pepper

FOR THE TARTLETS

150 g / 5 oz / 1 sheet ready-made shortcrust pastry
plain (all-purpose) flour, for dusting
30 g / 1 oz / ¼ stick unsalted butter
2 apples, cored, peeled and sliced
4 banana shallots, finely sliced
1 tsp caster sugar
salt and pepper

631

SERVES 4

Salt-Cod and Ratatouille

- Flash-fry the vegetables in a large frying pan set over a moderate heat, using fresh olive oil for each batch.
- Transfer the vegetables to a slow cooker when each batch is done.
- Rub the salt-cod fillets with the olive oil and season a little.
- Sit on top of the vegetables in the slow cooker.
- Cover with a lid and cook on a medium setting for 4 hours until the fish is cooked and the vegetables are soft.
- Remove the salt cod from the slow cooker and pat dry.
- Spoon the vegetables onto two serving plates before sitting 2 cod fillets on top of each plate.
- Garnish with a little more seasoning and some chives before serving.

PREPARATION TIME :
15-20 MINUTES

COOKING TIME :
4 HOURS 20 MINUTES

INGREDIENTS

110 ml / 4 fl. oz / ½ cup olive oil
1 large courgette (courgette), diced
2 medium aubergines, diced
2 red peppers, deseeded and diced
1 green pepper, deseeded and diced
1 onion, finely chopped
2 cloves of garlic, minced
salt and pepper

GARNISH
2-3 chive stalks, halved

Salt-Cod with Passata

632

Add 250 ml / 9 fl. oz / 1 cup passata to the slow cooker along with the vegetables.

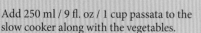

633

SERVES 4

Vegetable Casserole

PREPARATION TIME :
10 MINUTES

COOKING TIME : 6 HOURS

INGREDIENTS

30 ml / 1 fl. oz / 2 tbsp sunflower
or olive oil
2 medium onions, sliced
2 garlic cloves, crushed
1 carrot, chopped
1 celery stick, chopped
100 g / 4 oz cauliflower florets
3 tbsp dry white wine
400 g / 14 oz / 2 cups canned
tomatoes, chopped
4 beef tomatoes, skinned and sliced
2 green and 2 red peppers, sliced
1 tbsp Espelette pepper
1 tsp oregano
300 ml / 10 ½ fl. oz / 1 ¼ cups
vegetable stock
½ tsp sugar
salt and black pepper

- Heat the oil in a pan and gently sweat the onions, garlic, celery and carrot for 5 minutes stirring regularly.
- Mix in the espelette pepper and stir for 2 minutes.
- Add wine and boil off the alcohol for 2 minutes.
- Pour in the canned tomatoes and add the sliced beef tomatoes, cauliflower, peppers, oregano and sugar.
- Pour in the vegetable stock and bring to the boil
- Place casserole into the slow cooker and cook on medium for 4 to 8 hours.
- At the end of cooking, taste and add salt and black pepper as required.
- Spoon into serving dishes and garnish with chopped parsley.

Paprika Vegetable Casserole   **634**

Replace the Espelette pepper with the same
quantity of smoked paprika.

635

SERVES 6

Bacon and Cabbage Hotpot

PREPARATION TIME :
30 MINUTES

COOKING TIME : 4½ HOURS

INGREDIENTS

450 g / 1 lb / 3 cups bacon, chopped
200 g / 7 oz / 1 ⅓ cups smoked bacon
1 onion, chopped
1 can / 400 g haricot beans
1 celery stick, finely chopped
1 carrot, thinly sliced
1 red pepper, thinly sliced
½ Savoy (curly) cabbage, shredded and
blanched
2 garlic cloves
400 g / 14 oz / 2 cups canned tomatoes,
chopped
25g goose fat or 2 tbsp olive oil
1 tbsp oregano
1 clove, lightly crushed
2 tsp lemon juice
450 ml / 16 fl. oz / 2 cups stock
salt and pepper

GARNISH
30 ml / 2 tbsp chopped parsley

- Heat the oil and fry (sauté) the bacon and transfer to the crockpot
- Sweat the onion, garlic, celery, red pepper and carrot with a little salt for 5 minutes, stirring occasionally, then transfer to the slow cooker.
- In the saucepan mix the stock, tomatoes, oregano, lemon juice, cabbage and haricot beans. Stir well and bring to the boil.
- Transfer to the slow cooker and mix well with the other ingredients.
- Cover and cook on a medium setting for 4 hours.
- Pour into a casserole dish before serving and sprinkle with parsley.

Bacon and Kidney Bean Hotpot   **636**

Kidney beans may be used to replace haricot
beans if preferred.

637

SERVES 4

Lamb and Onion Stew

Lamb Stew
with Parsley

638

Stir through 2 tbsp finely
chopped flat-leaf parsley before
ladling into the casserole dish
at the end.

Lamb Stew
with Olives

639

Add 55 g / 2 oz / ⅓ cup pitted
black olives to the slow cooker
before cooking.

PREPARATION TIME :
15-20 MINUTES

COOKING TIME :
6 HOURS 20 MINUTES

INGREDIENTS

55 ml / 2 fl. oz / ¼ cup sunflower oil
900 g / 2 lb / 6 cups lamb neck fillet,
cut into 2" cubes
30 g / 1 oz / 2 tbsp plain
(all-purpose) flour
1 large onion, finely chopped
3 large carrots, peeled and diced
150 g / 5 oz / 1 cup pearl onions,
peeled
125 ml / 4 ½ fl. oz / ½ cup
dry white wine
500 ml / 18 fl. oz / 2 cups lamb stock
1 bouquet garni
salt and pepper

- Heat the sunflower oil in a casserole dish over a moderate heat.
- Season then sear the lamb in batches until golden brown in colour.
- Remove to a plate lined with kitchen paper to drain.
- Add the baby / pearl onions to the dish and saute for a few minutes.
- Remove to a separate plate lined with kitchen paper.
- Add the onion and carrot to the dish, reduce the heat and sweat with a little seasoning for 10-12 minutes, stirring occasionally.
- Increase the heat a little, add the lamb back to the dish, along with the baby onions and sprinkle the flour on top.
- Stir well to coat everything in the flour.
- Deglaze the base of the dish with the white wine, stirring until the wine has reduced by three-quarters.
- Add the bouquet garni and stock, stir thoroughly before pouring into a slow cooker.
- Cover and cook on a medium setting for 6 hours.
- Adjust the seasoning to taste and discard the bouquet garni.
- Ladle back into a casserole dish and serve.

640

SERVES 6-8 Tripe and Bacon Casserole

PREPARATION TIME :
15 MINUTES

COOKING TIME : 8 HOURS

INGREDIENTS

1 kg / 2 ¼ lb tripe cubed
1 calf's foot, de-boned and chopped
200 g / 7 oz / 1 ⅓ cup bacon lardons
3 onions, sliced
800 g / 1 lb 12 oz / 5 ⅓ cups carrots
1 bouquet garni
1 clove, crushed
125 ml / 4 ½ fl. oz / ½ cup Calvados
or apple brandy
250 ml / 9 fl. oz / 1 cup white wine
salt and pepper

GARNISH
2 tbsp flat-leaf parsley, chopped

- Pre-warm the slow cooker.
- Mix all the ingredients together in a large pan and bring to the boil.
- Place in the slow cooker and cook on medium heat for approximately 8 hours.
- Serve hot sprinkled with parsley

Tripe and Jelly 641

Drain and allow to chill. Use the juices to prepare an Aspic Jelly, mix in the meat and chill in the fridge until set. Serve cold.

642

SERVES 4 Sautéed Tuna with Rhubarb

PREPARATION TIME :
20 MINUTES

COOKING TIME : 4 HOURS

INGREDIENTS

4 Albacore or white tuna steaks
30 ml / 2 tbsp vegetable oil
500 ml / 18 fl. oz / 2 cups of dry white
wine
250 ml / 9 fl. oz / 1 cup vegetable
stock
1 tsp caster (superfine) sugar
3 cloves garlic, crushed
1 bay leaf, torn
1 tsp of ground coriander
5 spring onions (scallions),
sliced finely
1 tsp fennel seed, powdered
1 tsp whole fennel seed
½ red chilli, finely chopped
2 fennel, finely sliced
110 g / 4 oz rhubarb, cut into chunks
salt and pepper to taste

GARNISH
coriander

- Put the wine, stock, sugar, bay leaf, coriander, fennel seeds, powder and leaves, and rhubarb into the slow cooker and cook on medium for 4 hours then turn off, taste and adjust seasoning. If rhubarb is too tart–add further sugar to taste and stir.
- In a shallow pan, heat the oil and fry the tuna steaks until golden.
- Add the garlic, spring onions (scallions) and chilli to the pan and cook, stirring for a further 3 minutes.
- To serve, spoon rhubarb and fennel sauce into the centre of the plate and place the tuna steak and spring onion mixture on top.
- Sprinkle with coriander leaves and serve immediately.

Sweet Sauteed Tuna 643

Add 1 tbsp of rice vinegar to the rhubarb and fennel sauce at the end of cooking, for a more 'sweet and sour' sauce.

644

SERVES 4-6 # Roast Chicken with Chips

- Oil and preheat the slow cooker. Line with 2 folded strips of foil that intersect and overhang the slow cooker (to be used to lift out the chicken after cooking).
- Brush the chicken with oil or fat, and sprinkle with herbs.
- Place breast side up in slow cooker with lid on and cook on low for 8 hours.
- Remove the chicken and place breast side up on a roasting dish. Roast in a hot oven 220°C (200° fan) / 425F / gas 7 for 30 minutes .
- At the same time, coat the vegetable chips in hot oil and roast in a separate roasting tin for 45 minutes, turning them over once during cooking.
- 15 minutes before the chips are ready, remove the chicken and set aside under foil to rest.
- Carve the chicken and serve with vegetable chips.

Chicken with Beetroot Chips 645

Beetroot also works well in the roasted chips mix.

PREPARATION TIME :
25 MINUTES

COOKING TIME : 8 HOURS

INGREDIENTS

1.75 kg / 4 lb chicken, tied at legs and wings
30 ml / 2 tbsp goose fat or vegetable oil
½ tsp dried oregano
½ tsp dried thyme
450 g / 1 lb / 3 cups potatoes, peeled and cut into chips
450 g / 1 lb / 3 cups carrots, peeled and cut into chips
450 g / 1 lb / 3 cups parsnips, peeled and cut into chips
125 ml / 4 ½ fl. oz / ½ cup olive oil
salt

646

SERVES 4 # Rabbit with Herbs and Vegetables

- Heat the oil and fry (sauté) the rabbit joints until golden brown. Remove and set aside
- In the remaining oil, fry the bacon, celery, onion, carrot and garlic for 10 minutes.
- Cover with wine and stock and bring to the boil
- Transfer the stock, lemon juice, rabbit, herbs and vegetables to the slow cooker and mix well.
- Cover and cook on a low setting for 8 hours.
- 30 minutes before the end of cooking, boil the potatoes with a pinch of salt in a saucepan until tender but not breaking, then add these to the rabbit casserole and mix well.
- Spoon ½ cup of the juice from the pot, and mix with the cornflour (cornstarch) until thickened. Add this back to the casserole and stir through to thicken.
- To serve sprinkle with parsley.

Chicken with Herbs and Vegetables 647

Substitute the rabbit for a whole chicken and cook in the same way.

PREPARATION TIME :
30 MINUTES

COOKING TIME : 8 HOURS

INGREDIENTS

1 rabbit, jointed
200 g / 7 oz smoked streaky bacon, chopped
1 onion, chopped
1 celery stick, finely chopped
4 carrot, thinly sliced
3 garlic cloves
2 tbsp olive oil
1 tbsp oregano
2 tsp lemon juice
2 large sprigs of rosemary
150 ml / 5 fl. oz / ⅔ cup white wine
450 ml / 16 fl. oz/ 2 cups stock
2 toss cornflour (cornstarch)
salt and pepper
450 g / 1 lb / 3 cups new potatoes, peeled

GARNISH
2 tbsp chopped parsley

648

SERVES 4

Lamb Red Curry

Lamb Green Curry

649

Replace the red curry paste with the same volume of green curry paste for lamb green curry.

Creamy Red Curry

650

Replace half of the stock with 250 ml / 9 fl. oz / 1 cup coconut milk for a creamier curry.

PREPARATION TIME :
15-20 MINUTES

COOKING TIME :
4 HOURS 20 MINUTES

INGREDIENTS

55 ml / 2 fl. oz / ¼ cup groundnut oil
675 g / 1 lb 8 oz / 4 ½ cups lamb shoulder, diced
150 g / 5 oz / 2 cups baby spinach leaves
2 medium white potatoes, diced
1 onion, finely sliced
1 tbsp ginger, minced
3 cloves garlic, minced
500 ml / 18 fl. oz / 2 cups lamb stock
110 g / 4 oz / ⅔ cup Thai red curry paste
1 tbsp brown sugar
1 tbsp fish sauce
juice of 1 lime
pepper

- Heat the groundnut oil in a large casserole dish set over a moderate heat.
- Seal the diced lamb in batches until golden brown all over, moving each batch to a slow cooker.
- Reduce the heat under the dish before adding the onion, ginger and garlic to the dish.
- Saute for 4-5 minutes, stirring occasionally.
- Add the paste and fry gently for 1-2 minutes, stirring occasionally.
- Add the potato to the dish, then cover with the stock and stir well.
- Pour over the lamb in the slow cooker and cover with a lid.
- Cook on a medium setting for 4 hours.
- Once the lamb and potato are soft, adjust the seasoning with the sugar, lime juice, fish sauce and pepper.
- Stir in the spinach until wilted.
- Spoon into a serving dish and allow to stand for a few minutes before serving.

651

SERVES 4

Autumn Turkey Casserole

- Coat the turkey in the sunflower oil and season generously.
- Heat a large casserole dish over a moderate heat until hot and seal the turkey in batches until golden brown in colour all over.
- Transfer each batch to a slow cooker when done.
- Reduce the heat under the casserole dish and add the butter.
- Saute the onion, carrot and turnip in the butter for 4-5 minutes, stirring occasionally.
- Spoon into the slow cooker and cover with the stock.
- Cover with a lid and cook on a medium setting for 6 hours.
- Adjust the seasoning to taste after 6 hours before spooning into individual cast-iron serving dishes using a slotted spoon.

Autumn Veal Casserole   652

Replace the turkey with 900 g / 2 lb / 6 cups veal fillet that has been diced into 2" cubes.

PREPARATION TIME :
15 MINUTES

COOKING TIME :
6 HOURS 15-20 MINUTES

INGREDIENTS

55 ml / 2 fl. oz / ¼ cup sunflower oil
1 tbsp unsalted butter
4 turkey breasts, diced
600 g / 1 lb 5 oz / 4 cups pearl onions, peeled and halved
450 g / 1 lb / 3 cups carrots, peeled and sliced
1 small turnip, peeled and diced
500 ml / 18 fl. oz / 2 cups chicken stock
salt and freshly ground black pepper

653

SERVES 4

Tuna Tagine with Spices

- Pre-warm the Slow cooker or Crockpot
- Heat the oil and fry the onion, peppers and garlic until softened.
- Add the spices, stir well and cook through for 3 minutes.
- Add the lemon juice, dates, honey and tinned tomatoes and stir. Bring gently to the boil
- Mean while fry the tuna lightly on both sides to seal.
- Place the tuna and the hot spicy stock and vegetables into the slow cooker and cook on a low setting for 3 hours.
- Ten minutes before the end of cooking, stir in the chopped coriander.
- Serve hot with rice, couscous or pitta bread.

Tangy Monkfish Tagine   654

The tuna may be replaced by any other firm fish. For example Monkfish works well with this dish.

PREPARATION TIME 10 MINUTES

COOKING TIME 45 MINUTES

INGREDIENTS

4 tuna Steaks
4 garlic cloves, crushed
60 ml / 2 fl. oz / ¼ cup olive or vegetable oil
1 large onion, finely chopped
1 red pepper finely sliced
1 green pepper finely sliced
400 g / 14 oz / 2 cups canned tomatoes, chopped
50 g / 2 oz dates finely chopped
10 ml / 1 tbsp clear honey
1 lemon, zest and juice
2 tbsp coriander, chopped finely

SPICES

1 level tsp each of ground cumin, cinnamon, ginger, smoked paprika, turmeric.

655

SERVES 4

Milan-style Oxtail

- Coat the oxtail in the olive oil and season generously.
- Heat a large casserole dish over a moderate heat until hot.
- Seal the oxtail in batches until golden brown.
- Transfer the sealed oxtail to a slow cooker and reduce the heat under the dish a little.
- Add the carrot, garlic, celery and sauté with a little seasoning for 2-3 minutes stirring frequently.
- Stir in the tomato puree and beef stock.
- Add the rosemary, thyme and bay leaf then pour into the slow cooker.
- Cover with a lid and cook on a low setting for 8 hours until the oxtail is soft and can be pulled apart easily between your fingers.
- Adjust the seasoning to taste and ladle into serving dishes. Garnish with rosemary leaves before serving.

PREPARATION TIME: 15 MINUTES

COOKING TIME: 8 HOURS

INGREDIENTS

75 ml / 3 fl. oz / ⅓ cup olive oil
900 g / 2 lbs oxtail, cut into slices
2 cloves garlic, minced
4 carrots, peeled and diced
2 sticks celery, sliced
1 tbsp tomato puree
500ml / 18 fl. oz / 2 cups beef stock
1 sprig rosemary
1 sprig thyme
1 bay leaf

GARNISH
1 tbsp rosemary leaves

Provençal-style Pate

656

SERVES 4

Slowly-cooked Beef Chop

657

SERVES 4

PREPARATION TIME: 20 MINUTES

COOKING TIME:
4 HOURS 40 MINUTES

INGREDIENTS

20cm x 15cm / 8 x 6" squares of pig's caul, rinsed in cold water
4 tbsp olive oil
300 g / 10 ½ oz / 4 cups Swiss chard

300 g / 10 ½ oz / 2 cups pork shoulder, diced
150 g / 5 oz / 1 cup pancetta, cut into lardons
150 g / 5 oz / 1 cup pork liver, soaked in milk for a few hours then drained
55g / 2 oz / ⅓ cup pork back fat, diced
6 cloves garlic, crushed
2 sprigs thyme
2 sprigs rosemary

- Dry and dice the pork liver. Heat a large saucepan over a moderate heat until hot and add the back fat.
- Sauté for a few minutes until it starts to render, then add the pork shoulder, pancetta, liver and seasoning.
- Cook for a few minutes stirring occasionally before spooning into a slow cooker. Cook on a low setting for 4 hours.
- After 4 hours, strain the meat and set to one side. Preheat the oven to 190°C (170° fan) / 375F / gas 5.
- Heat some of the olive oil in a pan then add the Swiss chard and wilt with some seasoning until soft.
- Drain and press well to extract the excess liquid. Finely chop the Swiss chard and and mix with the meat mixture.
- Form into 8 rough balls and wrap in the pig's caul.
- Secure using toothpicks then arrange in a roasting tray.
- Add the garlic and herbs and drizzle with the remaining olive oil and seasoning.
- Roast for 15-20 minutes until golden brown.

PREPARATION TIME :10 MINUTES

COOKING TIME :
4 HOURS 20 MINUTES

INGREDIENTS

30 ml / 1 fl. oz / 2 tbsp sunflower oil
30 g / 1 oz / ¼ stick unsalted butter
2 x 450 g / 1 lb rib-eye steaks, with

bone attached
3 bay leaves
a few sprigs of rosemary
salt and pepper

- Rub the steaks with the oil and season generously.
- Heat a large frying pan set over a high heat until hot and smoking.
- Seal the steaks until golden brown in colour on both sides.
- Transfer to a slow cooker, add the herbs and cover with a lid.
- Cook on a medium setting for 4 hours.
- Remove after 4 hours and pat dry.
- Heat a large frying pan over a moderate heat until hot and melt half of the butter.
- Add the steaks to the butter, one at a time, using fresh butter for each steak until lightly coloured all over.
- Remove from the pan and let the steaks rest for a few minutes before serving.

658
SERVES 2

Pigeon and Kumquat Tagine

- Heat the oil and fry the pigeons all over until golden brown. Remove and place in the slow cooker.
- In the remaining oil, fry the onion, and garlic until softened and add the spices, stir well and cook through for 3 minutes.
- Add the stock, lemon juice, honey and tinned tomatoes and stir. Bring gently to the boil
- Place the pigeons and vegetables, with the boiling spicy stock liquid into the slow cooker and cook on a low setting for 6 hours.
- 30 minutes before the end of cooking, stir in the chickpeas, kumquats and coriander.
- Serve hot with rice, couscous or pitta bread.

Guinea Fowl Tagine
659

Pigeons may be replaced easily with Guinea Fowl if desired, and cooked in the same way.

PREPARATION TIME :20 MINUTES

COOKING TIME : 6 HOURS

INGREDIENTS

2 x whole prepared pigeons
4 garlic cloves, crushed
60 ml / 2 fl. oz / ¼ cup olive oil
1 large onion, finely chopped
400 g / 14 oz / 2 cups canned chopped tomatoes
2 tbsp clear honey
1 lemon, zest and juice
400 g / 14 oz / 2 cups canned chickpeas, drained
800 ml / 1 pint 12 fl. oz / 3 ½ cups chicken stock
juice of ½ lemon
2 tbsp coriander, roughly chopped
325 g / 11 oz / 3 cups kumquats

SPICES
1 level tsp each of ground coriander, ground cumin, cinnamon, ginger, sweet paprika, turmeric and ½ level tsp cayenne pepper and salt. 2 cloves crushed

660
SERVES 4

Lamb and Bacon Casserole

- Heat the oil and fry (sauté) the lamb cubes until brown and transfer to the slow cooker.
- Sweat the onions, garlic and carrots for 5 minutes. Cover with the tinned tomatoes, white wine, stock and herbs. Boil for 20 minutes.
- Transfer all the ingredients to the slow cooker.
- Cover and cook on a low setting for 8 hours.
- Taste and adjust seasoning
- Pour into a casserole dish before serving and sprinkle with parsley.

Lamb Casserole with Dumplings
661

Serve with rosemary herbed dumplings added 20 minutes before end of cooking.

PREPARATION TIME :10 MINUTES

COOKING TIME : 8 HOURS 30 MINUTES

INGREDIENTS

1 kg / 2 lb 2 oz fillet neck of lamb cut into 2 cm cubes
110 g / 4 oz / ⅔ cup streaky bacon
30 ml / 2 tbsp vegetable oil
2 garlic cloves, minced
1 tsp tomato puree
450 g / 1 lb / 2 cups canned chopped tomatoes
150 ml / 5 fl. oz / ⅔ cup white wine
150 ml / 5 fl. oz / ⅔ beef or chicken stock
2 sprigs of rosemary or 1 tsp dried rosemary
2 carrots, peeled and thinly sliced
1 bunch thyme
salt and ground black pepper

662

SERVES 4

Chicken with Olives

PREPARATION TIME :
20 MINUTES

COOKING TIME : 6 HOURS

....

INGREDIENTS

1 chicken jointed into 4 quarters
100 g / 4 oz / ⅔ cup bacon lardons
30 ml / 2 tbsp vegetable oil
3 garlic cloves, minced
150 ml / 5 fl. oz / ⅔ cup white wine
150 ml / 5 fl. oz / ⅔ cup chicken stock
2 tsp thyme, chopped
2 tsp basil, chopped
200 g / 7 oz / 2 cups green olives
50 g / 2 oz / ½ cup baby onions, blanched
50 g / 2 oz / ⅔ mushrooms, chopped
salt and ground black pepper

GARNISH
fresh parsley

- Heat the oil and fry (sauté) the chicken pieces until brown and transfer to the slow cooker.
- Sweat the onions, garlic, mushrooms and lardons for 5 minutes. Cover with the wine, stock, and herbs and bring to the boil.
- Transfer all the ingredients to the slow cooker, add the olives and stir gently to mix.
- Cover and cook on a low setting for 6 hours.
- Taste and adjust seasoning.
- Pour into a casserole dish before serving and sprinkle with finely shredded parsley.

Chicken with Stuffed Olives   663

This recipe also works well with stuffed olives for a slightly different flavour.

664

SERVES 4

Pork with Fromage Frais

PREPARATION TIME :15 MINUTES

COOKING TIME : 8 HOURS
30 MINUTES

....

INGREDIENTS

1.5 kg / 3 lb 5 oz boneless pork roasting joint
30 ml / 2 tbsp vegetable oil
1 garlic clove, minced
1 medium onion, sliced
150 ml / 5 fl. oz / ⅔ cup dry chicken stock
2 tbsp fresh sage, chopped
200 g / 7 oz / 2 cups pitted green olives
4 large or beef tomatoes sliced
salt and ground black pepper
2 tbsp fromage frais

GARNISH
fresh sage leaves

- Wipe the pork joint and rub salt and pepper into it.
- Heat the oil and fry (sauté) the pork until brown and transfer to the slow cooker.
- Sweat the onions and garlic for 5 minutes. Cover with the stock and bring to the boil.
- Transfer all the ingredients to the slow cooker, placing the pork joint on top of all the other ingredients
- Cover and cook on a low setting for 8 hours. Remove from pot and rest covered for 20 minutes.
- Stir the fromage frais into the olive mixture and warm through.
- Taste the mixture and adjust seasoning as necessary.
- Carve the pour, and spoon over the olive mixture to serve. Garnish with fresh sage leaves.

Cider Pork with Fromage Frais   665

Half a glass of cider may be added to the recipe at the pre slow-cooker stage.

666

SERVES 4

Chicken and Green Pepper Casserole

Chicken and Mixed Pepper Casserole

667

Replace the green pepper with a mix of red, yellow and green pepper slices to add colour.

Chicken and Coriander Casserole

668

Stir in a cup of chopped fresh coriander (cilantro) 2 minutes before serving for added flavour.

Chicken and Jalapeno Casserole

669

Substitute the green pepper for 1 large, chopped jalapeno pepper for a spicier casserole.

PREPARATION TIME :
25 MINUTES

COOKING TIME : 8 HOURS

INGREDIENTS

4 whole chicken legs or 1 chicken jointed
Salt and freshly ground pepper
30 ml / 1 fl. oz / 2 tbsp vegetable oil
2 tbsp butter
2 large garlic cloves, minced
¼ tsp cayenne pepper
6 spring onions (scallions), thinly sliced
3 green peppers, thinly sliced
4 beef tomatoes, skinned and chopped
500 ml / 1 pint / 2 cups chicken stock
250ml / ½ pint / 1 cup vegetable stock
1 tbsp tomato paste

GARNISH
1 cup chopped parsley leaves

- Warm the slow cooker.
- Heat the butter and oil in a heavy based pan over a medium heat.
- Add the chicken pieces and brown all over–remove and leave to the side.
- Gently fry the spring onions (scallions) and garlic for 3 minutes.
- Add the sliced peppers and stir well for 2 minutes.
- Stir in the cayenne pepper and cook for 1 further minute.
- Return the chicken to the pan, pour over the chicken and vegetable stock.
- Add the tomato paste and tomatoes, stir well and bring to the boil.
- Pour the casserole into the slow cooker and cook for 8 hours on a medium setting.
- Taste and adjust seasoning.
- Garnish with parsley leaves and serve.

670

SERVES 4

Chicken with Black Olives

PREPARATION TIME: 10 MINUTES

COOKING TIME : 6 HOURS 15 MINUTES

INGREDIENTS

4 chicken breasts with skin on or 1 chicken jointed into 4 quarters
pinch of saffron strands soaked in 3 tbsp of warm milk
1 lemon, zest and juice
30 ml / 2 tbsp vegetable oil
2 medium onions, sliced
4 vine tomatoes, quartered
30 ml / 2 tbsp dry white wine
30 ml / 2 tbsp chicken stock
100 g / 4 oz / 1 cup black Kalamata olives sliced
salt and ground black pepper

GARNISH
fresh parsley

- Pre-warm the slow cooker.
- Heat the oil and fry (sauté) the chicken pieces until brown and transfer to the slow cooker.
- Lightly fry the onions for 5 minutes. Combine with the wine, stock, and lemon zest and juice.
- Transfer all the ingredients to the slow cooker with the olives and the strained saffron milk and stir gently to mix.
- Cover with the lid and cook on a low setting for 6 hours.
- Taste and adjust seasoning.
- Pour into a casserole dish before serving and sprinkle with finely shredded parsley.

Chicken with Stuffed Olives
671

This recipe also works well with stuffed olives for a slightly different flavour.

672

SERVES 4

Stewed Vegetables with Sage

PREPARATION TIME: 15 MINUTES

COOKING TIME: 4 HOURS

INGREDIENTS

4 tbsp olive oil
2 large red peppers, deseeded and chopped
300 g / 10 ½ oz / 2 cups parsnips, peeled and quartered
300 g / 10 ½ oz / 2 cups carrots, peeled and quartered
2 tbsp flaked (slivered) almonds, lightly toasted
handful sage leaves
3 sage leaves, cut chiffonade

- Combine the parsnips and carrots in a large mixing bowl.
- Add the olive oil and seasoning and toss well.
- Heat a large frying pan set over a moderate heat until hot then pan-fry the carrots and parsnips for 3-4 minutes until lightly coloured, tossing and stirring occasionally.
- Transfer the contents of the frying pan to a slow cooker and add the peppers and the sage leaves.
- Cook on a medium setting for 4 hours until the vegetables are soft and tender.
- Spoon into serving bowls using a slotted spoon and garnish with the finely sliced sage and almonds before serving.

Stewed Vegetables with Thyme
673

Replace the sage with thyme and substitute the almonds for toasted, chopped almonds.

674

SERVES 4

Capon in White Truffle

- Grease and preheat the slow cooker.
- Clean and pat the capon dry, then brush with oil and sprinkle with salt and pepper.
- Place in a hot wok and seal until golden in colour all over. Remove the chicken and place to the side.
- Lightly fry the garlic, cauliflower and juniper berries in the truffle oil for 3 minutes, then spoon into the slow cooker.
- Rest the chicken on top, breast side up. Place the lid on and cook on low heat for 6 hours.
- Warm the cream through in a pan for 10 minutes without boiling, add the cooked pasta then pour this mixture over the capon and slow cook on low for a further hour.
- Season to taste. Remove the chicken and vegetables and serve on a plate or carver.

PREPARATION TIME :
25 MINUTES

COOKING TIME : 7 HOURS

INGREDIENTS

1.75 kg / 4lb Capon, cleaned and trussed
30 ml / 2 tbsp vegetable oil
2 garlic cloves, crushed
100 ml / 4 fl. oz / ¾ cup white wine
100 ml / 4 fl. oz / ¾ cup stock
150 g / 5 oz / 1 cup cauliflower florets
568 ml / 1 pint / 2 cups double cream
15 ml / 1 tbsp white truffle oil
350 g / 12 oz cooked pasta shells
15 ml / 1 tbsp juniper berries
salt and black pepper

Cheesy Capon

675

Parmesan shavings over the final dish work very well and add a cheesy twist.

676

SERVES 4

Pheasant and Quince Tagine

- Pre-warm the slow cooker.
- Heat the oil and fry the pheasant pieces until golden brown, remove to the side.
- Gently fry the quince pieces until lightly browned, remove to the side
- Adding more oil if required, cook the spices (except the coriander), garlic and chilli flakes in the remaining oil, stir well and cook through for 3 minutes.
- Add the lemon zest and juice, honey, stock and passata and stir. Bring gently to the boil
- Place al the ingredients into the slow cooker and cook on low for 8 hours to let the flavours meld.
- At the end of cooking, stir in the chopped fresh coriander gently.
- Serve hot with rice, couscous or pitta bread.

PREPARATION TIME :
30 MINUTES

COOKING TIME : 8 HOURS

INGREDIENTS

2 x pheasants, jointed and prepared
60 ml / 4 tsp / ¼ cup Olive or vegetable oil
4 garlic cloves, crushed
¼ tsp chilli flakes
1 tsp ginger powder
1 tsp cumin
1 tsp turmeric
1 tsp cinnamon
tsp paprika
1 x 440 g / 15 ½ oz can passata or pureed tomatoes
½ ltr good stock
1 lemon zest and juice
bunch of fresh coriander chopped
1 green pepper finely sliced
10 ml / 2 tbsp clear honey
2 lb quince, blanched, peeled and quartered lengthways and drizzled with lemon juice

Pheasant and Apple Tagine

677

The quince may be replaced with the equivalent quantity of apple slices with no impairment to flavour.

678
SERVES 6

Leg of Lamb with Potatoes

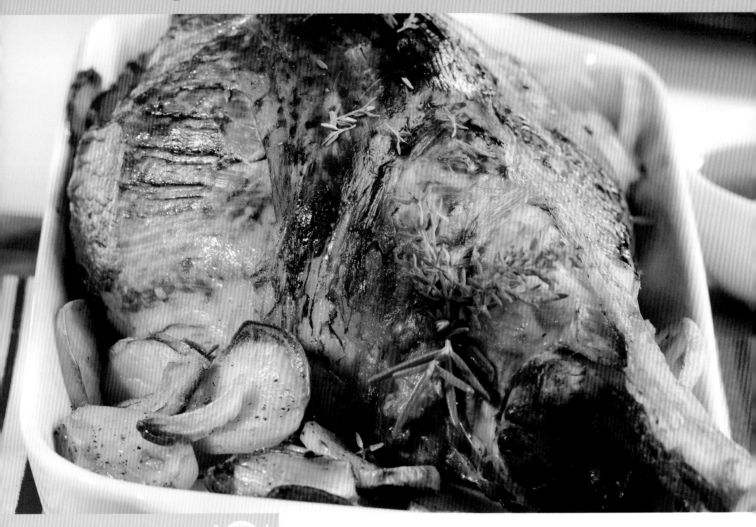

Minted Lamb with Potatoes
679

The garlic and rosemary may be replaced with finely chopped mint leaves.

Lamb with Rich Gravy
680

Add 2 cups of red wine to the slow Cooker at the start of the cooking process for rich flavoured meat and gravy.

Leg of Lamb with Butternut Squash
681

Replace the potato with half a deseeded butternut squash. Roast with thyme for 20 minutes until golden.

PREPARATION TIME :
15 MINUTES

COOKING TIME : 6 - 8 HOURS

INGREDIENTS

1 leg of lamb, cleaned and trimmed
2 tbsp goose fat or vegetable oil
2 tbsp fresh rosemary
3 garlic cloves, crushed
with a little oil

SAUTÉ POTATOES
1.5 kg / 3 ⅓ lbs waxy potatoes
(eg Charlotte, Maris Piper, King Edwards) boiled for 5 minutes, cooled and sliced thickly
3 tbsp goose fat or vegetable oil
Salt

- In a large thick-based pan, heat the fat or oil and sear the leg of lamb all over until browned.
- Put the lamb into the slow cooker, spread evenly with the garlic and oil paste and sprinkle with rosemary.
- Cover with the lid and cook for 6 to 8 hours on a low setting.
- Turn off the slow cooker and leave the lid off, allowing lamb to rest.
- Meanwhile heat oil in a wok or frying pan, and sauté the sliced cooked potatoes until golden brown. Drain on kitchen paper sprinkle with salt and keep warm in the oven.
- Using the lamb juices, make a gravy. Slice the meat and serve with the sauté potatoes and gravy immediately.

682

SERVES 4

Salt-Cod with Rice

- Drain the salt-cod from the soaking water and pat dry with kitchen towel and dust with flour
- Heat the oil in a pan and gently sauté the cod for 3 minutes until golden. Place into the slow cooker.
- In the remaining oil, add crushed garlic cloves and onions and sauté for further 2 minutes. Cover with wine and boil to reduce a little.
- Rinse and shred spinach, adding it to the wine mixture with the puree and capers and cook until the spinach has wilted. Add all ingredients to the slow cooker and cook on low for 4 hours.
- 15 minutes before the end of cooking, add the chick peas and dill weed, stir through and replace the lid, allowing to warm for 15 minutes.
- Adjust the seasoning to taste after 4 hours.
- Spoon into serving dishes and garnish with dill.
- Serve immediately.

PREPARATION TIME :
15 MINUTES

COOKING TIME : 4 HOURS

INGREDIENTS

600 g / 1 lb 5 oz / 3 cups salt cod (soaked overnight in water)
450 g / 1 lb canned chickpeas
1 red onion, finely chopped
30 ml / 1 fl. oz / 2 tbsp Olive or Sunflower Oil
300 g / 10 ½ oz / 2 cups spinach
3 cloves of garlic
1 cup dry white wine
450 g / 1 lb passata
60 ml / 4 tbsp tomato puree or paste
3 tsp green salted capers
250 ml / 9 fl. oz / 1 cup vegetable stock
salt and pepper to taste
2 tbsp dill weed, finely chopped

GARNISH
several sprigs of dill

684

SERVES 4

Spicy Leg of Lamb

- Wipe the leg of lamb and rub the goose fat into the skin
- Rub all over with the herbs and spices mixed with the olive oil and butter and sit in the slow cooker
- Surround with the onions slices.
- Cover and cook on a low setting for 8 hours.
- Preheat the oven to 190°C (170° fan) / 375F / gas 5. Remove the lamb and set in a roasting tray. Place in the top of a hot oven for 30 minutes.
- Remove and let it rest, covered, for 15 minutes before carving.
- Meanwhile, use the slow cooker juices to make a gravy.

PREPARATION TIME :
20 MINUTES

COOKING TIME : 8 HOURS

INGREDIENTS

2 kg / 2 lb 8 oz leg of lamb
30 ml / 2 tbsp goose fat
salt and ground black pepper
2 sprigs of fresh rosemary
2 cloves of garlic, crushed with salt
1 tbsp ground cumin
1 tbsp thyme leaves, finely chopped
½ tsp smoked paprika
1 large onion, finely sliced
2 tbsp olive oil
1 knob of butter
½ tsp ground coriander

GARNISH
sprinkle of smoked paprika

Mustard Leg of Lamb

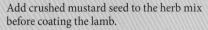

685

Add crushed mustard seed to the herb mix before coating the lamb.

686

SERVES 4

Roasted Bass with Tomatoes

PREPARATION TIME: 15 MINUTES

COOKING TIME: 3 HOURS 20 MINUTES

....

INGREDIENTS

8 sea bass fillets, pin-boned and skinned
110ml / 4 fl. oz / ½ cup olive oil
450 g / 1 lb / 2 ½ cups tomatoes, halved
2 bay leaves
1 tsp coriander seeds, lightly roasted
1 tbsp tarragon, finely chopped
1 tbsp flat-leaf parsley, finely chopped
4 sprigs oregano, to garnish

- Place the tomatoes, bay leaves, coriander seeds, half of the olive oil and some seasoning in a slow cooker.
- Cook on a medium setting for 3 hours until the tomatoes are soft and stewed.
- Preheat the oven to 190°C (170° fan) / 375F / gas 5.
- Rub the sea bass fillets with the olive oil and season well.
- Arrange on a roasting tray and roast for 6-8 minutes until firm yet springy to the touch and starting to flake.
- Once the tomatoes are ready, stir the chopped herbs through them and ladle onto serving plates with some of the herb sauce.
- Sit the sea bass fillets on top and garnish with a sprig of oregano before serving.

Roasted Hake with Olives

687

Substitute the sea bass for hake, using four 200 g / 7 oz fillets, one per serving. Add 55 g / 2 oz chopped black olives to the tomatoes as well as a tablespoon of capers.

688

SERVES 4

Provençal-style Stew

PREPARATION TIME: 20 MINUTES

COOKING TIME :
6 HOURS 20 MINUTES

....

INGREDIENTS

4 tbsp sunflower oil
900 g / 2 lbw / 6 cups chuck steak, cut into cubes
250 g / 9 oz / 1 ⅔ cups preserved green olives, drained
110g / 4 oz / ⅔ cup pancetta, cut into lardons
2 onions, roughly chopped
2 cloves garlic, roughly chopped
450 g / 1 lb / 2 ½ cups tomatoes, quartered
250ml / 9 fl. oz / 1 cup beef stock
250ml / 9 fl. oz / 1 cup red wine
1 bay leaf
3 sprigs of thyme

- Coat the steak in the oil and season generously.
- Heat a large frying pan over a moderate heat until hot.
- Seal the beef in batches until golden brown, moving each batch to the slow cooker.
- When you have finished sealing the beef, reduce the heat under the pan and sauté the lardons of pancetta for 2-3 minutes, stirring occasionally.
- Add the onions and garlic and cook them until they are starting to soften.
- Deglaze the pan with the red wine, then transfer everything to the slow cooker. Add the bay leaf, thyme, tomatoes, olives and beef stock.
- Cook in the slow cooker on a medium setting for 6 hours until the beef is tender and can be pulled apart easily between your fingers.
- Adjust the seasoning to taste before ladling into serving bowls. Serve immediately.

Provençal-style Stew with Olives

689

Change the green olives for pitted black olives.

690

SERVES 4

Sautéed Rice with Shrimps

Sautéed Rice with Cream

691

Instead of using chopped coriander, stir through chopped flat-leaf parsley and 55ml / 2 oz / ¼ cup double cream instead.

Chicken and Sautéed Rice

692

Replace the prawns (shrimps) for 2 large chicken breasts that have been diced.

Sautéed Prawns with Rice

693

Substitute the shrimps for 300 g / 10 ½ oz / 2 cups raw prawns and cook the same.

PREPARATION TIME: 15 MINUTES

COOKING TIME: 4 HOURS

....

INGREDIENTS

2 tbsp olive oil
200 ml / 7 fl. oz / 1 cup basmati rice
400 ml / 14 fl. oz / 2 cups chicken stock
300 g / 10 ½ oz / 2 cups raw prawns (shrimps), tails intact
250 g / 9 oz / 2 cups peas, fresh or frozen
1 stalk lemongrass, very finely sliced
1 green chilli pepper, deseeded and finely chopped
1 bay leaf
coriander, finely chopped

- Heat half of the olive oil in a large frying pan over a moderate heat until hot.
- Sauté the chilli pepper, lemongrass and rice in the oil for a minute, stirring frequently.
- Transfer everything to a slow cooker and cover with the stock and the bay leaf.
- Cook on a low setting for 4 hours until the rice has absorbed the stock and is tender, stirring half way through.
- Meanwhile, heat the remaining olive oil in a large frying pan over a moderate heat until hot.
- Season the prawns (shrimps) then pan-fry them for a minute, tossing occasionally.
- Add the rice and peas and reduce the heat a little, making sure everything is warmed through.
- Discard the bay leaf, stir through the chopped coriander (cilantro) and adjust the seasoning to taste.
- Spoon onto serving plates and garnish with any remaining coriander (cilantro) before serving.

694

SERVES 4

Roast Duck

PREPARATION TIME :
15 MINUTES

COOKING TIME : 8 HOURS

INGREDIENTS

1.75 kg / 4 lb duck
salt, pepper and paprika
30 ml / 2 tbsp sesame oil
30 ml / 2 tbsp goose fat
1 red onion, chopped small
4 oranges, halved
120 ml / 4 ½ fl. oz / ½ cup Cointreau
1 tbsp clear honey
50 g / 4 oz carrots, very thinly sliced
150 ml / 5 fl. oz / ⅔ cup chicken stock
2 tsp sesame seeds, toasted

GARNISH
spring onions sliced lengthways
basil, to garnish

- Grease and warm the slow cooker.
- Clean and pat the duck dry.
- Place in the slow cooker, on a bed of carrots, halved oranges and red onion.
- Allow to cook with lid on for 8 hours at a low heat.
- Check internal temperature has reached 160 F.
- When cooking complete, remove duck and place in a roasting tray, baste with a spoonful of oil for the tray. Sprinkle with Chinese 5 Spice powder and sprinkle with sesame seeds and bake at 220°C (200° fan) / 425F / 8 gas for 25 minutes.
- Place duck on vegetable sauce from the slow cooker and serve on a plate or carver with slices of orange.

695

SERVES 4

Rose Veal Blanquette

PREPARATION TIME :
25 MINUTES

COOKING TIME : 6 HOURS

INGREDIENTS

900 g / 2 lb of rose veal, diced
30 ml / 2 tbsp vegetable oil
150 g / 5 oz / 1 cup bacon lardons
150 g / 5 oz / 1 ½ cups spring onions, rough chopped
150 g / 5 oz / 1 ½ cups leeks, rinsed, chopped and blanched
150 g / 5 oz / 1 ½ cups carrots, peeled, sliced and blanched
2 garlic cloves, crushed
200 ml / 7 fl. oz dry white wine

FOR THE SAUCE
small quantity of chicken stock
50 g / 2 oz / ½ stick butter
50 g / 2 oz / ¼ cup plain (all-purpose) flour
300 ml / 1 ¼ cups milk
60 ml / 4 tbsp thick cream
½ lemon, juiced
salt and black pepper

- Heat the oil and fry (sauté) the veal pieces until golden brown. Remove and set aside
- In the remaining oil, fry the onion, lardons, spring onions (scallions), sliced leeks and garlic. Pour over the wine and boil off the alcohol for 5 minutes.
- Place the veal and vegetables into the slow cooker.
- Make a roux or white sauce, by melting the butter, mixing in the flour and allowing to cook out, then slowly adding the milk and enough chicken stock to form a 'coating sauce'.
- Once cooked and thickened, take off the heat, add the cream, and lemon juice then mix the sauce with the contents of the slow cooker gently.
- Cook on low heat, covered with a lid, for 6 hours.
- Taste when done and season accordingly.
- Serve hot.

Red Pepper Rose Veal Blanquette 696

Adding thinly sliced red pepper before slow cooking gives colour and flavour

SERVES 4

Roast Duck with Plums

- Heat the oil and fry (sauté) the duck legs until brown and transfer to the slow cooker.
- Fry the spices, garlic and sugar gently on low in the remaining fat for 3 minutes. Use the soy sauce and stock to mix with the spices and transfer to the slow cooker.
- Surround the duck with the plums, mushrooms and onions and replace the lid. Cover and cook on a low setting for 8 hours, stir once thoroughly during cooking.
- Pour into a casserole dish before serving.

PREPARATION TIME :
15 MINUTES

COOKING TIME : 8 HOURS

INGREDIENTS

4 large duck legs
30 ml / 1 fl. oz / 2 tbsp goose fat or vegetable oil
1 garlic clove, minced
2 tbsp brown sugar
30 ml / 1 fl. oz / 2 tbsp chicken stock
30 ml / 1 fl. oz / 2 tbsp dark soy sauce
1 tsp chilli flakes
50 g / 2 oz baby onions, blanched
50 g / 2 oz mushrooms, chopped
10 ripe plums, halved and destoned
3 tsp Chinese 5-spice powder
1 star anise, whole
1 tsp cinnamon, ground
salt and ground black pepper

Roast Duck with Honey

698

Replace the sugar in this recipe with 2 tbsp of honey or Golden Syrup and cook in the same way.

SERVES 2

Stuffed Chicken Breast

- Working on a flat surface, flatten the breast by butterflying them.
- Prepare a mixture of about 15 basil leaves, mozzarella, 3 sliced fresh tomatoes and finally sliced sun-dried tomatoes.
- Place half of the mixture on each butterflied breast and bring the sides of the breast around the filling. Secure using wooden toothpicks to keep everything tight.
- Peel, deseed and cut the 2 remaining fresh tomatoes. Sauté the onion in olive oil. Preheat the oven to 190°C (170° fan) / 375F / gas 5.
- In a baking dish put the tomatoes, onions and white wine. Salt and pepper. Place the breasts on this bed.
- Bake for 45 minutes before moving to a slow cooker to finish cooking for 3 hours on a medium setting.
- Serve with fresh pasta and decorate with fresh basil leaves.

PREPARATION TIME: 15 MINUTES

COOKING STIME: 3 HOURS

INGREDIENTS

2 chicken breasts (not too thick, skin on)
1 ball of mozzarella
3 sun-dried tomatoes
20 fresh basil leaves
5 small ripe tomatoes
1 onion, chopped
240 ml / 1 cup of dry white wine
olive oil
salt and pepper

700

MAKES 18

Roast Beef in a Pastry Crust

Roast Beef Pastry with Mushrooms

701

The pate may be replaced with a mixture of finely chopped mushrooms that have been cooked in Marsala wine with some seasoning.

PREPARATION TIME :20 MINUTES

COOKING TIME :
8 HOURS 30 MINUTES

INGREDIENTS

1.75 kg / 4lb rolled beef fillet
vegetable oil or goose fat
salt and pepper
100 g / 4 oz chicken liver or pork pate
200 g / 7 oz ready-made puff pasty
for glazing - 1 egg and 1 tbsp water mixed
1 small bunch of chive stalks, finely chopped

- Oil and season the beef joint and place in a slow cooker.
- Cook on low for 2 to 4 hours depending on how you would like your beef cooked.
- Remove the beef and set to one side to cool slightly.
- Meanwhile, roll out the pastry into a large rectangle with the short side in front of you.
- Combine the chicken liver/pork pate with the chopped chives in a small bowl and mix well.
- Spread a thin layer of the pate over the central rectangular section.
- Place the cooled joint of beef on the pastry and pate base. Make sure you have removed any string used to tie the joint.
- Roll up the beef and seal the ends using a pastry brush dampened with water, making sure you seal the ends well.
- Brush the outside of the pastry case with a mix of 1 egg and 1 tbsp water to glaze and make several diagonal cuts to the top to allow the release of steam.
- Preheat the oven to 190°C (170° fan) / 375F / gas 5.
- Place the beef pastry parcel on a tray and bake for 30 minutes or until the pastry is golden.
- Slice and serve immediately with gravy or sauce.

702
SERVES 6

Roast Pork with Onion

- Wipe the pork joint. Mix together the honey, herbs, and mustard and brush this over the pork joint.
- Heat the oil and fry (sauté) the pork until golden brown all over.
- Transfer to the slow cooker.
- Fry the onions and garlic for 5 minutes. Mix in the stock, vinegar, brown sugar and bring to the boil for 15 minutes stirring gently continuously.
- Spoon the confit around the pork joint in the slow cooker.
- Cover and cook on a low setting for 8 hours.
- Carve the pork, and spoon over the confit mixture to serve. Garnish with fresh sage leaves.

PREPARATION TIME :
25 MINUTES

COOKING TIME : 8 HOURS

INGREDIENTS

1.5 kg / 3 lb 5 oz boneless pork
roasting joint
30 ml / 2 tbsp clear honey
30 ml / 2 tbsp mild or Dijon mustard
1 tsp thyme, fresh chopped or dried
1 tsp sage, fresh chopped or dried
salt and ground black pepper
3 medium onions, thinly sliced
120 ml / 4 fl. oz / ½ cup chicken
stock
2 tbsp white wine vinegar
1 garlic clove, minced
1 tbsp brown sugar

Roast Pork with Wine   703

Add 2 tbsp of white wine to the confit mixture
and cook the same.

704
SERVES 6

Roast Beef with Apricot

- Wipe the beef joint and season.
- Heat the oil and fry (sauté) beef until golden brown all over.
- Remove to the slow cooker.
- Fry the mango chutney with the dried apricots and spread over the outside of the beef with a spatula or knife.
- Cover and cook on a low setting for 8 hours.
- Remove from pot and rest, covered for 20 minutes.
- Sprinkle with flaked almonds and serve.

PREPARATION TIME :15 MINUTES

COOKING TIME : 8 HOURS

INGREDIENTS

1.5 kg / 3 lb 5 oz boneless beef fillet
roasting joint
60 g / 2 oz / 4 tbsp mango chutney
60 g / 2 oz / 4 tbsp dried apricots,
finely chopped
30 g / 1 oz / 2 tbsp almond flakes,
lightly toasted
salt and ground black pepper

GARNISH
fresh parsley

Roast Duck with Apricot   705

Substitute the beef fillet with a whole duck
and cook the same.

706

SERVES 4

Guinea Fowl Casserole

PREPARATION TIME: 10 MINUTES

COOKING TIME: 6 HOURS

INGREDIENTS

2 tbsp sunflower oil
1 guinea fowl, cleaned and trussed
1 Savoy cabbage, outer leaves removed
500ml / 18 fl. oz / 2 cups chicken stock
½ tsp dried thyme
4 thyme sprigs

- Heat a large frying pan over a moderate heat until hot.
- Rub the guinea fowl with the oil and season generously with salt and pepper then seal until golden brown.
- Transfer to a slow cooker.
- Cut the Savoy cabbage into chunks and arrange in and around the guinea fowl in the cooker.
- Add the bunch of thyme sprigs and dried thyme and cover with the stock.
- Braise in the slow cooker on a medium setting for 6 hours until the guinea fowl is tender and the juice runs clear from the thickest part of the thigh when pierced.
- Transfer to a casserole dish and garnish with more salt and pepper before serving.

Poussin Casserole   707

Use two poussin instead of the guinea fowl and cook in the same way.

708

SERVES 4

Seafood Casserole

PREPARATION TIME :
30 MINUTES

COOKING TIME : 4 HOURS

INGREDIENTS

450 g / 1 lb of monkfish cubed
4 king prawns, shelled with tails
8 green-lipped mussels, fresh, scrubbed, de-bearded and tapped to check if alive
220 g / 8 oz clams and juice
220 g / 8 oz crabmeat
4 spring onions (scallions) sliced
1 lemon
30 ml / 1 fl. oz / 2 tbsp vegetable oil
2 garlic cloves, crushed
1 tsp dried parsley
200 ml / 7 fl. oz / 1 cup white wine
100 ml / 3 ½ fl. oz / ½ cup fish stock
50 g / 2 oz / ½ stick butter
50 g / 2 oz plain (all purpose) flour
110 ml / 4 fl. oz / ½ cup double cream
salt and pepper

- Heat the oil and fry (sauté) the monkfish pieces until golden brown.
- In the remaining oil, fry the onions and garlic until softened and add the herbs.
- Mix in the remaining seafood, cover with wine, bring to the boil with a tight fitting lid, and boil for 6 minutes.
- Remove lid and check the mussels. If any remain unopened, discard them.
- Transfer all ingredients (except the cream) to the slow cooker and cook on a medium setting for 4 hours.
- Stir in the cream gently.
- Sprinkle with chopped parsley and serve.

Seafood and Chicken Casserole   709

To add a meaty flavour, add 2 cooked chicken breasts to the slow cooker.

710

SERVES 4

Daube Aveyronnaise

- Heat a large, heavy-based casserole dish over a moderate heat. Sauté the pancetta until golden and crispy, stirring occasionally. Transfer to a plate lined with kitchen paper to drain.
- Add the sunflower oil, then season and sear the beef, in batches if necessary, until golden brown.
- Remove from the dish to drain, then add the carrots and sauté for 2-3 minutes, stirring occasionally.
- Add all the beef and pancetta back to the dish and sprinkle the flour on top, stirring well to coat. Add the wine and let it reduce by half.
- Cover with the stock and then bring to the boil. Add the thyme sprigs before pouring into a slow cooker.
- Cover with a lid and cook on a medium setting for 8 hours.
- Adjust the seasoning before ladling into serving bowls.

PREPARATION TIME : 15 MINUTES

COOKING TIME :
8 HOURS 15 MINUTES

INGREDIENTS

55 ml / 2 fl. oz / ¼ cup sunflower oil
675 g / 1 lb 8 oz / 4 ½ cups beef
braising steak, cubed
125 ml / 4 ½ fl. oz / ½ cup red wine
150 g / 5 oz / 1 cup pancetta
2 medium carrots, peeled and sliced
30 g / 1 oz / 2 tbsp plain (all-purpose)
flour
500 ml / 18 fl. oz / 2 cups beef stock
a few thyme sprigs
salt and pepper

Tripe Stew with Cider

711

SERVES 4

PREPARATION TIME :
10-15 MINUTES

COOKING TIME :
8 HOURS 10-15 MINUTES

INGREDIENTS

55 ml / 2 fl. oz / ¼ cup sunflower oil
675 g / 1 lb 8 oz / 4 ½ cups beef tripe,
trimmed and sliced
750 ml / 1 pint 6 fl. oz / 3 cups
good-quality cider
250 ml / 9 fl. oz / 1 cup beef stock
salt and pepper

- Coat the trip in the oil and season generously.
- Heat a large casserole dish over a moderate heat until hot.
- Flash-fry the tripe in batches for a minute, transferring each completed batch to a slow cooker when finished.
- Add the stock, cider and seasoning and cover with a lid.
- Braise on a medium setting for 8 hours until the trip is tender.
- Adjust the seasoning to taste before ladling into soup bowls.
- Serve immediately.

Chicken with Saffron and Figs

712

SERVES 4

PREPARATION TIME :
15 MINUTES

COOKING TIME :
5 HOURS 15 MINUTES

INGREDIENTS

55 ml / 2 fl. oz / ¼ cup olive oil
1 small chicken, jointed and trimmed
2 large Maris Piper potatoes, peeled
and cut into wedges
1 tsp saffron threads
500 ml / 18 fl. oz / 2 cups chicken
stock
110 g / 4 oz / ⅔ cup dried figs
1 tbsp tomato puree
1 tsp ras al hanout
1 tsp ground cumin
½ tsp ground cinnamon
½ tsp smoked paprika
1 tbsp honey
salt and pepper

GARNISH
sprig of flat-leaf parsley

- Coat the chicken pieces in half of the oil and season generously.
- Heat a large casserole dish over a moderate heat until hot.
- Seal the chicken in the dish until golden brown in colour all over.
- Remove to a slow cooker and reduce the heat under the dish a little.
- Add the remaining oil and saute the potato and figs for a few minutes.
- Add the ground spices, tomato puree and honey and stir well.
- Cover with the infused stock, stir thoroughly and pour into the slow cooker.
- Cook on a medium setting for 5 hours until the chicken is cooked through and the potato is soft.
- Adjust the seasoning to taste when ready and spoon into a roasting dish for presentation.
- Garnish with the parsley before serving.

713

SERVES 2

Mussels in Cream and Turmeric

PREPARATION TIME: 20 MINUTES

COOKING TIME : 4 HOURS

....

INGREDIENTS

450 g / 1 lb fresh mussels, scrubbed, de-bearded and tapped to check if alive
4 spring onions (scallions) sliced diagonally
1 lemon
30 ml / 2 tbsp vegetable oil
1 tsp ground turmeric
½ tsp chilli (chili) flakes
2 garlic cloves, crushed
1 tsp dried parsley
100 ml / 4 fl. oz dry white wine
100 ml / 4 fl. oz double cream
salt and black pepper

GARNISH
chopped fresh parsley

- Heat the oil and fry (sauté) the monkfish pieces until golden brown.
- In the remaining oil, and lightly fry the onions and garlic until softened.
- Add the herbs, chilli and turmeric and stir cooking for a further minute.
- Pour in the wine to deglaze the pan and boil.
- Tip the mussels (cleaned and checked) and cover with a lid. Boil for 5 minutes.
- Remove lid and check the mussels. If any remain unopened, discard them.
- Transfer all ingredients (except the cream) to the slow cooker and cook on a low setting for 4 hours.
- Stir in the cream gently.
- Adjust seasoning and sprinkle with parsley before serving.

Mussels with Cumin

714

Add a teaspoon of cumin seeds at the start and cook the same.

715

SERVES 6

Pork with Camembert Sauce

PREPARATION TIME :
30 MINUTES

COOKING TIME : 8 HOURS

....

INGREDIENTS

1 ½ kg / 3 lb 3 oz boneless pork roasting joint
salt and pepper

SAUCE
30 ml / 2 tbsp butter
1 clove garlic, minced
8 sage leaves, chopped
1 tsp tarragon, chopped
50 g / 2 oz hazelnuts, blanched and finely chopped
15 ml / 1 tbsp mild or Dijon mustard
60 ml / 2 fl. oz / ¼ cup chicken stock
150 g / 5 oz / 1 ½ Camembert, chopped

- Wipe the pork joint and season with salt and pepper.
- Heat the oil and fry (sauté) the pork until golden brown all over.
- Transfer to the slow cooker.
- Cover and cook on a low setting for 8 hours.
- Remove from pot and rest covered for 20 minutes.
- Meanwhile, to make the sauce, fry the onions and garlic gently for 5 minutes.
- Pour over the stock, hazelnuts, mustard, herbs, butter and Camembert and gently simmer stirring gently continuously for
  10 minutes. Remove from heat and stir in the cream.
- Adjust seasoning to taste.
- Carve pork and serve with the sauce.
- Garnish with fresh tarragon leaves.

Pork with Brie Sauce

716

This sauce works equally well with Brie, as a replacement for the Camembert if preferred

717

SERVES 4

Wild Boar with Juniper

Wild Boar with Pasta 718

This is a traditional Italian recipe, so serve with cooked pasta for that authentic feel. Garnish with Parmesan cheese.

Soy Wild Boar with Juniper 719

Add 1 tbsp of dark soy sauce for a richer flavour.

PREPARATION TIME :
35 MINUTES

COOKING TIME : 8 HOURS
....

INGREDIENTS

1.75 kg / 4lb boned joint or leg of wild boar, trimmed and cubed
30 ml / 2 tbsp goose fat or vegetable oil
1 onion, sliced
1 carrot, finely sliced
1 stick or celery, finely sliced
2 garlic cloves, crushed
35g / 1.5 oz / 3 tbsp juniper berries (if dried then soak in a spoon of oil overnight)
150ml / 5 fl. oz / ⅔ cup chicken stock
150ml / 5 fl. oz / ⅔ cup full-bodied red wine
4 baby cauliflower, blanched in boiling water for 5 minutes
1 tbsp tomato paste
3 bay leaves, torn
salt and black pepper

- Heat the oil and fry (sauté) the wild boar chunks until golden brown. Remove and set aside.
- In the remaining oil, fry the onion, celery, carrot and garlic for 10 minutes.
- Cover with wine and allow the wine to boil off the alcohol for 5 mintues.
- Add the tomato puree, bay leaves, juniper berries and stock and bring to the boil.
- Transfer the meat and onions to the slow cooker, and pour over the liquid.
- Cover and cook on a low setting for 8 hours.
- One hour before the end, add the baby cauliflower and coat with sauce. Replace the pot lid.
- Serve hot.

720

SERVES 4

Oxtail in Red Wine

PREPARATION TIME :
25 MINUTES

COOKING TIME : 8 HOURS

INGREDIENTS

1.3 kg / 3 lb 2 oz beef oxtail, cubed
plain (all-purpose) flour for dusting
1 bottle dry red wine (un-oaked)
3 cloves of garlic, crushed
2 medium onions, finely diced
30 ml / 2 tbsp goose fat or
vegetable oil
2 carrots, peeled, chopped and
blanched for 5 minutes
1 celery stalk, washed and chopped
500 ml / 18 fl. oz / 2 cups beef stock
2 sprigs of thyme
1 bay leaf crushed
salt and ground black pepper
2 tsp cornflour

GARNISH
fresh parsley

- Heat the oil in a heavy pan. Dust the oxtail pieces in seasoned flour and fry (sauté) until brown.
- Transfer to the slow cooker.
- Fry the garlic, onion, celery, carrot and herbs lightly.
- Pour over the red wine to deglaze the pan and boil without a lid to reduce by half. Return the oxtails to the wine sauce and pour into the slow cooker.
- Cover and cook on a low setting for 8 hours, stirring once thoroughly during cooking.
- Taste and adjust seasoning. The sauce may be thickened if required, with cornflour.
- Pour into a casserole dish before serving sprinkled with parsley.

Oxtail with Baby Potatoes   721

Adding halved, blanched baby potatoes to the recipe and cook the same.

722

SERVES 4

Roast Suckling Pig with Apples

PREPARATION TIME: 30 MINUTES

COOKING TIME : 8 HOURS

INGREDIENTS

4 lb / 1 ½ kg suckling pig portions
4 Granny Smith apples, peeled,
cored, sectioned and coated with
lemon juice
30 ml / 2 tbsp clear honey
30 ml / 2 tbsp oil
1 knob butter
100 g / 4 oz carrots, sliced and
blanched for 5 minutes
50 g / 2 oz fennel bulb, shredded
100 g / 4 oz baby new potatoes with
skins on, blanched for 5 minutes
1 tsp sage, fresh chopped or dried
salt and ground black pepper
1 medium onion, thinly sliced
120 ml / 4 oz / ½ cup chicken stock
30 ml / 2 tbsp white wine vinegar

- Arrange the suckling pig joints, skin down in a heavy pan with butter and oil and fry until golden brown.
- Arrange the vegetables in the bottom of the slow cooker, sit the browned meat on top and pour around it the chicken stock, wine vinegar and herbs.
- Cover and cook on a low setting for 8 hours.
- Remove from pot and rest covered for 20 minutes.
- Meanwhile put a knob of butter in a pan and gently fry the sliced apples until starting to soften and catch colour. Add the honey to coat.
- Use the meat juices to make a sauce, thickening if required.
- Carve the pork and serve with the cooked apples.

Glazed Suckling Pig   723

The apples can be pureed and spooned onto the meat for an alternative texture.

724

SERVES 4

Cod and Stew with Tomatoes

- Warm the slow cooker.
- Heat the oil in a pan and sauté the onion and garlic. Stir in the turmeric and cook through for 1 minute.
- Add the white wine and boil deglaze pan and burn off alcohol.
- Add fish stock coloured with saffron and bring gently to the boil.
- Place the tomato quarters, potatoes and baby shallots into the slow cooker.
- Pour over the liquid stock mixture and gently sit the cod fillets on top.
- Cover and cook on a medium setting for 4 hours.
- Adjust the seasoning to taste.
- Spoon into serving dishes and garnish with the parsley and freshly ground black pepper.

PREPARATION TIME :
25 MINUTES

COOKING TIME : 4 HOURS

INGREDIENTS

600 g / 1 lb 5 oz / 4 cups cod fillets, skinned and boned
1 onion finely chopped
120 ml / 4 fl. oz / ½ cup white wine
4 whole tomatoes, peeled and quartered
4 cloves of garlic, minced
1 tsp turmeric
8 baby shallots, peeled and blanched
500 g / 1 lb 2 oz potatoes, peeled, halved and boiled for 8 minutes
15 ml / 1 tbsp sunflower oil
15 ml / 1 tbsp butter
1 pinch saffron soaked in 120 ml /
4 ½ fl. oz / ½ cup fish stock
salt and pepper

GARNISH
4 tbsp fresh parsley, chopped

725

SERVES 4

Guinea Fowl Casserole

- Heat the oil and fry the Guinea Fowl (Guinea Hen) portions until golden brown. Remove from heat and place to one side.
- In the remaining fat, fry the onion and carrots for 3 minutes. Stir in the flour and cook for 1 minutes.
- Pour over the wine, honey, orange juice and zest and herbs and bring to the boil until slightly thickened.
- Place the sauce and vegetables into the slow cooker and spoon the guinea fowl pieces on top skin side upwards.
- Place the lid on tightly. Cook on a low setting for 8 hours. Taste the sauce and adjust seasoning.
- Serve immediately by setting the guinea fowl portions onto a serving dish and spooning the sauce over the top. Finishing off by garnishing with slices of orange.

PREPARATION TIME :
20 MINUTES

COOKING TIME : 8 HOURS

INGREDIENTS

2 x 1 kg / 2 lb 4 oz guinea fowl, halved to give 4 portions
60 ml / 4 tsp / ¼ cup olive oil
2 onions, finely chopped
2 carrots, chopped and blanched
1 tbsp plain (all-purpose) flour
1 tbsp clear honey
3 unwaxed oranges, zest and juice
¼ cinnamon stick
2 bay leaf
salt and black pepper
250 ml / 9 fl. oz / 1 cup red wine
½ chicken stock cube, good quality

GARNISH
braised orange slices

Cointreau Guinea Fowl Casserole   726

Add 1 tbsp of Cointreau to the final sauce before serving.

727

SERVES 4

Chinese Pork with Spices

Apple Chinese Pork

728

This recipe also works well replacing the cider with apple juice

Rice Wine
Chinese Pork

729

1 tbsp of Rice Wine may be added to give it a little extra kick

Chinese Pork
with Pears

730

Substitute the apples for 2 firm pears and cook the same.

PREPARATION TIME 10 MINUTES

COOKING TIME 45 MINUTES

INGREDIENTS

1.5 kg / 3 lb 3 oz boneless pork roasting joint cut into 2 inch chunks
30 ml / 2 tsp vegetable oil
3 garlic cloves, minced
5 ml / 1 tsp tomato puree
2 carrots, peeled and thinly sliced
6 Spring onions (scallions) sliced
1 ½ tsp Chinese 5 spice powder
30 ml / 2 tbsp Dark soy sauce
15 ml / 1 tbsp honey
1 tbsp fresh ginger, grated, or 1 tsp of powdered ginger
salt and ground black pepper
5 new potatoes scrubbed, blanched and sliced thickly
2 medium firm apples, cored and sliced in circles
150 ml / ¼ pt / ⅔ cup dry apple cider
150 ml / ¼ pt / ⅔ cup chicken stock

GARNISH
2 spring onions finely shredded

- Pre-warm the slow cooker.
- Heat the oil and fry (sauté) the pork pieces until brown and transfer to the slow cooker.
- Sweat the onions, garlic, potatoes, and carrots for 5 minutes. Cover with the tomato puree, cider, stock, honey and soy sauce and bring to the boil.
- Transfer all the ingredients to the slow cooker, add the apples and stir gently to mix.
- Cover and cook on a low setting for 8 hours.
- Taste and adjust seasoning.
- Pour into a casserole dish before serving and sprinkle with finely shredded spring onions.

731

SERVES 4

Vegetable and Pear Casserole

- Warm the slow cooker.
- Blanch all the hard vegetables for 5 minutes, drain and dry
- Heat the oil in a pan and gently sweat the onions, garlic, and all the vegetables and pear pieces.
- Add the vinegar, stock, tomato paste, herbs and cider and bring to the boil for 5 minutes.
- Place casserole into the slow cooker and cook on medium for 6 hours.
- At the end of cooking, taste and add salt and black pepper as required.
- Spoon into serving dishes and garnish with chopped parsley.

PREPARATION TIME: 25 MINUTES

COOKING TIME : 6 HOURS

INGREDIENTS

30 ml / 2 tbsp sunflower or olive oil
1 medium onion, peeled and sliced in circles
1 garlic clove, crushed
2 carrots, roughly chopped and blanched for 5 minutes
1 celery stick, chopped
100 g / 4 oz sweet potato sliced
100 g / 4 oz salsify, peeled and sliced
100 g / 4 oz shredded Savoy Cabbage
100 g / 4 oz cauliflower florets
1 tbsp tomato puree
4 beef tomatoes, skinned and sliced
3 tbsp cider vinegar
150 ml / 5 fl. oz / ½ cup dry cider
2 tbsp parsley, chopped
150 ml / 5 fl. oz / ½ cups vegetable stock
2 conference pears, cored and quartered
salt and black pepper

Casserole with Pear Calvados
732

Add 1 tbsp of pear brandy to the casserole and cook the same, for a sweeter taste.

733

SERVES 4

Veal Stuffed with Olives

- Pre-warm the slow cooker.
- Prepare stuffing by mixing the chopped olives, egg, lemon zest, shallots, fried bacon lardons, breadcrumbs and herbs. Combine thoroughly.
- Roll the veal flat, between 2 sheets of cling film. Season with salt and pepper and place a spoonful of stuffing in each, rolling the stuffing up within the meet and securing with string or a toothpick.
- Heat the oil and fry (sauté) the veal paupiettes until golden brown. Remove and place in the slow cooker.
- Pour in flour and fry off for 1 minute.
- Add the tinned tomatoes, whole green olives, chilli (chilli) flakes, lemon juice, and cook, stirring for 4 minutes.
- Cook on medium heat, covered with a lid, for 6 hours.
- Taste when done and season accordingly.

PREPARATION TIME :
15 MINUTES

COOKING TIME : 6 HOURS

INGREDIENTS

8 thin slices of veal
20 green olives, finely chopped
12 green olives, whole
1 egg
2 shallots finely diced
120 g / 4 oz bacon lardons, fried
2 garlic cloves minced
2 tbsp fine breadcrumbs
1 tbsp plain (all-purpose flour)
1 tbsp thyme, fresh chopped
1 tbsp rosemary fresh chopped
30 ml / 2 tbsp vegetable oil
2 x 400 g can chopped tomatoes with garlic and basil
¼ tsp chilli (chilli) flakes
1 lemon, zested and juice

GARNISH
sprig of rosemary

Veal Stuffed with Mushrooms
734

Swap the olives for sliced chestnut mushrooms and cook in the same way.

735

SERVES 6

Spicy Roast Tuna Pot

PREPARATION TIME : 20 MINUTES

COOKING TIME : 4 HOURS

INGREDIENTS

1 kg / 2 ½ lb fresh tuna fillet
15 ml / 1 tbsp vegetable oil
1 star anise, whole
¼ tsp chilli (chilli) flakes
3 spring onions (scallions) finely chopped
100 g / 4 oz porcini mushrooms, sliced
2 tbsp mixed Italian herbs
4 garlic cloves, minced
1 bay leaf
1 tsp ground coriander
½ tsp ground cloves
1 x 400 g can chopped tomatoes
80 ml / 2 ½ fl. oz / ⅓ cup white wine vinegar
salt and ground black pepper

GARNISH
fresh Basil

- Pre-warm the slow cooker.
- Heat the oil and fry (sauté) the tuna fillet. Add the cloves, coriander, garlic, a little salt and some ground black pepper to the tuna and turn regularly until brown all over, leave to one side.
- In the pan, heat the tomatoes, chilli flakes, star anise, onions, herbs, bay leaf, cloves and white wine vinegar for 5 minutes and place into the slow cooker.
- Sit the tuna fillet on top and scrape any ingredients remaining in the pan around the tuna.
- Cover with the lid and cook on a low setting for 4 hours for a rare finish to the fish.
- Taste and adjust seasoning.
- Serve tuna with the sauce spooned over and garnished with fresh basil.

Spicy Vinegar Tuna Pot   736

The vinegar may be replaced successfully with dry white wine if preferred.

737

SERVES 4

Mushroom and Vegetable Stew

PREPARATION TIME :
25 MINUTES

COOKING TIME : 6 HOURS

INGREDIENTS

60 ml / 2 fl. oz / 4 tbsp olive oil
2 medium onions, sliced
1 stick of celery, rough chopped
2 garlic cloves, crushed
2 carrots, sliced and blanched
2 small turnips, cubed and blanched
2 parsnips, sliced and blanched
¼ butternut squash, chopped
4 large beef tomatoes, quartered
2 potatoes, cubed and boiled
700 g / 1 ½ lb mixed mushrooms 2 green peppers, sliced
1 tbsp tomato paste
1 tbsp thyme, chopped
2 bay leaves, crushed
½ tbsp oregano, chopped
½ tbsp parsley, chopped
1 lemon, zested and juice
salt and black pepper to taste
700 ml / 1 ½ pt / 3 cups good vegetable stock

- Warm the slow cooker.
- Heat the oil in a large wok or heavy pan and sauté all the vegetables, herbs and garlic.
- Add the stock, tomato paste, lemon juice, tomatoes and seasoning and bring to the boil for 5 minutes.
- Pour all the ingredients into the slow cooker and cook on medium for 6 hours to allow flavours to infuse.

Seasonal Vegetable Stew   738

Vegetables can be chosen according to season, but remember that all woody vegetables (i.e. those grown underground) need blanching for at least 5 minutes before cooking.

739

SERVES 4

Monkfish Tajine

Fruity Monkfish Tajine 740

The peaches may be replaced
with dates, raisins and sultanas.

Tangy Monkfish Tajine 741

For a slightly tangier tagine,
replace the peaches with limes,
lemons and oranges.

Chilli Monkfish Tajine 742

For a slightly hotter tagine,
double the chilli flakes to 1 tsp.

PREPARATION TIME :
25 MINUTES

COOKING TIME : 4 HOURS

INGREDIENTS

1 ½ kg / 3 ⅓ lb / 6 ½ cups Monkfish,
skinned and cubed
flour for dusting
4 garlic cloves, crushed
60 ml / 4 tsp / ¼ cup olive or
vegetable oil
½ tsp chilli flakes
1 tsp ginger powder
1 tsp cumin
1 tsp turmeric
1 tsp cinnamon
½ tsp paprika
½ tsp fennel seed
1 x 440 g / 15 ½ oz can chopped
tomatoes
½ ltr good stock
1 lemon zest and juice
bunch of fresh coriander, chopped
1 red pepper finely sliced
10 ml / 2 tbsp clear honey
1 x 440 g / 15 ½ oz can peaches sliced

- Pre-warm the slow cooker.
- Heat the oil and fry the onion, peppers and garlic until
  softened.
- Add the spices and chilli flakes, stir well and cook
  through for 3 minutes.
- Add the lemon juice, honey, stock and tinned tomatoes
  and stir. Bring gently to the boil.
- Mean while dust the monkfish in flour and fry lightly
  on both sides until golden.
- Place the monkfish and the hot spicy stock and
  vegetables into the slow cooker and cook on a low
  setting for 4 hours.
- Ten minutes before the end of cooking, stir in the
  chopped coriander and sliced peaches.
- Serve hot with rice, couscous or pitta bread.

743
SERVES 4

Suckling Pig with Herbs

PREPARATION TIME: 30 MINUTES

COOKING TIME : 8 HOURS

INGREDIENTS

4 lb / 1 ⊠ kg boned and tied into a joint
30 ml / 2 tbsp oil
1 knob butter
3 tbsp sage, fresh
3 large sprigs of rosemary
2 tbsp juniper berries
2 tbsp capers
salt and ground black pepper
1 medium onion, thinly sliced
1 clove garlic crushed
120 ml / 4 oz / ½ cup chicken stock
120 ml / 4 oz / ½ cup thick cream
2 tbsp white wine vinegar

- Score the suckling pig skin with a sharp knife, rub in seasoning and arrange the suckling pig, skin down in a heavy pan with butter and oil and fry until golden brown. Place skin side up in the slow cooker.
- In the heavy pan, fry the onions and garlic for 3 minutes. Add the herbs and berries with the knob of butter and cook for 3 minutes.
- Pour the stock, vinegar and cream into the heavy pan and deglaze the pan. Bring slowly to a simmer.
- Pour into the slow cooker.
- Arrange the vegetables in the bottom of the slow cooker, sit the browned meat on top and pour around it the liquid stock.
- Cover and cook on a medium setting for 8 hours.
- Preheat the oven to 230°C (210° fan) / 450F / gas 8.
- Remove from the slow cooker and roast the oven for 20 minutes to create crackling.

Suckling Pig with Apples

 744

Place 2 diced eating apples into the slow cooker before cooking and serve alongside the pork.

745
SERVES 6

Bouillabaisse with Rouille Sauce

PREPARATION TIME :
15-20 MINUTES

COOKING TIME :
5 HOURS 35 MINUTES

INGREDIENTS

110ml / 4 fl. oz / ½ cup olive oil
450 g / 1 lb / 3 cups gurnard, filleted and cut into large chunks
450 g / 1 lb / 3 cups red mullet, filleted and cut into large chunks
450 g / 1 lb / 3 cups monkfish tail, cut into large chunks
500ml / 18 fl. oz / 2 cups fish stock
150 g / 5 oz / 1 cup Charlotte potatoes, halved
4 tbsp Pernod (pastis)
4 sprigs thyme

GARNISH
1 baguette, cut into thin slices

- Place the fish in a bowl and coat with the olive oil.
- Season generously, then heat a large frying pan over a moderate heat until hot. Seal the fish chunks in batches.
- Remove from the pan and place in the slow cooker.
- Once you have finished sealing the fish, deglaze the pan using the Pernod.
- Pour on top of the fish, add the potatoes and cover everything with the stock and thyme sprigs.
- Cook in the slow cooker on a medium setting for 5 hours.
- Once the fish and potatoes are cooked, turn off the slow cooker and let them rest as you prepare the garnish.
- Preheat the oven to 200°C / 400F / gas 6.
- Toast the baguette slices for 4 minutes until golden.
- Spoon the fish and potatoes into serving bowls.
- Serve with the toasted baguette slices on the side.

Bouillabaisse with Hake

746

if Monkfish is not available, it can be substituted with Hake, Cod or Turbot. You can use Grey Mullet instead of the Red Mullet as well.

747

SERVES 4

Roast Duckling with Tagliatelle

- Grease and warm the slow cooker.
- Clean and pat dry the duck. Prick the skin evenly with a fork.
- Rub salt into skin.
- Heat goose fat in a heavy pan and brown the duck all over.
- Place in the slow cooker and sprinkle coat with plum sauce and honey mixture. Sprinkle with 5 spice powder.
- Cook with for 6 hours on medium.
- Remove duck from slow cooker, place on a trivet and roast in a very hot over for 220°C (200° fan) / 425F / gas 7 for 25 minutes to make the skin crisp.
- Meanwhile cook and drain the tagliatelle. Whilst in the pan, add the basil and sesame oil and mix through.
- Carve the duck and serve hot, with tagliatelle to the side.

PREPARATION TIME :
25 MINUTES

COOKING TIME : 6 HOURS

INGREDIENTS

1 ¾ kg / 4 lb duck. Ask your butcher to fillet and reform meat
30 ml / 2 tbsp goose fat
salt, pepper and 1 tsp 5-spice powder
30 ml / 1 tbsp plum sauce
30 ml / 1 tbsp honey
2 tbsp fresh Basil, finely chopped
2 tbsp sesame oil
450 g / 1 lb cooked and drained tagliatelle

GARNISH
Spring onions sliced lengthways

Roast Chicken with Tagliatelle   748

This recipe works extremely well with chicken or goose, instead of duck.

749

SERVES 6

Roast Pork with Mustard

- Pre-warm the slow cooker.
- Wipe the pork joint and season with salt, pepper and paprika.
- Heat the oil and fry (sauté) the pork until golden brown all over.
- Mix the mustard and cream and spread all over the pork
- Transfer to the slow cooker.
- Cover and cook on a medium setting for 6 hours.
- Remove from pot, place on a trivet and bake in 230°C (210° fan) / 450F / gas 8 for 25 minutes until crisp on the outside.
- Meanwhile, to make the gravy, using cornflour (cornstarch) to thicken juices in the crockpot. Adjust seasoning to taste.
- Carve pork and serve with the sauce.

PREPARATION TIME :
15 MINUTES

COOKING TIME : 6 HOURS

INGREDIENTS

1 ½ kg / 3 lb 3 oz boneless pork roasting joint
salt, pepper and paprika
15 ml / 1 tbsp mild or Dijon mustard
15 ml / 1 tbsp thick cream

Roast Pork with Chipotle Mustard   750

Omit the French mustard for chipotle pepper for a spicier dish.

751

SERVES 4

Pork with Mustard Crust

Pork with Stuffing Crust

752

Packet stuffing mix can also be used, instead of the mustard crust.

Prune Stuffed Pork

753

The pork may be sliced open and stuffed with prunes, prior to slow cooking.

PREPARATION TIME :
20 MINUTES

COOKING TIME : 6 HOURS

INGREDIENTS

1½ kg / 3 lb 3 oz boneless pork roasting joint
30 ml / 2 tsp vegetable oil
175 ml / 8 pt / ⅓ cup dry chicken stock
salt and ground black pepper

CRUST
30ml / 2 tbsp butter
2 garlic cloves, crushed
1 tsp paprika
3 tsp fresh sage, chopped finely
100 g / 4 oz / 2 cups fine dry breadcrumbs
salt and pepper
45 ml / 3 tbsp mild French mustard

GARNISH
Fresh sage leaves

- Pre-warm the slow cooker.
- Wipe the pork joint and rub salt and pepper into it.
- Heat the oil and fry (sauté) the pork until brown and transfer to the crockpot
- Transfer the meat and the stock slow cooker
- Cover and cook on a low setting for 8 hours then check the internal temperature of the pork to ensure it has reached at least 160o F.
- Remove from pot and pat dry all over with kitchen towel.
- Mix the crust ingredients with the butter, and rub this firmly into the outside of the pork joint.
- Place this in a hot oven for 20 minutes or until the crust starts to turn golden brown.
- Meanwhile, use the slow cooker juices to make a gravy.

754

MAKES 18 # Veal and Olive Stew

- Pre-warm the slow cooker.
- Heat the oil and fry (sauté) the veal pieces until golden brown. Remove and set aside
- In the remaining oil, fry the onion, lardons, leeks and carrots
- Stir in the flour and cook for 2 minutes
- Pour over the wine and boil off the alcohol for 3 minutes.
- Add the stock, white wine vinegar, olives and passata and bring to the boil.
- Place all ingredients (except the cream) into the slow cooker
- Cook on low heat, covered with a lid, for 8 hours.
- Taste when done and season accordingly
- Remove from heat and stir in the cream thoroughly.
- Serve hot.

PREPARATION TIME :
15 MINUTES

COOKING TIME : 8 HOURS

INGREDIENTS

900 g / 2 lb / 8 cups of veal diced
30 ml / 2 tbsp vegetable oil
150 g / 6 oz / ¾ bacon lardons
150 g / 6 oz / ¾ leeks, rinsed and chopped and blanched for 5 minutes
150 g / 6 oz / ¾ carrots, peeled, sliced and blanched for 5 minutes
225 g / 8 oz green olives
1 tbsp plain (all-purpose) flour
1 tbsp sundried tomato puree
2 garlic cloves, crushed
1 small glass dry white wine
225 g / 8 oz tomato passata or pureed tomatoes
150 ml ¼ pt / 2.3 cup chicken stock
60 ml / 4 tbsp thick cream
1 tbsp white wine vinegar
Salt and black pepper

Veal Stew with Garlic Olives   **755**

stuffed olives can be a good substitute for the plain olives. Try garlic stuffed olives for a flavour boost.

756

SERVES 4 # Cod with Garlic, Onions, Peppers and Chilli

- Warm the slow cooker.
- Drain the Salt-Cod from the soaking water and pat dry with kitchen towel and dust with seasoned flour
- Heat the oil in a pan and gently sauté cod pieces for 3 minutes each side until golden. Keep to one side
- In the remaining oil, add crushed garlic cloves, chilli, spring onions, tomatoes, lemon grass paste and ginger and sauté for 4 minutes. Pour in the rice wine and stock. Bring to the boil for 2 minutes.
- Transfer all ingredients to the slow cooker.
- Cover and cook on medium for 4 hours stirring once during cooking.
- Adjust the seasoning to taste after 4 hours.
- Serve immediately in individual bowls with jasmine rice.

PREPARATION TIME :
20 MINUTES

COOKING TIME : 4 HOURS

INGREDIENTS

600 g / 1 lb 5 oz / 3 cups salt cod (soaked overnight in water, drained and dried)
1 tbsp seasoned plain (all-purpose) flour for dusting
2 red chilli (chilli) peppers, deseeded and finely stripped
5 spring onions (scallions) finely chopped
30 ml / 1 fl. oz / 2 tbsp olive oil
3 cloves of garlic
3 tbsp saki or rice wine
250 ml / 9 fl. oz / 1 cup fish or chicken stock
4 ripe tomatoes, blanched, peeled and chopped
½ tsp ground ginger
½ tsp lemongrass
salt and pepper to taste

Peppers and Chilli Monkfish   **757**

The salt cod may be replaced with the equivalent weight in Monk Fish, cubed.

758
SERVES 4

Veal and Vegetable Casserole

- Coat the veal in the oil and season generously.
- Heat a large casserole dish over a moderate heat until hot.
- Seal the veal in batches until golden brown in colour all over.
- Transfer to a slow cooker when ready.
- Add the vegetables, rosemary and seasoning and cover with a lid.
- Cook on a low setting for 4 hours until the veal is tender and cooked.
- Adjust the seasoning to taste before spooning into a casserole dish with a glass lid for presentation.
- Serve immediately.

PREPARATION TIME :
15 MINUTES

COOKING TIME :
4 HOURS 10 MINUTES

INGREDIENTS

30 ml / 1 fl. oz / 2 tbsp sunflower oil
450 g / 1 lb / 3 cups veal fillet, diced
225 g / 8 oz / 2 cups asparagus spears, trimmed and halved
150 g / 5 oz / 1 cup pearl onions
150 g / 5 oz / 1 ½ cups mangetout
4 Globe artichoke hearts, quartered
2-3 sprigs of rosemary
salt and pepper

Loin of Pork with Roast Shallots

759
SERVES 4

PREPARATION TIME :20 MINUTES

COOKING TIME :
6 HOURS 30 MINUTES

INGREDIENTS

55 ml / 2 fl. oz / ¼ cup sunflower oil
900 g / 2 lb piece of pork loin roast, bone in
12 shallots, peeled and halved
1 tsp caster (superfine) sugar
2 large carrots, peeled and cut into small batons
2 large sticks of celery, cut into batons
30 g / 1 oz / 2 tbsp sesame seeds
2-3 sprigs of rosemary, finely chopped
salt and pepper
2.5g / ½ tsp caster sugar
350 g / 12 oz / 1 ½ cup sliced basil, to garnish

- Rub the loin with the oil and season generously with salt and pepper.
- Combine the rosemary and sesame seeds in a shallot dish and roll the pork loin in the mixture to form a crust.
- Preheat the oven to 200°C (180° fan) / 400F / gas 6.
- Arrange the vegetables in the base of a roasting tray and sit the pork on top.
- Roast for 20 minutes.
- Remove after 20 minutes and transfer everything to a slow cooker, making sure the pork is sat on top of the vegetables.
- Cover with a lid and cook on a medium setting for 6 hours; it should be at least 60°C / 140F on a meat thermometer.
- Remove from the slow cooker and arrange the vegetable on a a serving platter.
- Sit the pork loin on top before serving.

Salt-Cod with Rice

760
SERVES 4

PREPARATION TIME :15 MINUTES

COOKING TIME : 4 HOURS

INGREDIENTS

600 g / 1 lb 5 oz / 3 cups salt cod (soaked overnight in water)
1 x 440g / 15 ½ oz can chick peas
1 red onion, finely chopped
30 ml / 1 fl. oz / 2 tbsp olive oil
300 g / 10 oz / 2 cups spinach
3 cloves of garlic
1 cup dry white wine
1 x 440g / 15 ½ oz passata
60 ml / 4 tbsp tomato puree or paste
3 tsp green salted capers
250 ml / 9 fl. oz / 1 cup vegetable stock
salt and pepper
2 tbsp dill weed, finely chopped

- Drain the Salt-Cod from the soaking water and pat dry with kitchen towel and dust with flour
- Heat the oil in a pan and gently sauté Cod pieces for 3 minutes each side until golden. Place into the slow cooker
- In the remaining oil, add crushed garlic cloves and onions and sauté for further 2 minutes. Cover with wine and boil to reduce a little.
- Rinse and shred spinach, adding it to the wine mixture with the puree and capers and cook until spinach is wilting.
- Add all ingredients to the slow cooker and cook on low for 4 hours.
- 15 minutes before the end of cooking, add the chick peas and dill weed, stir through and replace the lid, allowing to warm for 15 minutes.
- Adjust the seasoning to taste after 4 hours.
- Spoon into serving dishes and garnish with dill weed.
- Serve immediately.

Lamb Meatball and Sesame Seed Tagine

SERVES 4 · 761

- Mix meatball ingredients, hand roll into 20 small balls and fry them in batches until thoroughly cooked
- Heat the oil and fry the onion, herbs and garlic until softened.
- Add the spices and chilli flakes, stir well and cook through for 3 minutes.
- Add the stock, honey and tinned tomatoes and stir thoroughly. Bring gently to the boil. Add the dried fruit and simmer for 5 minutes.
- Place the spicy liquid into the slow cooker, and pile the cooked meatballs on top and cook on a low setting for 6 hours.
- 10 minutes before the end of cooking, stir in the chopped coriander
- Serve hot with rice, couscous or pitta bread.

Spicy Lamb Tajine — 762

For a slightly spicier tagine, add ¼ tsp chilli flakes or double the harissa paste.

PREPARATION TIME :20 MINUTES

COOKING TIME : 6 HOURS

INGREDIENTS

MEATBALLS
500 g / 15 ½ oz lamb mince
2 tsp ground cumin
2 tbsp ground coriander
2 garlic cloves minced
1 lemon, zested and juice
1 egg lightly beaten with fork
30 ml / 2 tbsp fresh mint chopped
60 ml / 4 tsp / ¼ cup vegetable oil

SAUCE
4 garlic cloves, crushed
1 medium onion, finely sliced
½ tsp chilli flakes
1 tsp cumin, 1 tsp turmeric
1 tsp cinnamon, ½ tsp paprika
½ tsp fennel seed, 1 tsp harissa paste
1 x 440g / 15.5 oz can tomatoes
120 ml / 4 fl. oz / ½ cup beef stock
1 handful of fresh mint chopped
10 ml / 2 tbsp clear honey
125 g s / 4 oz / ½ cup stoned dates
125 g s / 4 oz / ½ cup dried apricots

Lamb and Orange Tagine

SERVES 4 · 763

- Pre-warm the slow cooker.
- Heat the oil and fry the lamb cubes until brown and sealed. Set to one side.
- Add more oil and sauté the onion, herbs, spices, chilli flakes and garlic for 3 minutes.
- Add the stock, honey and orange juice and zest and stir thoroughly. Bring gently to the boil. Add the dates and segmented orange and simmer for 5 minutes.
- Place the spicy tagine sauce and lamb pieces into the slow cooker. Stir well and cook on a low setting for 8 hours.
- 10 minutes before the end of cooking, stir in the chopped coriander
- Serve hot with rice, couscous or pitta bread.

Spicy Lamb and Orange Tajine — 764

For a slightly spicier tagine, add 2 tsp chilli flakes before slow cooking

PREPARATION TIME :25 MINUTES

COOKING TIME : 8 HOURS

INGREDIENTS

800 g / 28 oz lamb, diced
60 ml / 4 tsp / ¼ cup vegetable oil
4 garlic cloves, minced
1 medium onion, finely sliced
1 tsp ground ginger
1 tsp cumin, 1 tsp turmeric
½ tsp ground cinnamon
1 star anise
2 tsp ground cumin
2 tbsp ground coriander
2 garlic cloves minced
2 unwaxed oranges zested and juice
2 unwaxed oranges peeled, pithed and segmented
400 ml / ¾ pt / 1.5 cups beef or chicken stock
¼ tsp chilli flakes
10 ml / 2 tbsp clear honey
125 g s / 4 oz / ½ cup stoned dates, finely chopped
30 ml / 2 tbsp fresh coriander

765

SERVES 4

Roast Cockerel and Prunes

PREPARATION TIME :10 MINUTES

COOKING TIME : 6 HOURS

....

INGREDIENTS

1.75 kg / 4 lb young cockerel /
chicken jointed
salt, pepper and paprika
350 g / 12 oz prunes, chopped
1 medium onion, finely chopped
30 ml / 2 tbsp goose fat or vegetable
oil
150 ml / 1.4 pt / ⅔ cup chicken stock
2 garlic cloves, minced
1 pinch saffron soaked in 2 tbsp milk
2 tsp ground cumin
2 tsp cinnamon
1 tsp ginger
1 tbsp coriander
1 tbsp honey
120 g / 4 oz / 0.5 cup ground almonds
ground black pepper
basil, to garnish

- Grease and warm the slow cooker..
- Clean, pat dry and brush the chicken / cockerel pieces
  with oil and sprinkle with salt pepper and paprika.
- Place in wok or heavy pan in hot oil and fry until
  golden brown. Remove and place to the side.
- Fry the onions, garlic, spices, fruit, milk with saffron
  and almonds in the remaining fat.
- Cover with stock and honey and bring to the boil
- Place all ingredients into the slow cooker and cook
  on low heat for 6 hours.
- When cooking finished, check sauce for thickness
  and seasoning, stir in the ground almonds and adjust
  seasoning as necessary before serving.

766

MAKES 18

Sweet & Sour Chicken and Prune Tagine

PREPARATION TIME :20 MINUTES

COOKING TIME : 6 HOURS

....

INGREDIENTS

4 large chicken joints with skin on
salt, pepper and paprika for dusting
30 ml / 2 tbsp vegetable oil

SAUCE
3 garlic cloves, minced
100 ml / 4 fl. oz / ½ cup soy sauce
100 ml / 4 fl. oz / ½ cup white wine
vinegar
100 ml / 4 fl. oz / ½ cup sherry
100 ml / 4 fl. oz / ½ cup chicken
stock
4 tbsp soft brown sugar
3 tbsp cornflour
1 lb dried prunes, soaked overnight
in apple or orange juice
1 lemon, zested and juiced
1 onion, finely sliced
1 tsp Chinese 5 spice powder
1 tsp fresh powdered ginger

GARNISH
2 spring onion finely shredded
lemon slices

- Heat the oil and fry (sauté) the chicken pieces until
  brown and transfer one side.
- Meanwhile, prepare the sauce. Fry the onion and garlic.
  Reserving the soy sauce and cornflour to one side, add
  all the other ingredients to the pan and bring to the boil
- Transfer to the slow cooker. Place the chicken breasts
  over the prunes. Cover and cook on low for 6 hours.
- Remove the chicken breasts to a warm plate to rest.
- Pour the sauce into a saucepan and bring to a simmer.
- Mix the cornflour and soy sauce to combine, and add to
  the saucepan stirring all the time to thicken.
- To serve, spoon the sauce onto individual plates. Cut
  each chicken breast into diagonal slices and reform on
  the sauce.
- Garnish with lemon slices and shredded spring onions
  sprinkled over.

Spicy Sweet & Sour Chicken   767

Add 1 tsp of chilli flakes to make a spicier
version of this dish.

768

SERVES 6

Roast Pork with Potatoes

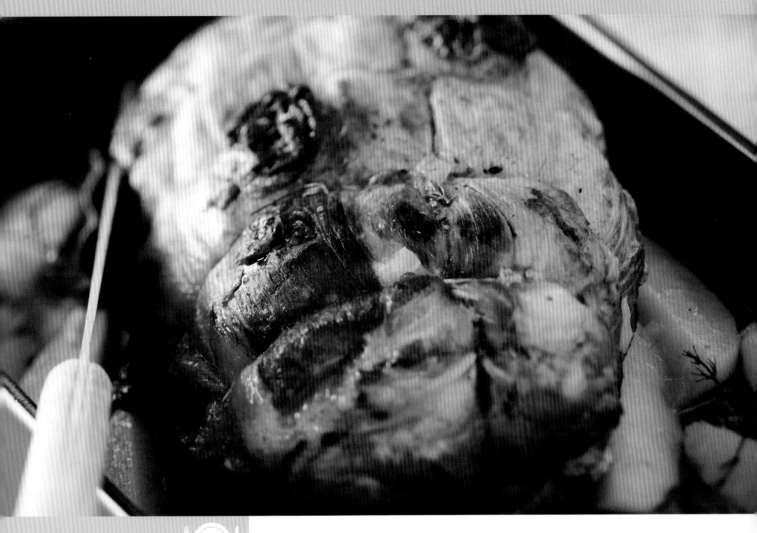

Roast Pork with Dry Prunes

769

Tinned prunes without the juice are a good alternative to dried prunes.

Prune Stuffed Pork

770

The pork may be sliced open and stuffed with the prunes, prior to slow cooking.

Roast Pork with Butternut Squash

771

Replace the potatoes with half de-seeded butternut squash. roast with thyme for 20 minutes until golden.

PREPARATION TIME: 15 MINUTES

COOKING TIME: 5 HOURS

INGREDIENTS

4 tbsp groundnut oil
2 kg / 4 ½ lb rolled shoulder of pork, butterflied
1 kg / 1 lb / 4 cups Charlotte potatoes, halved
110g / 4 oz / ⅔ cup prunes
300ml / 10 ½ fl. oz / 1 ⅓ cup chicken stock
4 sprigs of thyme, leaves stripped from the stems

- Open up the shoulder of pork and season the inside.
- Arrange most of the prunes in the middle, then re-roll the shoulder around the prunes.
- Tie securely with kitchen twine and season the outside generously.
- Heat the groundnut oil in a large frying pan set over a high heat until hot.
- Seal the shoulder in the oil until golden brown.
- Place the potatoes, thyme leaves and sprigs and the remaining prunes in a slow cooker.
- Sit the pork on top and pour in the chicken stock.
- Cook the pork on a high setting for 5 hours until it is firm yet slightly springy to the touch; it should ready at least 65C (160F) on a meat thermometer.
- Once cooked, spoon the potatoes into a roasting tray along with the prunes and thyme.
- Sit the pork shoulder on top before serving.

213

772

SERVES 4

Lamb with Yellow Peppers and Beans

PREPARATION TIME :
25 MINUTES

COOKING TIME : 8 HOURS

INGREDIENTS

1 leg of lamb of size to fit into slow cooker, bone removed
For Lamb stuffing:-
225 g / 8 oz fresh parsley minced
55 g / 2 oz fresh mint minced
8 cloves of garlic minced
30 g / 1 oz butter
For Flageolet Beans and Peppers:-
1 x 400 g can cooked flageolet beans
2 tbsp fresh mint chopped
1 tbsp olive oil
1 knob butter
3 yellow peppers sliced
2 tbsp chicken stock
salt and pepper

- Pre-warm the slow cooker.
- Mix up the lamb stuffing ingredients in a food processor and past inside the boned joint. Bind the joint with string or a skewer to hold
- Heat the oil and fry the lamb all over until brown and sealed.
- Place in the slow cooker
- In the pan used to fry the lamb, melt the knob of butter and olive oil and braise the beans and peppers with the mint and a pinch of salt and pepper. Add the stock.
- Pour the bean and pepper mixture around the lamb, cover and cook on a low setting for 8 hours.
- When done, lift lamb onto a roasting rack and roast in a hot oven at 180 F or Gas Mark 7 / 8 for 30 minutes to crisp up exterior of joint. During this time replace the lid onto the slow cooker to maintain heat. When the lamb is done, place on a serving surrounded with the beans and peppers.

773

SERVES 4

Sausages with Split Peas

PREPARATION TIME :
20 MINUTES

COOKING TIME : 4 HOURS

INGREDIENTS

2 coils of Cumberland sausage, cut into pieces
30 ml / 2 tbsp vegetable oil
1 x 400 g can of precooked split peas / green lentils
1 small carrot, scrubbed, sliced and blanched for 5 minutes
1 onions, thinly sliced
100 ml / 3 fl. oz / ½ cup white wine
100 ml / 3 fl. oz / ½ cup strong chicken stock
2 medium boiled potatoes, sliced
1 leek, rinsed and cut into 1" pieces
2 sticks celery, chopped
1 bay leaf
bouquet garni
salt and ground black pepper

GARNISH
2 tbsp flat leafed parsley

- Pre-warm the slow cooker.
- Heat the oil and fry (sauté) the sliced sausage until brown and transfer to the crockpot
- Sweat the onions, potato, celery, leek and carrot for 5 minutes then add to the slow cooker.
- Deglaze the pan with the white wine, boil for 5 minutes, scraping side of pan with wooden spoon and adding the cloves and bouquet garni.
- Add all ingredients to the slow cooker and stir well.
- Cover and cook on a medium setting for 4 hours.
- Taste and adjust seasoning
- Pour into a casserole dish before serving and sprinkle with parsley

SERVES 4 775

Lamb Shank with Garlic and Brandy

- Pre-warm the slow cooker.
- Wipe the veal portions and season with salt and pepper.
- Heat the oil and fry (sauté) the veal until golden brown all over.
- Transfer to the crockpot
- In a saucepan lightly fry the onion and garlic. Cover with the other ingredients omitting the cornflour and soy sauce and bring to the boil.
- Transfer liquid to the stock covering the veal.
- Adjust seasoning of the sauce to taste and thicken with a mixture of cornflour (cornstarch) and soy sauce as required
- Plate up the veal shank and serve with the sauce spooned over
- Garnish with fresh orange slices and parsley.

PREPARATION TIME :
30 MINUTES

COOKING TIME : 8 HOURS

INGREDIENTS

1.1 kg (2.5 lb) Veal knuckle or shank, sawn into 8 ½ cm (3 in) pieces
salt and pepper
1 large onion finely chopped
1 x 400 g can chopped tomatoes
2 tbsp tomato puree
175 ml (6 fl. oz) ¾ cup Orange Juice
2 oranges, peeled, de-pithed and cut into thin slices
1 orange zested and juice
15 ml / 1 tbsp brandy or cognac
120 ml / 4 oz / ½ cup beef stock
1 tbsp balsamic vinegar
1 tbsp cornflour (cornstarch)
1 tbsp soy sauce
2 tsp brown or Demerara sugar

GARNISH
fresh orange slices and parsley.

SERVES 4 776

Veal Colombo

- In a dish, stir the oil onto the veal pieces, then coat with Colombo powder. Leave in the fridge for 2 hours.
- Pre-warm the slow cooker.
- Heat the oil and fry (sauté) the veal until golden brown and transfer to the crockpot
- Fry the onions and garlic for 5 minutes then add the rest of the ingredients, mixing well and bringing to the boil.
- Immediately transfer to the slow cooker, cover and cook on a medium setting for 4 hours.
- To serve, spoon onto individual serving dishes.

PREPARATION TIME :
30 MINUTES

COOKING TIME : 4 HOURS

INGREDIENTS

1.5 kg / 3.3 lb veal fillet cut into 8 portions or strips
salt and ground black pepper
4 tbsp Colombo powder (see note below)
Oil for frying
1 medium onions, thinly sliced
1 garlic clove, minced
30 ml / 2 tbsp lime juice
1 small red chilli (chili) finely sliced
50 g / 2 oz sweet dried banana chips
1 x 400 g can coconut milk
bouquet garni
250 ml / 8 fl. oz / 1 cup chicken stock
1 green pepper finely sliced
100 g / 4 oz broccoli florets
4 baby corn on cobs - halved
1 tsp brown sugar

777

SERVES 6

Oven Roast Veal

Horseradish Veal Joint   778

Add 2 tbsp grated horseradish to the cream and mustard mixture before coating the veal joint.

Mild Mustard Veal Joint   779

Use mild wholegrain mustard instead of the English Mustard if preferred.

Oven Roast Veal with Mushroom Sauce   780

Sauté in a pan 1 chopped onion, 1 chopped garlic clove, and 225 g / 8 oz button mushrooms. Once done, add crème fraîche and cover the veal.

PREPARATION TIME :
35 MINUTES

COOKING TIME : 8 HOURS

INGREDIENTS

1 ¾ kg / 4lb joint of veal, boned and rolled
30 ml / 2 tbsp goose fat or beef dripping
90 ml / 6 tbsp thick / double cream
30 ml / 2 tbsp English mustard
30 ml / 2 tbsp vegetable oil

- Oil and Warm the slow Cooker.
- In a large thick-based pan, heat the goose fat or dripping and sear the veal joint until golden brown all over and remove to the slow cooker
- Cover with the lid and cook on low for 6 hours.
- In the last hour, prepare the roast potatoes.
- Heat the oven to 200°C (180° fan) / 450F / gas 8
- Remove the veal from the slow cooker, allow to cool slightly and pat dry with kitchen paper. Place in a roasting tin, brushed with 1 tsp of oil.
- Mix the cream, mustard and oil together and brush over the veal joint.
- Roast in the top of the hot oven for 30 minutes or until golden.
- Remove and rest for 20 minutes covered before carving and serving.

781

Caramelized Pork with Basil Leaves

- Combine the marinade ingredients and coat the pork joint. Cover with cling film and refrigerate for 2 to 4 hours
- Pre-warm the slow cooker.
- Season the pork with salt and pepper.
- Heat the oil and fry (sauté) the pork until golden brown all over. Pour into the base of the pan the granulated sugar and water and heat until boiling and reduced to a sticky syrup. Coat the pork entirely and cook all over for a further 10 minutes.
- Transfer to the slow cooker
- Cover and cook on a low setting for 8 hours then check the internal temperature of the pork to ensure it has reached at least 160o F. Remove from pot and rest covered for 20 minutes.
- Carve the pork and serve with any juices (thicken with cornflour / cornstarch if desired.

PREPARATION TIME : 20 MINUTES

COOKING TIME : 8 HOURS

....

INGREDIENTS

1.5 kg / 3lb 3oz boneless pork loin roasting joint
salt and pepper
2 tbsp goose fat or vegetable oil
4 tbsp granulated sugar
2 tablespoons water

MARINADE

1 tbsp soft Demerara sugar
1 lemon, zested and juice
1 orange zest and juice
2 tbsp olive oil
½ teaspoon chilli flakes
5 spring onions, (scallions) slices diagonally

782

Veal Casserole in Cream and Mushroom Sauce

- Pre-warm the slow cooker.
- Heat the oil and fry (sauté) the veal until golden brown and transfer to the slow cooker.
- Fry the onions, paprika, mushrooms and garlic for 5 minutes.
- Add the brandy and boil away.
- Mix in the bay leaves, stock and cream and bring to the boil.
- Immediately transfer to the slow cooker coating the veal joint.
- Cover and cook on a low setting for 8 hours.
- To serve, spoon onto individual serving dishes.

PREPARATION TIME : 30 MINUTES

COOKING TIME : 8 HOURS

....

INGREDIENTS

1.5 kg / 3.3 lb veal fillet joint
salt and ground black pepper
Oil for frying

SAUCE

1 medium onions, thinly sliced
2 garlic cloves, minced
200 g / 8 oz mushrooms, sliced
125 ml / 4 fl. oz / ½ cup chicken stock
250 ml / 8 fl. oz / 1 cup thick cream
1 tbsp brandy
1 tsp paprika
2 bay leaves

783

SERVES 2

Duckling & Clementine Casserole

**PREPARATION TIME :
15 MINUTES**

COOKING TIME : 8 HOURS

INGREDIENTS

1 duckling per 2 person
salt, pepper and paprika
30 ml / 2 tbsp sesame oil
30 ml / 2 tbsp goose fat
1 onion, finely chopped
4 small clementines, peeled
2 garlic cloves, minced
1 tbsp each ground coriander, cumin,
paprika and ginger
120 ml / 4 fl. oz / ½ cup Cointreau
15 ml / tbsp clear honey
300 ml / 10 fl. oz / 1 cups chicken
stock
100 ml / 3 fl. oz / ½ cups orange juice

GARNISH
Spring onions sliced lengthways

- Grease and warm the slow Cooker..
- Clean, pat dry the duck. Season and fry until golden brown
- Place in the slow cooker
- Fry onion and garlic until softened.
- Pour in spices and mix well. Fry for 2 minutes.
- Mix in the Cointreau, orange juice, stock, clementines and honey and bring to the boil for 5 minutes.
- Pour the sauce around the duckling. Cover with the lid and allow to cook for 8 hours at a low heat.
- Check internal temperature has reached 160 F.
- When cooking complete, remove duck and place in a roasting tray, baste with a spoonful of oil from the tray. Bake in a very hot oven (220 F or gas marked 8) for 20 minutes.
- To serve, move duckling to a serving dish, surround with the clementines and sauce and sprinkle with chopped spring onions.

784

SERVES 6

Marinated Pork Fillet

**PREPARATION TIME : 12 HRS
MARINATING AND 25 MINUTES**

COOKING TIME : 8 HOURS

INGREDIENTS

1.5 kg / 3 lb 3 oz boneless pork
roasting joint
90 ml / 6 tbsp calvados
1 eating apple, eg Pink Lady, cored
and thinly sliced

MARINADE

30 ml / 2 tbsp clear honey
2 lemons zested and juice
90 ml / 6 tbsp olive oil
1 tsp sage, fresh chopped or dried
1 sprig rosemary
salt and pepper
2 tbsp red wine vinegar
1 garlic clove, minced
1 tbsp brown sugar

- Wipe the pork joint and season
- Mix together the marinade ingredients and smother pork. Cover and refrigerate overnight.
- Pre-warm the slow cooker.
- Heat the oil and fry (sauté) the pork with a little marinade until golden brown all over.
- Transfer to the crockpot, surrounded with sliced apple and calvados.
- Cover and cook on a low setting for 8 hours then check the internal temperature of the pork to ensure it has reached at least 160o F. Remove from pot and rest covered for 20 minutes.
- Carve the pork, and spoon over the juices to serve. Garnish with fresh sage leaves.

785

SERVES 4

Spicy Boar Stew

Spicy Boar and Apple Stew

786

Adding a peeled and slice apple to this recipe really bring out the pork flavour.

Creamy Boar Stew

787

Stirring a spoon or two of crème fraiche into the sauce before serving give a creamy but still spicy alternative

Boar Stew with Raisins

788

Simmer 100 g / 3 ½ oz plump raisins with the boar chunks.

PREPARATION TIME :
25 MINUTES

COOKING TIME : 8 HOURS

INGREDIENTS

1 ¾ kg / 4lb boned joint or leg of wild boar trimmed and chopped into 2 inch square pieces
30 ml / 2 tbsp vegetable oil
2 onions, sliced
4 carrots, finely sliced on the diagonal and blanched for 5 minutes
1 stick or celery, finely sliced
2 leeks, cleaned and sliced and blanched for 5 minutes
1 garlic cloves, crushed
½ red cabbage, washed and chopped
300ml / ½ pint / 1 ⅓ cups chicken stock
2 bay leaves
1 tbsp tomato paste
2 tbsp cumin seeds
1 tbsp turmeric
½ tsp chilli flakes
Salt and black pepper

- Pre-warm the slow cooker.
- Heat the oil and fry (sauté) the wild boar chunks until golden brown. Remove and set aside
- In the remaining oil, fry the onion, celery, leeks, carrot, garlic and red cabbage for 10 minutes.
- Cover with stock and boil for 5 minutes.
- Add the tomato paste, bay leaves and bring to the boil
- Transfer the meat and stock mixture to the slow cooker.
- Cover and cook on a low setting for 8 hours.
- If required, thicken the sauce with a little cornflour.
- Serve hot with game chips and a selection of potatoes and vegetables.

789

SERVES 4

Veal and Carrot Stew

PREPARATION TIME:

15 MINUTES

COOKING TIME : 8 HOURS

INGREDIENTS

1 kg / 2 lb fillet of rose veal, cubed
Plain (all-purpose) flour for dusting
30 ml / 2 tbsp vegetable oil
1 clove garlic, minced
300 ml / ½ pt / 1¼ cups beef stock
1 glass dry white wine
2 tbsp tomato paste
1 whole clove
0.5 kg / 1 lb chopped carrots
blanched for 5 minutes.
2 bay leaves
bouquet garni
2 large onions, sliced
1 x 440ml / 15.5 oz can chopped
tomatoes
salt and ground black pepper

GARNISH

chives, washed and snipped
basil, to garnish

- Pre-warm the slow cooker.
- Heat the oil in a pan. Dust the veal cubes with flour and seasoning and fry (sauté) until brown.
- Transfer to the slow cooker.
- Sweat the onions, garlic and carrots for 5 minutes. Stir in the tomato paste , herbs, wine and stock and bring to the boil.
- Pour over the veal in the slow cooker. Cover and cook on a low setting for 8 hours.
- Taste and adjust seasoning.
- Pour into a casserole dish before serving and sprinkle chopped chives

790

SERVES 4

Tubetti with Mince and Red Onion

PREPARATION TIME :

25 MINUTES

COOKING TIME : 4 HOURS

INGREDIENTS

8 dried cannelloni tubes

FILLING

250 g / 1 lb minced beef
2 tbsp olive oil
150 g / 6 oz / ¾ bacon lardons
2 red onions finely shredded
1 carrot, shredded
1 celery stick finely chopped
2 cloves garlic
1 glass red wine
1 bay leaf
1 x 400 g can chopped tomatoes
200ml beef stock
1 green pepper
250 g / 8oz grated Parmesan and
cheddar mixed
400 g white sauce

- Pre-warm the slow cooker.
- Heat the oil and fry (sauté) the onions, lardons, mince, carrot, celery and garlic until golden brown.
- Add the wine and boil to reduce by half.
- Pour over the tomatoes, beef stock, peppers and bay leaf and boil for 5 minutes.
- Use the ragu to stuff the cannelloni tubes and place side by side in bottom of slow cooker dish
- Pour over the white sauce and cheeses mixed together. Sprinkle with salt and pepper.
- Cook on low heat, covered with a lid, for 8 hours.
- Serve hot and garnish with coriander.

791

MAKES 18

Caramelized Pork Spare-ribs

- Mix the marinade ingredients together in a pan and bring to the boil. Coat the spare ribs and refrigerate for 4 hours.
- Pre-warm the slow cooker.
- Transfer the ribs to the crockpot and cover and cook on a medium setting for 8 hours
- Remove from the slow cooker and set on a rack in a very hot oven 200 F or Gas Mark 8 for 25 minutes. Brush oil on the tomatoes and roast these for 20 minutes alongside the ribs.
- Carve and serve hot.
- Garnish with fresh basil leaves.

PREPARATION TIME :
25 MINUTES

COOKING TIME : 6 HOURS

INGREDIENTS

1 kg / 2 lb pork spare ribs
Cherry tomatoes on the vine
Olive oil

MARINADE: -
1 tsp salt
2 tbsp onion finely chopped
3 garlic cloves, minced
2 tbsp sugar
¼ tsp black pepper
3 tbsp of soy sauce
1 tbsp vegetable oil

GARNISH
Fresh basil leaves.

792

SERVES 4

Roasted Winter Vegetables

- Pre-warm the slow cooker.
- Heat the oil in a pan and fry (sauté) all vegetables and garlic turning regularly for 5 minutes.
- Mix in the Rosemary and give a good sprinkling of freshly ground black pepper.
- Transfer to the slow cooker.
- Cover and cook on a medium setting for 4 hours stirring once halfway through cooking.
- Taste and adjust seasoning.
- Pour into a serving dish and garnish with 2 whole chives.

PREPARATION TIME: 20 MINUTES

COOKING TIME : 4 HOURS

INGREDIENTS

1.5 kg / 3 lb mixed vegetables, chopped and blanched for 5 minutes
45 ml / 3 tbsp olive oil
3 clove garlic, minced
45 ml / 3 tbsp vegetable stock
2 bay leaves
2 tbsp chopped rosemary
ground black pepper

GARNISH
2 whole chives

793

SERVES 4

Leek and Prawn Stew

Prawn and Flageolet Stew

794

The beans may be replaced for flageolet beans

Prawn and Conchigliette Stew

795

The beans may be replaced with pasta (shells)

Prawn and Couscous Stew

796

Replace the beans with 100 g / 3.5 oz couscous and use as a bed for the stew.

PREPARATION TIME :

30 MINUTES

COOKING TIME : 5 HOURS

....

INGREDIENTS

2 x 440g / 15 ½ oz cans broad beans
1 onion, finely chopped
30 ml / 1 fl. oz / 2 tbsp Olive or Sunflower Oil
300 g / 10 oz / 2 cups Dublin Bay Prawns with shells on
300 g / 10 oz / 2 cups Littleneck clams, cleaned and checked alive by tapping
3 cloves of garlic
150 ml / ½ pt / ¾ cup dry white wine
150 ml / ½ pt / ¾ cup chicken stock
Salt and Pepper to taste
1 lemon zested and juice
2 tbsp fresh parsley, chopped

GARNISH
Several sprigs of parsley
Paprika for sprinkling

- Warm the slow Cooker..
- Heat the oil in a pan and gently sauté the onion and garlic.
- Add the wine, parsley, beans and stock and bring to the boil
- Place in the slow cooker for hours on low.
- Remove contents of slow cooker, into a wok and bring to the boil.
- Add the clams and prawns, cover with a lid, and boil for 5 minutes.
- Check clams, if any are unopened this means they are dead and must be removed.
- Spoon the Stew into bowls and serve sprinkled with parsley and alongside fresh crusty bread and butter.

797

SERVES 4

Thai Chicken Curry with Coconut Milk

- Pre-warm the slow cooker.
- Heat the oil and fry (sauté) the chicken until just turning colour. Add all the spices and the curry paste and fry for 3 minutes stirring continuously.
- Add the Thai fish sauce, brown sugar, coconut milk and stock and bring gently to the boil.
- Transfer immediately to the slow cooker.
- Cover with the lid and cook on a high setting for 4 hours.
- Taste and adjust seasoning
- Serve in individual bowls sprinkled with finely chopped coriander and accompanied with jasmine rice.

PREPARATION TIME :
20 MINUTES

COOKING TIME : 4 HOURS

INGREDIENTS

4 chicken breasts sliced or 1 chicken jointed into 8 pieces (marinated)
1 tbsp vegetable oil
115g / 4 oz / ½ cup Thai green curry paste
2 x 1" pieces of lemongrass
2 whole cloves
1 star anise, whole
1 tbsp Thai fish sauce
1 tbsp soft brown sugar
1 cinnamon stick
1 large bay leaf, torn
1 x 400 g can of coconut milk
5 spring onions (scallions) roughly chopped
120 ml / 4 fl. oz / ½ cup of chicken stock
8 basil leaves
3 sprigs of fresh coriander

798

SERVES 4

Provençal-style Rolled Pork

- Pre-warm the slow cooker.
- Roll and tie the pork belly and cut into 4 portions
- Heat the oil and fry (sauté) the pork pieces until golden brown. Remove and set aside
- In the remaining oil, fry the onion, garlic, lardons, courgettes and peppers stirring all the time
- Stir in the flour and cook for 2 minutes
- Pour over the stock, olives and passata and herbs and bring to the boil.
- Place all ingredients into the slow cooker
- Cook on low heat, covered with a lid, for 6 hours.
- Taste when done and season accordingly
- Remove the pork and score the skin finely with a very sharp knife. Place them the right way up, on an oiled roasting dish and place in a hot oven at 200 F or gas mark 8 for 20 to 25 minutes to crisp up crackling.
- Serve hot.

PREPARATION TIME :
55 MINUTES

COOKING TIME : 6 HOURS

INGREDIENTS

1.5 kg / 3lb 5 oz pork belly (skin on)
45 ml / 3 tbsp vegetable oil or goose fat
75 g / 3 oz / ⅓ cup bacon lardons
150 g / 6 oz / ¾ cup courgettes diced
150 g / 6 oz / ¾ cup red pepper
150 g / 6 oz / ¾ cup green pepper
75 g / 3 oz / ⅓ cup green stoned olives
1 tbsp sundried tomato puree
1 x 400 g can chopped tomatoes
1 tbsp plain (all-purpose) flour
3 garlic cloves, crushed
120 ml ¼ pt / ½ cup chicken stock
2 sprigs rosemary
1 tsp dried oregano
Salt and black pepper

799

SERVES 4

Rabbit Fricassée

PREPARATION TIME :15 MINUTES

COOKING TIME :
8 HOURS 15 MINUTES

INGREDIENTS

30 ml / 1 fl. oz / 2 tbsp olive oil
30 g / 1 oz / ¼ stick unsalted butter
1 large rabbit, jointed and trimmed
4 shallots, finely chopped
450 g / 1 lb / 3 cups new potatoes
150 g / 5 oz / 2 cups chestnut
mushrooms, chopped
500 ml / 18 fl. oz / 2 cups chicken
stock
250 ml / 9 fl. oz / 1 cup double cream
salt and pepper

- Heat a large casserole dish over a moderate heat until hot.
- Coat the rabbit pieces in the oil and season generously.
- Seal in batches until golden brown in colour all over before removing to a slow cooker.
- Reduce the heat under the casserole dish and add the butter.
- Sweat the shallot in the butter for 6-7 minutes, stirring occasionally, until softened then add the mushrooms.
- Add the stock and potatoes and stir thoroughly before pouring into a slow cooker.
- Cover with a lid and cook on a low setting for 8 hours until the rabbit is tender.
- Stir through the cream once the rabbit is cooked and adjust the seasoning to taste.
- Spoon into a casserole dish for presentation.

Cream and Parsley Rabbit

800

Add a small bunch of chopped flat-leaf parsley alongside the double cream.

801

SERVES 4

Turkey with Artichoke

PREPARATION TIME :
10-15 MINUTES

COOKING TIME :
4 HOURS 15 MINUTES

INGREDIENTS

55 ml / 2 fl. oz / ¼ cup olive oil
4 turkey escalopes, trimmed and
sliced
4 globe artichokes, trimmed down to
their hearts
225 g / 8 oz / 2 cups green beans,
trimmed
150 g / 5 oz / 1 ½ cups broad beans,
shelled
4 shallots, chopped
250 ml / 9 fl. oz / 1 cup chicken stock
salt and pepper

TO GARNISH
sprigs of thyme

- Coat the turkey slices in most of the oil and season generously.
- Halve the artichoke hearts and set to one side.
- Heat a large frying pan over a moderate heat until hot and seal the turkey in batches until golden brown in colour all over before removing to a slow cooker.
- Reduce the heat and add the remaining oil.
- Sauté the shallots for 5 minutes, stirring occasionally before adding the green beans and artichoke.
- Stir well then spoon into the slow cooker.
- Cover with the stock and cook on a medium setting for 3 hours.
- Add the broad beans after 3 hours and continue to cook for another hour.
- Adjust the seasoning to taste and spoon into a cast-iron serving dish.
- Garnish with the thyme sprigs before serving.

Turkey with Artichoke and Almonds

802

Add 55 g / 2 oz / ½ cup flaked (slivered) almonds to the slow cooker twenty minutes before serving.

SERVES 6

Country-style Roast Veal

- In a large thick-based pan, heat the fat or oil and sear the veal joint until golden brown all over and remove to one side
- In the same fat, fry off the bacon and onion until just starting to crisp
- Place the blanched carrots and celery in the base of the slow cooker then place the veal joint on top.
- Pour in the stock, and sprinkle over the herbs.
- Cover with the lid and cook on low for 8 hours.
- In the last hour, prepare the roast potatoes.
- Heat the goose fat or vegetable oil in a roasting tin, in a hot oven. Place the potatoes in the fat and baste. Roast for 1 hour, basting twice during cooking.
- Remove the veal from the slow cooker and place to one side to rest for 15 minutes, covered with silver foil
- Slice the meat and serve with the roasted potatoes and gravy immediately.

PREPARATION TIME :35 MINUTES

COOKING TIME : 8 HOURS

INGREDIENTS

1.75 kg / 4lb joint of veal, boned and rolled
30 ml / 2 tbsp vegetable oil
50 g / 2 oz lean bacon, rinded
1 onion, sliced
4 carrots, peeled and thinly chopped
4 sticks of celery, rinsed and chopped
1 garlic clove, crushed
sprig of rosemary
30 ml / 2 tbsp fresh thyme, chopped
150ml ¼ pint / ⅔ cup chicken stock
3 bay leaves
1.5 kgs / 3 lbs potatoes, boiled
5 tbsp vegetable oil

MAKES 18

Veal, Pumpkin and Honey

PREPARATION TIME :30 MINUTES

COOKING TIME : 6 HOURS

INGREDIENTS

900 g / 2 lb / 8 cups of veal fillet, diced
4 garlic cloves, crushed
1 tsp cayenne pepper
60 ml / 4 tsp / ¼ cup olive oil

1 large onion, finely chopped
1 x 400 g can of chopped tomatoes
450 g / 1 lb pumpkin, cubed
50 g / 2 oz / ½ cup prunes, chopped
2 tbsp clear honey
1 lemon, zest and juice
1 x 400 g can of chickpeas
800 ml / 27 fl. oz / 3 ½ cups stock
85 g / 3 oz / ½ cup blanched almonds
2 tbsp coriander, roughly chopped

- Toast the almonds for 5 minutes in a hot oven, then leave to cool.
- Heat the oil and fry the veal until golden brown. Remove and set aside.
- In the remaining oil, fry the onion, pumpkin and garlic until softened, stir well and cook through for 3 minutes.
- Add the stock, lemon juice, honey and tinned tomatoes and stir. Bring gently to the boil.
- Place the veal, prunes and vegetables, with the boiling spicy stock liquid into the slow cooker and cook on a low setting for 6 hours.
- Ten minutes before the end of cooking, stir in the chickpeas and coriander.
- Serve hot with rice, couscous or pitta bread.

SERVES 4

Guinea-fowl with Apple

PREPARATION TIME :30 MINUTES

COOKING TIME : 4 HOURS

INGREDIENTS

2 x 1 kg / 2lb Guinea Fowl (Guinea Hen)
60 ml / 4 tsp / ¼ cup Olive or vegetable oil
1 large onion, finely chopped
10 ml / 2 tbsp clear honey
1 lemon, zest and juice

3 cinnamon sticks
1 bay leaf
4 eating apples, cored and sliced into 4 sections
1 tbsp sage, crushed
salt and black pepper
150 ml / ¼ pt / ¾ cup dry cider
½ chicken stock cube, good quality
30 ml / 2 tbsp plain yoghurt

GARNISH
fresh sprig of sage

- Heat the oil and fry the guinea fowl until golden brown. Remove from heat and place in the slow cooker.
- In the remaining fat, fry the onion and brown.
- Pour over the cider and boil to reduce by half.
- Add the apples, herbs, spices and lemon juice and ½ stock cube and bring to the boil.
- Pour the apples and sauce over the guinea fowl, and place the lid on tightly. Cook on a low setting for 4 hours.
- When cooking complete, check the guinea fowl cooked with a thermometer, or pierce to see juices run clear.
- Stir in plain yoghurt to the sauce.
- Serve immediately garnishing with a sprig of fresh sage.

806

SERVES 4

Chicken with Confit Lemon

PREPARATION TIME :
15 MINUTES

COOKING TIME : 6 HOURS

INGREDIENTS

1 x 3 ½ lb chicken jointed or 8
chicken joints, skin on
30 ml / 2 tbsp vegetable oil
1 x 400 g jar green olives
1 small jar lemon confit in syrup
juice of 1 lemon
1 tbsp butter
2 large garlic cloves, minced
500 ml / 1 pint / 2 cups chicken stock
1 medium onion, finely chopped
60 ml / 2 oz / ¼ cup white wine
60 ml / 2 oz / ¼ cup cream
2 bay leaves
1 tsp brandy
1 green pepper, thinly sliced
1 red pepper, thinly sliced
salt and freshly ground pepper

GARNISH
lemon slices and parsley

- Warm the slow cooker.
- Heat the butter and oil in a heavy based pan over a medium heat
- Add the onions and garlic and soften, then add chicken pieces and brown all over–remove to the slow cooker
- Add the sliced peppers and stir well for 4 minutes
- Pour over the wine and boil to reduce by half.
- Add brandy, lemon juice, bay leaves and stock and bring to the boil.
- Pour into the slow cooker and cook for 6 hours on a low setting.
- Remove from the heat and stir in the cream.
- Taste and adjust seasoning
- Garnish with lemon slices parsley leaves and serve.

808

SERVES 6

Filleted Mignon with Pineapple

PREPARATION TIME : MARINADE OVERNIGHT PLUS 15 MINUTES

COOKING TIME : 8 HOURS

INGREDIENTS

1 kg / 2 ⊠ lb Fillet Mignon
60 ml / 6 tbsp beef stock
350 g can sliced pineapple rings,
drained and fried

MARINADE
30 ml / 2 tbsp clear honey
700 ml / 24 fl. oz / 3 cups pineapple
juice
180 ml / 6 fl. oz / ¾ cup soy sauce
180 ml / 6 fl. oz / ¾ cup sherry
100 ml / 4 fl. oz / ½ cup cider vinegar
55 g / 2 oz brown sugar
30 ml / 2 tbsp mild or Dijon mustard
2 cloves
½ stick cinnamon
1 garlic clove, minced
salt and ground black pepper
1 medium onion, finely chopped

- Mix the marinade ingredients together in a large bag. Insert the steak, seal and refrigerate overnight.
- Pre-warm the slow cooker.
- Wipe the fillet joint and fry all over to seal until browned. Place in the slow cooker cook on low for 8 hours.
- Remove the Pork joint and pop into a hot over 230 °C (210° fan) 450F / gas 8 for 20 minutes.
- Carve the pork, and spoon over the pineapple sauce mixture to serve. Garnish with slices of fried pineapple and sprinkled parsley.

Filleted Mignon with Apple   809

The pineapple may easily be replaced with
apple halves for a slightly less sweet flavour.

810

SERVES 4

Stuffed Chicken

Sweet Stuffed Chicken   811

Adding chopped peaches or nectarines to the stuffing; this adds a lovely fruity flavour to the finished dish

Mustard Stuffed Chicken   812

Use 1 tbsb of wholegrain mustard to stuff the chicken before filling its cavity.

Cream Cheese and Pepper Stuffed Chicken   813

Instead of the original stuffing, use 200 g / 7 oz cream cheese mixed with 1 sweet red pepper, sliced, and proceed to stuff the cavity of the chicken with black pepper and parsley.

PREPARATION TIME : 30 MINUTES

COOKING TIME : 6 HOURS

INGREDIENTS

1 chicken cleaned and dried
100 g / 4 oz / 2 cups bacon lardons
175 g / 6 oz / ¾ cup sausage-meat
2 garlic cloves, minced
2 tbsp basil, chopped
2 tbsp sun dried tomatoes or 1 tbsp sun dried tomato paste
Zest of 1 lemon
1 onion finely chopped
6 sage leaves, finely shredded
1 egg yolk
2 tbsp fresh breadcrumbs
salt and ground black pepper

GARNISH
Fresh sage sprigs and char grilled lemon slices

- Pre-warm the slow cooker.
- Clean and dry the chicken and wipe with vegetable oil.
- Sprinkle chicken with salt, pepper and paprika
- Heat the oil and fry (sauté) the chicken until brown then transfer to the crockpot
- Gently fry the garlic, lardons, onion and herbs for 5 minutes.
- Stir in the sun-dried tomato paste or pieces.
- In a separate bowl, fork mix with the sausage-meat. Add the breadcrumbs and lightly whipped egg and season with salt and pepper to taste
- Use this stuffing mixture to fill the chicken cavity.
- Transfer the stuffed chicken to the slow cooker.
- Cover with the lid and cook on a low setting for 6 hours.
- When cooked, move the chicken to a shallow roasting tin and brown in the oven on high, 200°C (180° fan) / 450F / gas 8 for 25 minutes.
- Allow the chicken to rest before carving and serving.

814

SERVES 4

Pear and Chocolate Crumble

PREPARATION TIME :
30 MINUTES

COOKING TIME : 6 HOURS

INGREDIENTS

200 g / 7oz / ¾ cup dark chocolate broken into pieces
200 g / 7oz / ½ cup dried breadcrumbs
200 g / 7oz / ½ cup brown sugar
¼ tsp Cinnamon
170 g / 6 oz / ¾ cup butter or margarine
zest and juice 1 orange
90 ml / 6 tbsp / ⅓ cup Calvados liqueur
8 ripe pears, peeled, cored and chopped into 1 inch chunks

GARNISH
orange zest strips
basil, to garnish

- Grease and warm the slow cooker.
- Poach pears in orange juice and Calvados for a few minutes.
- Rub the butter, sugar, orange zest and breadcrumbs together.
- Stir into the Pears and spoon into the slow cooker.
- Cook on high for 4 hours.
- Remove slow cooker from heat and stir in the chocolate pieces.
- Brown under a grill.
- Serve immediately with Chantilly cream or ice-cream.

White Chocolate Pear Crumble   815

White chocolate may be used to replace the dark chocolate in this recipe.

816

SERVES 4

Chilli con Carne

PREPARATION TIME :
20 MINUTES

COOKING TIME : 4 HOURS

INGREDIENTS

500 g / 1 lb lean beef mince
1 tbsp vegetable oil
½ tsp salt
1 large onion, finely chopped
1 red pepper, chopped
1 tsp hot chilli (chili) powder (or mild chilli powder if preferred)
1 tbsp paprika
2 tsp cumin
1 tsp oregano
3 garlic cloves
2 tbsp tomato puree
1 x 400 g can tinned chopped tomatoes
150ml / 5 fl. oz / ¾ cup water
1 beef stock cube
½ tsp sugar
1 x 400 g red kidney beans cooked

- Pre-warm the slow cooker.
- Sauté the onions, garlic and pepper until soft. Add the chilli, paprika and cumin, stir well and cook for a further 4 minutes.
- Add the mince and brown thoroughly.
- Pour over the water, sugar, oregano, tomatoes, and puree. Crumble in the stock cube and stir thoroughly.
- Transfer to the slow cooker.
- Cover and cook on a high setting for 3 ½ hours.
- Drain the kidney beans and stir into the chilli con carne. Replace lid and cook for a further ½ hour.
- Serve immediately with rice or grated cheese and tortilla chips.

Cheesy Chilli con Carne   817

Stir in some grated cheese and sprinkle on top, before serving.

818
SERVES 4
Meatballs with Eggs Tajine

- Combine meatball ingredients. Roll into 12 balls and refrigerate for 1 hour. Pre-warm the slow cooker.
- Heat the oil and fry the meatballs in batches, leaving to one side when browned.
- To make the sauce, sauté the onion, aubergine and garlic until soft. Add the Ras el Hanout spice mix and cinnamon and stir on the heat for 4 minutes.
- Add the chopped tomatoes, basil and honey. Pour the sauce into the slow cooker and gently spoon the meatballs into the sauce
- Cover and cook on high for 4 hours. Transfer to a saucepan. Stir in the chickpeas and heat for 5 minutes.
- Make four holes in the sauce and break one egg into each. Cover with a lid and simmer for 5 minutes until the eggs are set.
- Taste when done and season accordingly
- Remove from heat and serve with pitta bread.

Meatballs with Quail Eggs   819
The eggs in the sauce, my be replaced with 8 whole hardboiled quails eggs.

PREPARATION TIME :25 MINUTES

COOKING TIME : 4 HOURS

INGREDIENTS

500 g / 1 lb lamb mince
4 tbsp olive oil
50 g / 2 oz breadcrumbs
1 egg whipped with a fork
1 tbsp Parmesan, freshly grated
1 onion finely chopped
1 garlic cloves minced

SAUCE
4 eggs
2 garlic cloves
1 small aubergine, sliced and salted for 20 minutes then rinsed and dried
4 eggs
salt and black pepper
½ tsp cinnamon
2 tbsp honey
1 x 400 g chickpeas
1 tbsp basil, finely chopped
1 tsp Ras el Hanout spice mix
1 x 400 g can chopped tomatoes
3 tbsp of vegetable oil

820
SERVES 4
Beef Chorba with Risi Pasta

- Heat a slow cooker.
- In a separate pan, heat the onions and garlic until soft.
- Stir in the beef cube and brown all over
- Add the spices, chopped tomatoes, vegetables, lemon juice, Risi pasta and vegetable stock. Bring to the boil.
- Transfer into a slow cooker and cook on a low setting for 7 hours.
- Add the coriander and stir. Cook for a further hour. Adjust the seasoning to taste.
- Spoon into serving dishes and garnish with the coriander leaves.
- Serve immediately.

Lamb Chorba with Risi Pasta   821
Substitute the same quantity of beef for lamb.

PREPARATION TIME :
10 MINUTES

COOKING TIME : 8 HOURS

INGREDIENTS

500 kg / 1 lb / 3 cups steak, diced
30 ml / 2 tbsp olive oil
3 cloves garlic, minced
150 g / ½ cup / 1 onion, chopped
5 g / 1 tsp turmeric
1 x 400 g can chopped tomatoes
1 potato, chopped and blanched 1 turnip, chopped and blanched
30 ml / 2 tbsp lemon juice
2 carrots, chopped and blanched
2 celery stalks chopped
1 courgette chopped
pinch of Saffron
1 bunch fresh coriander (cilantro), chopped
55 g / 2 oz / ¼ cup pasta
850 ml / 1 ½ pint / 3 cup vegetable stock
salt and Pepper
coriander leaves

822

SERVES 4

Roast Leg of Turkey with Herbs

Cranberry Roast Turkey with Herbs

823

Add 2 tbsp cranberry sauce to the stock prior to cooking.

PREPARATION TIME :
20 MINUTES

COOKING TIME : 8 HOURS

INGREDIENTS

2 medium turkey legs
45 ml / 3 tbsp goose fat or vegetable oil
1 onion, finely chopped
60 ml / 4 tbsp chicken stock
5 g / 1 tsp sage, finely chopped
5 g / 1 tsp thyme, finely chopped
Zest of 1 lemon
Salt and pepper

GARNISH
Sprig of fresh herbs

- Warm the slow Cooker..
- Heat fat in a pan and sauté the turkey legs until golden. Place in the slow cooker.
- Sauté the onion for 3 minutes and cover with the stock, lemon zest, herbs and seasoning and bring to the boil for 2 minutes
- Pour into the slow cooker over the turkey legs.
- Place the lid over the pot and cook on low heat for 8 hours.
- Remove and place turkey legs in a roasting tin, and roast in a hot oven (220 F or Gas Mark 7 / 8) for 20 minutes.
- Rest and carve. Serve with thickened pan juices.

824

SERVES 4

Capon with Gribiche Sauce

- Warm the slow Cooker..
- Heat Oil in pan and sauté the capon until golden.
- Spread the vegetables, stock and herbs on the bottom of the slow cooker dish. Place the capon, skin side up, into the slow cooker and season.
- Place the lid over the pot and cook on low heat for 8–10 hrs or until juices run clear.
- Meanwhile make the Gribiche Sauce. Mix all the sauce ingredients together, mashing the egg with a fork. Keep in the refrigerator until the Capon is ready for serving.
- Place on a serving dish when cooked and garnish with parsley.
- Use juices to make a gravy and serve the Gribiche sauce to the side.

PREPARATION TIME :
30 MINUTES

COOKING TIME : 8 - 10 HOURS

INGREDIENTS

1.75 kg / 4lb capon cut into portions
30 ml / 2 tbsp vegetable oil
1 clove garlic, minced
225 g / 8 oz leeks, washed and sliced
225 g / 8 oz carrots, cut into batons
225 g / 8 oz chopped celery
250 ml / 8 fl. oz / 1 cup chicken stock
salt and pepper
6 tbsp sage leaves
for the sauce
250 ml / ½ pint / 1 cup mayonnaise
3 hard-boiled eggs chopped
1 tbsp Dijon mustard
5 g / 1 tbsp shallots, finely chopped
½ tbsp white wine vinegar
50 g / 2 oz baby cornichons, chopped
5 ml / tsp lemon juice
25 g / 1 oz capers, chopped
½ tsp tarragon, chopped
1 tsp chives, snipped

Guinea Fowl with Gribiche Sauce   825

Replace the capon with 2 small guinea fowl for this alternative

826

SERVES 4

Chicken Kiev

- Using a sharp knife, cut a pocket in the side of each chicken breast.
- Use a teaspoon to stuff the pocket with pesto, then press the edges firmly together.
- Place the flour, eggs and polenta on separate plates. Season the flour with salt and pepper.
- Dip each chicken breast into the flour, then the eggs, then the polenta, coating thoroughly each time.
- Heat the butter until foaming then add the chicken breasts and cook, turning regularly for about 20 minutes until cooked through.
- Serve hot with a salad.

PREPARATION TIME: 10 MINUTES

COOKING TIME: 20 MINUTES

INGREDIENTS

4 chicken breasts, skinned
8 tbsp pesto
75 g / 2 ¾ oz / ⅓ cup plain (all purpose) flour
3 eggs, beaten
250 g / 9 oz / 1 cup polenta
2 tbsp butter

Cheesy Chicken Kiev   827

Add 1 slice of mozzarella with the pesto inside the chicken breast.

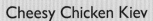

828

SERVES 4

Mushroom Soup

PREPARATION TIME: 15 MINUTES

COOKING TIME : 4 HOURS

....

INGREDIENTS

600 g mixed wild mushrooms, chopped
30 ml / 2 tbsp vegetable oil
salt and pepper
2 clove garlic, minced
1 large onion, finely chopped
110 g / 4 oz / ½ cup leeks, finely chopped
500 ml / 16 fl. oz / 2 cups beef stock
½ glass dry white wine
1 tbsp turmeric
2 medium potatoes, finely chopped
1 bay leaf
1 tbsp brandy
100ml / 3 fl. oz / ½ cup single cream
salt and ground black pepper

GARNISH
1 tbsp fine chopped mushrooms fried

- Pre-warm the slow cooker.
- Heat the oil in a pan. Fry the onion, garlic, leeks, turmeric and mushrooms for 8 minutes stirring gently
- Transfer to the crockpot
- Add all the other ingredients.
- Cover and cook on medium for 4 hours.
- Taste and adjust seasoning
- Serve in individual bowls and garnished with 1 tbsp chopped fried mushrooms

Mushroom Soup without Alcohol   829

Replace the wine and brandy with an equivalent measure of chicken or vegetable stock

830

SERVES 4

Octopus and Turnip Casserole

PREPARATION TIME :
300 MINUTES

COOKING TIME : 8 HOURS

....

INGREDIENTS

500 g / 1 lb baby octopus
1 pinch saffron soaked in 500 ml / 1 pt / 2 cups fish stock
4 tbsp white wine
2 tsp white wine vinegar
2 garlic cloves, minced
5 g / 1 tsp thyme
1 lemon, zest and juice
5 ml / 1 tbsp light soy sauce
170g / 6 oz bacon lardons
½ onion finely chopped
1 stick of lemon grass
170g / 6 oz / ¾ cup turnip, diced
110 g / 4 oz / ½ cup potato, diced
10 ml / 2 tbsp vegetable oil

GARNISH
4 tbsp fresh parsley, chopped

- Warm the slow Cooker..
- Heat the oil in a pan and gently sauté the onion, garlic, bacon, turnip, potato and octopus for 10 minutes.
- Add the stock, sugar, lemon grass, white wine, vinegar, thyme, lemon zest and juice and soy sauce. Bring to the boil
- Transfer to the slow cooker, cover with the lid and cook for 8 hours on low.
- Spoon into serving dishes and garnish with the parsley and freshly ground black pepper. Serve with rice or crusty bread.

Asian Octopus and   831
Turnip Casserole

For an Asian twist to this casserole, replace the wine with coconut cream and add 1 tbsp of green Thai curry paste to the mixture before slow cooking.

832

SERVES 4

Rabbit and Spring Vegetable Stew

PREPARATION TIME: 5 MINUTES

COOKING TIME: 1 HOUR

INGREDIENTS

1 rabbit, jointed
2 tbsp butter
2 tbsp olive oil
1 onion, finely chopped
500ml / 1 pint / 2 cups chicken stock
1 sprig thyme
200 g / 7 oz carrots, scrubbed
8 baby turnips, scrubbed
200 g / 6 ½ oz / ¾ cup peas

- Heat the butter in a casserole pan with the oil then seal the rabbit in batches on all sides. Remove to a plate.
- Cook the onion in the butter until soft and translucent. Return the rabbit to the pan.
- Pour over the stock and add the thyme. Bring to a simmer then cook for 20 minutes over a low heat.
- Add the carrots and turnips and cook for a further 20 minutes.
- Add the peas and cook for 5 minutes.
- Season with salt and pepper. If the sauce is too liquid, remove the rabbit and vegetables and reduce to the desired consistency, then return them to the pan to heat through before serving.

Rabbit and Sweetcorn Stew

833

Replace the peas with sweetcorn for a sweet and colourful twist.

834

SERVES 4

Vegetable and Cardamom Stew

PREPARATION TIME :
30 MINUTES

COOKING TIME : 4 HOURS

INGREDIENTS

900 g / 2 lb mixed / 8 cups vegetables,
diced (can include carrot, turnip,
swede, cauliflower, broccoli,
courgette (courgette), pumpkin, wild
mushrooms, potatoes etc) all finely
diced
60 ml / 4 tbsp vegetable oil
5g / 1 tsp cumin seed
15 g / 1 tbsp flour
1 l / 35 fl. oz / 4 cups vegetable or
chicken stock
10 ml / 2 tsp white wine vinegar
2 garlic cloves, minced
1 x 400 g can chickpeas, drained
10 cardamoms, lightly toasted

GARNISH
Sprig of Mint

- Warm the slow Cooker..
- Heat the oil in a pan and gently sauté all the vegetables,
  cumin seeds and garlic for 10 minutes stirring gently.
- Add the flour to the pan and stir in for a further 3
  minutes.
- Add the stock, vinegar, and cardamoms mixing well.
  Bring to the boil.
- Transfer to the slow cooker, cover with the lid and cook
  for 4 hours on medium.
- Add the chickpeas and stir. Cover the pan and slow
  cook for 15 minutes.
- Spoon into serving dishes and garnish with the mint.

Spicy Vegetable and Cardamom Stew

835

For extra spice, when frying the vegetables,
add 1 tsp of chilli (chili) flakes and 1 tbsp of
mild curry powder.

836

SERVES 4

Sausage Casserole

PREPARATION TIME :
25 MINUTES

COOKING TIME : 6 HOURS

INGREDIENTS

enough Morteau Sausage for 4
persons
30 ml / 2 tbsp vegetable oil
4 cloves
1 x 400 g can of chopped tomatoes
12 small carrots, scrubbed, trimmed
and blanched for 10 minutes
4 onions, sliced
1 chicken stock cube
150 ml / ¼ pt / ⅔ cup white wine
2 medium boiled potatoes, sliced
bouquet garni
salt and ground black pepper

GARNISH
2 tbsp flat leafed parsley

- Pre-warm the slow cooker.
- Heat the oil and fry (sauté) the sliced sausage until
  brown and transfer to the slow cooker.
- Sweat the onions, potato and carrots for 5 minutes then
  add to the slow cooker.
- Deglaze the pan with the white wine, boil for 5 minutes,
  scraping side of pan with wooden spoon and adding the
  cloves and bouquet garni.
- Pour into the slow cooker.
- Cover and cook on a low setting for 6 hours.
- Taste and adjust seasoning.
- Pour into a casserole dish before serving and sprinkle
  with parsley.

837

SERVES 4

Roast Beef and Potato Curry

- Pre-warm the slow cooker.
- Heat the oil and fry (sauté) the beef, onions and garlic until just turning colour. Add all the spices and herbs and fry for 3 minutes stirring continuously.
- Add the brown sugar, coconut cream, stock, puree and water and bring gently to the boil.
- Transfer immediately to the slow cooker.
- Cover with the lid and cook on a medium setting for 8 hours.
- Taste and adjust seasoning
- Serve in individual bowls sprinkled with finely chopped coriander and accompanied with Basmati Pilau rice.

PREPARATION TIME :
25 MINUTES

COOKING TIME : 8 HOURS

INGREDIENTS

800 g / 1¾ lb of roasted beef, sliced
2 tbsp vegetable oil
1 onion, finely chopped
½ tsp salt
15 g / 1 tbsp cumin
15 g / 1 tbsp ground coriander
15 g / 1 tbsp turmeric
5 g / 1 tsp ginger
5 g / 1 tsp chilli (chili) flakes
4 whole cloves
2 large bay leaves, torn
3 tbsp tomato, crumbled
500 ml / ½ pt water
½ tsp Demerara sugar
120 ml / 4 fl. oz / ½ cup of beef stock
45 ml / 3 tbsp coconut cream
8 basil leaves
½ bunch fresh coriander

Roast Chicken and Potato Curry

838

Suggested variation; This recipe works equally well with chicken pieces instead of beef.

839

SERVES 4

Stewed Apricots with Raspberries

- Combine the lemon juice, apricot halves, sugar and vanilla extract in a slow cooker.
- Cover with a lid and cook on a medium setting for 6 hours until the apricots are soft; make sure you stir them from time to time.
- Once soft and cooked, spoon into serving dishes and garnish with small handfuls of raspberries and a sprig of mint.
- This dish can be served warm or cold.

PREPARATION TIME :
10-15 MINUTES

COOKING TIME :
4 HOURS 5-10 MINUTES

INGREDIENTS

450 g / 1 lb / 3 cups apricots, destoned and halved
1 lemon, juiced
110 g / 4 oz / ½ cup caster (superfine) sugar
1 tsp vanilla extract
GARNISH
110 g / 4 oz / ⅔ cup raspberries
sprigs of mint leaves

Creamy Stewed Apricots

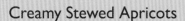

840

Stir 110 ml / 4 fl. oz / ½ cup double cream into the apricots before serving.

841

SERVES 4

Jambalaya with Prawns

Jambalaya with Pepperoni

842

The bacon and chorizo may be substituted for other spicy sausage, such as pepperoni

Vegetarian Jambalaya

843

For non–meat eaters, replace the chicken stock with vegetable stock and replace the meat with other fish, for eg diced and fried Monkfish cubes

PREPARATION TIME :
15 MINUTES

COOKING TIME : 8 HOURS

INGREDIENTS

900 g / 16 oz jasmine rice
2 tbsp vegetable oil
1 1 / 2 pints / 4 cups chicken stock
1 red chilli (chilli) finely chopped
75 g Spanish Chorizo in small cubes
2 rashers of streaky bacon, finely chopped
225 g / 8 oz prawns (shrimp), cooked and peeled
1 x 400 g can chopped tomatoes
1 clove garlic, minced
5 spring onions (scallions) sliced
1 tsp oregano, fresh or dried
1 tsp fresh basil
1 small pinch allspice
8 green olives, pitted and sliced
oil to grease dish
knob of butter

GARNISH
Sprig of Coriander leaf

- Grease the inside of the slow cooker.
- Fry the chorizo, bacon, chilli, onions and garlic gently until softened
- Add the rice to the pan and stir through the bacon mixture thoroughly on a medium heat for 3 minutes.
- Place this mixture into the slow Cooker with the chicken stock and herbs.
- Cook on low for 8 hours stirring once during cooking and replacing the lid tightly
- Add the olives and the prawns and fork through the rice, leave on low heat for a further hour or two.
- Fork through with the knob of butter to give the rice a gloss
- Serve immediately sprinkled with coriander leaf

844

SERVES 4

Duck and Vegetable Stew

- Heat a large casserole dish over a moderate heat until hot.
- Season the duck breasts and seal in the dish, skin side down until most of their fat has been rendered.
- Remove from the dish and transfer to a slow cooker.
- Add the chopped and diced vegetables to the casserole dish and saute in the rendered duck fat for 8-10 minutes, stirring occasionally until softened and lightly coloured.
- Spoon into the slow cooker and rearrange the duck breasts so that they sit on top of the vegetables.
- Cover with a lid and cook on a medium setting for 5 hours. Once the duck is ready, remove from the slow cooker and slice.
- Spoon the vegetables into serving dishes and sit the sliced duck on top.
- Garnish with a little more seasoning before serving.

PREPARATION TIME :
15 MINUTES

COOKING TIME : 5 HOURS 15-20 MINUTES

INGREDIENTS

2 large duck breasts, skin and fat
scored in a criss cross pattern
4 large carrots, peeled and chopped
2 leeks, chopped and washed
2 onions, chopped
1 small turnip, peeled and diced
250 ml / 9 fl. oz / 1 cup chicken stock
salt and freshly ground black pepper

Cherry and Duck Stew   845

stir through 150 g / 5 oz / 1 cup canned, drained cherries to the slow cooker 1 hour before the duck is ready.

846

SERVES 4

Scallops with Braised Chicory

- Heat the olive oil in a large casserole dish set over a medium heat until hot.
- Season the chicory with sugar, salt and pepper, tossing to coat them lightly.
- Saute in the casserole dish for 5-7 minutes, turning occasionally until lightly coloured.
- Remove from the dish and transfer to a slow cooker.
- Add the stock and scallops and cover with a lid.
- Braise in the slow cooker for 4 hours on a medium setting until the scallops are firm yet slightly springy to the touch.
- Adjust the seasoning to taste before spooning the braised chicory and scallops into serving dishes.
- Garnish with the saffron before serving.

PREPARATION TIME :
15 MINUTES

COOKING TIME : 4 HOURS 10 MINUTES

INGREDIENTS

55 ml / 2 fl. oz / ¼ cup olive oil
450 g / 1 lb / 3 cups queen scallops,
roe removed
8 chicory bulbs, halved
1 tsp caster (superfine) sugar
500 ml / 18 fl. oz / 2 cups vegetables
stock
salt and pepper

GARNISH
1 tbsp saffron threads

Orange Scallops with Chicory   847

Replace 125 ml / 4 ½ fl. oz / ½ cup of the stock with freshly squeezed orange juice.

848

SERVES 4

Beef and Carrot Stew

- Pre-warm the slow cooker.
- Heat the oil and fry (sauté) the beef cubes until brown and transfer to the slow cooker.
- Sweat the onions and carrots for 5 minutes.
- Transfer all the ingredients to crockpot with the herbs
- Cover and cook on a low setting for 8 hours.
- Taste and adjust seasoning.
- Pour into a casserole dish before serving and sprinkle with parsley.

PREPARATION TIME : 25 MINUTES

COOKING TIME : 8 HOURS

INGREDIENTS

1.75 kg / 4 lb silverside beef, cut into 2 cm cubes
30 ml / 2 tsp vegetable oil
4 cloves
1 x 400 g can of chopped tomatoes
300 ml / ½ pt / 1 ¼ cups water
12 small carrots, scrubbed, trimmed and blanched for 10 minutes
4 onions, sliced
150 ml ¼ pt / ⅔ cup beef stock
1 bunch thyme
salt and ground black pepper

849

MAKES 18

Roast Capon

PREPARATION TIME :
15 MINUTES

COOKING TIME : 8 HOURS

INGREDIENTS

1 ¾ kg / 4lb chicken
salt, pepper and paprika
30 ml / 2 tbsp goose fat or vegetable

oil
4 sage leaves
1 red onion, chopped small
8 baby carrots, scrubbed and blanched for 10 minutes
50 g / 4 oz / 1 cup frozen peas
150 ml / 1 ⬚ pt / ⅔ cup chicken stock

GARNISH
Spring onions sliced lengthways

- Grease and warm the slow Cooker..
- Clean, pat dry and brush the chicken with oil and sprinkle with salt pepper and paprika.
- Place in wok of hot oil and fry all over until golden brown. Remove the chicken and place to the side.
- Fry the onions in the remaining fat.
- Place the onions, peas, blanched carrots, sage and stock into the slow cooker. Rest the chicken on top of the vegetables, breast side up. Place the lid on and cook on low heat for 8 hours.
- Check internal temperature has reached 160 F.
- Remove the chicken and vegetables and serve on a plate or carver.

850

MAKES 18

Coq au Vin

PREPARATION TIME :
20 MINUTES

COOKING TIME : 6 HOURS

INGREDIENTS

1 chicken jointed into 4 quarters
100 g / 4 oz / 2 cups bacon lardons
30 ml / 2 tsp vegetable oil
3 garlic cloves, minced
1 bottle of French red wine
150 ml / ¼ pt / ⅔ cup chicken stock
2 tsp thyme, chopped

2 tsp basil, chopped
200 g / 8 oz / 2 cup green olives
50 g / 2 oz / ½ cup baby onions, blanched
50 g / 2 oz / ½ mushrooms, chopped
salt and ground black pepper
2 carrots, peeled and finely sliced
2 bay leaves, crushed
1 stalk of celery, washed and finely sliced

GARNISH
Fresh parsley

- Pre-warm the slow cooker.
- Heat the oil and fry (sauté) the chicken pieces until brown and transfer to the crockpot
- Sweat the onions, garlic, mushrooms and lardons for 5 minutes. Cover with the wine, stock, and herbs and bring to the boil.
- Transfer all the ingredients to crockpot and stir gently to mix.
- Cover and cook on a low setting for 6 hours.
- Taste and adjust seasoning
- Pour into a casserole dish before serving and sprinkle with finely shredded parsley

Pork, Prune and Carrot Casserole

851

SERVES 4

- Heat half of the olive oil in a large, heavy-based casserole dish set over a moderate heat until hot.
- Season then seal the pork chunks until golden brown in colour all over.
- Remove from the dish, then add the remaining olive oil and saute the onion, carrot and potato for 4-5 minutes, stirring occasionally.
- Add the pork and prunes to the dish, then pour in the cider and stock.
- Pour into a slow cooker and cover with a lid.
- Cook on a low setting for 6 hours until the pork is tender.
- Adjust the seasoning to taste before spooning into a casserole dish using a slotted spoon.
- Garnish with the saffron and serve immediately.

PREPARATION TIME :
15 MINUTES

COOKING TIME :
6 HOURS 20 MINUTES

INGREDIENTS

75 ml / 3 fl. oz / ⅓ cup olive oil
675 g / 1 lb 8 oz pork tenderloin, silver skin trimmed and cut into large chunks
2 large carrots, peeled and sliced diagonally
2 red onions, sliced
1 large potato, peeled and cut into wedges
200 g / 7 oz / 1 cup canned prunes, drained
250 ml / 9 fl. oz / 1 cup chicken stock
250 ml / 9 fl. oz / 1 cup cider
salt and pepper

GARNISH
1 tbsp saffron threads

Pork and Turnip Casserole

852

Replace the potato with 1 peeled and diced turnip.

Stew with Squid and Clams

853

SERVES 4

- Heat a large saucepan over a moderate heat until hot.
- Add the clams and 250 ml / 9 fl. oz / 1 cup water to the saucepan at the same time.
- Cover and let the steam cook the clams for 2-3 minutes.
- Strain the clams, reserving the cooking liquor and let them cool to one side for a few minutes.
- Pick the meat from the shells and place in a bowl.
- Heat the olive oil in a large frying pan set over a moderate heat until hot.
- Season the squid tubes and seal until lightly coloured.
- Transfer to a slow cooker and add the clam meat beans, fish stock, reserved cooking liquor, chilli and seasoning.
- Cover with a lid and cook on a low setting for 4 hours until the beans are soft. Adjust the seasoning to taste before spooning into serving bowls.
- Garnish with thyme before serving.

PREPARATION TIME :15 MINUTES

COOKING TIME : 4 HOURS
15 MINUTES

INGREDIENTS

30 ml / 1 fl. oz / 2 tbsp olive oil
450 g / 1 lb frozen squid tubes, thawed, rinsed and patted dry
300 g / 10 ½ oz / 2 cups little neck clams, cleaned
400 g / 14 oz / 2 cups canned haricot beans, drained
1 red chilli, deseeded and finely chopped
250 ml / 9 fl. oz / 1 cup fish stock
salt and pepper

GARNISH
a few sprigs of thyme, chopped

Stew with Saffron

854

Add 1 tsp saffron threads to the cooking liquor before pouring into the slow cooker.

855

SERVES 4

Seafood and Fennel Casserole

PREPARATION TIME :20 MINUTES

COOKING TIME :
6 HOURS 15 MINUTES

....

INGREDIENTS

450 g / 1 lb / 3 cups prawns, halved
lengthways
450 g / 1 lb / 3 cups queen scallops,
roe removed
150 g / 5 oz / 1 cup white fish fillet,
pin-boned and cut into small chunks
4 fennel bulbs, trimmed and sliced
125 ml / 4 ½ fl. oz / ½ cup dry white
wine
3 bay leaves
1 lemon, juiced
500 ml / 18 fl. oz / 2 cups fish stock
salt and pepper

GARNISH

sprigs of dill, chopped

- Heat the olive oil in a large casserole dish set over a moderate heat until hot.
- Season the prawns, scallops and white fish with a little seasoning before sautéing in the dish for 2 minutes, stirring occasionally.
- Transfer to a slow cooker and reduce the heat.
- Add the fennel and saute for a few minutes before deglazing the dish with the white wine, scraping the base of the pan well.
- Pour into the slow cooker and add the fish stock and bay leaves.
- Cover and cook on a low setting for 6 hours until the fennel is soft and the seafood is cooked through.
- Adjust the seasoning to taste using lemon juice, salt and pepper.
- Spoon into a casserole dish before garnishing with the dill. Serve immediately.

Creamy Seafood Casserole

856

Replace the prawns with the same weight of langoustine. Stir through 55 ml / 2 fl. oz / ¼ cup double cream into the slow cooker just before serving.

857

SERVES 4

Rabbit Cassoulet

PREPARATION TIME :
15 MINUTES

COOKING TIME : 6
HOURS 15 MINUTES

....

INGREDIENTS

30 ml / 1 fl. oz / 2 tbsp olive oil
1 rabbit, jointed
30 g / 1 oz / 2 tbsp plain (all-purpose)
flour
150 g / 5 oz / 1 cup smoked sausage,
sliced
400 g / 14 oz / 2 cups canned haricot
beans, drained
2 large vine tomatoes, diced
2 spring onions, chopped
500 ml / 18 fl. oz / 2 cups chicken
stock
salt and pepper

GARNISH

sprigs of lemon thyme

- Dust the rabbit pieces with the flour and some seasoning, shaking off any excess.
- Heat the olive oil in a large casserole dish set over a moderate heat until hot.
- Seal the rabbit pieces until golden brown in colour all over then remove them to a slow cooker.
- Add the beans, sausage, tomato, spring onion and stock and stir well.
- Cover with a lid and cook on a medium setting for 6 hours until the rabbit is cooked through.
- Adjust the seasoning to taste before spooning the cassoulet into serving dishes.
- Garnish with the thyme before serving.

Rabbit Crumble

858

After the rabbit is cooked, spoon the cassoulet into a casserole dish. Top with 55 g / 2 oz / ½ cup golden breadcrumbs and place in an oven for 10 minutes until golden brown.

859

SERVES 4

Sautéed Chicken with Peas

Sautéed Chicken with Mint

860

Replace the tarragon with a handful of fresh mint and cook the same.

Sautéed Chicken with Soup

861

Replace the stock, cream and wine, with a 440ml can of creamy chicken soup and cook the same.

PREPARATION TIME :
20 MINUTES

COOKING TIME : 8 HOURS

INGREDIENTS

1 chicken, jointed
100 g / 4 oz smoked bacon lardons
25 g / 1 oz goose fat or 2 tbsp olive oil
1 onion, chopped
2 tbsp Tarragon, finely chopped
150 ml / ¼ pt / ½ cup white wine
150 ml / ¼ pt / ½ cup chicken stock
150 ml / ¼ pt / ½ cup double cream
4 tbsp / 2 oz / ¼ cup Parmesan cheese, finely grated
225 g / 8 oz fresh peas
225 g / 8 oz fresh sugar snap peas
salt and pepper

GARNISH
fresh tarragon

- Pre-warm the slow cooker.
- Heat the oil and fry (sauté) the chicken joints until golden brown. Remove and set aside.
- In the remaining oil, fry the bacon and onion for 5 minutes and add to the slow cooker with the chicken joints.
- Put the wine in to the pan and boil to reduce by half. Add the chicken stock and bring to the boil.
- Pour over the chicken and bacon mixture in the slow cooker, add both types of peas and stir well.
- Cover and cook on a low setting for 8 hours.
- 10 minutes before the end of cooking, stir in the cream and Parmesan to taste and replace the lid.
- To serve sprinkle with fresh tarragon.

862

SERVES 4

Chicken and Dried Fruit Tajine

PREPARATION TIME :
10-15 MINUTES

COOKING TIME :
4 HOURS 15-20 MINUTES

INGREDIENTS

55 ml / 2 fl. oz / ¼ cup olive oil
4 chicken legs, jointed
4 ripe pears, peeled, cored and
quartered
2 lemons, sliced
110 g / 4 oz / ½ cup sultanas
2 tsp ras al hanout
1 tsp ground cumin
1 tsp ground coriander (cilantro)
½ tsp ground cinnamon
250 ml / 9 fl. oz / 1 cup chicken stock
1 tbsp honey
2 tbsp coriander (cilantro) leaves,
chopped
1 tsp saffron threads
salt and pepper

- Coat the chicken pieces in the olive oil and season.
- Heat a large casserole dish and seal the chicken until golden brown in colour all over.
- Transfer to a slow cooker and reduce the heat.
- Add the pears, lemon and sultanas sautéing for a few minutes, stirring occasionally.
- Add the ground spices and stir well before stirring in the honey and stock thoroughly.
- Pour everything into the slow cooker on top of the chicken and cover with a lid.
- Stir well before cooking on a medium setting for 4 hours until the chicken is cooked through.
- Once the chicken is cooked through, stir in the saffron, coriander and seasoning to taste.
- Spoon into serving dishes using a slotted spoon before serving.

Chicken, Dried Fruit and Almonds

863

Replace the sultanas with half of the weight of flaked (slivered) almonds.

864

SERVES 4

Red Kidney Beans and Bacon

PREPARATION TIME :
10 MINUTES

COOKING TIME :
6 HOURS 10-15 MINUTES

INGREDIENTS

30 ml / 1 fl. oz / 2 tbsp olive oil
900 g / 2 lb / 4 ½ cups canned kidney
beans, drained and rinsed
450 g / 1 lb piece of pork belly, cut
into large cubes
150 g / 5 oz / 1 cup smoked sausage,
sliced
150 g / 5 oz / 1 cup black pudding,
sliced
500 ml / 18 fl. oz / 2 cups ham stock
salt and pepper

- Heat the olive oil in a large casserole dish over a moderate heat until hot.
- Seal the pork belly, smoked sausage and black pudding in batches until golden brown all over.
- Transfer each batch to a slow cooker before adding the kidney beans and stock.
- Stir well and cover with a lid before cooking on a medium setting for 6 hours until the pork belly is soft.
- Adjust the seasoning to taste before spooning into a serving dish.
- Serve immediately.

Kidney Beans, Bacon and Tomato

865

Replace half of the stock with the same volume of passata.

866

SERVES 4

Lamb and Walnut Tajine

- Heat a large casserole dish over a high heat until hot.
- Coat the lamb in the oil and season generously with the ground spices and seasoning.
- Toss well and seal in batches in the casserole dish before transferring to a slow cooker.
- Add the sweet potato, honey, bay leaf and stock and stir well.
- Cover with a lid and cook on a low setting for 6 hours until the lamb is tender.
- Meanwhile, pulse the walnuts in a food processor until they resemble very fine breadcrumbs.
- Adjust the seasoning to taste before stirring through the walnuts.
- Spoon into serving dishes and serve immediately.

PREPARATION TIME :
10-15 MINUTES

COOKING TIME :
6 HOURS 10-15 MINUTES

INGREDIENTS

55 ml / 2 fl. oz / ¼ cup olive oil
900 g / 2 lb / 6 cups lamb shoulder, diced
2 large sweet potatoes, peeled and cut into 2" cubes
30 g / 1 oz / ¼ walnuts
2 tsp ras al hanout
1 tsp ground cinnamon
½ tsp ground nutmeg
½ tsp paprika
1 bay leaf
1 tbsp honey
500 ml / 18 fl. oz / 2 cups lamb stock
salt and pepper

Lamb, Walnut and Prune Tajine   867

Add 150 g / 5 oz / 1 cup canned, drained prunes to the slow cooker before cooking.

868

SERVES: 4

Vegetarian Bouillabaisse

- Heat the olive oil in a large saucepan set over a medium heat until hot.
- Sweat the fennel, leek, potato and carrots for 8-10 minutes, stirring occasionally until softened.
- Add the tomato puree and stir well, then add the stock and chopped tomatoes with some seasoning.
- Stir well before pouring into a slow cooker.
- Cover with a lid and cook on a medium setting for 4 hours until the vegetables are soft.
- Adjust the seasoning to taste before ladling into serving bowls and garnishing with a sprinkling of thyme leaves and a sprig of basil.

PREPARATION TIME :
10-15 MINUTES

COOKING TIME :
4 HOURS 20 MINUTES

INGREDIENTS

55 ml / 2 fl. oz / ¼ cup olive oil
4 fennel bulbs, trimmed and chopped
1 leek, sliced and washed
4 carrots, peeled and sliced
2 large white potatoes, peeled and diced
1 tbsp tomato puree
1 tsp saffron threads, infused in the stock
500 ml / 18 fl. oz / 2 cups vegetables stock
400 g / 14 oz / 2 cups canned chopped tomatoes
salt and pepper

GARNISH
sprigs of basil leaves
1 tbsp picked thyme leaves

Vegetarian Bouillabaisse with Olives   869

Add 55 g / 2 oz / ⅓ cup pitted black olives to the bouillabaisse before cooking in the slow cooker.

870

SERVES 6

Basque Chicken Casserole

Chicken Casserole with Stuffed Olives

871

Substitute the Spanish olives for stuffed olives and feta cheese.

Duck Casserole

872

The chicken may be replaced with either jointed duck or rabbit, cooking the same.

PREPARATION TIME :
25 MINUTES

COOKING TIME : 8 HOURS

INGREDIENTS

1 chicken jointed into 8 portions
50 g / 2 oz / 1 cups bacon lardons
30 ml / 1 fl. oz / 2 tbsp vegetable oil
100 g / 4 oz Spanish chorizo sausage, chopped to 1 cm cubes
3 garlic cloves, minced
30 ml / 1 fl. oz / 2 tbsp sun-dried tomato puree paste
150 ml / 5 fl. oz / ⅔ cup chicken stock
150 ml / 5 fl. oz / ⅔ cup dry white wine
2 tsp paprika powder
1 large bay leaf
bouquet garni
1 large carrot, chopped and blanched for 5 minutes
1 red pepper, cut into slivers
10 Spanish olives, whole
50 g / 2 oz baby onions, blanched
salt and ground black pepper

GARNISH
fresh parsley

- Pre-warm the slow cooker.
- Heat the oil and fry (sauté) the chicken pieces until brown and transfer to the slow cooker.
- Fry the onion, bacon, sausage, garlic, carrot and peppers for 5 minutes then stir in the paprika for a further minute.
- Cover with the wine, stock, tomato paste and herbs and bring to the boil.
- Transfer all the ingredients to slow cooker.
- Cover and cook on a low setting for 8 hours.
- At the end of cooking, stir in the olives and warm through.
- Pour into a casserole dish before serving and sprinkle with finely shredded parsley.

873

SERVES 4

Rabbit Stew with Macaroni

- Preheat the oven to 190°C (170° fan) / 375F / gas 5. Arrange the rabbit on a large roasting tray and drizzle with half of the olive oil and seasoning.
- Roast for 20 minutes in the oven until lightly coloured before removing and stripping the meat from the bones.
- Shred the meat and place in a slow cooker.
- Heat the remaining oil in a saucepan set over a moderate heat and saute the carrot, onion, garlic and bay leaf for 5 minutes. Add the chopped tomatoes, stock and macaroni to the slow cooker and stir well.
- Cook for 5 minutes until the macaroni starts to soften a little before pouring everything into the slow cooker.
- Stir well and cover with a lid before cooking for 4 hours on a medium setting.
- Adjust the seasoning to taste after 4 hours before spooning back into a casserole dish.
- Garnish with the parsley leaves before serving.

Rabbit Stew with Capers   874

Add 30 g / 1 oz / 2 tbsp drained baby capers to the stew before serving.

PREPARATION TIME :
15-20 MINUTES

COOKING TIME :
4 HOURS 30-35 MINUTES

INGREDIENTS

55 ml / 2 fl. oz / ¼ cup olive oil
2 small rabbits, jointed
2 large carrots, peeled and finely diced
1 onion, finely chopped
2 cloves of garlic, minced
1 bay leaf
300 g / 10 ½ oz / 1 ½ cup long macaroni
400 g / 14 oz / 2 cups canned chopped tomatoes
250 ml / 9 fl. oz / 1 cup chicken stock
salt and pepper

GARNISH
small handful of flat-leaf parsley leaves

875

SERVES 4

Duck Cassoulet

- Heat a pan over a moderate heat until hot before sauteing the pancetta for 3-4 minutes until golden.
- Meanwhile, score the fat of the duck breasts. Rub the duck with some of the olive oil and season generously.
- Seal in batches in the casserole dish until golden brown in colour all over. Reduce the heat before adding the remaining olive oil, the onion, tomato and beans.
- Stir well before adding the stock. Pour everything from the dish into the slow cooker and cover.
- Cook on a medium setting for 5-6 hours until the duck legs are cooked. Once the legs are cooked, spoon the cassoulet from the slow cooker into a roasting tray.
- Preheat the oven to 190°C (170° fan) / 375F / gas 5.
- Cut the breasts and place on top of the beans.
- Sprinkle with the breadcrumbs before roasting in the oven for 10 minutes.
- Remove and garnish with thyme.

Sausage Cassoulet   876

Add 150 g / 5 oz / 1 cup sliced smoked sausage to the slow cooker instead of the duck and cook the same.

PREPARATION TIME :
15 MINUTES

COOKING TIME :
5-6 HOURS 25-30 MINUTES

INGREDIENTS

55 ml / 2 fl. oz / ¼ cup olive oil
1 large duck, jointed
1 onion, finely chopped
2 large vine tomatoes, cored and diced
110 g / 4 oz / ⅔ cup pancetta, cut into lardons
400 g / 14 oz / 2 cups canned haricot beans, drained
400 g / 14 oz / 2 cups flageolet beans, drained
handful of breadcrumbs
250 ml / 9 fl. oz / 1 cup chicken stock
salt and pepper

GARNISH
a few sprigs of thyme

877

SERVES 4

Cod and Pepper Casserole

PREPARATION TIME :
15 MINUTES

COOKING TIME :
6 HOURS 15 MINUTES

INGREDIENTS

55 ml / 2 fl. oz / ¼ cup olive oil
4 x 225 g / 8 oz cod fillets
2 large red peppers, deseeded and
finely sliced
2 large green peppers, deseeded and
finely sliced
2 yellow peppers, deseeded and
finely diced
1 large onion, finely sliced
2 cloves of garlic, sliced
1 red chilli pepper, deseeded and
sliced
salt and pepper

GARNISH
sprigs of chervil

- Heat the oil in a large casserole dish set over a medium heat until hot.
- Add the onions, garlic and peppers and sweat with a little salt for 8-10 minutes, stirring occasionally, until softened.
- Spoon into a slow cooker and add the cod fillets and sliced chilli pepper on top.
- Cover with a lid and cook on a medium setting for 6 hours until the fish is firm yet springy to the touch.
- Adjust the seasoning to taste before spooning into a roasting tray for presentation, sitting the cod on top of the peppers.
- Garnish with the chervil before serving.

Cod Casserole with Saffron 878

Add 1 tsp saffron threads to the slow cooker before cooking.

879

SERVES 4

Mexican Casserole

PREPARATION TIME 10 MINUTES

COOKING TIME 45 MINUTES

INGREDIENTS

55 ml / 2 fl. oz / ¼ cup sunflower oil
900 g / 2 lb / 6 cups steak, diced into
2" cubes
400 g / 14 oz / 2 cups canned haricot
beans, drained
400 g / 14 oz / 2 cups canned butter
beans, drained
1 onion, finely chopped
2 cloves of garlic, minced
2 yellow peppers, deseeded and
evenly diced
2 red peppers, deseeded and chopped
2 large vine tomatoes, cored and
diced
1 tsp dried oregano
1 tsp dried basil
1 tsp paprika
500 ml / 18 fl. oz / 2 cups beef stock
2 sprigs of thyme
1 bay leaf
salt and pepper

- Coat the steak in the oil and season generously.
- Heat a large casserole dish over a moderate heat until hot and seal the steak in batches until golden brown in colour all over.
- Remove the sealed beef to a slow cooker.
- Reduce the heat under the dish a little before adding the onion, garlic and peppers.
- Sweat with a little salt until softened then add the tomato, dried herbs and paprika.
- Stir well before adding the beans, stock and herbs.
- Pour into the slow cooker and stir well before covering with a lid.
- Cook on a medium setting for 6 hours until the beef is starting to fall apart.
- Adjust the seasoning to taste before ladling back into a casserole dish for presentation.
- Serve immediately.

Chicken Mexican Casserole 880

Swap the beef steak for chicken breasts and cook in the same way.

881

SERVES 6

Lamb with Curry

Lamb Curry with Rosemary

882

Finely chopped rosemary may be added to the lamb coating mixture.

Crisp Lamb Curry

883

The lamb may be crisped in a hot oven for 20 minutes after the slow cooking process.

PREPARATION TIME :
15 MINUTES

COOKING TIME : 6 HOURS

....

INGREDIENTS

1 leg of lamb, cleaned and trimmed
30 ml / 2 tbsp goose fat or vegetable oil
30 ml / 2 tbsp clear honey
30 ml / 2 tbsp Dijon Mustard
15 ml / 1 tbsp curry powder
2 garlic cloves, crushed with a little oil

- Warm the slow cooker.
- In a large thick-based pan, heat the fat or oil.
- Spoon the honey, mustard, crushed garlic and curry powder in the pan and use it to coat the lamb all over. Sear the leg of lamb all over until browned.
- Place the lamb into the slow cooker.
- Cover with the lid and cook for 6 hours on a low setting.
- Remove the lamb from the slow cooker, and leave, covered to rest.
- Meanwhile, use the lamb juices to make gravy. Slice the meat and serve with vegetables of your choice and gravy immediately.

884

SERVES 4

Haddock Stew with Tomatoes

PREPARATION TIME :
15-20 MINUTES

COOKING TIME : 4 HOURS 25-30 MINUTES

INGREDIENTS

4 x 175 g / 6 oz skinless haddock fillets
150 g / 5 oz / 1 cup mussels, cleaned
30 ml / 1 fl. oz / 2 tbsp olive oil
1 onion, chopped
2 cloves garlic, minced
1 bay leaf
300 g / 10 ½ oz / 2 cups new potatoes
500 ml / 18 fl. oz / 2 cups vegetable stock
400 g / 14 oz / 2 cups canned chopped tomatoes
sprigs of thyme, to garnish
salt and pepper

- Parboil the potatoes in a large saucepan of boiling, salted water for 10 minutes. Drain and allow to cool.
- Heat the olive oil in a a large casserole dish over a medium heat.
- Saute the onion and garlic for 4-5 minutes, stirring occasionally, until softened.
- Add the chopped tomatoes, bay leaf and vegetables stock and stir well.
- Cut the potatoes in half, then add to the stew.
- Pour into a slow cooker and add the mussels and haddock. Cook on a medium setting for 4 hours.
- Remove the lid and discard any mussels that haven't opened. Discard the bay leaf, then adjust the seasoning.
- Spoon into serving bowls and remove the leaves from some of the thyme sprigs.
- Sprinkle on top, then garnish with sprigs of thyme before serving.

Haddock Stew with Olives 885

Add 55 g / 2 oz / ⅓ cup pitted black olives to the slow cooker before cooking.

886

SERVES 4

Pork Sauté

PREPARATION TIME :
15 MINUTES

COOKING TIME :
4 HOURS 15-20 MINUTES

INGREDIENTS

30 ml / 1 fl. oz / 2 tbsp olive oil
450 g / 1 lb piece of pork fillet, trimmed and diced
110 g / 4 oz / ⅔ cup chorizo slices
2 red peppers, deseeded and sliced
2 green peppers, deseeded and sliced
400 g / 14 oz / 2 cups canned chopped tomatoes
250 ml / 9 fl. oz / 1 cup passata
1 tsp paprika
½ tsp cayenne pepper
salt and pepper

GARNISH
1 tsp smoked paprika
sprig of flat-leaf parsley

- Coat the pork in the oil and season generously.
- Heat a large casserole dish over a moderate heat until hot and seal the pork in batches until golden brown in colour all over.
- Transfer the sealed pork to a slow cooker before reducing the heat under the dish a little.
- Add the peppers and fry for a few minutes with a little salt, stirring occasionally.
- Add the paprika and cayenne pepper and stir well before adding the chopped tomatoes and passata.
- Pour into the slow cooker and add the chorizo slices. Stir thoroughly before covering with a lid.
- Cook on a medium setting for 4 hours.
- Adjust the seasoning to taste before spooning into a cast iron casserole dish.
- Garnish with a sprinkle of smoked paprika and a sprig of parsley before serving.

Pork and Almond Sauté 887

Add 55 g / 2 oz / ½ cup flaked (slivered) almonds to the slow cooker before cooking.

888

SERVES 4

String Beef

- Coat the chunks of steak in the oil and season generously.
- Tie using kitchen string and arrange on a plate.
- Heat a large casserole dish over a moderate heat until hot and seal the beef in batches until golden brown in colour all over.
- Transfer the sealed beef to a slow cooker when done.
- Add the vegetables and stock and cover with a lid.
- Braise on a mediums setting for 6 hours.
- Adjust the seasoning to taste before ladling into serving dishes and serving immediately.

PREPARATION TIME :
15-20 MINUTES

COOKING TIME :
6 HOURS 10-15 MINUTES

INGREDIENTS

30 ml / 1 fl. oz / 2 tbsp sunflower oil
600 g / 1 lb 5 oz piece of rump steak, cut into large chunks
500 ml / 18 fl. oz / 2 cups beef stock
4 sticks celery, cut into batons
4 medium carrots, peeled and cut into batons
1 medium turnip, peeled and cut into batons
salt and pepper

Oriental String Beef

889

Change the sunflower oil for sesame oil for an Asian flavour. Season with soy sauce instead of salt.

890

SERVES 4-6

Roasted Gammon with Parsnips

- Preheat the oven to 190°C (170° fan) / 375F / gas 5.
- Rub the gammon joint with a little of the groundnut oil.
- Smear the crushed garlic on top, then season with salt, pepper, chopped rosemary and the sage leaves.
- Place in a roasting tray and scatter the parsnip and bay leaves around the joint.
- Drizzle the rest of the groundnut oil on the parsnips and season them.
- Cover the tray loosely with aluminium foil.
- Roast for 30 minutes then remove the tray from the oven and discard the aluminium foil.
- Transfer the contents of the roasting tray to a slow cooker and cook on a medium setting for 6 hours.
- Remove from the slow cooker and cover loosely with aluminium foil for 10 minutes to let it rest.
- Arrange on a serving plate with the parsnips and serve immediately.

PREPARATION TIME :
15-20 MINUTES

COOKING TIME :
6 HOURS 40-45 MINUTES

INGREDIENTS

1.35 kg / 3 lb piece of unsmoked gammon joint
2 large parsnips, peeled and sliced
55 ml / 2 fl. oz / ¼ cup groundnut oil
a few sage leaves
a few sprigs of rosemary, chopped
2 cloves of garlic, crushed
2 small bay leaves
salt and pepper

Roast Gammon with Chestnuts

891

Add 150 g / 5 oz / 1 ½ cups cooked chestnuts to the slow cooker before cooking.

892

SERVES 2

Lamb Shank with Brandy

Lamb Shank with Cinnamon

893

Add a pinch of cinnamon to the sauce and cook the same.

Lamb Shank with Wine

894

Replace the brandy for a ¼ cup of port wine and cook the same.

PREPARATION TIME :
30 MINUTES

COOKING TIME : 8 HOURS

INGREDIENTS

2 lamb shanks (one per person)
salt and pepper
30 ml / 2 tbsp rosemary, chopped
5 cloves of garlic, crushed
120 ml / 4 oz / ½ cup chicken stock
30 ml / 2 tbsp brandy or cognac
60 ml / 2 oz / ¼ cup beef stock
1 tbsp tomato puree
1 tsp balsamic vinegar
1 tsp soy sauce
½ tsp brown or Demerara sugar

- Pre-warm the slow cooker.
- Wipe the lamb shanks and season with salt and pepper.
- Heat the oil and fry (sauté) the pork until golden brown all over.
- Transfer to the slow cooker.
- Cover with all the other ingredients, stir well and cook on a low setting for 8 hours. Remove from pot and rest covered for 20 minutes.
- Adjust seasoning of the sauce to taste and thicken with cornflour (cornstarch) if required.
- Plate up the lamb shank and serve with the sauce spooned over.
- Garnish with fresh parsley leaves.

895

SERVES 4

Braised Pork with Beans

- Coat the pork pieces in the oil.
- Season with paprika, salt and pepper.
- Heat a large casserole dish over a moderate heat until hot and seal the pork until golden brown in colour all.
- Remove from the dish and transfer to a slow cooker.
- Add the beans and stock and stir well.
- Cover with a lid and cook on a medium setting for 6-7 hours until the beans are soft and the pork is cooked.
- Adjust the seasoning to taste before ladling into serving bowls and serving immediately.

PREPARATION TIME :
10-15 MINUTES

COOKING TIME :
6-7 HOURS 10 MINUTES

INGREDIENTS

55 ml / 2 fl. oz / ¼ cup sunflower oil
900 g / 2 lb piece of pork shoulder, boned and cut into 4 pieces
200 g / 7 oz / 1 cup black beans, soaked in water overnight then drained
750 ml / 1 pint 6 fl. oz / 3 cups ham stock
2 tsp paprika
salt and pepper

Pork with Beans in Stout

896

Replace 250 ml / 9 fl. oz / 1 cup of the stock with the same volume of good-quality stout.

897

SERVES 4

Duck, Apple and Dates

- Heat a large casserole dish. Season and seal the duck legs in the hot dish until golden brown in colour all over. Once browned, move to a slow cooker.
- Add the carrots, apples, dates and figs to the casserole dish and stir well.
- Reduce the heat a little before adding the ground spices and honey. Stir well and cover with the stock.
- Pour into the slow cooker, stir well and cover with a lid. Cook on a medium setting for 4-5 hours until the duck legs are cooked through.
- Adjust the seasoning before removing the slices of apple separately from the carrot, the dates and the figs.
- Arrange the apple slices on serving plates before spooning the carrots, dates and figs around the plate.
- Sit the duck leg on top and garnish with the thyme sprigs, leaves and more seasoning before serving.

PREPARATION TIME :
15 MINUTES

COOKING TIME :
4-5 HOURS 15-20 MINUTES

INGREDIENTS

4 duck legs, trimmed, skin lightly scored
450 g / 1 lb / 3 cups carrots, peeled and sliced
4 Bramley apples, peeled, cored and sliced
200 g / 7 oz / 1 ½ cups pitted dates
4 figs, quartered
2 tsp ras al hanout
1 tsp ground cinnamon
1 tsp ground cumin
1 tbsp honey
250 ml / 9 fl. oz / 1 cup chicken stock
salt and freshly ground black pepper

GARNISH
sprigs of thyme
1 tbsp picked thyme leaves

Duck Apple and Apricot

898

Replace the dates with the same volume of dried apricot halves and cook the same.

899

SERVES 4

Pigeon and Peas Casserole

PREPARATION TIME :
10 MINUTES

COOKING TIME :
4-5 HOURS 10-15 MINUTES

INGREDIENTS

30 ml / 1 fl. oz / 2 tbsp olive oil
1 large wood pigeon, cleaned and trimmed
450 g / 1 lb / 4 cups frozen petit pois, thawed
1 onion, sliced
250 ml / 9 fl. oz / 1 cup chicken stock
salt and pepper

TO GARNISH

sprig of flat-leaf parsley
leavesmozzarella
basil, to garnish

- Rub the pigeon with the oil and season generously.
- Meanwhile, heat a large casserole dish over a moderate heat until hot and seal the pigeon until golden brown in colour all over.
- Remove from the dish and transfer to a slow cooker.
- Reduce the heat under the casserole dish and saute the onion with some salt.
- Add the stock, stir well, and then pour into the slow cooker. Cook on a medium setting for 3 hours.
- Add the peas after 3 hours and stir well before cooking for a further 1-2 hours until the pigeon is cooked fully; the pigeon is ready when the juices run clear when the thickest part of the thigh is pierced.
- Remove it from the slow cooker and spoon the peas and onions into a casserole dish.
- Sit the pigeon on top and garnish with the parsley before serving.

Pigeon and Mushroom Casserole

900

Sauté 30 g / 1 oz button top mushrooms for 5 minutes then add to the casserole in the slow cooker half an hour before finished and spoon with the peas.

901

SERVES 4

Sea Bass Tajine

PREPARATION TIME :
10-15 MINUTES

COOKING TIME :
4 HOURS 15 MINUTES

INGREDIENTS

55 ml / 2 fl. oz / ¼ cup olive oil
1 large sea bass, gutted, cleaned and cut into thick steaks
2 red peppers, deseeded and sliced
1 green pepper, deseeded and sliced
110 g / 4 oz / ⅔ cup Kalamata olives
2 carrots, peeled and sliced
2 onions, slices
2 sprigs of thyme, leaves picked
2 tsp ras al hanout
1 tsp ground cinnamon
1 tsp saffron threads, infused in the stock
500 ml / 18 fl. oz / 2 cups fish stock
salt and pepper

- Heat the olive oil in a large casserole dish set over a moderate heat until hot.
- Season the sea bass and seal in the oil for 2-3 minutes until lightly coloured.
- Remove from the dish and reduce the heat. Continue to add the peppers, carrot and onion to the dish and saute for a few minutes.
- Add the ground spices, stir well, and add the olives and thyme.
- Cook for a few minutes before adding the infused stock and stirring again.
- Pour into the slow cooker and cover with a lid.
- Cook on a medium setting for 4 hours until the fish is cooked through and the peppers are slightly soft.
- Adjust the seasoning to taste before spooning into a serving dish.

Sweet Potato Tajine

902

Add 2 peeled and diced sweet potatoes to the slow cooker before cooking and cook the same.

Salt-cod Bouillabaisse

- Pre-warm the slow cooker.
- Heat the oil and fry the pheasant pieces until golden brown, remove to the side.
- Gently fry the quince pieces until lightly browned, remove to the side
- Adding more oil if required, cook the spices (except the coriander), garlic and chilli flakes in the remaining oil, stir well and cook through for 3 minutes.
- Add the lemon zest and juice, honey, stock and passata and stir. Bring gently to the boil
- Place al the ingredients into the slow cooker and cook on low for 8 hours to let the flavours meld.
- At the end of cooking, stir in the chopped fresh coriander gently.
- Serve hot with rice, couscous or pitta bread.

PREPARATION TIME: 15 MINUTES

COOKING TIME : 5 HOURS

INGREDIENTS

2 x pheasants, jointed and prepared
60 ml / 4 tsp / ¼ cup olive oil
4 garlic cloves, crushed
¼ tsp chilli flakes, 1 tsp ginger powder
1 tsp cumin, 1 tsp turmeric
1 tsp cinnamon, 1 tsp paprika
1 x 440 g / 15 ½ oz can passata
500 ml / 17 fl. oz stock
1 lemon, zest and juice
fresh coriander, chopped
1 green pepper finely sliced
10 ml / 2 tbsp clear honey
2 lb quince, peeled and quartered

Beef Stew with Salsify

PREPARATION TIME :25 MINUTES

COOKING TIME : 8 HOURS

INGREDIENTS

1.75 kg / 4 lb silverside beef, cut into 2 cm cubes
30 ml / 2 tbsp vegetable oil or lard
4 cloves
15 ml / 1 tbsp tomato puree

300 ml / 10 fl. oz / 1 ¼ cups water
100 g / 4 oz streaky bacon, chopped
200 g / 8 oz carrots, peeled, chopped
4 onions, sliced
150 ml / ¼ pt / ⅔ cup beef stock
1 tbsp plain (all-purpose) flour
1 tbsp Dijon Mustard
salt and pepper
450 g / 16 oz salsify, peeled and sliced

- Pre-warm the slow cooker.
- Heat the oil and fry (sauté) the beef cubes until brown and transfer to the slow cooker.
- Fry the onions, bacon and carrots for 5 minutes. Stir in the flour and fry for further minute.
- Pour the stock into the pan, with the puree and mustard and stir thoroughly. Bring to the boil.
- Transfer all the ingredients to slow cooker.
- Cover and cook on a low setting for 8 hours.
- 30 minutes before the end of cooking, boil the salsify in a pan of salty water for 20 minutes. Strain and serve with stew.
- Pour into a casserole dish and serve with a sprinkle of parsley.

Roast Leg of Lamb

PREPARATION TIME :
20 MINUTES

COOKING TIME : 8 HOURS

INGREDIENTS

1.5 kg / 3 lb leg of lamb
30 ml / 2 tbsp goose fat
salt and ground black pepper

2 sprigs of fresh rosemary
8 cloves of garlic, cut into slivers
1 knob of butter

GARNISH
Fresh rosemary sprigs and lemon slices

- Pre-warm the slow cooker.
- Wipe the leg of lamb and fry in the butter and fat until golden brown all over.
- Remove from the pan and sit inside the slow cooker on top of the rosemary sprigs.
- With a sharp knife make small cuts over the upper surface skin and insert a sliver of garlic clove in each. Sprinkle with salt and pepper.
- Cover and cook on a low setting for 8 hours.
- Remove the lamb and set in a roasting tray–place in the top of a hot oven set at 220°C (200° fan) 425F / gas 7 for 20 minutes to crisp up the skin.
- Remove and rest covered for 15 minutes before carving.
- Meanwhile, use the slow cooker juices to make a gravy after removing the rosemary sprigs.

906
SERVES 4
Sautéed Beef with Paprika

PREPARATION TIME :
10 MINUTES

COOKING TIME :
6 HOURS 15 MINUTES

....

INGREDIENTS

55 ml / 2 fl. oz / ¼ cup groundnut oil
900 g / 2 lb / 6 cups rump steak, diced
2 large onions, sliced
2 tbsp paprika
250 ml / 9 fl. oz / 1 cup beef stock
salt and pepper

GARNISH

30 g / 1 oz / 2 tbsp cocktail gherkins, thinly sliced
2 tbsp basil leaves, finely chopped
1 tsp smoked paprika

- Coat the beef in the oil and season generously with paprika, salt and pepper.
- Toss well and heat a large casserole dish over a moderate heat until hot.
- Seal the beef in batches, transferring the sealed beef to a slow cooker when finished.
- Add the onions, beef stock and a little more seasoning and stir well.
- Cover with a lid and cook on a medium setting for 6 hours.
- Adjust the seasoning to taste before spooning into a casserole dish for presentation.
- Sprinkle the smoked paprika on top and stir.
- Garnish with the gherkins and basil before serving.

Sautéed Chicken with Sour Cream
907

Replace the meat and beef stock with sliced chicken breasts and cook for the same duration. Garnish with sour cream before serving.

908
SERVES 4
Chicken and Fruit Tajine

PREPARATION TIME :
10-15 MINUTES

COOKING TIME :
5 HOURS 15-20 MINUTES

....

INGREDIENTS

55 ml / 2 fl. oz / ¼ cups olive oil
4 chicken legs, trimmed and jointed
600 g / 1 lb 5 oz / 4 cups new potatoes
150 g / 5 oz / 1 cup prunes
150 g / 5 oz / 1 cup dried figs
2 sticks of cinnamon
2 tsp ras al hanout
1 tsp ground cinnamon
1 tsp ground cumin
375 ml / 13 fl. oz / 1 ½ cups chicken stock
salt and pepper

GARNISH
a pinch of ras al hanout

- Coat the chicken pieces in the olive oil and season thoroughly.
- Heat a large casserole dish over a moderate heat until hot and seal the chicken legs until golden brown in colour all over before removing to a slow cooker.
- Reduce the heat under the casserole dish and add the potatoes, prunes, figs and cinnamon sticks.
- Stir well before adding the ground spices and stock.
- Stir thoroughly and pour into the slow cooker. Cover with a lid and cook on a medium setting for 5 hours.
- Adjust the seasoning to taste after 5 hours before spooning into serving dishes.
- Garnish with a pinch of ras al hanout before serving.

Chicken Tajine with Apples
909

Replace the cup of figs with the same weight of dried apple rings and cook the same.

910

SERVES 4

Cod wrapped in Bacon

Cod with Pancetta

911

Replace the streaky bacon with pancetta and cook the same.

Cod with Calvados

912

The wine may be replaced with half the quantity of calvados.

PREPARATION TIME :
25 MINUTES

COOKING TIME : 4 HOURS

INGREDIENTS

4 x 150 g / 5.5 oz Cod Fillets, skinned and boned
4 large slices of streaky bacon
15 ml / 1 tbsp sunflower oil
15 ml / 1 tbsp butter
For Rhubarb Sauce
½ medium onion finely chopped
1 tsp ground ginger
450 g / 1 lb young rhubarb stalks, chopped into 1 inch cubes
15 ml / 1 tbsp clear honey
15 ml / 1 tbsp white wine
¼ tsp chilli (chilli) flakes
salt and pepper

GARNISH
rhubarb leaves

- Warm the slow cooker.
- Wrap each cod fillet neatly with the bacon overlapping underneath the fillet
- Heat the oil in a pan and sauté the cod in bacon, lower side first. Gently turn over to sauté the upper sides, until bacon is thoroughly golden. If the bacon starts to unwrap, you can secure with a cocktail stick
- Gently remove the cod fillets onto a plate.
- Add the butter to the pan, gently frying the onion and rhubarb stalks.
- Stir in the ginger and chilli flakes and cook through for 1 minute.
- Add the white wine and honey, mixing thoroughly and bring to the boil. Stew the rhubarb for 5 minutes
- Pour over the rhubarb and liquid mixture into the slow cooker and very gently sit the cod fillets on top.
- Cover and cook on a low setting for 4 hours.
- Adjust the seasoning to taste.
- To serve, remove the bacon wrapped cod onto a serving dish and spoon the rhubarb sauce around. Serve immediately.

913

SERVES 4

Roast Pork

PREPARATION TIME :
15 MINUTES

COOKING TIME :
6 HOURS 15-20 MINUTES

....

INGREDIENTS

55 ml / 2 fl. oz / ¼ cup olive oil
900 g / 2 lb piece of pork loin roast
300 g / 10 ½ oz / 2 cups streaky
bacon rashers
1 large bunch of sage leaves
8 cloves of garlic, sliced
salt and freshly ground black pepper

- Rub the pork with the olive oil then wrap in the rashers of streaky bacon, overlapping them diagonally so that the loin is covered, tying securely using kitchen string.
- Heat a large frying pan over a moderate heat until hot then seal the pork until golden brown in colour all over.
- Remove to a slow cooker and reduce the heat.
- Saute the garlic and any remaining bacon for 2 minutes, stirring occasionally.
- Move the bacon and garlic to the slow cooker, then add the sage leaves and a little seasoning.
- Cover with a lid and cook on a medium setting for 6 hours until the pork reaches an internal temperature of at least 60°C / 140F.
- Remove the pork from the slow cooker and let it rest covered loosely with aluminium foil for 10 minutes.
- Spoon the bacon, garlic and sage into a casserole dish and sit the pork on top before serving.

Braised Cider Pork   **914**

Instead of dry cooking the pork, braise it in
500 ml / 18 fl. oz / 2 cups of cider.

915

SERVES 4

Pork with Orange Zest

PREPARATION TIME :
10-15 MINUTES

COOKING TIME :
6 HOURS 15 MINUTES

....

INGREDIENTS

30 ml / 1 fl. oz / 2 tbsp sunflower oil
30 g / 1 oz / ¼ stick unsalted butter
675 g / 1 lb 8 oz piece of boneless
rolled pork shoulder
2 tbsp good-quality marmalade
2 oranges, zest pared and julienned
2 onions, finely sliced
salt and pepper

- Rub the pork with the oil and brush with the marmalade.
- Season generously and heat a large frying pan over a moderate heat until hot.
- Seal the pork in the pan until golden brown in colour all over.
- Remove from the pan and place in a slow cooker.
- Reduce the heat under the casserole dish and add the butter.
- Saute the onion and orange zest with a little salt for 5-6 minutes, stirring occasionally.
- Spoon into the slow cooker and sit the pork on top.
- Cover with a lid and cook on a medium setting for 6 hours.
- Adjust the seasoning to taste after 6 hours and let it rest for 10 minutes before serving.

Pork with Added Prunes   **916**

Add 150 g / 5 oz / 1 cup prunes to the slow
cooker before cooking.

917

SERVES 4

Chicken, Mushroom and White Wine

- Rub the chicken pieces with the oil and season generously.
- Heat a large casserole dish and seal the chicken in batches until golden brown in colour, removing each completed batch to a slow cooker when done.
- Reduce the heat and add the butter to the dish.
- Saute the morels for a few minutes, stirring occasionally before deglazing the pan with the white wine.
- Let it reduce by half before adding the stock.
- Stir well and pour the contents of the dish into the slow cooker.
- Cover with a lid and cook on a medium setting for 5 hours until the chicken pieces are cooked through.
- Stir through the cream and adjust the seasoning to taste before pouring into a casserole dish for presentation.

PREPARATION TIME
15 MINUTES

COOKING TIME
5 HOURS 20 MINUTES

INGREDIENTS

30 ml / 1 fl. oz / 2 tbsp olive oil
30 g / 1 oz / ¼ stick unsalted butter
1 large chicken, jointed and trimmed
300 g / 10 ½ oz / 4 cups morels, brushed clean
250 ml / 9 fl. oz / 1 cup dry white wine
500 ml / 18 fl. oz / 2 cups chicken stock
125 ml / 4 ½ fl. oz / ½ cup double cream
salt and pepper

Chicken in Crème Fraiche   918

Replace the double cream with crème fraiche for a lighter casserole.

919

SERVES 4

Lentil and Sausage Soup

- Heat the olive oil in a large casserole dish set over a medium heat until hot.
- Saute the leek, garlic, carrots and bay leaves with a little salt for a few minutes.
- Add the sausage, lentils and potatoes and stir well.
- Cover with the stock before pouring into a slow cooker.
- Cover with a lid and cook on a medium setting for 6 hours.
- Adjust the seasoning to taste after 6 hours before ladling into serving bowls and serving.

PREPARATION TIME 15 MINUTES

COOKING TIME 6 HOURS AND 10 MINUTES

INGREDIENTS

30 ml / 1 fl. oz / 2 tbsp olive oil
1 bulb of garlic, lightly crushed
2 carrots, peeled and sliced
1 leek, halved and washed
400 g / 14 oz / 2 cups puy lentils
300 g / 10 ½ oz / 2 cups Charlotte potatoes, peeled and turned
250 g / 9 oz / 1 ⅔ cups smoked sausage, chopped
1.2 l / 2 pints / 4 ⅘ cups vegetables stock
2 bay leaves
salt and pepper

Lentil and Chorizo Soup   920

Replace the smoked sausage meat with chorizo.

921

SERVES 4

Roasted Chicken and Lemon

Roasted Chicken with Tarragon

922

Replace the rosemary and sage with tarragon.

Chicken Thighs with Lemon

923

Use skinless chicken thighs instead of chicken breasts and cook them whole.

Roasted Chicken with Orange

924

Replace the lemons with sliced orange wedges, and cook the same.

PREPARATION TIME: 10 MINUTES

COOKING TIME: 4 HOURS

INGREDIENTS

4 tbsp olive oil
4 chicken breasts, trimmed
2 lemons, sliced into discs
5-6 cloves garlic, lightly crushed
1 sprig rosemary, leaves finely chopped
2 sprigs sage, leaves picked

- Rub the chicken breasts with the olive oil.
- Season generously with salt, pepper and half of the rosemary.
- Heat a large frying pan over a moderate heat until hot and seal the chicken breasts until golden brown.
- Remove the chicken from the pan and add the lemon slices, searing them in batches.
- Place everything apart from half of the sage leaves in a slow cooker and cook on a high setting for 4 hours until the chicken is firm yet springy to the touch and cooked through.
- Spoon everything into a ceramic roasting tray and garnish with the reserved sage leaves and chopped rosemary.
- Serve immediately.

Sauteed Lamb with Olives

925

SERVES 4

- Coat the lamb in the oil and season generously. Meanwhile, heat a large casserole dish over a moderate heat until hot.
- Seal the lamb in bathes until golden brown. Once browned, transfer the sealed lamb to a slow cooker.
- Reduce the heat under the dish before adding the carrot and olives.
- Saute with a little seasoning for 2-3 minutes until the carrot starts to soften.
- Add the passata and infused stock and stir well. Pour into the slow cooker and add the olives.
- Cover with a lid and cook on a medium setting for 6 hours
- Adjust the seasoning to taste before spooning into serving dishes and garnishing with the chopped sage and sprigs of rosemary.

PREPARATION TIME :
10 MINUTES

COOKING TIME :
6 HOURS 15-20 MINUTES

INGREDIENTS

55 ml / 2 fl. oz / ¼ cup sunflower oil
900 g / 2 lb piece of boneless lamb shoulder, cut into 4 large pieces
150 g / 5 oz / 1 cup pitted black olives
2 carrots, peeled and sliced
400 ml / 14 fl. oz / 1 ⅔ cups passata
250 ml / 9 fl. oz / 1 cup lamb stock
½ tsp saffron threads, infused in the stock
salt and pepper

GARNISH
sprigs of rosemary
2 tbsp sage leaves, finely chopped

Sauteed Lamb with Olives and Shallots

926

Add 4 halved shallots to the dish at the same time as the carrot and cook the same.

Chicken Breast with Shallots

927

SERVES 4

- Coat the chicken breasts in half of the oil and season generously.
- Heat a griddle pan over a moderate heat until hot and seal the chicken in batches, until golden brown.
- Remove from the pan and transfer to a slow cooker. Heat a large saucepan over a medium heat until hot.
- Add the remaining oil and sweat the shallots with a little salt for 8-10 minutes, stirring occasionally until softened.
- Add the balsamic vinegar and sugar and stir before spooning into the slow cooker.
- Cover the slow cooker with a lid and cook on a medium setting for 4 hours.
- Adjust the seasoning to taste. Once the chicken is cooked, spoon the shallots onto a serving plate.
- Sit the chicken on top and garnish with the tarragon, celery leaf and more seasoning.

PREPARATION TIME :
15 MINUTES

COOKING TIME :
4 HOURS 15-20 MINUTES

INGREDIENTS

55 ml / 2 fl. oz / ¼ cup olive oil
4 skinless chicken breasts, trimmed
6 shallots, roughly sliced
2 cloves of garlic, minced
1 tsp caster (superfine) sugar
55 ml / 2 fl. oz / ¼ cup balsamic vinegar
salt and freshly ground black pepper

GARNISH
1 tbsp tarragon leaves, roughly chopped
sprigs of celery leaf

Braised Chicken with Shallots

928

Add 500 ml / 18 fl. oz / 2 cups chicken stock to the slow cooker to braise the chicken instead.

929

SERVES 4

Minced Meat Loaf

PREPARATION TIME :
10-15 MINUTES

COOKING TIME :
4-5 HOURS 15-20 MINUTES

....

INGREDIENTS

30 ml / 1 fl. oz / 2 tbsp olive oil
650 g / 1 lb 8 oz / 4 ½ cups beef mince
2 shallots, finely sliced
2 cloves of garlic, minced
2 tsp ground cumin
1 tsp ground coriander
1 tsp dried oregano
1 small bunch of tarragon, finely
chopped
salt and pepper

GARNISH

small handful of red chard leaves
2 chive stalks, halved
sprigs of chervil

- Combine the beef, shallot, garlic, ground spices, dried oregano, tarragon and season contents in a large mixing bowl.
- Mix together well using your hands until you have a homogenous mixture.
- Shape the beef into a loaf shape and coat in the olive oil.
- Season the outside generously before heating a large frying pan over a moderate heat until hot.
- Seal the meat loaf in the oil until golden brown in colour all over.
- Transfer to a slow cooker and cover with a lid.
- Cook on a medium setting for 4-5 hours until the internal temperature of the meat loaf is at least 60°C / 140F.
- Remove from the slow cooker and garnish with the chard, chive and chervil before serving.

Lamb Meat Loaf   930

Replace the beef mince, and instead, use lamb mince of the same weight, dividing the mixture into 6 rolled kebab shapes before sealing and cooking.

931

SERVES 4

Rose Veal and Orange Tajine

PREPARATION TIME :
15-20 MINUTES

COOKING TIME :
6 HOURS 15-20 MINUTES

....

INGREDIENTS

55 ml / 2 fl. oz / ¼ cup olive oil
450 g / 1 lb / 3 cups rose veal fillet,
trimmed and diced
2 orange, halved and sliced
4 shallots, peeled and halved
2 cloves of garlic, lightly crushed
2 large carrots, peeled and sliced
2 medium white potatoes, peeled
and diced
1 small head of broccoli, prepared
into small florets
2 tsp ras al hanout
1 tsp ground cumin
1 tsp ground cinnamon
½ tsp paprika
250 ml / 9 fl. oz / 1 cup beef stock
1 tbsp honey
salt and pepper

- Coat the veal in half of the oil and season generously.
- Heat a large casserole dish over a moderate heat until hot and seal the veal in batches until golden brown in colour all over.
- Transfer to a slow cooker and reduce the heat under the casserole dish.
- Add the remaining oil and saute the shallot, garlic, carrot and potato for a few minutes, adding the ground spices.
- Stir well, and then add the broccoli, orange, stock and honey.
- Pour everything from the casserole dish into the slow cooker and cover with a lid.
- Cook on a medium setting for 6 hours until the veal is tender and cooked.
- Adjust the seasoning to taste before spooning into serving tajines.

Spicy Rose Veal   932

For a spicier dish, add 1 tsp Tabasco sauce with a pinch of crushed chillies to the slow cooker after cooking.

933

SERVES 4

Mild Chicken Curry

Mild Turkey Curry   934

Replace the chicken with turkey for a lean version of this recipe.

Low-fat Chicken Curry   935

Use reduced fat coconut milk and yoghurt for a healthy alternative.

PREPARATION TIME : 30 MINUTES

COOKING TIME : 6 HOURS

INGREDIENTS

4 chicken breasts, sliced
1 tbsp vegetable oil
1 star anise, whole
5 ml / 1 tsp cinnamon, ground
1 x large can of coconut milk
5 spring onions, chopped
1 tbsp poppy seeds, soaked in coconut milk
1 tbsp garam masala powder
salt and ground black pepper
120 ml / 4 fl. oz / ½ cup of stock

MARINADE
180 ml / 6 fl. oz thick plain yoghurt
1 lemon, zest and juice
¼ tsp turmeric, ¼ tsp cumin
1 tbsp coriander powder
¼ tsp red chilli flakes, ½ tsp ginger
2 garlic cloves, minced

PASTE
1 green chilli, deseeded and chopped
3 cloves of garlic, minced
1 tsp powdered ginger

- Marinade the chicken pieces in the marinade ingredients for approximately 4 hours or over night.
- Pre-warm the slow cooker.
- Heat the oil and fry (sauté) the star anise, cinnamon, chopped onions until just turning colour. Add the paste ingredients and cook for 2 minutes, then add the chilli flakes.
- Add the marinated chicken pieces and cook for 5 minutes, stirring continuously.
- Pour over the stock and bring to the boil for 5 minutes. Stir in the coconut milk with poppy seeds and lemon juice.
- Transfer all the ingredients to the slow cooker.
- Cover with the lid and cook on a medium setting for 6 hours.
- Taste and adjust seasoning.
- Stir in the garam masala.
- Serve in individual bowls sprinkled with finely chopped coriander and accompanied with jasmine rice.

261

936

SERVES 4

Lamb with Mushrooms

PREPARATION TIME :
15 MINUTES

COOKING TIME :
5 HOURS 15 MINUTES

INGREDIENTS

900 g / 2 lb piece of boneless lamb leg
30 ml / 1 fl. oz / 2 tbsp olive oil
30 g / 1 oz / ¼ stick unsalted butter
300 g / 10 ½ oz / 4 cups cep
mushrooms, brushed clean
salt and pepper

GARNISH
sprigs of flat-parsley

- Butterfly the leg of lamb using a sharp knife. Season inside generously and heat a large frying pan until hot.
- Melt the butter a knob at a time, saute the mushrooms and season. Remove and arrange on a lined plate.
- Fill the inside of the lamb with half of the sauteed mushrooms. Roll the lamb around the mushrooms and tie securely using kitchen string.
- Coat the outside of the lamb with oil and season.
- Heat a large, clean frying pan and seal the lamb until golden. Place in a slow cooker and add the mushrooms.
- Cook on a medium setting for 5 hours until the lamb is cooked medium.
- Remove the lamb from the slow cooker and let it rest for 10 minutes covered loosely with aluminium foil before serving with the mushrooms on the side.
- Garnish with the parsley before serving.

Lamb with Apricot — 937

Replace the cep mushrooms in the middle of the lamb with 150 g / 5 oz / 1 cup chopped dried apricot halves.

938

SERVES 4

Vegetables with Turmeric

PREPARATION TIME :
15-20 MINUTES

COOKING TIME :
4 HOURS 15 MINUTES

INGREDIENTS

55 ml / 2 fl. oz / ¼ cup olive oil
1 large courgette (courgette), cut into
ribbons using a vegetable peeler
2 large carrots, peeled and cut into
ribbons using a vegetable peeler
2 large beef tomatoes, sliced
2 onions, sliced
2 cloves of garlic, minced
1 aubergine (aubergine), halved
and sliced
1 tsp ras al hanout
1 tsp turmeric
1 tbsp honey
250 ml / 9 fl. oz / 1 cup vegetable
stock
salt and pepper

GARNISH
small handful of picked flat-leaf
parsley leaves

- Heat some of the olive oil in a large casserole dish set over a moderate heat.
- Sauté the vegetables in batches for a few minutes each, apart from the tomato.
- Use fresh oil for each batch and move each completed batch to a slow cooker when done.
- Add the tomato slices to the slow cooker once all the vegetables have been sautéed.
- Add the ground spices, honey and seasoning and stir well.
- Cover with the stock and cover with a lid.
- Cook on a medium setting for 4 hours.
- Adjust the seasoning to taste after 4 hours and transfer to serving dishes using a pair of tongs.
- Garnish with the parsley leaves before serving.

Vegetables with Curry — 939

Replace the turmeric with mild curry powder.
Add a large handful of sultanas to the slow
cooker before cooking.

940

SERVES 4 Petit Sale with Lentils

- Rub the gammon with the oil and heat a large casserole dish over a moderate heat until hot.
- Chop half of the pearl onions.
- Seal the gammon and the smoked sausage pieces until golden brown in colour all over before removing to a slow cooker.
- Reduce the heat under the casserole dish and add the whole and chopped onions, sauteing them for a few minutes stirring frequently.
- Add the lentils, stock and bouquet garni and stir well.
- Pour into the slow cooker and cover with a lid.
- Cook on a medium setting for 6 hours until the gammon is cooked through.
- Adjust the seasoning to taste and discard the bouquet garni before ladling the lentils into a roasting tray.
- Sit the meat and onions on top and garnish with a fresh bouquet garni.

Petit Sale with White Wine 941

Replace 125 ml / 4 ½ fl. oz / ½ cup of the stock with the same volume of dry white wine.

PREPARATION TIME :
15 MINUTES

COOKING TIME :
6 HOURS 10 MINUTES

INGREDIENTS

30 ml / 1 fl. oz / 2 tbsp olive oil
300 g / 10 ½ oz / 2 cups smoked sausage, chopped
450 g / 1 lb piece of gammon on the bone, trimmed
1 bouquet garni
4 pearl onions, blanched and peeled
400 g / 14 oz / 2 cups puy lentils
500 ml / 18 fl. oz / 2 cups ham stock
salt and pepper

GARNISH
1 bouquet garni

942

SERVES 6 Rose Veal with Ham

- Combine the breadcrumbs, egg, ham, lemon zest, parsley and seasoning in a food processor. Pulse until it comes together.
- Remove from the processor and bring together in a bowl. Lay the veal belly on a flat surface and spread the stuffing out.
- Roll the veal belly into a cylinder and tie securely at 1" intervals using string. Season with oil generously.
- Heat a large frying pan and seal until golden brown.
- Move to a slow cooker and cook on medium for 6 hours.
- Turn off the slow cooker when the veal is ready.
- Blanche the turnip and carrots in a saucepan of boiling, salted water for 3 minutes and refresh in water.
- Quarter the carrots and pat the turnip and carrot dry.
- Melt the butter in a pan. Saute the vegetables with a little seasoning. Arrange the veal on a serving platter and garnish with the vegetables before serving.

Rose Veal with Stuffing 943

Replace the ham in the stuffing with the same weight of chopped, cooked chestnuts.

PREPARATION TIME :20 MINUTES

COOKING TIME :
6 HOURS 20 MINUTES

INGREDIENTS

30 ml / 1 fl. oz / 2 tbsp olive oil
1.35 kg / 3 lb piece of rose veal belly,
parsley, finely chopped
1 small egg, beaten
225 g / 8 oz / 2 cups fresh breadcrumbs
110 g / 4 oz / ⅔ cup Corsican ham, sliced
1 lemon, zested
salt and pepper

GARNISH
30 g / 1 oz / ¼ stick unsalted butter
350 g / 12 oz / 3 cups baby turnips, peeled and halved
150 g / 5 oz / 1 cup baby Chantenay carrots
6 vine cherry tomatoes
salt and pepper

944

SERVES 4

Seafood Casserole with Pastry

Seafood Casserole with Brandy

945

Two tbsps of brandy can be used to replace the white wine in the recipe and give stronger flavours.

Seafood Casserole with Vegetables

946

Additional vegetables, such as peas, mushrooms and carrot (blanched) work well with this recipe.

PREPARATION TIME :
40 MINUTES

COOKING TIME : 4.5 HOURS

INGREDIENTS

450 g / 1 lb / 4 cups of mixed firm fish, eg monkfish or cod cut into large chunks
120 g / 4 oz smoked haddock
220 g / 1 small can prawns, drained
220 g / 1 small can mussels, drained
220 g / 1 small can clams and juice
220 g / small can crabmeat
225 g / 8 oz crabsticks, cut into cubes
4 spring onions sliced
juice of 1 lemon
30 ml / 2 tbsp vegetable oil
1 tsp dried parsley
100 ml / ¼ pint / ½ cup white wine
100 ml / ¼ pint / ½ cup fish stock
50 g / 2 oz / ¼ cup butter
6 tbsp double cream
50 g / 2 oz / ¼ cup plain flour
salt and black pepper
1 pack puff pastry

- Pre-warm the slow cooker.
- Heat the oil and fry (sauté) the onions and garlic until softened.
- Stir in the flour and butter cook for 2 minutes.
- Gradually add the stock and wine and fish. Bring to the boil for 8 minutes, adding parsley in the last minute.
- Transfer all ingredients (except the cream) to the slow cooker and cook on a Medium setting for 4 hours.
- Check for seasoning and stir in the cream gently.
- Sprinkle with chopped parsley and allow to cool for 30 minutes.
- Pour the casserole into an ovenproof casserole.
- Roll out the puff pastry and top the casserole, glazing the pastry with a whisked egg yolk.
- Bake at the top of a hot oven 220°C (200° fan) / 425 F / gas 7 for 25 minutes or until the pastry is golden and the fish casserole bubbling beneath.
- Serve immediately.

947

SERVES 4

Lamb Tajine with Fruit

- Coat the lamb in most of the oil and season generously.
- Heat a large casserole dish over a moderate heat until hot then seal the lamb in batches until golden brown in colour over.
- Remove to a slow cooker and reduce the heat under the casserole dish a little.
- Add the remaining oil and saute the onion and garlic for 5 minutes, stirring frequently.
- Add the harissa and ground spices and stir well.
- Add the stock, prunes and apricot halves then pour into the slow cooker and stir again thoroughly.
- Cover with a lid and cook on a medium setting for 6 hours until the lamb is cooked and tender.
- Adjust the seasoning to taste before spooning into a tajine.
- Garnish with pine nuts and parsley before serving.

PREPARATION TIME :

15 MINUTES

COOKING TIME :

6 HOURS 15-20 MINUTES

INGREDIENTS

75 ml / 3 fl. oz / ⅓ cup olive oil
900 g / 2 lb / 6 cups diced lamb leg
110 g / 4 oz / ⅔ cup prunes
110 g / 4 oz / ⅔ cup dried apricot halves
2 onions, sliced
2 cloves of garlic, sliced
1 tbsp harissa
1 tsp ras al hanout, 1 tsp ground cumin
½ tsp ground cinnamon, ½ tsp paprika
500 ml / 18 fl. oz / 2 cup lamb stock
salt and pepper

GARNISH
30 g / 1 oz / ¼ cup pine nuts
sprigs of flat-leaf parsley

Lamb Tajine with Armanac

948

Stir through 30 ml / 1 fl. oz / 2 tbsp Armagnac into the slow cooker before cooking for a richer prune flavour.

949

SERVES 4

Chicken Cari

- Heat the oil in a large casserole dish set over a medium heat until hot.
- Sweat the onion, garlic and ginger for 8-10 minutes until softened and starting to colour.
- Add the ground spices and dried herbs and stir well.
- Add the chicken, potato, passata and coconut milk and stir again.
- Pour into a slow cooker and cover with a lid.
- Cook on a medium setting for 6 hours until the chicken is cooked through.
- Adjust the seasoning to taste before spooning back into a frying pan for presentation.

PREPARATION TIME :

15 MINUTES

COOKING TIME :

6 HOURS 15 MINUTES

INGREDIENTS

55 ml / 2 fl. oz / ¼ cup vegetable oil
4 skinless chicken breasts, diced
2 large white potatoes, peeled and diced
2 large onions, finely chopped
4 cloves of garlic, minced
piece of ginger, peeled and finely chopped
2 tsp ground cumin
1 tsp paprika
1 tsp dried oregano
½ tsp cayenne pepper
250 ml / 9 fl. oz / 1 cup passata
400 ml / 14 fl. oz / 1 ⅔ cups coconut milk
salt and pepper

Chicken Cari with Saffron

 950

Add 1 tsp of saffron threads to the slow cooker before cooking.

951

SERVES 4

Chicken Curry with Yoghurt

PREPARATION TIME :
10-15 MINUTES

COOKING TIME :
5 HOURS 15 MINUTES

....

INGREDIENTS

45 ml / 1 ½ fl. oz / 3 tbsp vegetable oil
4 skinless chicken breasts, diced
3 onions, finely sliced
2 cloves of garlic, sliced
piece of ginger, peeled and finely chopped
1 tbsp Madras curry powder
1 tsp ground cumin
1 tsp turmeric
1 tsp chilli powder
250 ml / 9 fl. oz / 1 cup chicken stock
125 ml / 4 ½ fl. oz / ½ cup water
55 ml / 2 fl. oz / ¼ cup plain yoghurt
salt and pepper

TO GARNISH

1 tbsp picked coriander
(cilantro) leaves

- Heat the oil in a large saucepan set over a medium heat until hot.
- Sweat the onion, garlic and ginger with a little salt for 8-10 minutes until softened.
- Add the ground spices and stir well.
- Add the stock, water and chicken and stir well.
- Pour into a slow cooker and cover with a lid before cooking on a medium setting for 6 hours until the chicken is cooked through.
- Stir through the yoghurt once the chicken is cooked and adjust the seasoning to taste.
- Spoon into serving bowls and garnish with the coriander leaves before serving.

Chicken Curry with Peas 952

Add 150 g / 5 oz / 1 ½ cups thawed frozen petit pois to the slow cooker about an hour before the chicken is ready.

953

SERVES 4

Creamy Chicken with Peas

PREPARATION TIME : 10 MINUTES

COOKING TIME :
4-5 HOURS 10-15 MINUTES

....

INGREDIENTS

30 ml / 1 fl. oz / 2 tbsp olive oil
1 tbsp butter
1 medium chicken, jointed and trimmed
125 ml / 4 ½ fl. oz / ½ cup dry white wine
350 g / 12 oz / 3 cups frozen petit pois, thawed
500 ml / 18 fl. oz / 2 cups chicken stock
250 ml / 9 fl. oz / 1 cup double cream
450 g / 1 lb / 3 cups baby carrots
1 sprig of rosemary
salt and freshly ground black pepper

- Coat the chicken pieces in the oil and season generously.
- Heat a large casserole dish over a moderate heat until hot.
- Seal the chicken in batches until golden brown in colour all over before removing to a slow cooker.
- Reduce the heat under the casserole dish a little before adding the butter.
- Sauté the carrots for 3 minutes, stirring occasionally.
- Add the peas and deglaze the dish with the white wine, stirring the base well.
- Add the stock, cream and rosemary and stir well.
- Pour into the slow cooker and cover with a lid.
- Cook on a medium setting for 4-5 hours until the chicken is cooked through.
- Adjust the seasoning to taste before ladling the casserole into a serving dish.
- Garnish with salt and pepper before serving.

Creamy Chicken with Parsnips 954

Change the baby carrots for the same weight of parsnips that have been peeled and quartered.

955

SERVES 4

Cod Tripe with Chickpeas

- Drain the salt-cod or tripe from the soaking water and pat dry with kitchen towel and dust with flour.
- Heat the oil in a pan and sauté the codpieces, dusted in flour for 3 minutes each side until golden - remove with a slotted spoon into the slow cooker.
- Gently sauté the onion and garlic until golden brown.
- Add the white wine and boil deglaze pan and burn off alcohol.
- Add fish stock coloured with saffron and peas and bring gently to the boil.
- Pour into the slow cooker and cook on a low setting for 6 hours.
- Pour in the chickpeas and allow to warm through thoroughly. Adjust the seasoning to taste.
- Spoon into serving dishes and garnish with the parsley and freshly ground black pepper. Serve immediately with crusty bread or vegetables.

PREPARATION TIME : 25 MINUTES

COOKING TIME : 6 HOURS

INGREDIENTS

600 g / 1 lb 5 oz salt cod tripe
plain (all purpose) flour for dusting
1 onion finely chopped
1 x 400 g can cooked chickpeas
120 ml / 4 fl. oz / ½ cup white wine
4 cloves of garlic, minced
15 ml / 1 tbsp sunflower oil
15 ml / 0.5 fl. oz / 1 tbsp butter
1 pinch saffron soaked in 120 ml / 4 fl. oz / 0.5 cup fish stock
100 g / 4 oz peas
salt and pepper

956

SERVES 4

Cassoulet

PREPARATION TIME: 20 MINUTES

COOKING TIME : 4 HOURS

INGREDIENTS

4 good quality pork and herb sausages
4 small lean pork chops, chopped into cubes
50 g / 2 oz / 2 tbsp bacon lardons
30 ml / 1 fl. oz / 2 tbsp sunflower or olive oil
1 medium onion, peeled and sliced in circles
1 garlic clove, crushed

2 carrots, roughly chopped and blanched for 5 minutes
1 celery stick, chopped
1 tbsp tomato puree
4 beef tomatoes, skinned and sliced
1 x 400 g can cannellini or haricot beans, drained
1 x 400 g can of butter beans, drained
2 tbsp parsley, chopped
230 ml / 8 fl. oz / 1 cups Vegetable Stock
bouquet garni
salt and black pepper to taste

GARNISH

2 tbsp parsley (chopped)

- Heat the oil in a heavy pan and brown the sausages, cubes of pork and bacon lardons. Place in slow cooker.
- In the remaining oil, fry the carrot, onion, garlic and celery.
- Pour the vegetable stock over and bring to the boil. Add the tomatoes and puree, beans and parsley. When boiling, transfer to the slow cooker, add the bouquet garni and stir thoroughly.
- Cook on high for 4 hours.
- At the end of cooking, taste and add salt and black pepper as required.
- Spoon into serving dishes and garnish with chopped parsley.

957

SERVES 6

Chickpeas with Cod

PREPARATION TIME : 15 MINUTES

COOKING TIME : 4 HOURS

INGREDIENTS

750 g / 1 ½ lb fresh or frozen (thawed) cod fillet
1 x 400 g can chick peas
300 g / 10 oz boiled potatoes
4 garlic minced

4 tbsp parsley, chopped
½ tsp chilli flakes
25 ml / 1 fl. oz vegetable oil
300 ml / 10 fl. oz water or fish stock
1 tbsp butter
4 tomatoes peeled and chopped
½ green pepper chopped
1 tsp turmeric
salt and ground black pepper

- Pre-warm the slow cooker.
- Heat the oil and butter and fry (sauté) the garlic, pepper and tomatoes gently. Stir in the parsley, turmeric and chilli and cook for 4 minutes. Pour into the slow cooker.
- Gently place the cod pieces, seasoned with salt and pepper on top and pour the drained tin of chick peas around the fish.
- Cover with the lid and cook on a low setting for 4 hours.
- Taste and adjust seasoning
- Serve tuna with the sauce spooned over, in individual dishes.

958

SERVES 4

Beef Rolls with Tagliatelle

PREPARATION TIME :
15 MINUTES

COOKING TIME :
5 HOURS 20 MINUTES

INGREDIENTS

55 ml / 2 fl. oz / ¼ cup olive oil
675 g / 1 lb 8 oz / 4 ½ cups beef mince
8 rashers streaky bacon
2 cloves of garlic, minced
1 tsp dried oregano
½ tsp dried basil
½ tsp paprika
55 g / 2 oz / ½ cup Parmesan, grated
400 g / 14 oz / 4 cups dried tagliatelle
salt and pepper

- Combine the beef mince, half of the olive oil, Parmesan, garlic, dried herbs, paprika and seasoning in a large mixing bowl.
- Mix together well using your hands. Divide the mixture into 8 and shape into short kebabs.
- Roll each in a rasher of streaky bacon and secure using a toothpick.
- Heat a large casserole dish and seal the beef rolls for a few minutes until golden in colour on the outside.
- Move to a slow cooker and cook on a medium setting for 5 hours. Once cooked, turn off the slow cooker and cook the pasta according to the packet instructions.
- Drain and toss in the remaining olive oil before spooning onto serving plates.
- Top with the beef rolls before and serve immediately.

Beef Rolls with Tomato

959

Add 150 g / 5 oz / 1 ½ cups vine cherry tomatoes to the slow cooker.

960

SERVES 4

Chicken and Olive Tajine

PREPARATION TIME :
10 MINUTES

COOKING TIME :
5 HOURS 15 MINUTES

INGREDIENTS

55 ml / 2 fl. oz / ¼ cup olive oil
4 chicken legs, jointed
1 onion, finely chopped
4 cloves of garlic, finely chopped
1 tsp ras al hanout
1 tsp ground cinnamon
1 tsp ground cumin
1 tsp paprika
½ tsp turmeric
500 ml / 18 fl. oz / 2 cups chicken stock
150 g / 5 oz / 1 cup Kalamata olives
2 tbsp picked flat-leaf parsley leaves, finely chopped
salt and pepper

- Coat the chicken in most of the olive oil and season generously.
- Heat a large casserole dish over a moderate heat until hot and seal the chicken in batches until golden brown in colour all over.
- Remove to a slow cooker and reduce the heat under the casserole dish a little.
- Add the remaining oil and sauté the onion and garlic for 5 minutes, stirring occasionally.
- Add the ground spices and stir well before adding the olives, stock and parsley.
- Stir well before pouring into the slow cooker on top of the chicken.
- Cover with a lid and cook on a medium setting for 5 hours until the chicken is cooked through.
- Adjust the seasoning to taste before spooning into a tajine and serving.

Chicken, Olive and Honey Tajine

961

Add 2 tbsp hone to the slow cooker before cooking.

962

SERVES 4

Roast Chicken with Mushrooms

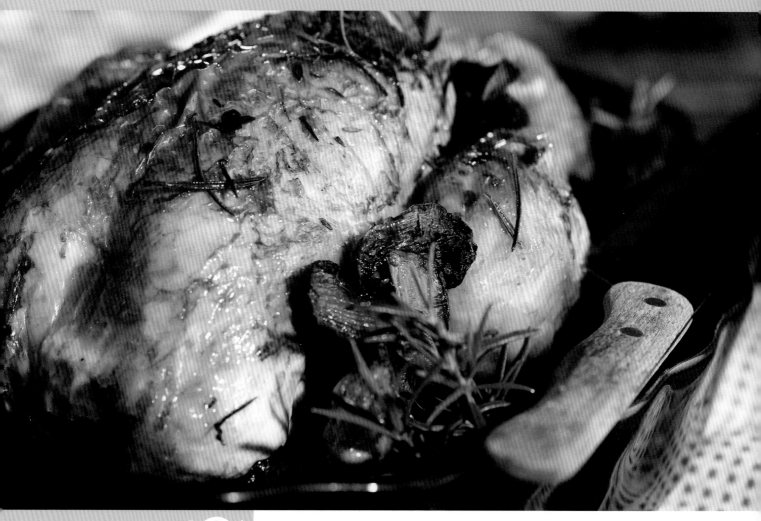

Chicken Breast with Onions

963

The Chicken may be replaced with 4 Chicken breasts and the onion then added to the pot for cooking.

Garlic Chicken with Mushrooms

964

Add 8 halved garlic cloves to the pot if you like a more garlicky flavour to your chicken.

PREPARATION TIME :
20 MINUTES

COOKING TIME : 8 HOURS

INGREDIENTS

1 ¾ kg / 4lb chicken
30 ml / 2 tbsp goose fat or vegetable oil
1 large onion, quartered
salt, pepper and paprika
3 sprigs of rosemary, chopped into 1" pieces
100 g / 4 oz mushrooms, brushed and sliced

- Warm the slow cooker.
- Wipe the chicken with oil and sprinkle the salt, pepper and paprika over the chest. Place the onion pieces within the cavity.
- Heat oil in pan and fry the chicken for 5 minutes each side. Remove and put to one side.
- Use remaining oil to fry the seasoned sliced mushrooms until brown.
- Place the chicken and mushrooms into the slow cooker. Make little incisions in the skin and insert 1" pieces of rosemary just beneath the skin.
- Place the lid over the pot and cook on low heat for 8 hours.
- Remove chicken and leave to rest for 10 minutes.
- Meanwhile, use the juices in the crockpot to make a gravy, cornflour (cornstarch) may be used to thicken if necessary.

965

SERVES 4

Pork with Bacon and Sage

PREPARATION TIME :
15 MINUTES

COOKING TIME :
6 HOURS 20-25 MINUTES

INGREDIENTS

30 ml / 1 fl. oz / 2 tbsp sunflower oil
1 tbsp butter
900 g / 2 lb piece of pork loin roast
12 rashers back bacon
1 large handful of picked sage leaves
300 g / 10 ½ oz / 2 cups pearl onions,
peeled and halved
4 canned artichoke hearts, drained
and chopped
300 g / 10 ½ oz / 2 cups baby carrots
150 g / 5 oz / 1 cup new potatoes,
halved
150 g / 5 oz / 1 ½ cups frozen petit
pois, thawed
500 ml / 18 fl. oz / 2 cups ham stock
salt and pepper

TO GARNISH
sprig of sage leaves

- Preheat the oven to 200°C (180° fan) / 400F / gas 6.
- Wrap the pork in the bacon and thread the sage leaves through the bacon, using a sharp knife to help make incisions.
- Tie the pork using kitchen string at 2" intervals and rub in the oil all over.
- Season generously before sitting on a roasting tray.
- Roast for 20 minutes, then transfer to a slow cooker.
- Add the vegetables, stock and butter and cover. Arrange the pork so that it sits on top of the vegetables. Cook on a medium setting for 6 hours.
- Remove the pork from the slow cooker and adjust the seasoning of the vegetables according to taste.
- Spoon the vegetables onto a serving platter before sitting the pork on top.
- Garnish with a sprig of sage leaves before serving.

Pork wrapped in Bacon and Tarragon
966

Use tarragon sprigs instead of the sage leaves.

967

SERVES 4

Beef Casserole with Dumplings

PREPARATION TIME :
15 MINUTES

COOKING TIME :
6 HOURS 20-25 MINUTES

INGREDIENTS

55 ml / 2 fl. oz / ¼ cup sunflower oil
600 g / 1 lb 5 oz / 4 cups braising
steak, cut into 1" cubes
1 onion, finely chopped
450 g / 1 lb / 3 cups carrots, peeled
and sliced
450 g / 1 lb / 3 cups white potatoes,
peeled and diced
250 ml / 9 fl. oz / 1 cup good-quality
ale
500 ml / 18 fl. oz / 2 cups beef stock
salt and pepper

FOR THE DUMPLINGS
500 g / 1 lb 2 oz / 3 ⅓ cups beef mince
110 g / 4 oz / 1 cup shredded suet
salt and pepper

TO GARNISH
sprigs of flat-leaf parsley

- Make the dumplings by combining the beef mince, suet and seasoning in a large mixing bowl.
- Mix well with your hands. Shape into large balls by moulding between your palms. Arrange in a slow cooker in an even layer.
- Coat the beef with half of the oil and season generously before heating a large casserole dish.
- Seal the beef in batches, then transfer to a slow cooker.
- Reduce the heat a little under the casserole dish and add the remaining oil.
- Sauté the carrots, potato and onion with a little seasoning for 5 minutes, stirring occasionally.
- Add the ale and let it reduce, stirring the base and sides well before adding the stock.
- Pour everything into the slow cooker and cook on a medium setting for 6 hours.
- Adjust the seasoning and garnish with parsley.

Beef Casserole with Pearl Barley
968

Replace the dumplings with 200 g / 7 oz / 1 cup pearl barley that has been soaked in water overnight.

SERVES 4

Herb and Meatball Tagine

- Mix meatball ingredients, hand roll into small 1" meatballs and fry them in batches until thoroughly cooked
- Heat the oil and fry the onion, herbs and garlic until softened.
- Add the spices and chilli flakes, stir well and cook through for 3 minutes.
- Add the prunes and tinned tomatoes and stir thoroughly. Bring gently to the boil.
- Place the spicy liquid into the slow cooker, and pile the cooked meatballs on top and cook on a medium setting for hours.
- Serve hot with rice or pitta bread.

PREPARATION TIME :
25 MINUTES

COOKING TIME :
4 HOURS

....

INGREDIENTS

MEATBALLS
450 g / 1 lb beef mince
100 g / 4 oz / 2 cups breadcrumbs
15 ml / 1 tbsp parsley
15 ml / 1 tbsp oregano
15 ml / 1 tbsp basil
1 tsp onion powder
salt and pepper
½ tsp ground nutmeg
1 garlic clove minced

2 tsp ground cumin
2 tbsp ground coriander
2 garlic cloves minced
1 egg lightly beaten
60 ml / 4 tsp / ¼ cup vegetable oil

SAUCE
4 prunes, chopped
2 garlic cloves, crushed
½ medium onion, sliced
1 tsp cumin
1 tsp turmeric
½ tsp cinnamon
½ tsp Cayenne pepper
1 tbsp paprika
1 x 440 g / 15 ½ oz can chopped tomatoes
salt and pepper

Salmon Steak with Grapes

970

SERVES 4

PREPARATION TIME :
20 MINUTES

COOKING TIME : 1 HOUR

....

INGREDIENTS

4 large salmon fillets
1 medium onion, finely sliced
250 ml / 8 fl. oz / 1 cup dry white

wine
bunch of fresh dill
1 slice lemon
450 g / 1 lb seedless white grapes
salt and pepper

- Pre-warm the slow cooker.
- Heat the wine, dill, lemon, seasoning and grapes and simmer for 5 minutes
- Spoon the grape sauce mixture into the slow cooker
- Place an oiled layer of foil over the grapes and using a fish slice, gently position the salmon fillets onto the foil–skin side up
- Season the salmon.
- Place the lid on the pot and steam the fish on low for 1 hr.
- At the end of cooking, carefully lift out the foil with salmon on, place on a flat tin and flash under the grill for a few minutes.
- To serve, spoon the grape mixture onto 4 individual plates and gently place the salmon on top.
- Garnish with a toasted lemon slice and fresh parsley

Chicken Bouillabaisse

971

SERVES 4

PREPARATION TIME :
20 MINUTES

COOKING TIME : 6 HOURS

....

INGREDIENTS

4 chicken breast quartered
Plain (All Purpose) Flour for dusting
1 spring fresh rosemary
4 garlic cloves, minced
1 medium onion, finely sliced
0.5 kg / 1 lb celery sticks
2 tbsp butter
2 tbsp oil
4 plum tomatoes, blanched, peeled

and chopped
4 medium carrots, peeled and chopped and blanched for 5 minutes
½ unwaxed lemon, zested in strips, and juice
1 pinch saffron soaked in 100 ml / 4 fl. oz / ½ cup chicken stock
100 ml / 4 fl. oz / ½ cup dry white wine
2 tbsp pernod

GARNISH
4 tbsp fresh parsley, chopped

- Warm the slow Cooker..
- Heat the oil in a pan and gently sauté chicken pieces, onion and garlic for 5 minutes. Keep to one side.
- Melt butter and gently braise the celery for 10 minutes. Pour over the wine and boil to reduce by half.
- Add all ingredients to the slow cooker. Place the lid on and cook for 6 hours on low.
- Adjust the seasoning to taste after 4 hours.
- Spoon into serving dishes and garnish with the parsley and freshly ground black pepper.

972

SERVES 4

Beef Cheek, Onion and Carrot

PREPARATION TIME : 15 MINUTES

COOKING TIME : 8 HOURS 15 MINUTES

INGREDIENTS

55 ml / 2 fl. oz / ¼ cup sunflower oil
900 g / 2 lb / 6 cups beef cheek, roughly chopped
450 g / 1 lb / 3 cups pearl onion, blanched and peeled
2 carrots, peeled and julienned
125 ml / 4 ½ fl. oz / ½ cup good-quality red wine
500 ml / 18 fl. oz / 2 cups beef stock
salt and pepper

TO GARNISH

sprig of flat-leaf parsley

- Coat the beef cheek in the oil and season generously.
- Heat a large casserole dish over a moderate heat until hot and seal the beef in batches until golden brown in colour all over.
- Transfer the sealed beef to a slow cooker when completed.
- Reduce the heat under the casserole dish a little before adding the onions.
- Sauté for a few minutes before adding the wine.
- Let it reduce by half before adding the stock and the carrot.
- Pour into the slow cooker and cover with a lid.
- Cook on a medium setting for 8 hours until the beef cheek is starting to fall apart.
- Adjust the seasoning to taste before spooning the stew into a roasting dish for presentation.
- Garnish with a sprig of parsley before serving.

Beef and Ale Stew

973

Replace the wine with the same volume of ale.

974

SERVES 4

Bacon with Lentils

PREPARATION TIME :
15 MINUTES

COOKING TIME :
5 HOURS 15-20 MINUTES

INGREDIENTS

450 g / 1 lb / 3 cups gammon steak
450 g / 1 lb / 2 ½ cups Puy lentils
110 g / 4 oz / ⅔ cup rashers of smokey bacon
55 ml / 2 fl. oz / ¼ cup olive oil
2 onions, finely sliced
2 cloves garlic, minced
3 large carrots, peeled and sliced
2 bay leaves
3 sprigs of thyme
750ml / 1 pint 6 fl. oz / 3 cups chicken stock
salt and pepper

- Heat the olive oil in a large casserole dish over a medium heat until hot.
- Sweat the onion, garlic, carrot, bay leaves and thyme sprigs with a little salt for 6-7 minutes, stirring frequently, until softened and starting to colour.
- Add the bacon, gammon and lentils and stir well.
- Cover with the stock, then spoon the mixture into a slow cooker.
- Cover with a lid and cook on a low setting for 5 hours until the gammon is soft and starting to pull apart easily between your fingers and the lentils are soft and tender.
- Adjust the seasoning to taste and skim away any excess liquid; the casserole should be moist but not sodden.
- Spoon everything back into the casserole dish and serve immediately.

Vegetarian cheese with lentils.

975

You can make this a vegetarian version by substituting the gammon and bacon for Halloumi cheese and / or Paneer. Change the chicken stock to vegetable stock in this case.

976

SERVES 4

Quail Casserole with Cognac

- Prcheat the oven to 190°C (170° fan) / 375F / gas 5.
- Rub the quails with the olive oil and season the insides and outsides generously.
- Wrap the breasts with the bacon and tie securely using kitchen string.
- Arrange the quails in a high-sided roasting tray and roast for 20 minutes until browned on the outside.
- Remove from the oven and deglaze the tray with the Cognac. Add the stock and grapes and stir well.
- Arrange the quails in a slow cooker and pour the Cognac, stock and grapes on top.
- Cover the slow cooker with a lid and cook on a medium setting for 6 hours until the quails are cooked through.
- Adjust the seasoning to taste before removing the quails and arranging on a serving plate.
- Spoon the grapes and sauce around before serving.

PREPARATION TIME :
15 MINUTES

COOKING TIME :
6 HOURS 30 MINUTES

INGREDIENTS

75 ml / 3 fl. oz / ⅓ cup olive oil
2 quails, trimmed and trussed
4 rashers back bacon
300 g / 10 ½ oz / 2 cups seedless green grapes
55 ml / 2 fl. oz / ¼ cup Cognac
250 ml / 9 fl. oz / 1 cup chicken stock
salt and pepper

Creamy Cognac Quails

977

Stir 125 ml / 4 ½ fl. oz / ½ cup double cream into the slow cooker after cooking.

978

SERVES 4

Chablis Scallop and Oyster

- Drizzle the scallops with the olive oil and season well.
- Heat a large frying pan over a moderate heat until hot and seal the scallops in batches for 30 seconds on both side.
- Remove to a slow cooker and add the stock, wine, potato, leek, carrot and chives.
- Stir well and cover with a lid.
- Cook on a low setting for 6 hours, adding the oysters to the slow cooker after 5 ½ hours.
- Adjust the seasoning to taste before ladling into serving bowls and garnishing with the parsley.

PREPARATION TIME :
15 MINUTES

COOKING TIME :
6 HOURS 10 MINUTES

INGREDIENTS

55 ml / 2 fl. oz / ¼ cup olive oil
8 queen scallops, roe removed
10 rock oysters, opened and chilled
500 ml / 18 fl. oz / 2 cups fish stock
250 ml / 9 fl. oz / 1 cup Chablis
300 g / 10 ½ oz / 2 cups new potatoes, peeled and halved
1 large carrot, peeled and diced
1 leek, sliced and washed
3-4 chive stalks, finely chopped
salt and pepper

GARNISH
sprigs of flat-leaf parsley

DESSERTS

979

SERVES 4-6

Roasted Prickly Pears

Roasted Pineapple

980

Swap the 4 pears with a pineapple, peeled and cubed, and cook in the same way.

Roasted Oranges

981

Swap the 4 pears for 4 peeled oranges for a citrus kick.

PREPARATION TIME: 15 MINUTES

COOKING TIME: 4 HOURS

INGREDIENTS

4 prickly pears
225 g / 8oz / 1 cup caster (superfine) sugar
110 g / 4oz / 1 stick butter
¾ tsp cinnamon
3 tbsp lemon juice

- Wash the prickly pears thoroughly and place in the slow cooker.
- Mix the sugar, cinnamon and lemon juice together.
- Rub over the prickly pears, making sure the fruit is properly covered.
- Cut the butter into chunks and scatter evenly around the pears in the pot.
- Replace the lid and cook on a low setting for 4 hours.
- Once cooked leave to cool slightly and arrange on a plate.
- If the cooking liquor is a little thin reduce in a pan to a syrupy consistency.
- Spoon the cooking sauce around the pears and serve.

982

SERVES 6

Orange Custard Cream

- Wash the fruit and arrange in the base of your slow-cooker with the dried fruit.
- In a large bowl mix the orange juice, zest, cider, sugar and cinnamon together.
- Pour the mixture over the fruit, cover with the lid and cook slowly on low setting for around 3-4 hours.
- Make the orange custard by heating the milk with the orange zest and vanilla pod, heat until just boiling.
- Beat the sugar with the egg yolks until pale.
- Pour the milk onto the egg yolks stirring steadily, remove the vanilla pod.
- Return the milk to the pan (cleaned) and cook over a low heat stirring continuously until the custard coats the back of a spoon.
- Strain through a sieve and add the Grand Marnier and orange essence. Allow to cool and serve with stewed fruit when ready.

PREPARATION TIME: 40 MINUTES

COOKING TIME: 4 HOURS

INGREDIENTS

3 large cooking apples, peeled and cored
2 pears, cored
3 apricots
150 ml / 5 fl. oz / ¾ cup orange juice
1 tsp. grated orange rind
75 g / 2 ½ oz / ½ cup currants
120ml / 4 fl. oz / ½ cup apple cider
¼ tsp cinnamon
90 g / 3 ½ oz / ⅓ cup brown sugar
570 ml / 1 pint / 2 ¼ cups whole milk
finely grated zest of 1 large orange
1 vanilla pod
4 tbsp caster (superfine) sugar
6 egg yolks
2 tbsp Grand Marnier
2 drops, orange essence

Chocolate Custard Cream

983

Make a chocolate version by adding 55 g / 2oz / 1 / 3 cup of dark chocolate instead of the orange, added during cooking out time.

984

SERVES 6

Spicy Stewed Mirabelle Plums

- Wash the plums carefully.
- In a bowl mix the orange juice together with the brown sugar, cinnamon, star anise, ground nutmeg and crushed cardamom.
- Place the plums in the slow cooker together with the sugar, juice and spice mix.
- Add the orange peel slice and vanilla pod (whole)
- Cook in the slow cooker on a low setting for 3-4 hours.
- Serve with cream as an optional extra.

PREPARATION TIME: 10 MINUTES

COOKING TIME: 4 HOURS

INGREDIENTS

24 Mirabelle plums
240 ml / 9 fl. oz / 1 cup orange juice
50g / 2oz / ⅓ cup brown sugar
1 tsp ground cinnamon
1 star anise
½ tsp ground nutmeg
1 vanilla pod
2 cardamon pods, crushed
3 slices of orange peel

Spicy Stewed Victoria Plums

985

Suggested variations; you can use other types of plums such as Victoria, in which case use only 12 plums for the above recipe.

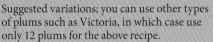

986

SERVES 4

Stewed Fruit with Red Wine

PREPARATION TIME: 20 MINUTES

COOKING TIME: 3-4 HOURS

INGREDIENTS

75 g / 3 oz / ½ cup dried apricot halves
225 g / 8 oz / 1 ½ cups dried prunes
3 figs cut into quarters
460 ml / 16 fl. oz / 1 ¾ cups honey
180 ml / 6 fl. oz / ¾ cup red wine
1 cinnamon stick
300 ml / 10 ½ fl. oz / 1 ¼ cups orange juice

- Chop up the dried fruits to preferred eating size and place in the bottom of a slow cooker.
- Combine the liquid ingredients together and pour over the fruits in the slow cooker.
- Add the cinnamon stick and orange peel.
- Cover and cook on a low heat for 3-4 hour until the fruit is tender.
- Once cooked remove the fruit from the cooker and place in a serving dish.
- If preferred reduce the remaining cooking liquor in a pan to a slight syrup consistency.
- Leave the fruit to cool once cooked to just above room temperature for flavour to develop.

Stewed Fruit with Port 987

Use port instead of the red wine for a richer, fuller and sweeter flavour.

988

SERVES 6

Rice Pudding with Raisins

PREPARATION TIME: 15 MINUTES

COOKING TIME: 2 HOURS

INGREDIENTS

150 g / 5 oz / ¾ cup short grain rice
360 ml / 12 fl. oz / 1 ½ cups double cream
240 ml / 8 fl. oz / 1 cup water
100 g / 3 ½ oz / ½ cup raisins
½ tsp salt
1 tsp vanilla extract
½ tsp cinnamon

TO SERVE
150 g / 5 oz / ¾ cup white chocolate drops or chopped white chocolate

- Mix all the rice pudding ingredients together in a bowl.
- Place the mixed ingredients into the slow cooker.
- Cook on high setting for 2-2½ hours.
- Check the rice pudding is tender if not continue cooking until it is ready.
- Shortly before serving stir through the white chocolate chips.
- Wait for the chocolate chips to melt slightly before serving.

Rice Pudding with Cranberries 989

Instead of using raisins why not try chopped dried cranberries which work well with white chocolate.

990

SERVES 4

Stewed Pears with Cinnamon

Cranberry Stewed Pears

991

You can poach the pears in cranberry juice to give the fruit a pinkish hue.

Stewed Rhubarb with Cinnamon

992

Replace the pears with 16 sticks of rhubarb, roughly chopped to 2cm chunks and cooked the same.

Stewed Pears with Ginger

993

In place of the cinnamon add 1 tbsp of finely grated fresh ginger.

PREPARATION TIME: 10 MINUTES

COOKING TIME: 2-3 HOURS

INGREDIENTS

60g / 2oz / ⅓ cup light brown sugar
½ tsp ground cinnamon
1 cinnamon stick
480 ml / 17 fl. oz / 2 cups white grape juice
4 pears
zest and juice of 1 lemon

- Peel the pears carefully to maintain shape and be sure to keep stem in tact.
- Combine the sugar, cinnamon, grape juice together in a bowl.
- Carefully rub the pears with the lemon juice to help prevent discolouration during cooking time.
- Stand the pears up in the base of your slow cooker.
- Pour the cinnamon and juice mix around the pears.
- Add the cinnamon sticks.
- Cover and cook on a low setting for 2-3 hours.
- Once cooked remove the pears to a serving dish together with the cinnamon stick.
- Pour the cooking liquor into a pan and reduce by one third.
- Pour the reduced cooking liquor over the pears and serve.

994

SERVES 6

Stewed Plums

Stewed Pears

 995

Small pears work well in this recipe. Replace the port with sweet Madeira such as Malmsey.

Stewed Plums with Ice Cream

996

Add 2 scoops of vanilla ice-cream to compliment the plums.

Stewed Plums with Mulled Wine

 997

Replace the red wine with mulled wine and cook the same.

PREPARATION TIME: 10 MINUTES

COOKING TIME: 2-2 ½ HOURS

INGREDIENTS

200 ml / 7 fl. oz / 1 cup port
200 ml / 7fl. oz / 1 cup red wine
1 cinnamon stick
1 star anise
zest and juice of 2 oranges
500 g / 1 lb 2 oz / 3 cups plums, halved and pitted

- Wash the plums, after halving and pitting them place them in the base of a slow cooker.
- Mix the red wine with the port together with the spices and the juice.
- Pour over the plums and cover, cook on a low setting for 2-2 ½ hours or until the plums are tender.
- Once cooked remove the plums from the slow cooker and peel if preferred.
- Reserve the cooking liquor.
- Arrange in a serving dish.
- Pour the cooking sauce into a pan and reduce to a syrup like consistency, until shiny and slightly thicker in look and feel.
- Cover the plums with the reduced sauce and serve.

998

SERVES 6

Roast Vanilla Peaches

- Wash and cut the peaches in half and remove the stone.
- Mix the sugar, water and orange juice together.
- Arrange the peaches face down into the slow cooker.
- Pour the sugar and orange juice mix over the peaches.
- Cut the butter up into small cubes and dot around the peaches in the base of the slow cooker so that they are evenly spaced.
- Split the vanilla pods in half and arrange close to the peaches.
- Cook on a low setting for 2 hours until the peaches are tender.
- Remove the peaches to a serving dish.
- Spoon the cooking juice over the peaches or reduce in a pan over a high heat for more of a syrup consistency.

PREPARATION TIME: 10 MINUTES

COOKING TIME : 2 HOURS

INGREDIENTS

6 peaches, slightly under ripe
225 g / 8 oz / 1 cup caster (superfine) sugar
3 tbsp water
225 ml / 8 fl. oz / 1 cup orange juice
2 vanilla pods split
50 g / 2 oz / ½ stick unsalted butter

Roast Vanilla Apricots

999

Apricots also work well in this recipe, use 12 slightly underripe apricots instead of the peaches.

1000

SERVES 4-6

Cherries with Vanilla Prune Ice Cream

- Stir the pitted cherries with the water, sugar, vanilla and cherry brandy. Place in the slow cooker and cook on a high setting for 2 hours.
- Put the sugar, water and vanilla pod into a pan. Dissolve the sugar over a low heat slowly. Beat the egg yolks well.
- Half whip the cream. When the sugar has dissolved turn up the heat and boil. Take out the vanilla pod scraping out the seeds and adding to the sugar syrup.
- Whisk the egg yolks and carefully add to the sugar syrup. Whisk until the mixture is very thick.
- Cool, whisking every now and then. Fold in half the cream, then the chopped prunes then the remaining cream
- When the ice cream is nearly frozen whisk again and then freeze until hard.
- Serve the cherries warm or at room temperature with the vanilla prune ice cream.

PREPARATION TIME: 10 MINUTES

COOKING TIME : 2 HOURS

INGREDIENTS

480 g / 1 lb 1 oz / 3 cups fresh cherries, pitted
1 vanilla pod split lengthways
1 cup caster (superfine) sugar
180 ml / 6 fl. oz / ¾ cup water
60 ml / 2 fl. oz / ¼ cup cherry brandy (optional)

FOR THE ICE CREAM

300 g / 10 ½ oz / 2 cups pitted prunes, roughly chopped
70 g / 2 ½ oz / ⅓ cup sugar
1 vanilla pod split lengthways
3 egg yolks
425 ml / 15 fl. oz / 1 ¾ cup double cream

Cherries with Vanilla and Date Ice Cream

1001

Swap the prunes for dates and prepare the ice cream in the same way.

1002

SERVES 6

Spicy Stewed Plums

PREPARATION TIME: 10 MINUTES

COOKING TIME: 4 HOURS

INGREDIENTS

12 plums, ripe
240 ml / 8 fl. oz / 1 cup orange juice
50 g / 2oz / ⅓ cup brown sugar
1 tsp ground cinnamon
½ tsp ground nutmeg
1 vanilla pod, split lengthways
2 cardamon pods, crushed
1 cinnamon stick

- Wash and halve the plums, removing the stones.
- Place in the slow cooker face down.
- Mix the sugar, orange juice and spices together with the seeds of the vanilla pod.
- Pour the mixture over the 4 hours.
- Once cooked, remove the plums and pour the cooking liquor into a heavy based pan.
- Reduce the liquor to a syrupy consistency.
- Once the plums have cooled slightly remove the skins and place in a serving dish.
- Cover the plums with the reduced cooking juice and serve with the vanilla pod and cinnamon stick for garnish.

Spicy Stewed Apricots
1003

Swap the plums for 12 apricots and cook in the same way.

1004

SERVES 4-6

Roasted Figs

PREPARATION TIME:15 MINUTES

COOKING TIME: 2-3 HOURS

INGREDIENTS

12 figs
480 ml / 16 fl. oz / 2 cups
Banyuls wine
50 g / 2 oz / ⅓ cup brown sugar
½ tsp ground cinnamon
½ tsp ground nutmeg
1 lemon zested

- Wash the figs carefully and arrange tip facing upwards in the base of a slow cooker.
- Mix the Banyuls wine with the brown sugar, cinnamon, nutmeg and lemon zest.
- Pour the mix over the figs and cover the slow cooker and cook for 2-3 hours until the figs are tender.
- Remove the figs from the cooking liquor and leave to cool slightly.
- When the figs have cooled a little and have hardened slightly cut into quarters from top to bottom.
- Arrange the fruit in a serving dish.
- Pour the cooking juice over the figs and serve.

Roasted Figs with Port
1005

Use black figs if green figs are not available and replace the Banyuls with port and cook the same way.

1006

SERVES 6

Vanilla Apples and Pears

Spicy Plums and Pears 1007

Replace the apples with plums and replace the grape juice with port or a spicy red wine. You can use star anise instead of the cinnamon stick.

PREPARATION TIME: 10 MINUTES

COOKING TIME: 2 HOURS

INGREDIENTS

60 g / 2 oz / ⅓ cup light brown sugar
½ tsp ground cinnamon
1 cinnamon stick
480 ml / 17 fl. oz / 2 cups white grape juice
4 pears
4 apples
100 g / 3 ½ oz / ½ cup sultanas
60 g / 2 oz / ⅓ cup whole almonds
zest and juice of 1 lemon

- Peel, core, and quarter the pears and apples.
- Rub the lemon juice over the fruit to prevent discolouration.
- Arrange the fruit evenly on the bottom of a slow cooker.
- Scatter the almonds around the fruit together with the cinnamon stick, vanilla pod and lemon zest.
- Mix the sugar, white grape juice and cinnamon together and pour over the fruit, whole spices and almonds.
- Cover the fruit and spice mix and cook on a low setting for 2 hours.
- Arrange the fruit, spices and almonds on a serving dish pouring the cooking juice over it and serve.

1008

SERVES 4

Figs with Cream Stuffing

PREPARATION TIME: 20 MINUTES

COOKING TIME: 2 HOURS

INGREDIENTS

6 green figs
480 ml / 17 fl. oz / 2 cups sweet sherry
50 g / 2 oz / ⅓ cup brown sugar
½ tsp ground cinnamon
½ tsp ground nutmeg
1 lemon zested
150 ml / 5 fl. oz / ¾ cup double cream
1 tbsp icing sugar

- Wash the figs and place standing up in the slow cooker.
- Mix the sugar with the sherry and the spices.
- Pour over the figs and cover for 2 hours on a low setting.
- Once cooked remove the figs and place on a serving plate.
- Reduce the cooking liquor until it a rose coloured syrupy consistency.
- Slice the top third of each fig off, and scoop a little of the flesh out and put into a bowl.
- Scoop out the flesh of the 2 extra figs and add this to the other fig filling into a bowl.
- Mix the cream with the icing sugar and lightly whip.
- Add the cream to the fig mixture and gently stir so as not to break the filling up too much.
- Fill the figs with the creamed mixture and replace the top of the figs and serve in the tagine if desired.
- Spoon the syrup around and over the figs and serve.

Mission Figs with Stuffing

1009

If green figs aren't available use black Mission figs and Marsala wine instead of the sweet sherry.

1010

SERVES 4

Apple Crumble

PREPARATION TIME: 20 MINUTES

COOKING TIME: 4 HOURS

INGREDIENTS

3 large bramley apples (or any cooking apple)
125 g / 4 ½ oz / ¾ cup plain (all-purpose) flour
125 g / 4 ½ oz / 1 stick butter
125 g / 4 ½ oz / ⅔ cup, soft brown sugar
2 tbsp Golden Syrup
juice of half a lemon
60 g / 2 oz / ¼ cup rolled oats

- Wash and peel the apples, core and cut into chunks.
- Cover the apples with the lemon juice to prevent discolouration during the cooking process.
- Place at the bottom of your slow cooker and cover with the golden syrup.
- Make the crumble by gently rubbing the butter and flour together until the mixture resembles breadcrumbs.
- Add the oats and sugar to the mix.
- Cover the apples with the crumble mix evenly.
- Cook on a low setting for 4 hours, serve warm.

Apple and Blackberry Crumble

1011

Add half a cup of black fruits to the apples such as blackberries and cover with the crumble mix.

1012

SERVES 4

Warm Roast Apples

- Cut the apples in half lengthways and arrange face down on the base of the slow cooker.
- Cover with the apple juice and dot with butter.
- Cook on a low heat for 2-2½ hours until the apples are tender but still hold their shape.
- To make the cream, in a heavy based saucepan combine the butter, both sugars and golden syrup together.
- Heat over a high heat for around 3 minutes, carefully agitating the pan but not stirring it.
- Add half the cream and enough sea salt to taste, being careful not to burn your tongue.
- Pour the sauce into a bowl and leave to cool.
- When the apples are ready to be served whip the remaining cream until thick and the mix with the caramel sauce, adding more or less to your taste.
- Place in a piping bag and pipe onto the plate used to serve the apples.

PREPARATION TIME: 30 MINUTES

COOKING TIME: 2-2½ HOURS

INGREDIENTS

4 eating apples e.g Pink Lady or Braeburn
120 ml / 4 fl. oz / ½ cup apple juice
2 tbsp unsalted butter

75 g / 3 oz / ⅔ stick butter
55 g / 2 oz / ⅓ cup brown sugar
55 g / 2 oz / ¼ cup caster (superfine) sugar
4 tbsp Golden Syrup
250 ml / 9 fl. oz / 1 cup double cream
¾ tsp sea salt

1013

SERVES 6

Stewed Pears with Chocolate

PREPARATION TIME: 30 MINUTES

COOKING TIME: 2-2 ½ HOURS

INGREDIENTS

6 pears
90 g / 3oz / ½ cup brown sugar
115 ml / 4 fl. oz / ½ cup maple syrup
1 tbsp butter
zest of 1 small orange
¼ tsp ground ginger
For the sauce:
300 g/ 10 oz / 2 cups of good quality dark chocolate
180 ml/ 6 fl. oz / ¾ cup double cream
180 ml/6 fl. oz / ¾ cup full-fat milk
pinch of groud cinnamon
6 tbsp flaked (slivered) almonds

- Peel the pears being careful to keep the fruit in tact and keep the stalk in place.
- Stand the pears upright in the base of the slow cooker.
- Mix the other ingredients together and pour on to the pears.
- Cover and cook on a high heat setting for around 2-2 ½ hours or until tender.
- Fifteen minutes before serving the pears prepare the chocolate sauce.

- Chop the chocolate up and place in a heat resistant bowl.
- Heat up in a heavy based pan the cream, milk and cinnamon until boiling.
- Pour over the chocolate and stir gently until melted.
- When the pears are cooked place on a serving platter as desired and pour over the chocolate sauce and flaked (slivered) almonds.

1014

SERVES 4

Poached Pear in Pastry

PREPARATION TIME: 30 MINUTES

COOKING TIME: 2 HOURS

INGREDIENTS

4 Conference pears (or similar)
175g / 6 oz / ¾ cup sugar
3 tbsp honey
1 cinnamon stick

1 star anise
2 cardamon pods crushed
1 vanilla pod, split lengthways
juice of 1 lemon
strip of orange peel
2 cloves
1 packet puff pastry
2 eggs lightly beaten

- Peel the pears carefully, keeping the stalk intact.
- Cover the pears in the lemon juice to prevent discolouration.
- Mix the sugar, honey, orange peel and spices together and add the red wine.
- Pour over the pears in the slow cooker and cook for 2-4 hours on a low heat or until tender when pierced with a skewer.
- Once cooked reduce the cooking liquor in a pan until thick.
- Preheat oven to 180°C (160° fan) 375F, gas 5.
- Roll out the pastry to 3-4mm thickness and cut into triangles that will approximately fit the size of your pears.
- Working quickly place the pear in the centre of the pastry with a little of the cooking liquor and pinch together sealing with a little lightly beaten egg
- Once pinched together using a pastry brush glaze the rest of the pastry enveloped pears.
- Place on a baking sheet and bake for 20-25 minutes until golden brown.

SERVES 4

Stewed Fruit with Liquorice

1015

Sweet Stewed Fruit with Liquorice

1016

Replace the stone fruits with apples and pears, add 75 g of currants and or raisins for a sweeter dessert.

PREPARATION TIME: 15 MINUTES

COOKING TIME: 3 HOURS

INGREDIENTS

3 peaches, halved and stoned
3 nectarines, halved and stoned
150 ml / 5 fl. oz / ¾ cup orange juice
1 tsp grated orange rind
120 ml / 4 fl. oz / ½ cup apple cider
¼ tsp cinnamon
90 g / 3 ½ oz / ½ cup brown sugar
2 sticks fresh liquorice

- Arrange the fruits evenly in the slow cooker.
- Mix the juice, cider, sugar and spices together.
- Pour the juice and spices over the fruit and arrange the liquorice sticks around the fruits.
- Cover the fruit, juice, spices and liquorice stick and cook on a low setting for around 3 hours or until the fruit is tender.
- Arrange in a serving dish, and place the liquorice alongside as a garnish.

1017

SERVES 4

Spiced Caramelised Mangoes

- Cut the mangoes in half, peel and cut into rough chunks. Set to one side.
- Take a heavy based pan and warm over a medium heat.
- When the pan is hot add the sugar and leave for a few minutes.
- After about 5 minutes the sugar will start to melt and liquid will appear around the edges.
- Start to shake the pan to agitate the sugar and leave until around a quarter of the sugar has melted.
- Using a wooden spoon stir the sugar until it turns a dark amber colour.
- Remove from the heat and add the mango.
- Place the mango and the caramel into a slow cooker and add the spices.
- Cook on a low setting until the mango collapses which should take around 2 hours. Serve with the spices as a garnish if desired.

PREPARATION TIME: 30 MINUTES

COOKING TIME: 2 HOURS

INGREDIENTS

4 large ripe mangos
175 g / 6 oz / ¾ cup caster (superfine) sugar
1 cinnamon stick
2 star anise

Spiced Caramelised Apricots

1018

Replace the mangoes with apricots. Plunge into boiling water for 10 seconds then place in cold water to remove the skins more easily. Make sure all stones are removed first.

1019

SERVES 4

Pear Pudding

- Cover the pears in the lemon juice to prevent discolouration in the cooking process.
- Arrange the pears at the base of the slow cooker and dot the butter around the pears together with the apple juice and brown sugar.
- Cook on a low setting for 2 hours until tender.
- Preheat oven to 180°C (160° fan) 375F, gas 5
- In a food processor mix together all the dry ingredients, then add the eggs and vanilla extract.
- Blend until smooth and the mixture reaches dropping consistency.
- Once the pears are cooked arrange them in a baking dish.
- Cover them with the pudding batter and bake in the oven on the middle shelf for 30 minutes or until golden and firm to the touch.
- Leave to rest for 5-10 minutes before serving.

PREPARATION TIME: 30 MINUTES

COOKING TIME: 2 ½ HOURS

INGREDIENTS

4 pears, peeled quartered and cored
½ lemon, juiced
2 tbsp unsalted butter
120 ml / 4 fl. oz / ½ cup apple juice
2 tbsp soft brown sugar
125 g / 4 ½ oz / ¾ cup plain (all-purpose) flour
150 g / 5 oz / 1 ⅓ stick butter
1 tsp baking powder
¼ tsp bicarbonate of (baking) soda
2 eggs
2 tsp vanilla extract

Pear and Blackberry Pudding

1020

For a more wintery pudding add a handful of blackberries to the cooked pears before covering in the pudding batter.

1021

SERVES 4-6

Panettone Bread and Butter Pudding

PREPARATION TIME: 30 MINUTES

COOKING TIME: 2 HOURS

INGREDIENTS

12 medium slices of Panettone
30 g / 1 oz / 2 tbsp unsalted butter, softened
1 vanilla pod, split lengthways and seeds scraped out
720 ml / 1 pint 6 fl. oz / 3 cups whole milk
8 egg yolks
175 g / 6 oz / ¾ cup golden caster (superfine) sugar
30 g / 1 oz / 2 tbsp raisins
30 g / 1 oz / 2 tbsp sultanas

- Pour the milk into a pan and add the vanilla pod and seeds.
- Bring up to boiling point and leave to one side.
- Whisk together the sugar and egg yolks.
- Remove the vanilla pod from the milk and add the egg yolk and sugar mixture to the warm milk.
- Cook over a low heat until the mixture begins to thicken and will coat the back of a wooden spoon.
- Pour the mixture through a sieve to remove any cooked egg strands.
- Arrange the sliced Pannettone and extra currants and sultanas to the bottom of the slow cooker. Being careful that the slices overlap slightly.
- Pour the custard over the Pannettone and cover.
- Cook on a high heat setting for 1 ½ hours until the custard is set.
- Leave to cool slightly before serving.

Chocolate Bread and Butter Pudding

1022

You could use stale pain au chocolat instead of the Panettone, in which case slice 6 pain au chocolat and arrange in a similar way, do not add the currants or sultanas.

1023

SERVES 4-6

Bananas and Blood Oranges

PREPARATION TIME: 20 MINUTES

COOKING TIME: 2 HOURS

INGREDIENTS

4 bananas peeled and chopped
1 whole banana, for garnish
½ lemon juiced
4 blood oranges, peeled and segmented
1 tsp cinnamon
1 vanilla pod, split lengthways
240 ml / 8 fl. oz / 1 cup orange juice

- Coat the chopped bananas with a little of the lemon juice to prevent discolouration.
- Together with the blood oranges layer alternately at the bottom of the slow cooker so that the fruit is evenly spaced.
- Mix the cinnamon with the orange juice and add the seeds from the scraped vanilla pod.
- Pour the spiced juice mixture over the bananas and oranges.
- Cover and place on a low setting for 2 hours.
- Once cooked remove from the slow cooker into a mixing bowl.
- Combine the bananas and oranges together to form a thick stewed fruit mixture.
- Serve in bowls and top with banana slices and a pinch of cinnamon if desired.

Bananas with Orange and Grapefruit

1024

Swap half of the orange segments with segments of one grapefruit for a sharper tasting dessert.

1025

SERVES 4

Bananas with Almonds and Toffee

Bananas with Hazelnuts, Chocolate and Toffee Sauce

1026

Add a handful of chocolate chips to the slow cooker just before the end of cooking time. Use chopped hazelnuts instead of the flaked (slivered) almonds.

PREPARATION TIME: 20 MINUTES

COOKING TIME: 1 ½ – 2 HOURS

INGREDIENTS

6 slightly under ripe bananas
175 g / 6 oz / ¾ cup caster (superfine) sugar
55 g / 2 oz / ½ cup flaked (slivered) almonds
120 ml / 4 fl. oz / ½ cup double cream.

- Heat a heavy-based pan. When the pan is hot add the sugar and leave for a few minutes keeping a constant eye to see if the sugar changes colour.
- After 5 minutes the sugar will start to melt and liquid will appear around the edges.
- Start to shake the pan to agitate the sugar and leave until around a quarter of the sugar has melted.
- Using a wooden spoon start to stir the sugar gently until it turns a dark amber colour, which should take from beginning to end around 10 minutes.
- Slice the bananas into large chunks and arrange in the base of the slow cooker.
- Pour the caramel over the bananas and cover for around 1 ½ - 2 hours until the bananas are very soft.
- When cooked using a slatted spoon remove the bananas to a serving dish.
- Take the caramel sauce and in a pan start to heat gently, once hot again add the cream a little at a time to make the toffee sauce.
- Pour the sauce over the bananas and serve.

SERVES 4

Baked Spiced Apples

Baked Spiced Pears

Use pears instead of the apples. Use apple juice instead of cider if you wish, for a non-alcoholic version.

PREPARATION TIME: 20 MINUTES

COOKING TIME: 3 HOURS

INGREDIENTS

4 Pink Lady apples or similar
1 tsp cinnamon
85 g / 3 oz / ½ cup soft brown sugar
½ tsp ground mixed spice
½ tsp nutmeg
1 tsp vanilla extract
120 ml / 4 fl. oz / ½ cup apple cider
2 tbsp Demerara sugar (for garnish)

- Wash the apples making sure that the stalk remains attached to the fruit.
- Arrange the apples in the base of a slow cooker, slicing off the base of each apple if they do not stand up properly.
- Mix together the spices, sugar and apple cider.
- Pour the spices and sugar mix over the apples.
- Cover and cook for 3 hours or until the apples are tender but retain their shape.
- To serve arrange on a platter and spoon over the cooking juices.
- Sprinkle the Demerara sugar if desired.

1029
SERVES 6
Butter Toffee Rice Pudding

- Combine the milk and sugar for the rice pudding in a saucepan and bring to the boil over a moderate heat.
- Place the rice in a slow cooker and cover with the hot milk mixture. Stir well and cook on a medium setting for 6 hours, stirring occasionally until soft.
- Prepare the butter toffee by combining the condensed milk, sugar and butter in a saucepan.
- Bring the mixture to a simmer over a medium heat, stirring occasionally until the sugar has dissolved.
- Continue to cook the caramel until thickened.
- Remove from the heat and season to taste using sea salt.
- Pour into a square silicone tray and chill until firm.
- Once the rice pudding is done, remove the salted butter toffee from the fridge and cut into cubes.
- Place a few cubes of the toffee into the base of serving glasses and top with the rice pudding mixture, stirring to help melt the toffee. Serve immediately.

PREPARATION TIME : 10 MINUTES

COOKING TIME :
6 HOURS 10 MINUTES

INGREDIENTS

FOR THE BUTTER TOFFEE
400 g / 14 oz / 1 ⅔ cups condensed milk
110 g / 4 oz / ½ cup golden caster (superfine) sugar
110 g / 4 oz / 1 stick salted butter
a pinch of flaked sea salt

FOR THE RICE PUDDING
75 g / 3 oz / ⅓ cup arborio rice
750 ml / 1 pint 6 fl. oz / 3 cups whole milk
75 g / 3 oz / ⅓ cup caster (superfine) sugar

Strawberry Jam Rice Pudding
1030
Replace the toffee with 1 tbsp of strawberry jam in the base of each serving glass before topping with the rice pudding and stirring briefly.

1031
SERVES 4
Mango Sweet Soup

- Combine the tapioca, milk, sugar and salt in a large saucepan.
- Cook over a low heat, stirring frequently until the tapioca starts to absorb the milk and swell in size.
- Add the butter gradually to the pudding and continue cooking over a low heat, stirring constantly until the butter has been absorbed into the pudding.
- Fold through the pear and pour into a slow cooker.
- Cover with a lid and cook on a medium setting for 4 hours until the tapioca is thickened and creamy.
- Add the mango and mandarin flesh and stir thoroughly before spooning into serving bowls.
- Garnish with the julienned mandarin peel before serving.

PREPARATION TIME :
15 MINUTES

COOKING TIME :
4 HOURS 15-20 MINUTES

INGREDIENTS

110 g / 4 oz / 1 cup tapioca, soaked in cold water overnight then drained
1 ¼ l / 2 pints 4 fl. oz / 5 cups whole milk
110 g / 4 oz / 1 cup caster (superfine) sugar
55 g / 2 oz / ½ stick unsalted butter, cubed
a pinch of salt
1 large mango, de-stoned and flesh finely diced
2 eating pears, peeled, cored and finely diced
1 mandarin, peeled, skinned and finely diced

TO GARNISH
2 mandarins, zest pared and julienned

Exotic Fruit Pudding
1032
Replace the pears with kiwi fruit for an extra tangy taste.

1033

SERVES 4

Crumble Coco Passion

PREPARATION TIME :
10 MINUTES

COOKING TIME :
3 HOURS 15 MINUTES

INGREDIENTS

2 large mangoes, destoned and diced
450 g / 1 lb / 3 cups pineapple
chunks, drained
225 g / 8 oz / 2 cups seedless red
grapes
1 lime, sliced
1 lime, juiced
110 g / 4 oz / ⅔ cup desiccated
coconut
55 g / 2 oz / ¼ cup caster (superfine)
sugar

- Combine the mango, pineapple, lime slices and lime juice in a slow cooker.
- Cover with a lid and cook on a medium setting for 3 hours until the fruit is tender.
- Preheat the grill to hot.
- Spoon the softened fruit into heatproof serving bowls and sprinkle the grapes on top.
- Combine the coconut and sugar in a small mixing bowl and sprinkle on top of the fruit.
- Grill for 1-2 minutes until the coconut mixture starts to brown.
- Remove from the oven and serve immediately.

Double Coco Crumble Passion   **1034**

Once the coconut mixture is golden, sprinkle
1 tbsp of cocoa powder over the dish.

1035

SERVES 8

Strawberry Bread and Butter Pudding

PREPARATION TIME :
15-20 MINUTES

COOKING TIME :
3 HOURS 40-45 MINUTES

INGREDIENTS

FOR THE BREAD AND
BUTTER PUDDING
1 medium white sandwich loaf
(ideally 2-3 days old and slightly
stale)
150 g / 5 oz / 1 ½ sticks unsalted
butter, softened
750 ml / 1 pint 6 fl. oz / 3 cups whole
milk
110 g / 4 oz / ⅔ cup soft light
brown sugar
3 large eggs
1 tsp ground cinnamon

FOR THE ROAST STRAWBERRIES
450 g / 1 lb / 4 cups strawberries,
hulled and large ones halved
55 g / 2 oz / ½ cup icing
(confectioner's) sugar
½ tsp vanilla extract

- Combine the strawberries, icing sugar and vanilla extract and place spooning in a slow cooker.
- Cook on medium for 3 hours. Combine the milk, sugar and cinnamon in a saucepan.
- Cook over a moderate heat, stirring to dissolve the sugar. Remove from the heat and cool for 5 minutes.
- Meanwhile, cut the bread. Whisk the eggs then pour the warm milk over and whisk.
- Butter the inside of a baking dish with ½ stick of the softened butter. Butter the slices of bread.
- Arrange in the baking dish, layering if necessary. Pour over the milk and egg mixture. Preheat the oven to 190°C (170° fan) / 375°F / gas 5. Bake for 35-40 minutes.
- After 25 minutes, arrange the strawberries on a baking tray and bake for 15 minutes.
- Remove the bread and butter pudding and arrange.
- Top with strawberries before serving.

Grape Bread Pudding   **1036**

Replace the strawberries with the same
weight of white seedless grapes and follow the
same preparation method for them.

1037

SERVES 4-6

Cherry and Hazelnut Crumble

Cherry, Apple and Almond Crumble

1038

Replace the ground hazelnuts with almonds if preferred. Add a few roughly chopped apples to the cherries for a different texture and flavour.

Cherry Crumble with Orange

1039

Add a grated rind of orange to the topping of the crumble before sprinkling on the cherries.

Blackberry and Apple Crumble

1040

Replace the cherry and hazelnut with 225 g / 8 oz fresh blackberries and 4 large cooking apples and cook the same.

PREPARATION TIME: 25 MINUTES

COOKING TIME: 2 HOURS

INGREDIENTS

800 g / 1 lb 12 oz / 5 cups canned pitted black cherries, drained
240 ml / 9 fl. oz / 1 cup sour cream
55 g / 2 oz / ¼ cup brown sugar
1 egg lightly beaten
1 tsp vanilla extract

FOR THE CRUMBLE
75 g / 3 oz / ½ cup plain flour, sifted
110 g / 4 oz / 1 cup ground hazelnuts
88 g / 3 ½ oz / ½ cup brown sugar
125 g / 4 ½ oz / 1 stick butter, chilled and cubed

- Arrange the cherries on the bottom of your slow cooker so that they are evenly distributed.
- In a separate bowl mix the sour cream, sugar, egg and vanilla extract together.
- Pour the cream mix over the cherries.
- In a food processor mix together the flour, nuts, sugar and butter until the mixture resembles breadcrumbs.
- Crumble the mix over the cherries and cream, cover.
- Cook on a low setting for around 2 hours until the crumble sinks a little into the hot cherries.
- Leave to cool slightly before serving.

1041

MAKES 18

Chocolate Rice Pudding

- Combine the milk and sugar for the rice pudding in a saucepan and bring to the boil over a moderate heat, stirring frequently.
- Place the rice in a slow cooker and cover with the hot milk mixture.
- Stir well before covering with a lid.
- Cook on a medium setting for 6 hours, stirring occasionally until soft.
- Stir through the chopped chocolate and the salt after 6 hours until you have an even, homogenous, chocolate rice pudding.
- Spoon into serving bowls and serve immediately.

PREPARATION TIME :
10 MINUTES

COOKING TIME :
6 HOURS 10 MINUTES

INGREDIENTS

30 g / 1 oz / ¼ stick unsalted butter, softened
75 g / 3 oz / ⅓ cup pudding rice
55 g / 2 oz / ¼ cup caster (superfine) sugar
750 ml / 1 pint 6 fl. oz / 3 cups whole milk
175 g / 6 oz / 1 cup milk chocolate, chopped
a pinch of salt
basil, to garnish

Mango and Pineapple Crumble

1042

SERVES 4

PREPARATION TIME :
15 MINUTES

COOKING TIME :
4 HOURS 30 MINUTES

INGREDIENTS

FOR THE FRUIT COMPOTE
125 g / 4 ½ oz / ½ cup caster (superfine) sugar
1 pineapple, trimmed, cored and flesh diced
4 medium mangoes, destoned and flesh diced
1 lime, juiced

FOR THE CRUMBLE TOPPING
150 g / 5 oz / 1 cup plain (all-purpose) flour
110 g / 4 oz / ½ cup golden caster (superfine) sugar
110 g / 4 oz / 1 stick unsalted butter, cold and cubed
a pinch of salt

GARNISH
2 tbsp desiccated coconut
2.5g / ½ tsp caster (superfine) sugar

- Combine the sugar, pineapple, mango and lime juice in a slow cooker.
- Cook on a medium setting for 4 hours, stirring occasionally, until the fruit is soft. Preheat the oven to 190°C (170° fan) / 375F / gas 5.
- Combine the flour, sugar, salt and butter for the crumble topping in a food processor and pulse until it resembles breadcrumbs.
- Spoon the softened fruit into ovenproof serving bowls, then sprinkle the crumble topping on top.
- Bake for 20-25 minutes.
- Remove from the oven and let them stand for a few minutes before garnishing with the desiccated coconut.

Pear Baked Egg Custard

1043

SERVES 4

PREPARATION TIME :
10 MINUTES

COOKING TIME :
4 HOURS 45-50 MINUTES

INGREDIENTS

4 large eating pears, peeled, cored and halved

55 g / 2 oz / ¼ cup granulated sugar
125 ml / 4 ½ fl. oz / ½ cup water
8 medium egg yolks
75 g / 3 oz / ⅓ cup caster (superfine) sugar
500 ml / 18 fl. oz / 2 cups whipping cream
GARNISH
½ nutmeg, finely grated

- Combine the pear halves, granulated sugar and water in a slow cooker.
- Cover with a lid and cook on a medium setting for 4 hours, stirring occasionally, until the pear is tender.
- Once tender, drain and pat dry before arranging in a 2 lb baking dish.
- Preheat the oven to 170°C (150° fan) / 325 F / gas 3.
- Prepare the filling by whisking together the egg yolks and caster (superfine) sugar until pale and thick.
- Add the cream and mix well, then pass through a fine sieve into a saucepan and heat over a medium heat to blood temperature.
- Pour the custard into the baking dish on top of the pears and let it settle for a few minutes.
- Bake for 30-35 minutes until the custard is just set.
- Remove from the oven and garnish with nutmeg.

1044

SERVES 4

Creamy Hot Chocolate

- Combine the milk, cream and sugar in a large saucepan.
- Cook over a medium heat, stirring frequently until the sugar has dissolved.
- Place the chocolate chips in a slow cooker and pour the hot milk and cream mixture on top, stirring well until the chocolate melts.
- Cover with a lid and cook on a low setting for 2 hours.
- Stir through a pinch of salt after 2 hours.
- Ladle into serving bowls and serve hot alongside warm doughnuts.

PREPARATION TIME :
10 MINUTES

COOKING TIME :
2 HOURS 10 MINUTES

INGREDIENTS

750 ml / 1 pint 6 fl. oz / 3 cups whole milk
250 ml / 9 fl. oz / 1 cup double cream
110 g / 4 oz / ½ cup caster (superfine) sugar
175 g / 6 oz / 1 cup milk chocolate chips
a pinch of salt

Hot Chocolate and Marshmallow

1045

Once the hot chocolate is poured, cover with squirty cream and 1 tbsp of marshmallows.

1046

SERVES 4

Apples with Gingerbread Stuffing

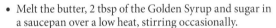

- Melt the butter, 2 tbsp of the Golden Syrup and sugar in a saucepan over a low heat, stirring occasionally.
- Sift together the flour, ground ginger, bicarbonate of soda and salt and stir the melted ingredients into the dry ingredients to make a dough.
- Add the rolled oats and stir again then turn the dough out onto a lightly floured surface and knead gently for a few minutes.
- Score the outsides of the apples with a sharp knife and fill their centres with the gingerbread stuffing.
- Arrange in a slow cooker and cook on a medium setting for 4 hours. Remove from the slow cooker and arrange in a baking dish, pouring the remaining Golden Syrup around them.
- Preheat the oven to 190°C (170° fan) / 375F / gas 5. Bake the apples for 15 minutes until golden brown on top.
- Remove from the oven and let them stand for a few minutes before serving.

PREPARATION TIME :
10-15 MINUTES

COOKING TIME :
4 HOURS 20 MINUTES

INGREDIENTS

4 large Golden Delicious apples, cored and hollowed out a little
150 g / 5 oz / 1 cup plain (all-purpose) flour
75 g / 3 oz / ⅔ stick unsalted butter, softened
55 g / 2 oz / ¼ cup golden caster (superfine) sugar
175 g / 6 oz / ½ cup Golden Syrup
30 g / 1 oz / 2 tbsp rolled oats
a little plain (all-purpose) flour, for dusting
1 tsp bicarbonate of soda
1 tsp ground ginger
a pinch of salt

Apples with Raisin Stuffing

1047

Replace the oats in the stuffing with 55 g / 2 oz / ¼ cup raisins.

1048

MAKES 18

Carrot Crumble

Mango Crumble 1049

Replace the carrots with 4 mangoes, peeled and halved and cook in the same way.

Carrot and Berry Crumble 1050

Replace the black pudding with the same weight of blackberries for a vegetarian, fruity twist.

Pineapple Crumble 1051

Replace the weight of carrots for pineapple and cook the same.

PREPARATION TIME :
10-15 MINUTES

COOKING TIME :
3 HOURS 25-30 MINUTES

INGREDIENTS

30 ml / 1 fl. oz / 2 tbsp olive oil
1 tbsp unsalted butter
450 g / 1 lb / 3 cups carrots, peeled and sliced
225 g / 8 oz / 1 ½ cups black pudding, sliced
1 onion sliced
salt and pepper

FOR THE CRUMBLE
150 g / 5 oz / 1 cup plain (all-purpose) flour
75 g / 3 oz / ⅔ cup butter, chilled and cut into cubes
75 g / 3 oz / ⅔ cup Parmesan, grated
salt and pepper

GARNISH
sprigs of oregano
basil, to garnish

- Heat the olive oil in a large saucepan set over a moderate heat until hot.
- Sweat the onion and carrot with a little seasoning for 10 minutes, stirring occasionally.
- Add the black pudding after 10 minutes and stir well.
- Spoon into a slow cooker and cover with a lid.
- Cook on a low setting for 3 hours until the carrot is tender.
- Turn off after 3 hours and set to one side.
- Preheat the oven to 190°C (170° fan) / 375F / gas 5.
- Combine the flour, butter and a little seasoning in a food processor.
- Pulse until you have a mixture that resembles fine breadcrumbs.
- Pour into a mixing bowl and stir through the Parmesan.
- Spoon the carrot and black pudding into heatproof serving bowls.
- Sprinkle the crumble on top and arrange the bowls on baking trays.
- Bake for 8-10 minutes until the crumble is cooked and crunchy on top.
- Remove from the oven and garnish with oregano before serving.

SERVES 4

Crumble-style Baked Apple

- Arrange the halved apples in a slow cooker and drizzle with the honey.
- Cover with a lid and cook on a medium setting for 4 hours until softened.
- Remove the apple halves from the cooker once softened and pat dry before arranging on a baking tray.
- Preheat the oven to 190°C (170° fan) / 375 F / gas 5.
- Combine the flour, sugar, salt and butter in a food processor.
- Pulse until the mixture resembles breadcrumbs, then stir through the oats.
- Spoon the crumble mixture into the cored apple halves and bake for 20-25 minutes until golden brown in colour and crunchy.
- Remove from the oven and let them stand for a few minutes before serving.

PREPARATION TIME :
10-15 MINUTES

COOKING TIME :
4 HOURS 30-35 MINUTES

INGREDIENTS

4 Bramley apples, halved horizontally and cored
110 g / 4 oz / ⅔ cup plain (all-purpose) flour, sifted
55 g / 2 oz / ½ cup rolled oats
110 g / 4 oz / ⅔ cup soft light brown sugar
110 g / 4 oz / 1 stick unsalted butter, cold and cubed
1 tbsp honey
a pinch of salt

Spiced Apple Crumble Bake
1053

Add 1 tsp of ground mixed all-spice and ½ tsp of ground cinnamon to the food processor before pulsing, for a spicy flavour.

SERVES 4

Apples with Almonds

- Combine the butter, sugar, vanilla extract and salt in a saucepan.
- Cook over a medium heat, until the sugar has dissolved and you have an even, smooth sauce.
- Fill the cored apples with the ground almonds and arrange upright in a slow cooker.
- Pour the sauce over and around them and cover with a lid. Cook on a medium setting for 4 hours.
- Turn the slow cooker off once the apples are soft and sprinkle their tops with the flaked almonds.
- Preheat the grill to hot.
- Arrange on a grilling tray and flash under the grill for a minute or so until golden brown in colour on top.
- Remove from the grill and arrange on a serving plate, pouring any of the sauce from the slow cooker around them.

PREPARATION TIME :
10-15 MINUTES

COOKING TIME :
4 HOURS 15 MINUTES

INGREDIENTS

4 Golden Delicious apples, cored
110 g / 4 oz / 1 stick unsalted butter, softened
175 g / 6 oz / 1 cup soft light brown sugar
55 g / 2 oz / ½ cup ground almonds
½ tsp vanilla extract
a pinch of salt

GARNISH
2 tbsp flaked (slivered) almonds

Index

Index

Index

Index